Simple Heuristics
That Make
Us Smart

Gerd Gigerenzer

Peter M. Todd

and the ABC Research Group

OXFORD
UNIVERSITY PRESS

OXFORD
UNIVERSITY PRESS

Oxford New York

Athens Auckland Bangkok Bogotá Buenos Aires Calcutta
Cape Town Chennai Dar es Salaam Delhi Florence Hong Kong Istanbul
Karachi Kuala Lumpur Madrid Melbourne Mexico City Mumbai
Nairobi Paris São Paulo Shanghai Singapore Taipei Tokyo Toronto Warsaw

and associated companies in
Berlin Ibadan

First published in 1999 by Oxford University Press, Inc.
198 Madison Ave., New York, New York 10016

First issued as an Oxford University Press paperback, 2001

Oxford is a registered trademark of Oxford University Press

Library of Congress Cataloging-in-Publication Data
Gigerenzer, Gerd.
    Simple heuristics that make us smart / Gerd Gigerenzer, Peter M.
Todd, and the ABC Research Group.
        p.   cm.
    Includes bibliographical references and indexes.
    ISBN 0-19-512156-2; ISBN 0-19-514381-7 (pbk.)
    1. Heuristic. I. Todd, Peter M.   II. ABC Research Group.
III. Title.
BD260.G54   1999
128'.33—dc21   98-51084

9 8 7 6

Printed in the United States of America
on acid-free paper

Simple Heuristics

That Make Us Smart

EVOLUTION AND COGNITION

General Editor: Stephen Stich, Rutgers University

Published in the Series

Simple Heuristics That Make Us Smart
Gerd Gigerenzer, Peter M. Todd, and the ABC Research Group

Dedicated, simply, to our families.

Preface

This book is an invitation to participate in a journey into largely unknown territory. The journey ventures into a land of rationality that is different from the familiar one we know from many stories in cognitive science and economics—tales in which humans live in a world with unlimited time and knowledge, where the sun of enlightenment shines down in beams of logic and probability. The new land of rationality we set out to explore is, in contrast, shrouded in a mist of dim uncertainty. People in this world have only limited time, knowledge, and computational capacities with which to make inferences about what happens in the enigmatic places in their world.

How can one be rational in a world where vision is limited, time is pressing, and decision-making experts are often unavailable? In this book we argue that rationality can be found in the use of fast and frugal heuristics, inference mechanisms that can be simple and smart. The laws of logic and probability play little if any role in the performance of these components of the mind's adaptive toolbox—these heuristics are successful to the degree they are ecologically rational, that is, adapted to the structure of the information in the environment in which they are used to make decisions.

We set out on this journey as a disparate group of people from various fields that often do not talk to each other, including psychology, mathematics, computer science, economics, and evolutionary biology. The trick was to put everyone in one boat, where there was no escape from talking and working together or from learning the language and the skills of the others. The boat and its long-term funding was provided by the unique policy of the Max Planck Society, which allowed us to take on a challenging project with an uncertain outcome by adopting a research perspective of many, many years. Much of the exploration described in this book was carried out at the Max Planck Institute for Psychological Research in Munich; further forays into the vast unexplored territory of ecological rationality have taken place in our new home at the Max Planck Institute for Human Development in Berlin. We have only been on our journey for fewer than three years, but in that time we have seen new horizons and made new discoveries in the world of heuristics, making the time right for a first report from the field.

Our group's name, the ABC research group, is short for the Center for Adaptive Behavior and Cognition. This name also has a second meaning that is central to the topic of this book: We study the ABCs of decision-making heuristics—that is, the basic building blocks from which these inference mechanisms are made.

The chapters in this book tell the story of our explorations in a way that reflects our feelings and mounting excitement during the long trek. We stumbled over the surprising performance of a variety of simple heuristics, and the reasons behind their successful behavior, only after long and painful stretches of lack of insight and failed conjectures. We started off believing our results just could not be true (a sentiment many of our colleagues were quick to share, and slower than we to abandon), only to end up realizing that there are good reasons for these findings to be true. To reflect our progress from bafflement and disbelief to happy certainty, some early chapters will report our first puzzling findings, while later chapters will put the pieces together into the bigger picture.

This book is meant to excite and inspire intellectual adventurers who love to explore and dare rather than playing it safe and sticking to received wisdom. This is not to say that we present only daring, unwise results—we marshal the evidence of experiments, real-world simulations, and the safe haven of proofs. But we have also undertaken bold adventures, such as the (lucrative) decision to throw one of our heuristics at the stock market to see whether it could make any money.

We have made forays into several different regions of the new territory of ecological rationality, from the chaos of the stock market to the intricacies of mate choice. But what is most important is the guiding vision that has given us the overall direction that we follow. We may have seen only the coastal regions of the new territory, and we may have placed some of the heuristics mistakenly on our growing map, but we believe that the land of fast and frugal heuristics is the right direction in which to head.

The individual chapters in this book are all multiauthored, reflecting the interdisciplinary collaboration among researchers that gave birth to each separate expedition. Successful interdisciplinary collaboration is still a rare event even in these days of proliferating interdisciplinary.groups. Part of our success came from the attitudes that the individual researchers brought with them: After an initial phase of puzzlement ("What could I learn from a mathematician?"), intellectual curiosity and trust—that is, the feeling that one can challenge and disagree but still be respected and remain friends—won out. Also crucial, though, was establishing an environment in which these attitudes could evolve: everyone with offices near each other and the doors left open, and coffee and tea every afternoon at 4 P.M. These are some of the features that made our journey enjoyable as well as productive.

Any journey into new territory must build upon the past explorations of others, and draw upon the knowledge and guidance of current adventuresome experts. We have been inspired both by the ideas, and by the title, of Donald Norman's book *Things That Make Us Smart* (1993). We are grateful to our colleagues who read through drafts of earlier versions of individual chapters and gave us helpful feedback: Gregory Ashby, Peter Ayton, Talia Ben-Zeev, Jim Bettman, Greg Brake, Arndt Bröder, Ed Bukszar, Nick Chater, Edgar Erdfelder, Klaus Fiedler, Bruno Frey, William M. Goldstein, Karl Grammer, Nigel Harvey, Reid Hastie, Wolfgang Hell, Oswald Huber, Helmut Jungermann, Peter Juslin, Timothy Ketelaar, Jack Knetsch, Asher Koriat, Jane Lancaster, Pat Langley, Barbara Mellers, Richard Nisbett, Richard Olsen, John Payne, Stuart Russell, Peter Sedlmeier, Thor Sigvaldason, Tom Stewart, Richard Thaler, Ryan Tweney, Kim Vicente, Tom Wallsten, X. T. Wang, Elke Weber, and Kevin Weinfurt.

Special thanks go to Valerie M. Chase, Elke Kurz, Catrin Rode, and William Wimsatt, who read drafts of the entire book, and to Donna Alexander, Andreas Deters, Martin Dieringer, Timmo Köhler, Ulrich Kuhnert, Torsten Mohrbach, Marianne Müller-Brettel, Brady Richards, Rüdiger Sparr, Anita Todd, Ahn Vu, and Jill Vyse, who helped us with collecting data and editing the manuscript.

This book is the starting point of an ongoing research program; for further developments and results, we invite you to visit our Center's website at http://www.mpib-berlin.mpg.de/abc/.

Welcome to our journey.

Berlin
July 1998

Gerd Gigerenzer
Peter Todd

Contents

The ABC Research Group

The Center for Adaptive Behavior and Cognition (ABC) is an interdisciplinary research group founded in 1995 to study the psychology of bounded rationality and how good decisions can be made in an uncertain world.

Patricia M. Berretty
Department of Psychology
University of Illinois
603 E. Daniel Street
Champaign, IL 61820
USA
email: pberrett@s.psych.uiuc.edu

Bernhard Borges
c/o Coopers and Lybrand
830 Post Road East
Westport, CT 06880
USA
email: borges@ibm.net

Philip W. Blythe
Center for Adaptive Behavior and
  Cognition
Max Planck Institute for
  Human Development
Lentzeallee 94
14195 Berlin
Germany
email: blythe@mpib-berlin.mpg.de

Seth Bullock
Center for Adaptive Behavior and
  Cognition
Max Planck Institute for
  Human Development
Lentzeallee 94
14195 Berlin
Germany
email: bullock@mpib-berlin.mpg.de

Jean Czerlinski
Department of Sociology
University of Chicago
Social Sciences 306-310
1126 East 59th Street
Chicago, IL 60637
USA
email: jfczerli@midway.uchicago.edu

Jennifer Nerissa Davis
Center for Adaptive Behavior and
    Cognition
Max Planck Institute for
    Human Development
Lentzeallee 94
14195 Berlin
Germany
email: davis@mpib-berlin.mpg.de

Gerd Gigerenzer
Center for Adaptive Behavior and
    Cognition
Max Planck Institute for
    Human Development
Lentzeallee 94
14195 Berlin
Germany
email: gigerenzer@mpib-berlin.mpg.de

Daniel G. Goldstein
Center for Adaptive Behavior and
    Cognition
Max Planck Institute for
    Human Development
Lentzeallee 94
14195 Berlin
Germany
email: goldstein@mpib-berlin.mpg.de

Adam S. Goodie
Department of Psychology
University of Georgia
Athens, GA 30602-3013
USA
email: goodie@egon.psy.uga.edu

Ralph Hertwig
Center for Adaptive Behavior and
    Cognition
Max Planck Institute for
    Human Development
Lentzeallee 94
14195 Berlin
Germany
email: hertwig@mpib-berlin.mpg.de

Ulrich Hoffrage
Center for Adaptive Behavior and
    Cognition
Max Planck Institute for
    Human Development
Lentzeallee 94
14195 Berlin
Germany
email: hoffrage@mpib-berlin.mpg.de

Kathryn Blackmond Laskey
Department of Systems Engineering
George Mason University
Fairfax, VA 22030-4444
USA
email: klaskey@gmu.edu

Laura Martignon
Center for Adaptive Behavior and
    Cognition
Max Planck Institute for
    Human Development
Lentzeallee 94
14195 Berlin
Germany
email: martignon@mpib-berlin.mpg.de

Geoffrey F. Miller
Centre for Economic Learning and
    Social Evolution (ELSE)
University College London
Gower Street
London WC1E 6BT
UK
email: uctpgfm@ucl.ac.uk

Andreas Ortmann
Department of Economics
Bowdoin College
Brunswick, ME 04011
USA
email: aortmann@bowdoin.edu

Jörg Rieskamp
Center for Adaptive Behavior and
    Cognition
Max Planck Institute for
    Human Development
Lentzeallee 94
14195 Berlin
Germany
email: rieskamp@mpib-berlin.mpg.de

Peter M. Todd
Center for Adaptive Behavior and
    Cognition
Max Planck Institute for
    Human Development
Lentzeallee 94
14195 Berlin
Germany
email: ptodd@mpib-berlin.mpg.de

Gregory M. Werner
School of Cognitive and
    Computing Sciences
University of Sussex
Brighton, Falmer BN1 9QH
UK
email: gwerner@ix.netcom.com

Part I

THE RESEARCH AGENDA

1

Fast and Frugal Heuristics

The Adaptive Toolbox

Gerd Gigerenzer
Peter M. Todd

Truth is ever to be found in simplicity, and not in the multiplicity and confusion of things. As the world, which to the naked eye exhibits the greatest variety of objects, appears very simple in its internal constitution when surveyed by a philosophical understanding, and so much the simpler by how much the better it is understood.

Isaac Newton

A man is rushed to a hospital in the throes of a heart attack. The doctor needs to decide quickly whether the victim should be treated as a low-risk or a high-risk patient. He is at high risk if his life is truly threatened, and should receive the most expensive and detailed care. Although this decision can save or cost a life, the doctor does not have the luxury of extensive deliberation: She or he must decide under time pressure using only the available cues, each of which is, at best, merely an uncertain predictor of the patient's risk level. For instance, at the University of California, San Diego Medical Center, as many as 19 such cues, including blood pressure and age, are measured as soon as a heart attack patient is admitted. Common sense dictates that the best way to make the decision is to look at the results of each of those measurements, rank them according to their importance, and combine them somehow into a final conclusion, preferably using some fancy statistical software package.

Consider in contrast the simple decision tree in figure 1-1, which was designed by Breiman and colleagues (Breiman et al., 1993) to classify heart attack patients according to risk using only a maximum of three variables. A patient who has a systolic blood pressure of less than 91 is immediately classified as high risk—no further information is needed. Otherwise, the decision is left to the second cue, age. A patient under 62.5 years old is classified as low risk; if he or she is older, then one more cue (sinus tachycardia) is needed to classify that patient as high or low risk.

3

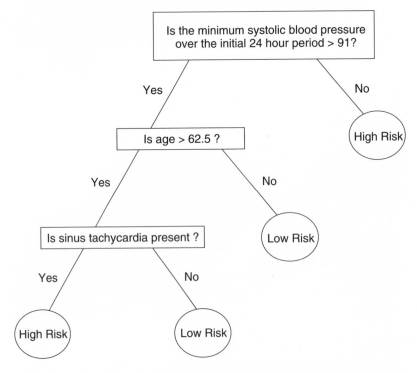

Figure 1-1: A simple decision tree for classifying incoming heart attack victims as high-risk or low-risk patients (adapted from Breiman et al., 1993).

Thus, the tree requires the doctor to answer a maximum of three yes/no questions to reach a decision rather than to measure and consider 19 predictors, letting life-saving treatment proceed all the sooner.

This decision strategy is simple in several respects. First, it ignores the great majority of possible measured predictors. Second, it ignores quantitative information by using only yes/no answers to the three questions. For instance, it does not care how much older or younger the patient is than the 62.5-year cutoff. Third, the strategy is a step-by-step process; it may end after the first question and does not combine (e.g., weight and add) the values on the three predictors. Asking at most three yes/no questions is a fast and frugal strategy for making a decision. It is fast because it does not involve much computation, and it is frugal because it only searches for some of the available information. Its simplicity raises the suspicion that it might be highly inaccurate, compared to standard statistical classification methods that process and combine all available predictors. Yet it is actually more accurate in classifying heart attack patients according to risk status than are some rather complex statistical classification methods (Breiman et al., 1993). The more general form of this counterintuitive finding—that fast and frugal decision making can be as accurate as strategies that use all available information and expensive computation—forms one of the bases of our research program.

This book is about fast and frugal heuristics for making decisions—how they work, and when and why they succeed. These heuristics can be seen as models of the behavior of both living organisms and artificial systems. From a descriptive standpoint, they are intended to capture how real minds make decisions under constraints of limited time and knowledge. From an engineering standpoint, these heuristics suggest ways to build artificially intelligent systems—artificial decision makers that are not paralyzed by the need for vast amounts of knowledge or extensive computational power. These two applications of fast and frugal heuristics do not exclude one another—indeed, the decision tree in figure 1-1 could be used to describe the behavior of an unaided human mind or could be built into an emergency-room machine.[1]

Visions of Rationality: From Demons to Bounded Rationality

Humans and animals make inferences about their world with limited time, knowledge, and computational power. In contrast, many models of rational inference view the mind as if it were a supernatural being possessing demonic powers of reason, boundless knowledge, and all of eternity with which to make decisions. Such visions of rationality often conflict with reality. But we can use them as points of comparison to help clarify our own vision of *ecological rationality*—rationality that is defined by its fit with reality. We start by considering two conceptual revolutions. The first is the demise of the dream of certainty and the rise of a calculus of uncertainty: that is, probability theory. This revolution is known as the *probabilistic revolution* in science and everyday life (Gigerenzer et al., 1989; Krüger et al., 1987). The second revolution, which this book is meant to advance, concerns the way minds deal with an uncertain world. We propose replacing the image of an omniscient mind computing intricate probabilities and utilities with that of a bounded mind reaching into an adaptive toolbox filled with fast and frugal heuristics.

Let us briefly sketch the first revolution, as it concerns our views about mind and rationality. For two millennia following Aristotle, the Western intellectual tradition distinguished between two kinds of knowledge. One was demonstrative proof, the other probable reasoning. The first provided

---

1. Decision trees such as the one in this example are easy to use, but their construction in the first place is based on quite extensive computations. In this book we will see how fast and frugal heuristics can get around this costly construction phase.

certainty, while the second produced only uncertain knowledge. During the Reformation and the Counter-Reformation of the sixteenth century, traditional sources of certainty—particularly religion and philosophy—came under attack simultaneously. As a result, the domain of demonstrative proof shriveled, while that of probable reasoning grew (Daston, 1988). By the mid-seventeenth century, a new pragmatic rationality emerged that abandoned traditional ideals of certainty. It was a modest view, expressed by the calculus of probability invented during the same period. The modesty of this vision stemmed from an acceptance that humble humans can attain only uncertain knowledge about themselves and their world. To be rational, then, required taming life's uncertainty. Blaise Pascal's famous wager (1669/1962) illustrates some moral consequences of this new rationality. In an atmosphere of unwavering religious certainty that God had to exist, Pascal asked: Is it rational to believe in him? Pascal proposed that one should sacrifice worldly pleasures to enhance one's uncertain prospect of salvation, because no matter how small the probability of God's existence, the payoff of living a Christian life is eternal afterlife, and the expected reward—the (perhaps small) probability of salvation multiplied by its infinite value—is still infinite. The other alternative—eternal damnation—is infinitely awful, no matter what its probability. The new rationality expressed by the calculus of probability was not just an intellectual revolution of thought, but also one in moral and religious attitudes.

The probabilistic revolution has shaped our picture of the mind in fields ranging from cognitive science to economics to animal behavior. Mental functions are assumed to be computations performed on probabilities and utilities (Gigerenzer & Murray, 1987). In this view, the laws of probability describe or prescribe sound reasoning, judgment, and decision making. Probabilistic conceptions of the mind have led to many elegant theories, but also to thorny problems. The moment one moves beyond simple constrained settings such as ones that psychologists and computer scientists study to real-world situations that people actually live through, the time, knowledge, and computation that probabilistic models demand grow unfeasibly large. As a consequence, when these models meet the rigors of reality, they turn into a psychology more applicable to supernatural beings than to mere humans.

In this book, we push for a second revolution, which provides a bold vision of rationality. Our premise is that much of human reasoning and decision making can be modeled by fast and frugal heuristics that make inferences with limited time and knowledge. These heuristics do not involve much computation, and do not compute probabilities and utilities. They are models of bounded rationality. This second theoretical upheaval embraces the earlier probabilistic revolution's emphasis on uncertainty without sharing its focus on probability theory, either as a description or as an attainable norm of human behavior. The four major visions of rationality that continue to struggle with each other in this second upheaval are shown in figure 1-2.

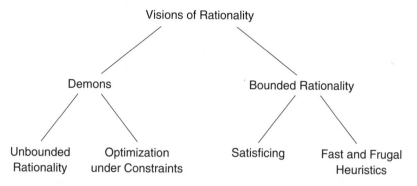

Figure 1-2: Visions of rationality.

Rationality comes in many forms. The first split in figure 1-2 separates models that assume the human mind has essentially unlimited demonic or supernatural reasoning power from those that assume we operate with only bounded rationality. There are two species of demons: those that exhibit *unbounded rationality*, and those that *optimize under constraints*. Unbounded rationality encompasses decision-making strategies that have little or no regard for the constraints of time, knowledge, and computational capacities that real humans face. Unbounded rationality is traditionally modeled by probability theory. Its best-known realizations are the maximization of expected utility and Bayesian models. There are also two main forms of bounded rationality: satisficing heuristics for searching through a sequence of available alternatives, and fast and frugal heuristics that use little information and computation to make a variety of kinds of decisions. We will illustrate these four conceptions of rationality by considering a commonly faced decision problem, showing where the demons may lurk.

A couple of years after completing his historic scientific voyage on the *Beagle*, the 29-year-old Charles Darwin turned his mind to more domestic issues. He scrawled the following notes in pencil on a scrap of paper, divided into two columns like a balance sheet and headed "This is the Question":

MARRY

Children—(if it please God)—constant companion, (friend in old age) who will feel interested in one, object to be beloved and played with—better than a dog anyhow—Home, and someone to take care of house—Charms of music and female chit-chat. These things good for one's health. Forced to visit and receive

Not MARRY

No children, (no second life) no one to care for one in old age. . . . Freedom to go where one liked—Choice of Society *and little of it.* Conversation of clever men at clubs.—Not forced to visit relatives, and to bend in every trifle—to have the expense and anxiety of children—perhaps quarrelling.

relations *but terrible loss of time.*
My God, it is intolerable to think of
spending one's whole life, like a neu-
ter bee, working, working and nothing after all.—No, no won't do.—
Imagine living all one's day solitarily
in smoky dirty London House.—
Only picture to yourself a nice soft
wife on a sofa with good fire, and
books and music perhaps—compare
this vision with the dingy reality of
Grt Marlboro' St.

Loss of time—cannot read in the eve-
nings—fatness and idleness—anxiety
and responsibility—less money for
books etc—if many children forced
to gain one's bread.—(But then it is
very bad for one's health to work too
much)
Perhaps my wife won't like London;
then the sentence is banishment and
degradation with indolent idle fool—

(Darwin, 1887/1969, pp. 232–233)

Darwin concluded that he should marry, writing "Marry—Marry—
Marry Q. E. D." decisively beneath the first column. On the reverse side of
the page he considered the consequences of his decision for his personal
freedom, ending with the insight: "There is many a happy slave." The
following year, Darwin married his cousin, Emma Wedgwood, with whom
he eventually had 10 children. How did Darwin decide to marry, based
on the possible consequences he envisioned—children, loss of time, a
constant companion? He did not tell us. But we can use his "Question"
as a thought experiment to illustrate various visions of rationality.

Unbounded Rationality

When Darwin was just a 5-year-old child, dreamy and quiet and showing
no signs of his later genius, the astronomer-philosopher Pierre Simon de
Laplace (1814/1951) was contemplating the ultimate genius, an omniscient superintelligence he characterized as follows:

> Given . . . an intelligence which could comprehend all the forces by
> which nature is animated and the respective situation of the beings
> who compose it—an intelligence sufficiently vast to submit these
> data to analysis . . . nothing would be uncertain and the future as
> the past, would be present to its eyes. (Laplace, 1814/1951, p. 4)

Laplace was areligious, and the superintelligence he imagined was a
secularized version of God. John Locke (1690/1959) had contrasted the
omniscient God with us humble humans living in the "twilight of probability"; Laplace secularized this opposition with his fictitious superintelligence. From the perspective of God and Laplace's superintelligence alike,
Nature is deterministic and certain; but for humans, Nature is fickle and
uncertain. Mortals cannot know the world, but must rely on uncertain
inferences, on bets rather than on demonstrative proof. Although omni-
science and certainty are not attainable for any real system, the spirit of
Laplace's superintelligence has survived nevertheless in the vision of unbounded rationality.

Imagine that Darwin had attempted to resolve his Question by maximizing his subjective expected utility. To compute his personal expected utility for marrying, he would have had to determine *all* the possible consequences that marriage could bring (e.g., children, constant companion, and an endless stream of further possibilities not included in his short list), attach quantitative probabilities to each of these consequences, estimate the subjective utility of each consequence, multiply each utility by its associated probability, and finally add all these numbers up. The same procedure would have to have been repeated for the alternative "not marry." Finally, he would have had to choose the alternative with the higher total expected utility. To acquire reliable information about the consequences and their probabilities and utilities, Darwin might have had to invest years of research—time he could have spent studying barnacles or writing *Origin of Species*.

Unbounded rationality is a strange and demanding beast. On one hand, researchers who envision rationality in this way accept the difference between God, or Laplace's superintelligence, and mere mortals. Humans must make inferences from behind a veil of uncertainty, but God sees clearly; the currency of human thought is probabilities, whereas God deals in certitude. On the other hand, when it comes to how they think these uncertain inferences are executed, those who believe in unbounded rationality paint humans in God's image. God and Laplace's superintelligence do not worry about limited time, knowledge, or computational capacities. The fictional, unboundedly rational human mind does not either—its only challenge is the lack of heavenly certainty. In figure 1-2, unbounded rationality appears in a class of models of reasonableness labeled "demons." We use the term in its original Greek sense of a divine (rather than evil) supernatural being, as embodied in Laplace's superintelligence.

Proponents of unbounded rationality generally acknowledge that their models assume unrealistic mental abilities, but nevertheless defend them by arguing that humans act *as if* they were unboundedly rational. On this interpretation, the laws of probability do not describe the process but merely the outcome of reasoning. Another common defense is that this theory exhibits mathematical beauty and convenience. Finally, some proponents simply say, "don't quarrel with success" (see Conlisk, 1996; Selten, 1991).

The greatest weakness of unbounded rationality is that it does not describe the way real people think. Not even philosophers, as the following story illustrates. One philosopher was struggling to decide whether to stay at Columbia University or to accept a job offer from a rival university. The other advised him: "Just maximize your expected utility—you always write about doing this." Exasperated, the first philosopher responded: "Come on, this is serious."

Because of its unnaturalness, unbounded rationality has come under attack in the second half of the twentieth century. But when one (unboundedly rational) head has been chopped off, another very similar one has usually sprouted again in its place: its close demonic relative, optimization under constraints.

Optimization Under Constraints

To think is to take a risk, a step into the unknown. Our inferences, inevitably grounded in uncertainty, force us to "go beyond the information given," in Jerome Bruner's famous phrase. But the situation is usually even more challenging than this, because rarely is information given. Instead we must *search* for information—cues to classify heart attack patients as high risk, reasons to marry, indicators of stock market fluctuation, and so on. Information search is usually thought of as being internal, performed on the contents of one's memory. But it is important to recognize that much information search is external, looking through the knowledge embodied in the surrounding environment. This external search includes seeking information in the socially distributed memory spanning friends and experts and in human artifacts such as libraries and the Internet.

The key difference between unbounded rationality and the three other visions in figure 1-2 is that the latter all involve *limited information search*, whereas models of unbounded rationality assume that search can go on indefinitely. In reasonable models, search must be limited because real decision makers have only a finite amount of time, knowledge, attention, or money to spend on a particular decision. Limited search requires a way to decide when to stop looking for information, that is, a *stopping rule*. The models in the class we call "optimization under constraints" assume that the stopping rule optimizes search with respect to the time, computation, money, and other resources being spent. More specifically, this vision of rationality holds that the mind should calculate the benefits and costs of searching for each further piece of information and stop search as soon as the costs outweigh the benefits (e.g., Anderson & Milson, 1989; Sargent, 1993; Stigler, 1961). The rule "stop search when costs outweigh benefits" sounds plausible at first glance. But a closer look reveals that optimization under constraints can require even more knowledge and computation than unbounded rationality (Vriend, 1996; Winter, 1975).

To see this point, imagine the unboundedly rational Darwin and a Darwin who optimizes under constraints, both of them trying to decide whether to marry. The unboundedly rational Darwin has to search for all the possible consequences of marrying and not marrying before choosing the alternative with the higher subjective expected utility. Now suppose that the Darwin who attempts to optimize under constraints has already listed two consequences of marriage, having a constant companion and children, and estimates of their respective probabilities and utilities. Before he proceeds to a third consequence, he must calculate whether the benefits of continuing the information search will outweigh its costs—if not, then he can stop his search at this point. To compute the benefit of further search, this poor Darwin would again have to consider what all the third consequences could be, estimate their utilities and probabilities, calculate how much each one could change his ultimate decision, and average all of these to come up with the expected benefit of continuing his search. The same calculation has to be performed before each further consequence is considered. Thus, calculating the benefits of further search demands the same kind of knowledge that the unboundedly rational Darwin needs. But the Darwin who tries to optimize under constraints is not finished yet—he must also determine the costs of continuing search. These include, for instance, the opportunity costs: The optimizing Darwin must determine all the other things he could be doing during the time he would be considering his decision (such as dissecting another barnacle), and what the cost of continuing to deliberate his Question instead of pursuing those other activities would be. At the end, this leads to an infinite regress. The optimizing Darwin would need to determine not only what the opportunity costs are, but also the second-order costs for making all these cost-benefit calculations, and so on (Conlisk, 1996). Even the unboundedly rational Darwin could make a decision faster than this.

Recall that the very motivation for replacing unbounded rationality by optimization under constraints was to build empirically more realistic models that respect the limitations of human minds. The paradoxical approach of optimization under constraints is to model "limited" search by assuming that the mind has essentially unlimited time and knowledge with which to evaluate the costs and benefits of further information search. The dream of optimization, threatened in its instantiation in unbounded rationality, is thus salvaged by being incorporated into an apparent competitor. When solving Darwin's Question or other real-world problems, constrained optimization invites unbounded rationality to sneak in through the back door.

Of course, few would argue that real humans have the time and knowledge necessary to perform the massive computations required of either of these imaginary demonic Darwins. Instead, these visions of rationality are usually presented as lofty ideals that human reasoning *should* aspire to. But such aspirations can make real human reasoning look flawed and irrational in comparison. In our view, it is these aspirations that are flawed—we will argue that reasoning can be powerful and accurate without requiring unlimited time and knowledge.

What certain forms of optimization under constraints can offer—in contrast to unbounded rationality—is an analysis of the structure of environments. For instance, in Anderson's rational analysis framework (Anderson, 1990; Oaksford & Chater, 1994) constraints from the environment are used to modify one's understanding of what is optimal behavior in a particular context. Such an analysis does not directly address the question of what mental mechanisms could possibly yield behavior approaching the optimal norm, but at least it allows us to create a more realistic standard for assessing proposed mechanisms.

Instead of the demonic visions of reason, we turn to the idea of bounded rationality. Many, if not most, researchers in cognitive science, economics, and animal behavior interpret the term "bounded rationality" as synonymous with optimization under constraints, a (mis)use we strongly reject. This interpretation may be responsible for the frequent dismissal of bounded rationality in favor of good old-fashioned demonic visions. The economist Thomas Sargent (1993), for instance, in interpreting bounded rationality as optimization under constraints, argues that when one models people as "bounded" in their rationality, one's models use a greater number of parameters and become more demanding mathematically. He believes that the reason why researchers (particularly economists) stick with models incorporating unbounded rationality is that their desire for models with fewer parameters is not met by the bounded approach: "a reduction is not what bounded rationality promises" (p. 4). But this is a misleading interpretation of bounded rationality—rationality need not be optimization, and bounds need not be constraints.

Bounded Rationality: Satisficing

The "father" of bounded rationality, Herbert Simon, has vehemently rejected its reduction to optimization under constraints: "bounded rationality is not the study of optimization in relation to task environments" (Simon, 1991, p. 35). In personal conversation, he once remarked with a mixture of humor and anger that he had considered suing authors who misuse his concept of bounded rationality to construct ever more complicated and unrealistic models of human decision making.

Simon's vision of bounded rationality has two interlocking components: the limitations of the human mind, and the structure of the environments in which the mind operates. The first component of his vision means that models of human judgment and decision making should be built on what we actually know about the mind's capacities rather than on fictitious competencies. In many real-world situations, optimal strategies are unknown or unknowable (Simon, 1987). Even in a game such as chess, where an optimal (best) move does in fact exist at every point, no strategy can calculate that move in a reasonable amount of time (either by human minds or computers), despite the well-defined nature of the possibilities to be searched. In less well-defined natural situations, our hope of identifying a usable optimal strategy is even further diminished. Because of the mind's limitations, humans "must use approximate methods to handle most tasks" (Simon, 1990, p. 6). These methods include recognition processes that largely obviate the need for further information search, heuristics that guide search and determine when it should end, and simple decision rules that make use of the information found. We explore these classes of methods at length in this book.

The second component of Simon's view of bounded rationality, environmental structure, is of crucial importance because it can explain when and why simple heuristics perform well: <u>if the structure of the heuristic is adapted to that of the environment.</u> Simon's (1956a) classic example concerns foraging organisms that have a single need, food. One organism lives in an environment in which little heaps of food are randomly distributed; it can get away with a simple heuristic, that is, run around randomly until a heap of food is found. For this, the organism needs some capacity for vision and movement, but it does not need a capacity for learning. A second organism lives in an environment where food is not distributed randomly but comes in hidden patches whose locations can be inferred from cues. This organism can use more sophisticated strategies, such as learning the association between cues and food, and a memory for storing this information. The general point is that to understand which heuristic an organism employs, and when and why the heuristic works well, one needs to look at the structure of the information in the environment. Simon (1956a) was not the only one to make this important point; it was made both before his work (e.g., Brunswik, 1943) and at various times since (e.g., Anderson, 1990; Shepard, 1990), including the extreme statement that only the environment need be studied, not the mechanisms of the mind (e.g., Gibson, 1979). But in general the second part of Simon's (1956a) paper title, "Rational choice and the structure of environments," has been neglected in mainstream cognitive sciences (sometimes even by Simon himself—see Simon, 1987).

We use the term "ecological rationality" to bring environmental structure back into bounded rationality. A heuristic is ecologically rational to the degree that it is adapted to the structure of an environment (see below). Thus, simple heuristics and environmental structure can both work hand in hand to provide a realistic alternative to the ideal of optimization, whether unbounded or constrained.

One form of bounded rationality is Simon's concept of <u>satisficing</u>—a word that originated in Northumbria (a region in England on the Scottish border), where it meant "to satisfy." Satisficing is a method for making a choice from a set of alternatives encountered sequentially when one does not know much about the possibilities ahead of time. In such situations, there may be no optimal solution for when to stop searching for further alternatives—for instance, once Darwin decided to marry, there would be no optimal way of deciding when to stop looking for prospective marriage partners and settle down with a particular one (see chapter 13 for more on satisficing in mate search). Satisficing takes the shortcut of setting an adjustable aspiration level and ending the search for alternatives as soon as one is encountered that exceeds the aspiration level (Simon, 1956a, 1990).

Satisficing is evident in the behavior of firefighter commanders who make life-and-death decisions under extreme time pressure: Rather than surveying all of the alternative courses of action to combat the flames in, say, the basement of a four-story apartment building, they seem to pick one possible action, play it quickly through in a mental simulation, and if it works well enough—that is, if its outcome exceeds a predetermined aspiration level for success—they act it out without ever considering other alternatives. If the outcome of the mental simulation does not meet their aspiration level, they go on to the next alternative, repeating the simulation process until a satisfactory course of action is found (Klein, 1998).

Bounded Rationality: Fast and Frugal Heuristics

Satisficing is a way of making a decision about a set of alternatives that respects the limitations of human time and knowledge: It does not require finding out or guessing about all the options and consequences the future may hold, as optimization under constraints does. However, some forms of satisficing can still require a large amount of deliberation on the part of the decision maker, for instance to set an appropriate aspiration level in the first place, or to calculate how a current option compares to the aspiration level (Simon, 1956b). Rather than let unrealistic mental computation slip back into our picture of human rationality, we narrow our focus still more to concentrate on fast and frugal heuristics for decision making.

Fast and frugal heuristics employ a minimum of time, knowledge, and computation to make adaptive choices in real environments. They can be used to solve problems of sequential search through objects or options, as in satisficing. They can also be used to make choices between simultaneously available objects, where the search for information (in the form of cues, features, consequences, etc.) about the possible options must be limited, rather than the search for the options themselves. Fast and frugal heuristics limit their search of objects or information using easily computable stopping rules, and they make their choices with easily computable decision rules. We thus see satisficing and fast and frugal heuristics as two overlapping but different categories of bounded rationality: There are some forms of satisficing that are fast and frugal, and others that are computationally unreasonable; and there are some fast and frugal heuristics that make satisficing sequential option decisions, and some that make simultaneous option choices. We consider fast and frugal heuristics to represent bounded rationality in its purest form.

How would a fast and frugal Darwin settle his marriage quandary? One way that he could make his decision between the two alternatives—to marry or not—with little time and knowledge would be to employ a form of one-reason decision making, in which he need only find a single piece of information to determine his decision. Indeed, the passage immediately before Darwin's "Q. E. D." can be read to suggest that there was only one decisive reason for his choice in favor of marriage, that of having a constant companion: "Imagine living all one's day solitarily in smoky dirty London House.—Only picture to yourself a nice soft wife on a sofa. . . . " There is a sound reason why a person might base a decision on only one reason rather than on a combination of reasons: Combining information from different cues requires converting them into a common currency, a conversion that may be expensive if not actually impossible. For instance, to make his decision on the basis of several cues combined into one assessment of each option, Darwin would have to decide how many conversations with clever friends are equivalent to having one child, and how many hours in a smoky abode can be traded against a lifetime of soft moments on the sofa. Standard models of optimization, whether constrained or unbounded, assume that there is a common currency for all beliefs and desires, namely, quantitative probabilities and utilities. Although this is a mathematically convenient assumption, the way we look at the world does not always conform to it. Some things do not have a price tag, and cannot be reduced to and exchanged for any common currency (Elster, 1979). Love, true friendship, military honors, and PhD's, for example, are supposed to be priceless, and therefore incommensurable with items for sale in a shopping mall. When reasons cannot be converted to a single currency, the mind has little choice but to rely on a fast and frugal strategy that bases its decision on just one good reason. As we will see, however, incommensurability is not the only reason for one-reason decision making (chapters 4–6).

Before we take a closer look at fast and frugal heuristics, let us sum up our discussion so far. Bounded rationality has become a fashionable term in many quarters, and a plethora of proposed examples have been thrown together under this term, including optimization under constraints. Figure 1-2 helps to make clear the distinctions between bounded rationality and the demonic visions of rationality. Unbounded rationality is not concerned with the costs of search, while bounded rationality explicitly limits search through stopping rules. Optimization under constraints also limits search, but does so by computing the optimal stopping point, that is, when the costs of further search exceed the benefits. In contrast, bounded rationality "bets" on simple heuristics for search and stopping rules that do not attempt to optimize. Finally, the purest form of bounded rationality is found in fast and frugal heuristics, which perform limited search through objects (in satisficing) or cues and exploit environmental structure to yield adaptive decisions.

The ABCs of Fast and Frugal Heuristics: A New Research Program

This book promotes the view of bounded rationality as the way that real people make the majority of their inferences and decisions. It is also a useful framework for developing decision-making heuristics for artificial agents. The program of studying boundedly rational heuristics involves (a) designing computational models of candidate simple heuristics, (b) analyzing the environmental structures in which they perform well, (c) testing their performance in real-world environments, and (d) determining whether and when people really use these heuristics. The results of the investigatory stages (b), (c), and (d) can be used to inform the initial theorizing of stage (a). The different stages of this research program rest on multiple methods, including theoretical modeling of heuristics, computer simulation of their performance, mathematical analysis of the fit between heuristics and specific environments, and laboratory experimentation. We now consider each of the four stages in turn.

Computational Models

A computational model of a heuristic specifies the precise steps of information gathering and processing that are involved in generating a decision, such that the heuristic can be instantiated as a computer program. For a fast and frugal heuristic, this means the computational model must specify principles for guiding a search for alternatives, information, or both, stopping that search, and making a decision.

Heuristic Principles for Guiding Search   Decisions must be made between alternatives, based on information about those alternatives. In many situations, those alternatives and pieces of information may need to be found through active search. The heuristic principles for guiding search, whether across alternatives or information, are what give search its direction (if it has one). For instance, search for cues can be simply random, or in order of some precomputed criterion related to their usefulness (see chapter 6), or based on a recollection about which cues worked previously when making the same decision (see chapter 4). Search for alternatives can similarly be random or ordered. Fast and frugal search-guiding principles do not use extensive computations or knowledge to figure out where to look next.

Heuristic Principles for Stopping Search   In our conception of bounded rationality, the temporal limitations of the human mind (or that of any realistic decision-making agent) must be respected as much as any other constraints. This implies in particular that search for alternatives or information must be terminated at some point. Moreover, the method for determining when to stop search should not be overly complicated. For example, one simple stopping rule is to cease searching for information and make a decision as soon as the first cue or reason that favors one alternative is found (see chapter 4). This and other cue-based stopping rules do not need to compute an optimal cost-benefit trade-off as in optimization under constraints; in fact, they need not compute any costs or benefits at all. For search across alternatives, simple aspiration-level stopping rules can be used, as in Simon's original satisficing notion (Simon, 1956a, 1990; see also chapter 13).

Heuristic Principles for Decision Making   Once search has been guided to find the appropriate alternatives or information and then been stopped, a final set of heuristic principles can be called upon to make the decision or inference based on the results of the search. These principles can also be very simple and computationally bounded. For instance, a decision or inference can be based on only one cue or reason, whatever the total number of cues found during search (see chapters 2–6). Such one-reason decision making does not need to weight or combine cues, and so no common currency between cues need be determined. Decisions can also be made through a simple elimination process, in which alternatives are thrown out by successive cues until only one final choice remains (see chapters 8 and 11).

These heuristic principles are the building blocks, or the ABCs, of fast and frugal heuristics. Given that the mind is a biological rather than a logical entity, formed through a process of successive accrual, borrowing, and refinement of components, it seems reasonable to assume that new heuristics are built from the parts of the old ones, rather than from scratch (Pinker, 1997; Wimsatt, in press). In this light, we have used two main methods to construct computational models of fast and frugal heuristics: combining building blocks and nesting existing heuristics. Heuristic principles can be combined in multiple ways, such as the several guises in which we find one-reason decision making throughout this book, though of course not arbitrarily. For instance, a fast and frugal heuristic for two-alternative choice that stops information search at the first cue on which the alternatives differ must also use a decision principle based on one-reason decision making. Whole fast and frugal heuristics can themselves be combined by nesting one inside another. As an example, the recognition heuristic (see chapters 2 and 3) works on the basis of an elementary cognitive capacity, recognition memory, but it can also serve as the first step of heuristics that draw on other capacities, such as recall memory (see chapters 4 and 5). Recognition memory develops earlier than recall memory both ontogenetically and evolutionarily, and the nesting of heuristics can similarly be seen as analogous to the addition of a new adaptation on top of an existing one.

We have formulated the fast and frugal heuristics in this book as precise step-by-step models that are highly *transparent*: It is easy to discern and understand just how they function to make decisions. Because they involve few free parameters and a minimum of computation, each step of the algorithm is open to scrutiny. These simple heuristics stand in sharp contrast to more complex and computationally involved models of mental processes, which may generate good approximations to human behavior but are also often rather opaque. For instance, the resurgence of connectionism in the 1980s brought forth a crop of neural networks that were respectable models for a variety of psychological phenomena, but whose inner workings remained mysterious even to their creators. Only with effort has the fascination with these black-box connectionist models been overcome, and new methods developed to allow us to see inside them (Regier, 1996; Rumelhart & Todd, 1993). The temptation of the black magic associated with black-box methods exists in other related domains, such as the use of complicated and opaque statistical packages to analyze behavior (Boyd & Richerson, 1985; Gigerenzer, 1993). Transparent models of fast and frugal heuristics avoid misunderstanding and mystification of the processes involved, even if they do sacrifice some of the allure of the unknown.

Ecological Rationality

Traditional definitions of rationality are concerned with maintaining internal order of beliefs and inferences, as we will see in the next section. But real organisms spend most of their time dealing with the external disorder of their environment, trying to make the decisions that will allow them to survive and reproduce (Tooby & Cosmides, 1998). To behave adaptively in the face of environmental challenges, organisms must be able to make inferences that are fast, frugal, and accurate. These real-world requirements lead to a new conception of what proper reasoning is: ecological rationality. Fast and frugal heuristics that are matched to particular environmental structures allow organisms to be ecologically rational. The study of ecological rationality thus involves analyzing the structure of environments, the structure of heuristics, and the match between them, as we will see throughout this book.

How is ecological rationality possible? That is, how *can* fast and frugal heuristics work as well as they do, and escape the trade-offs between different real-world criteria including speed and accuracy? The main reason for their success is that they make a trade-off on another dimension: that of generality versus specificity. While coherence criteria are very general—logical consistency, for instance, can be applied to any domain—the correspondence criteria that measure a heuristic's performance against the real world require much more domain-specific solutions. What works to make quick and accurate inferences in one domain may well not work in another. Thus, different environments can have different specific fast and frugal heuristics that exploit their particular information structure to make adaptive decisions. But specificity can also be a danger: If a different heuristic were required for every slightly different decision-making environment, we would need an unworkable multitude of heuristics to reason with, and we would not be able to generalize to previously unencountered environments. Fast and frugal heuristics avoid this trap by their very simplicity, which allows them to be robust in the face of environmental change and enables them to generalize well to new situations.

Exploiting Environment Structure   Fast and frugal heuristics can benefit from the way information is structured in environments. In chapter 10, for instance, we will meet a fast and frugal heuristic for quantitative estimation that relies on the skewed distributions of many real-world variables such as city population size—an aspect of environment structure that traditional statistical estimation techniques would either ignore or even try to erase by normalizing the data. Standard statistical models, and standard theories of rationality, aim to be as general as possible, so they make as broad and as few assumptions as possible about the data to which they will be applied. But the way information is structured in real-world environments often does not follow convenient simplifying assumptions. For instance, whereas most statistical models are designed to operate on data sets where means and variances are independent, Karl Pearson (1897) noted that in natural situations these two measures tend to be correlated, and thus each can be used as a cue to infer the other (Einhorn & Hogarth, 1981, p. 66). While general statistical methods strive to ignore such factors that could limit their applicability, evolution would seize upon informative environmental dependencies such as this one and exploit them with specific heuristics if they would give a decision-making organism an adaptive edge.

Robustness   How can simple domain-specific heuristics ever be about as accurate as complex general strategies that work with many free parameters? One answer lies in not being *too* specific. Simple heuristics are meant to apply to specific environments, but they do not contain enough detail to match any one environment precisely. General strategies that can be made to conform to a broad range of environments, on the other hand, can end up being too highly focused to be of much real use—having a large number of free parameters to fiddle with can be a hindrance. Imagine a compulsive Weather Channel watcher with too much time on his hands who decides to record the daily fluctuations in temperature and rainfall where he lives for a year. If he uses this exact daily data to determine his wardrobe choices the following year, wearing shorts this April 15 because it was hot and dry last April 15, he will often end up cold and wet. As accurate as his detailed weather model may be for describing the particular pattern for which it was constructed, its predictive value in other situations—other times or other locations—may be minimal. This failure of generalization, a phenomenon known as *overfitting* (e.g., Geman et al., 1992; Massaro, 1988b), stems from assuming that every detail is of utmost relevance. In contrast, if our weather watcher had used many fewer parameters in his model, for instance just recording the average weekly temperature and rainfall and using that to infer how to dress accordingly a year later, he could have made much more accurate (weekly) predictions and ended up more comfortable, adapting to the general trends that occur year after year. As we will show in various chapters, models with many free parameters, from multiple linear regression to neural networks, can suffer from trying to be like the compulsive rain spotter.

Thus, there is an important difference between the two typical applications of a strategy, *fitting* (fit a strategy to a given set of data) and *generalization* (use a strategy to predict new data). In fitting, it is usually true that the more parameters a model has, and the more information (cues) it uses, the better it will fit given data. In generalization, in contrast, more is not necessarily better. A computationally simple strategy that uses only some of the available information can be more robust, making more accurate predictions for new data, than a computationally complex, information-guzzling strategy that overfits.

Robustness goes hand in hand with speed, accuracy, and especially information frugality. Fast and frugal heuristics can reduce overfitting by ignoring the noise inherent in many cues and looking instead for the "swamping forces" reflected in the most important cues. Thus, simply using only one or a few of the most useful cues can automatically yield robustness. Furthermore, important cues are likely to remain important. The informative relationships in the environment are likely to hold true when the environment changes—for instance, April is likely to be associated with showers in northern locations year after year. In contrast, the random fluctuations of noise and even the effects of smaller systematic factors may well frequently alter—for instance, May flowers may depend on many variable factors such as temperature, rainfall, seed dispersal, and insect pests that collectively change more from one year to the next. Because of this pattern, fast and frugal heuristics that pay attention to systematic informative cues while overlooking more variable uninformative cues can ride out environmental change without suffering much decrement in performance. Laplace's superintelligence would never overfit because it does not have to make uncertain predictions. But models of inference that try to be like a Laplacean superintelligence are doomed to overfitting, when they swallow more data than they can digest.

Studying ecological rationality enables us to go beyond the widespread fiction that basing decision making on more information and computation will always lead to more accurate inferences. This ideology dominates much research, leading to computational models of cognition that are based on information-hungry statistical methods (Gigerenzer & Murray, 1987), and more generally to evaluative judgments about what is good and bad cognition. For instance, many "dual process" theories in cognitive and social psychology characterize reasoning with dichotomies such as analytic versus heuristic, argumentative versus suggestive, rule-based versus associative, and mindful versus mindless (e.g., Evans, 1989; Sloman, 1996). The unquestioned assumption behind these theories is that the more laborious, computationally expensive, and nonheuristic the strategy, the better the judgments to which it gives rise. This more-is-better ideology ignores the ecological rationality of cognitive strategies. Consequently, it comes as a surprise to the dichotomy makers when people perform bet-

ter by violating one of these ideological dictums, for instance when people
make better judgments by relying on their intuition than when they reason
(Wilson & Schooler, 1991), or when someone's forecasts of stock earnings
decrease in accuracy as new information is added (Davis et al., 1994), or
when simple intuitive strategies do well on Bayesian inferences (McKenzie, 1994; see also Ambady & Rosenthal, 1992). There is a point where too
much information and too much information processing can hurt. Cognition is the art of focusing on the relevant and deliberately ignoring the
rest. We take the same approach to modeling cognition.

Performance in Real-World Environments

As mentioned earlier, bounded rationality is often characterized as a view
that takes into account the cognitive limitations of thinking humans—an
incomplete and potentially misleading characterization. If we want to understand how real human minds work, we must look not only at how our
reasoning is "limited" compared to that of supernatural beings, but also
at how our minds are adapted to real-world environments. This two-sided
conception of bounded rationality should inform our choice of criteria by
which to evaluate the performance of heuristics.

One set of criteria that is often used to evaluate judgments and decisions is the laws of logic and probability theory. For instance, if judgments
are consistent (e.g., I always think that event A is more likely than B) and
transitive (I think A is more likely than B, B is more likely than C, and
therefore that A is more likely than C), this is taken as an indication that
the underlying decision strategies are rational. If such criteria are violated,
this is typically held to be a sign of irrationality on the part of the decision
maker. These laws of logic and probability are called *coherence* criteria
because they are primarily concerned with the internal logical coherence
of judgments rather than with how well they help us to make useful decisions in the real world. If you believe there is a probability of 90% that
Elvis is still alive and a probability of 10% that he is not, your beliefs are
at least coherent, in that you give the two opposite possibilities together
a 100% chance, as probability theory says you must. But if they lead you
to spend long hours in cornfields waiting for his UFO to land, these beliefs are not doing you much real-world good. Instead of considering these
issues of content and real-world adaptiveness, most experimental research
programs aimed at demonstrating the rationality or (usually) irrationality
of humans and animals have used the abstract coherence criteria. For instance, many claims that there are systematic irrational fallacies in human
reasoning are based entirely on a violation of some rule or other of logic
or probability (e.g., Tversky & Kahneman, 1983; Wason, 1983). Similarly,
it has been claimed that monkeys are rational (McGonigle & Chalmers,
1992) following the observation that squirrel monkeys make choices that
conform to transitivity.

This book adopts a different, adaptive view of rational behavior. We do not compare human judgment with the laws of logic or probability, but rather examine how it fares in real-world environments. The function of heuristics is not to be coherent. Rather, their function is to make reasonable, adaptive inferences about the real social and physical world given limited time and knowledge. Hence, we should evaluate the performance of heuristics by criteria that reflect this function. Measures that relate decision-making strategies to the external world rather than to internal consistency, such as accuracy, frugality, and speed, are called *correspondence* criteria (Hammond, 1996a). As Egon Brunswik (1957) observed, the mind and the environment are like a husband and wife who must come to terms with each other by mutual adaptation. However, owing to the focus on coherence in much research on reasoning and decision making, the couple has become estranged. Our aim is to get this couple corresponding again, even if they cannot be coherent.

Indeed, the two kinds of criteria, coherence and correspondence, can sometimes be at odds with each other. For instance, in social situations, including some competitive games and predator-prey interactions, it can be advantageous to exhibit inconsistent behavior in order to maximize adaptive unpredictability and avoid capture or loss (Driver & Humphries, 1988). In chapters 4 and 5, we will meet a similarly illogical heuristic—the Minimalist heuristic—that violates transitivity but nevertheless makes fairly robust and accurate inferences in particular environments. Thus, intransitivity does not necessarily imply high levels of inaccuracy, nor does transitivity guarantee high levels of accuracy—logic and adaptive behavior are logically distinct.

To conclude: Heuristics are not simply hobbled versions of optimal strategies. There are no optimal strategies in many real-world environments in the first place. This does not mean, though, that there are no performance criteria in the real world. As a measure of the success of a heuristic, we compare its performance with the actual requirements of its environment, which can include making accurate decisions, in a minimal amount of time, and using a minimal amount of information. We have thus replaced the multiple coherence criteria stemming from the laws of logic and probability with multiple correspondence criteria relating to real-world decision performance. But there is a further difference between these two sets of multiple criteria: While *all* coherence criteria must be met for a decision method to be deemed rational, correspondence criteria can be considered in relation to each other. In some environments, for instance, it may be more important to make a decision quickly rather than focusing on accuracy. However, one of the surprising empirical results reported in this book is that simple heuristics need not always make such trade-offs. We will show that, when compared to some standard benchmark strategies, fast and frugal heuristics can be faster, more frugal, and more accurate at the same time. No trade-off need be considered.

Do People Use Fast and Frugal Heuristics?

The research program described so far encompasses three big questions: (1) What are reasonable heuristic principles for guiding search, stopping search, and making a decision using the results of that search? (2) When and why do these heuristics perform well, that is, how can they be ecologically rational? (3) How well do fast and frugal heuristics actually perform in real-world environments? Exploring these three questions is sufficient if we are interested in investigating new heuristics for various applied settings—the realms of artificial intelligence and decision-support systems, for instance. But if we are also concerned to discover the principles that guide natural human and animal behavior, we must add a fourth question to our research program: What is the evidence that humans or animals use specific fast and frugal heuristics?

We know rather little about the heuristic principles of limited search and stopping that people and animals use. One major reason for this is that the typical experimental task eliminates search in the first place (but see e.g., Connolly & Gilani, 1982; Payne et al., 1993; Saad & Russo, 1996). Researchers usually sidestep questions of search by using tasks in which all pieces of information—usually only two or three—are already conveniently laid out in front of the participant. We refer to this type of task as *inference from givens*, as opposed to *inference from memory* or inference from the external environment, both of which require search (Gigerenzer & Goldstein, 1996a). For instance, the majority of psychological studies of categorization use artificial objects (e.g., drawings of faces or fishes) that vary on only a few cues. To classify a new object, the participant is not supposed to perform a search for cues in memory or in the environment, but rather is expected merely to use the few immediately available cues presented in the stimuli (see chapter 11 for a discussion of this problem and a fast and frugal categorization heuristic designed to tackle more realistic multiple-cue situations). Theories of cognition and the experimental tasks used to test those theories often conspire hand in hand to overlook limited search and stopping rules. But experiments in which search is obviated are unsuitable for testing models of ecological and bounded rationality that rely on limited information search as a central component.

Ironically, one reason why so little attention has been devoted to heuristic principles of limited search may stem from the use of a fast and frugal heuristic itself. The *tools-to-theories heuristic* of scientific discovery (Gigerenzer, 1991a) predicts that the laboratory tools entrenched in the daily routine of cognitive scientists will tend to be adopted as models of mind. In the 1950s and 1960s, statistical methods of inference were institutionalized in experimental psychology, based on a mishmash of Fisher's null hypothesis testing and Neyman and Pearson's decision theory. None of these institutionalized tools dealt with search and stopping rules, in contrast to other well-known statistical tools that do (e.g., the sequential analysis of Wald, 1947). In accordance with the tools-to-theories heuristic, many researchers have since proposed theories that model cognitive processes after these institutionalized statistical tools, and that therefore also ignore the necessity of modeling search and stopping rules. For example, in his causal attribution theory, Kelley (1967) proposed that the mind attributes effects to causes in the same way that cognitive researchers generally do, that is, by calculating Fisher's analysis of variance. As another instance, in what became known as signal detection theory, Tanner and Swets (1954) suggested that the mind discriminates between two stimuli the way a statistician of the Neyman-Pearson school would test between two statistical hypotheses. As mentioned above, these statistical approaches of Fisher and Neyman-Pearson did not include the concept of search, and so, following the tools-to-theories explanation, this is why neither the cognitive theories stemming from these statistical tools nor the experimental tasks designed to test them consider search processes, a legacy we are left with today (Gigerenzer & Goldstein, 1996b; Gigerenzer & Murray, 1987).

In contrast to the lack of work on heuristic principles for guiding and stopping search, decision rules have been the focus of a great deal of research and theorizing. For instance, psychologists have asked whether children integrate information additively, multiplicatively, or in some other way (e.g., Gigerenzer & Richter, 1990), and whether adults integrate information by Bayes's rule or by averaging (e.g., Birnbaum & Mellers, 1983). But again these questions are typically investigated with experimental designs in which information is restricted to only two or three cues presented to participants, removing the need for any search. As a consequence, the results of these studies may not tell us much about the heuristic decision principles used in more realistic situations where information or alternatives must be actively sought.

Summary of the Research Program

The research program just described is designed to elucidate three distinct but interconnected aspects of rationality (see also Chase et al., 1998).

1. *Bounded rationality.* Decision-making agents in the real world must arrive at their inferences using realistic amounts of time, information, and computational resources. We look for inference mechanisms exhibiting bounded rationality by designing and testing computational models of fast and frugal heuristics and their psychological building blocks. The building blocks include heuristic principles for guiding search for information or alternatives, stopping the search, and making decisions.

2. *Ecological rationality.* Decision-making mechanisms can exploit the structure of information in the environment to arrive at more adaptively useful outcomes. To understand how different heuristics can be

ecologically rational, we characterize the ways information can be structured in different decision environments and how heuristics can tap that
structure to be fast, frugal, accurate, and otherwise adaptive at the same
time.

3. *Social rationality.* The most important aspects of an agent's environment are often created by the other agents it interacts with. Thus, predators must make crucial inferences about the behavior of their prey (see
chapter 12), males and females must make decisions about others they are
interested in mating with (chapter 13), and parents must figure out how
to help their children (chapter 14). Social rationality is a special form of
ecological rationality, and to study it we design and test computational
models of fast and frugal heuristics that exploit the information structure
of the social environment to enable adaptive interactions with other
agents. These heuristics can include socially adaptive building blocks,
such as emotions of anger and parental love and social norms, which can
act as further heuristic principles for search, stopping, and decision (we
return to this point below).

These three aspects of rationality look toward the same central goal:
to understand human behavior and cognition as it is adapted to specific
environments (ecological and social), and to discover the heuristics that
guide adaptive behavior.

How the ABC Research Program Relates to Earlier
Notions of Heuristics

The term "heuristic" is of Greek origin, meaning "serving to find out or
discover." From its introduction into English in the early 1800s up until
about 1970, "heuristic" referred to useful, even indispensable cognitive
processes for solving problems that *cannot* be handled by logic and probability theory (e.g., Groner et al., 1983; Polya, 1954). After 1970, a second
meaning emerged in the fields of psychology and decision-making research: overused, mostly dispensable cognitive processes that people often misapply to situations where logic and probability theory *should* be
applied instead (e.g., Tversky & Kahneman, 1974). We now explore the
twentieth-century changes in the concept of heuristic in a bit more detail,
and show how our own use of the term fits into the historical context.

In 1905, the 26-year-old Albert Einstein published his first fundamental paper in quantum physics, titled "On a heuristic point of view concerning the generation and transformation of light." In that Nobel prize-
winning paper, Einstein used the term "heuristic" to indicate that he considered the view he presented therein as incomplete, false even, but still
useful. Einstein could not wholeheartedly accept the quantum view of
light that he started to develop in this paper, but he believed that it was
of great transitory use on the way to building a more correct theory (Hol-

ton, 1988, pp. 360–361). As used by Einstein, then, a heuristic is an approach to a problem that is necessarily incomplete given the knowledge available, and hence unavoidably false, but which is useful nonetheless for guiding thinking in appropriate directions (see also Wimsatt, 1987).

A few decades later, Max Wertheimer (a close friend of Einstein's), Karl Duncker, and other Gestalt psychologists spoke of heuristic reasoning, but with a meaning slightly different from Einstein's. Gestalt psychologists conceptualized thinking as an interaction between inner mental processes and external problem structure. In this view, heuristic methods such as "looking around" and "inspecting the problem" are first used to guide the search for appropriate information in the environment, which is then restructured or reformulated by inner processes (e.g., Duncker, 1935/ 1945). It is in this tradition that Herbert Simon and Allen Newell modeled heuristics for search, replacing the somewhat vague methods of the Gestalt school with much more precise computational models. With the advent of information processing theory in cognitive psychology, a heuristic came to mean a useful shortcut, an approximation, or a rule of thumb for guiding search, such as a strategy that a chess master uses to reduce the enormous space of possible moves at each point in a game.

We use the term "heuristic" in the same positive sense as these earlier theorists, emphasizing its beneficial role in guiding search, and following Simon and Newell's emphasis on creating precise computational models. However, we break with the past tradition of using well-defined artificial settings for the study of heuristics, such as mathematical problems (Polya, 1954) or the games of chess and cryptarithmetic that Newell and Simon (1972) investigated. Instead, our research addresses how fast and frugal heuristics can make inferences about unknown aspects of real-world environments.

The research most closely related to the ABC program on fast and frugal heuristics is that on adaptive decision making and on simple classification rules in machine learning. In their work on the "adaptive decision maker," Payne, Bettman, and Johnson (1993) studied the trade-off between accuracy and effort for various choice strategies, including lexicographic rules and Elimination by Aspects (Tversky, 1972). Payne and colleagues emphasized that a decision maker has a multitude of strategies available and chooses among them depending on their costs and accuracy given constraints such as time pressure. This important work has many connections with our own program, as we will see throughout this book, but important differences will also become evident. One such distinction is that Payne and colleagues focused on preferences, such as between hypothetical job candidates or randomly generated gambles, rather than on inferences about the real world, such as which soccer team will win or which of two cities is larger. This is why they could not measure the accuracy of strategies in terms of their ability to predict real-world outcomes. Instead, they measured accuracy by how closely a strategy could match the predictions of a weighted additive rule, which is the traditional gold standard for rational preferences. As a consequence, in Payne, Bettman, and Johnson's research a heuristic can never be better than a weighted additive rule in accuracy (though it may require less computational effort). In contrast, by measuring the performance of all competing strategies against external real-world criteria, we find that fast and frugal heuristics can be more accurate than a weighted additive rule both in theory (chapter 4) and in practice (chapter 5). Research in machine learning similarly focuses on inferences about real-world environments, again allowing accuracy to be measured objectively. Work on simple classification rules that use only one or a few cues (e.g., Holte, 1993; Rivest, 1987) has demonstrated that fast and frugal methods can be accurate, as well as being robust generalizers owing to their limited parameter use.

A very different notion emerged in psychology in the early 1970s, emphasizing how the use of heuristics can lead to systematic errors and lapses of reasoning that indicate human irrationality. This "heuristics-and-biases" program launched by Tversky and Kahneman (1974) tainted the idea of simple mental mechanisms by attaching them to the value-laden "bias" term in a single inseparable phrase. Within this program, heuristics were often invoked as the explanation when errors—mainly deviations from the laws of probability—were found in human reasoning. Although Tversky and Kahneman (1974) repeatedly asserted that heuristics sometimes succeed and sometimes fail, their experimental results were typically interpreted as indicating some kind of fallacy, which was usually attributed to one of three main heuristics: representativeness (judgments influenced by what is typical), availability (judgments based on what comes easily to mind), or anchoring and adjustment (judgments relying on what comes first).

The heuristics-and-biases program suggests that ordinary people are cognitive misers who use little information and little cognition and thus are largely unable to estimate probabilities and risks. Some have taken this to mean that it might be best to cut the general public out of making important social and political decisions, such as those concerning the regulation of the nuclear industry and other potentially hazardous new technologies. In the words of a *Newsweek* article reporting on heuristics-and-biases research: "Most people . . . are woefully muddled information processors who often stumble along ill-chosen short-cuts to reach bad conclusions" (McCormick, 1987, p. 24). However, Tversky and Kahneman also argued that leaving decisions to experts may not be an improvement, as they can be subject to similar mistakes. Given this pessimistic view, it is hard to know where to turn for reasonable decisions.

The narrowly defined "fallacies" discussed by the heuristics-and-biases program have not only been deemed irrational, but have also been interpreted as signs of the bounded rationality of humans (e.g., Thaler, 1991, p. 4). Equating bounded rationality with irrationality in this way is as serious a confusion as equating it with optimization under constraints. Bounded rationality is neither limited optimality nor irrationality.

Our research program of studying fast and frugal heuristics shares some basic features with the heuristics-and-biases program. Both emphasize the important role that simple psychological heuristics play in human thought, and both are concerned with finding the situations in which these heuristics are employed. But these similarities mask a profound basic difference of opinion on the underlying nature of rationality, leading to very divergent research agendas: In our program, we see heuristics as the way the human mind can take advantage of the structure of information in the environment to arrive at reasonable decisions, and so we focus on the ways and settings in which simple heuristics lead to accurate and useful inferences. In contrast, the heuristics-and-biases approach views heuristics as unreliable aids that the limited human mind too commonly relies upon despite their inferior decision-making performance, and hence researchers in this tradition seek out cases where heuristics can be blamed for poor reasoning. We discuss two important distinctions here that follow from this basic difference; for a more detailed analysis, see Gigerenzer (1991b, 1994, 1997; Gigerenzer & Murray, 1987), and for arguments in favor of each side, see the debate between Kahneman and Tversky (1996) and Gigerenzer (1996).

The first distinction is that the ABC program opts for computational models of heuristics instead of vague labels. After three decades of research, the heuristics-and-biases program has generated only nebulous, if plausible, proposals for simple mechanisms of (poor) reasoning, primarily the three heuristics mentioned earlier, representativeness, availability, and anchoring. These one-word labels at once explain too little and too much: too little, because the underlying processes are left unspecified, and too much, because, with sufficient imagination, one of them can be fit to almost any empirical result post hoc. For instance, "base-rate neglect," or ignoring the frequency with which different alternatives occur in the environment when making decisions about them, is commonly attributed to the representativeness heuristic. However, the opposite result, overweighting of base rates (or "conservatism," Edwards, 1968), is as easily "explained" by anchoring (on the base rate) and adjustment (Gigerenzer & Murray, 1987). There are two ways a theory can fail: by being wrong, or by being not even wrong, but merely indeterminate and imprecise. The heuristics-and-biases program has too often fallen into the latter category. But we would rather risk the former fate, because indeterminate theories hinder scientific progress by resisting attempts to prove, disprove, or improve them. In this book, we therefore propose computational models of heuristics, putting our theoretical cards on the table so that others can see them—and even pick them up and play with them.

The second distinction is a normative one. The ABC program dispenses with the focus on coherence criteria (e.g., the laws of probability) as the yardsticks of rationality. Instead, we study the correspondence-based performance of heuristics in real-world environments, situations where optimal coherent strategies are often not known or not feasible. In contrast, proponents of the heuristics-and-biases program typically assume that each reasoning task has exactly one normative answer, which is derived by applying a law of probability in a content-blind way, without looking at the specifics of the task or environment. Our view liberates fast and frugal heuristics from their role in the heuristics-and-biases program as the harbingers of coherence-defined irrationality and holds them up as tools for adaptive and accurate decision making in real environments.

To summarize the place of our research in its historical context, the ABC program takes up the traditional notion of heuristics as an essential cognitive tool for making reasonable decisions. We specify the function and role of fast and frugal heuristics more precisely than has been done in the past, by building computational models with specific principles of information search, stopping, and decision making. We replace the narrow, content-blind norms of coherence criteria with the analysis of heuristic accuracy, speed, and frugality in real-world environments as part of our study of ecological rationality. Finally, whereas the heuristics-and-biases program portrays heuristics as a frequent hindrance to sound reasoning, rendering *Homo sapiens* not so sapient, we see fast and frugal heuristics as enabling us to make reasonable decisions and behave adaptively in our environment—*Homo sapiens* would be lost without them.

The Adaptive Toolbox

Gottfried Wilhelm Leibniz had a beautiful dream. He dreamed of a universal logical language, the Universal Characteristic, that would replace all reasoning (Leibniz, 1677/1951). The Universal Characteristic had two parts: (1) an alphabet of human thought, that is, a system of primitive characters that stand for irreducible simple concepts and form an inventory of real things; and (2) a calculus of reasoning that combines the elements of this alphabet. While Robert Boyle had searched for the alphabetic elements of chemistry, Leibniz aimed for an even more ambitious target: understanding the universal language in which God had written the book of nature. He saw such knowledge of God's creation as the most important goal anyone could strive for. Leibniz believed that the Universal Characteristic would put an end to scholarly bickering and clamorous controversy—people could stop shouting at one another and settle matters peacefully by sitting down with pencil and paper and saying, "Let's calculate." All matters of science and morality would be solved, and we would live in the best of all possible worlds. Young Leibniz made the optimistic prediction about the Universal Characteristic's development period that "a few selected persons might be able to do the whole thing in five years" (Leibniz, 1677/1951, p. 22). (Similar sentiments have been uttered over the years concerning psychology and artificial intelligence.) For some time, many Enlightenment thinkers believed that the mathematical theory of probability could make Leibniz's dream a reality. But by the 1840s, mathematicians had given up the task of reducing rational reasoning to a general calculus as thankless and even antimathematical (Daston, 1988). However, as we saw earlier in our discussions of demons, there are still many theorists in a variety of fields to this day who have not given up the logic of this dream.

The multitude of simple concepts making up Leibniz's alphabet of human thought were all to be operated on by a single general-purpose tool such as probability theory. But no such universal tool of inference could be found. Just as a mechanic will pull out specific wrenches, pliers, and spark-plug gap gauges for each task in maintaining a car's engine rather than merely hitting everything with a large hammer, different domains of thought require different specialized tools. This is the basic idea of the *adaptive toolbox*: the collection of specialized cognitive mechanisms that evolution has built into the human mind for specific domains of inference and reasoning, including fast and frugal heuristics (see also Bettman, 1979; Cosmides & Tooby, 1992; Payne et al., 1993). The notion of a toolbox jumbled full of unique one-function devices lacks the beauty of Leibniz's dream of a single all-purpose inferential power tool. Instead, it invokes the more modest but surprising abilities of a "backwoods mechanic and used parts dealer" (as Wimsatt, in press, describes Nature) who can provide serviceable solutions to most any problem with just the things at hand.

The adaptive toolbox contains psychological (as opposed to morphological or physiological) adaptations (Tooby & Cosmides, 1992). These include so-called "lower order" perceptual and memory processes which can be fairly automatic, such as depth perception, auditory scene analysis, and face recognition, as well as "higher order" processes that are based on the "lower" processes and can be at least partly accessible to consciousness. Higher order mental processes include the examples we have discussed earlier of inferring whether a heart attack victim should be treated as a high- or low-risk patient and deciding whether or not to marry. The focus of this book is on fast and frugal heuristics for higher order cognitive processes that call upon lower order processes of cue perception and memory.

Lower order perceptual and memory processes such as face and voice recognition are complex and difficult to unravel, in part because they make use of massively parallel computations. No one has yet managed to build a machine that recognizes faces as well as a 2-year-old child. Now consider a higher order decision mechanism that makes inferences based on these processes, the recognition heuristic introduced in chapter 2. This fast and frugal heuristic uses recognition to make rapid inferences about unknown aspects of the world: For instance, food whose taste one recognizes is probably safer than unrecognized food, and a university whose name one has heard of probably provides a more prestigious education than one whose name is unfamiliar. Although the mechanisms of recognition memory may be intricate and complex, the recognition heuristic can be described as an algorithm just a few steps long. We do not need to know precisely how recognition memory works to describe a heuristic that relies on recognition. This example illustrates an apparently paradoxical thesis: *Higher order cognitive mechanisms can often be modeled by simpler algorithms than can lower order mechanisms.*

This thesis is not new. It has been proposed in various forms over the past century, as for example by proponents of the Würzburg school of psychology in the early twentieth century (Kusch, 1999) and more recently by Shepard (1967a). The thesis has limits as well, of course: Some higher order processes, such as the creative process involved in Darwin's development of the theory of natural selection, are probably beyond the grasp of fast and frugal heuristics. But we believe that simple heuristics can be used singly and in combination to account for a great variety of higher order mental processes that may at first glance seem to require more complex explanation, as we will show throughout this book.

Emotions, Social Norms, and Imitation

Although we focus on cognitive heuristics in this book, it is important to point out that emotions can also function as heuristic principles for guiding and stopping information search. For instance, falling in love can be seen as a powerful stopping rule that ends the current search for a partner (at least temporarily) and strengthens commitment to the loved one. Similarly, feelings of parental love, triggered by one's infant's presence or smile, can be described as a means of preventing cost-benefit computations with respect to proximal goals, so that the question of whether it is worthwhile to endure all the sleepless nights and other challenges associated with baby care simply never arises. Emotions are good examples of building blocks in the adaptive toolbox that are substantially domain-specific rather than domain-general (Tooby & Cosmides, 1990): For instance, while parental love is designed to help parents to solve the adaptive task of protecting and providing for their offspring, disgust functions to address the adaptive challenge of avoiding being sickened by spoiled food. There is no general-purpose all-encompassing emotion.

Social norms and social imitation can also help us make decisions with limited time and knowledge. Following heuristics such as "eat what older and experienced conspecifics eat" or "prefer mates picked by others" can speed up decision making by reducing the need for direct experience and information gathering. These forms of social rationality can be found throughout the animal world: For instance, female guppies have a tendency to copy the mate choices of other female guppies that is powerful enough to reverse their prior preferences for one male over another (Dugatkin, 1996), and female quail use a related form of mate copying (Galef & White, 1998). In humans, in addition to individual and media-fueled mate copying, academic hiring sometimes seems to follow a similar heuristic.

Thus the adaptive toolbox contains decision-making heuristics that employ emotions, norms, and imitation in addition to the cognitive building blocks outlined earlier. These additional heuristic principles are particularly important in the realm of social rationality.

How Are Heuristics Selected?

How does the mind choose which heuristic in the adaptive toolbox to apply to a specific problem? There may not be as much choice as it initially seems. The most important reason for this is that specific tasks call for specific tools—that is, each heuristic is specialized for certain classes of problems, which means that most of them are not applicable in a given situation. There are two (overlapping) forms of domain specificity used throughout this book that can determine heuristic choice: specific adaptive tasks, such as mate choice or parental investment; and specific inference tasks, such as categorization or estimation. Clearly, a heuristic designed to make a choice between two alternatives will not be suitable for categorization, nor will a mate choice heuristic help in judging habitat quality. The domain-specific bins in the adaptive toolbox could often hold only a single appropriate tool.

In cases where there *is* more than one applicable heuristic, the knowledge that the decision maker has can be used to select the heuristic. For instance, if a person knows that certain cues can be used to decide between two options, but not which cues are better indicators than others, she does not have enough information (about how to order the cues) to apply a fast and frugal heuristic we call Take The Best (chapter 4). However, she can use the even simpler Take The Last heuristic, which only needs to know what cues to use, and not what order to use them in. If she does not even know any cues to use, but at least recognizes one option and not the other, she can still apply what is perhaps the simplest fast and frugal heuristic: the recognition heuristic (chapter 2). In this way, the level of knowledge can make further selections among domain-specific heuristics in the adaptive toolbox.

Other external factors, such as time pressure and success, may further help to select heuristics (Johnson & Payne, 1985). There are also certain situations in which it is adaptive to alternate between multiple strategies, either randomly, yielding unpredictable *protean* behavior that can be useful when engaging competitors or fleeing from predators (Driver & Humphries, 1988), or systematically, yielding individual differences in decisions that help avoid conflicts such as everyone crowding into the local bar on the same night each week (Arthur, 1994). We assume that all of the factors involved in selecting decision-making mechanisms from the adaptive toolbox will themselves be used in a fast and frugal manner to make the tool choice, rather than being handed over to a hidden computationally elaborate demon who undermines the spirit of fast and frugal cognition by optimizing heuristic choice.

The tools in the adaptive toolbox are made from more primitive components, including the heuristic principles of information search, stopping, and decision discussed earlier. New tools can also be fashioned from old tools, much as a handle added to a chopping stone creates an axe. Thus, for instance, the Take the Best heuristic presented in chapter 4 is made from the more primitive (and probably earlier evolved) recognition heuristic of chapter 2 along with additional heuristic principles. This constructive view applied to the mental tools themselves distinguishes the adaptive toolbox image from the similar metaphor of the mind as a Swiss army knife (Cosmides & Tooby, 1992). Both analogies emphasize that the mind uses a collection of many specifically designed adaptive strategies rather than a few general-purpose power tools, but the toolbox metaphor puts more emphasis on the possibility of recombining tools and building blocks and the nesting of heuristics.

Beyond Demons and Nightmares

In the world of academic thought, there are powerful demons that few people would want to tangle with, such as irrationality and mysticism. But there are also demons that some researchers seem to love, inviting them into mental theories at every opportunity—unbounded rationality and optimization under constraints sitting at the top of the demonic hierarchy. These popular demons embody characteristics that are unquestionably desirable, such as being able to calculate the future, but nonetheless absolutely unattainable for mortal humans. Why have so many social scientists idealized our human knowledge and abilities in ways aspiring to the characteristics of some Supreme Being, rather than reflecting our more real limitations? Is it an intellectual holdover from the pre-Darwinian view of humankind as distinct from the rest of Nature?

The fascination with what is optimal in thought and behavior does reflect a certain sense of beauty and morality. Leibniz's dream of a universal calculus exhibits the aesthetics and the moral virtue of this ideal, as does Laplace's omniscient superintelligence. Cognitive scientists, economists, and biologists have often chased after the same beautiful dreams by building elaborate models endowing organisms with unlimited abilities to know, memorize, and compute. These heavenly dreams, however, tend to evaporate when they encounter the physical and psychological realities of the waking world. Mere mortal humans cannot hope to live up to these dreams, and instead appear irrational and dysfunctional when measured against their fantastic standards. On earth, heavenly dreams become nightmares.

In the face of this nightmarish dilemma, many researchers have still preferred to keep dreaming that humans can approximate these exacting standards, rather than surrender to an ungodly picture of human irrationality and stupidity. The choice, however, is not between an unrealistic dreaming rationality and a realistic nightmare irrationality. There is a third vision that dispenses with this opposition: rationality through simplicity, and accuracy through frugality.

This book is the story of our successes and unresolved challenges in understanding how minds can be fast, frugal, and accurate at the same time, making adaptive inferences about an unknown world through uncertain cues. It is also the story of an interdisciplinary group who set out to journey together from the land of demons to the land of ecologically rational beings, learning the use of multiple methods of inquiry and the value of multiple points of view from each other. When we began our travels almost three years ago, we never imagined how fascinating the voyage would be, nor the many new things our eyes would see.

Part II

IGNORANCE-BASED DECISION MAKING

2

The Recognition Heuristic

How Ignorance Makes Us Smart

Daniel G. Goldstein
Gerd Gigerenzer

Human thought consists of first, a great capacity for recognition, and second, a capability for selective search.

Herbert A. Simon

On a country road in Scotland, MacGregor sees his old schoolmate MacAlister and calls out to him. MacAlister hesitates. He recognizes MacGregor's face, but has no idea of his name, where they had met before, or anything else. MacGregor expresses surprise that his old classmate would "tartle," that is, hesitate in getting beyond a sense of mere recognition. As this useful Scottish verb helps to demonstrate, recognition and recall memory can break apart. Sometimes this break can be permanent, as in the case of R.F.R., a 54-year-old policeman who developed amnesia so grave that he even had difficulty identifying his wife and mother in photographs (Warrington & McCarthy, 1988). It would seem that R.F.R. had lost his capacity for recognition. Had he? In an experiment, he was presented photographs of famous people and of strangers he had never seen before and was asked to point out the famous ones. He performed as though his memory were unimpaired. Even though he lacked the recall memory to name people (such as his mother) in photographs, he retained a normal recognition memory, and this allowed him to indicate the famous faces he had seen before.

Like R.F.R. and the tartling Scotsman, as we wander through a stream of sights, sounds, tastes, odors, and tactile impressions, we have little trouble knowing what we have encountered before, even when we cannot recall more information. Our sense of recognition is argued to constitute a specialized memory system that can be impaired independently of other memory capacities. For instance, elderly people suffering memory loss (Craik & McDowd, 1987; Schonfield & Robertson, 1966) and patients suffering certain kinds of brain damage (Schacter & Tulving, 1994; Squire et al., 1993) have problems saying what they know about an object, even where they have encountered it, but can act in a way that shows that they have encountered the object before. Similarly, laboratory research has demonstrated that recognition memory continues to encode information even in divided-attention learning tasks that are too distracting to allow more substantial memories to be formed (Jacoby et al., 1989). Mere recognition, this essentially binary feeling that we have or have not experienced something before, is a minimal state of knowledge. Why do minds encode it? What is mere recognition good for?

In this chapter, we introduce the simplest heuristic in this book, the *recognition heuristic*, which exploits the vast and efficient capacity of recognition to make inferences about unknown aspects of the world. The processes underlying face, voice, and name recognition are anything but simple, and are still far from understood in cognitive science. However, their output is available to us as a simple signal, recognition, which can be exploited by a very simple heuristic. The recognition heuristic is so frugal that it actually requires a beneficial lack of knowledge to work. In this chapter, we define the heuristic in the form of a simple rule, which allows us to study its performance by means of simulation and mathematical analysis. We show that, under certain conditions, it leads to the counterintuitive *less-is-more effect*, in which a lack of recognition can be beneficial for making inferences. We also illustrate how to measure recognition, which allows us to study experimentally whether people actually use the recognition heuristic.

The term "recognition" has been used in many contexts, so let us be clear about the way in which we shall use it. MacAlister steps onto a bus. The passengers may fall into three classes corresponding to the three columns in figure 2-1. There may be passengers he does not recognize, that is, whom he is sure he has never seen before, represented by the leftmost column. There may be passengers he merely recognizes, but whom he cannot identify or recall anything about (those that make him tartle), represented by the center column. Finally, there may be people he can recognize and also identify (what their profession is, for instance), represented by the rightmost column.

With the term "recognition," as the striped line in figure 2-1 shows, we divide the world into the novel (the leftmost column) and the previously experienced (the two rightmost columns). For instance, landmark recognition, which serves the adaptive function of helping an organism find its way home, is based on the simple binary distinction between the novel and the previously experienced. Mere recognition needs to be distinguished from degrees of knowledge and what is referred to as "familiarity," such as in theories that postulate that attitudes toward objects become more positively inclined with repeated exposure (e.g., Zajonc,

RECOGNITION HEURISTIC

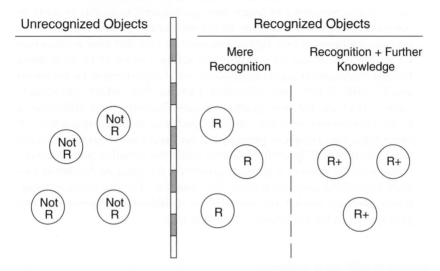

Figure 2-1: How the recognition heuristic applies to unrecognized, novel objects (Not R = not recognized), merely recognized objects (R), and objects about which something is known beyond recognition (R+). The distinction relevant for the recognition heuristic is that between unrecognized objects and everything else.

1968), and those that contend that the belief in an assertion increases with its repetition (e.g., Gigerenzer, 1984; Hasher et al., 1977). We will study heuristics that use knowledge beyond mere recognition beginning in chapter 4. Our use of the term "recognition" also needs to be distinguished from the very common usage that refers to a person's ability to verify whether an object was presented in a previous experimental session. Such studies often fail to touch upon the distinction between the novel and the previously experienced because the stimuli in these studies, mostly digits or common words, are *not* novel to the participant before the experiment. For example, "cat," a common word, would not be novel to someone before an experiment whereas "flink," a nonword, most probably would. In contrast, experiments that use never-before-seen photographs, as in the following examples, exemplify our sense of the word "recognition."

Recognition memory is vast, automatic, and save for déjà vu, reliable. Shepard (1967b) instructed participants to look through 612 pictures at their own pace and immediately afterward tested recognition memory with pairs of pictures, one previously presented and the other novel. Participants were able to recognize the previously presented pictures in 98.5% of all cases, on average. Standing (1973) increased the number of pictures (photographs and "striking" photographs preselected for their vividness) to 1,000 and limited the time of presentation to five seconds. In a test like Shepard's 48 hours later, participants were able to point to the previously presented picture 885 times (normal pictures) or 940 times (striking pictures). These figures become 770 and 880 after a correction for guessing. Standing then outdid himself by a factor of 10. In perhaps the most extensive recognition memory test ever performed, he presented people with 10,000 pairs of normal pictures from which participants chose correctly 8,300 times (6,600 with guessing correction). With respect to the performance with the "striking" pictures, Standing speculates, "if one million items could be presented under these conditions then 731,400 would be retained" (p. 210). Note that, while the retention percentage declines with the number of pictures presented, the absolute number of pictures recognized keeps increasing. We conjecture that the limits of recognition memory cannot be exceeded in a laboratory experiment, and perhaps not in the lifetime of a human being.

How to Benefit from Ignorance

The remarkable capacity for recognition in higher organisms is likely to have evolved for a number of adaptive functions. Consider the eating habits of wild rats, which exhibit strong *neophobia*, that is, a reluctance to eat foods they do not recognize (Barnett, 1963). This mechanism is adaptive in avoiding poisons: Every food a living rat has eaten has, necessarily, not killed it (Revusky & Bedarf, 1967). Norway rats prefer foods they recognize from having tasted them or from having smelled them on the breath of other rats (Galef, 1987; Galef et al., 1990). This heuristic for food choice is followed even if the rat whose breath is smelled happens to be sick at the time. That is, recognition dominates illness information. We will report later in this chapter on a related experiment with humans, in which recognition dominates conflicting information. Food choice in wild rats accords with the recognition heuristic, defined shortly.

In what follows, we describe the recognition heuristic and explore its inferential accuracy. We specify conditions under which this heuristic enables organisms with less knowledge to make more accurate inferences than organisms with more knowledge: a counterintuitive phenomenon we call the less-is-more effect. We start by introducing our "Drosophila" problem area—that is, an example that is well understood—for studying inference: geography.

Proper name recognition constitutes a specialized region in our cognitive system that can be impaired independently of other language skills (McKenna & Warrington, 1980; Semenza & Zettin, 1989; Semenza & Sgaramella, 1993). A person's knowledge of geography consists largely of proper names (those of cities, countries, mountains, and so on) and their assignment to real places on the earth. Geographical knowledge is always incomplete, which makes it an ideal field of inquiry for studies of recognition. We will analyze recognition by means of computer simulation, mathematical analysis, and experimentation. In several demonstrations, we use a geographical topic about which our participants (students at the University of Chicago) had incomplete knowledge: cities in Germany. In particular, we dealt with the class of 83 German cities with more than 100,000 inhabitants. Our American participants recognized only about a quarter of these cities, and yet they were able to exploit this lack of recognition, as we will see.

The task we examine is a common one: selecting a subset of objects from a larger set. In this chapter, we focus on the case of choosing one object from two. This task, two-alternative choice, besides being a staple of experimental psychology, is an elementary case to which many problems of greater complexity (multiple choice, for instance) are reducible. An example of a two-alternative choice question is: "Which is the stronger currency: the pound or the markka?" Or, in the realm of geography: "Which city has a larger population: Munich or Dortmund?"

The Recognition Heuristic

Consider the task of inferring which of two objects has a higher value on some criterion (e.g., which is faster, higher, stronger). The recognition heuristic for such tasks is simply stated: *If one of two objects is recognized and the other is not, then infer that the recognized object has the higher value.*

For instance, a person who has never heard of Dortmund but has heard of Munich would infer that Munich has the higher population, which happens to be correct. The recognition heuristic can *only* be applied when one of the two objects is not recognized, that is, under partial ignorance. Note that where recognition correlates negatively with the criterion, "higher" would be replaced with "lower" in the definition.

Recognition and the Structure of the Environment

The recognition heuristic is *domain-specific* in that it only works in environments where recognition is correlated with the criterion. How is the correlation between recognition and the criterion estimated? In some domains, the direction of this correlation can be genetically coded (as seems to be the case with the rat's inference that unrecognized food is suspect). In other domains, the direction of the correlation must be learned through experience. However, in cases of inference or prediction, the criterion is inaccessible to the organism. Though the criterion may be inaccessible, there are "mediators" in the environment that have the dual property of reflecting (but not revealing) the criterion and also being accessible to the senses, as figure 2-2 illustrates. A person may have no direct information

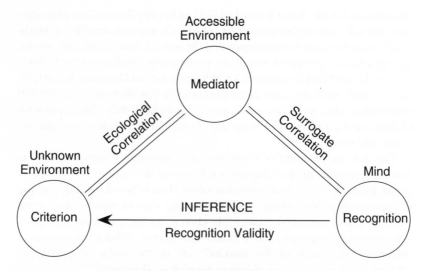

Figure 2-2: The ecological rationality of the recognition heuristic. The inaccessible criterion is reflected, but not revealed, by the mediator variable. The mediator influences the probability of recognition. The mind in turn uses recognition to infer the criterion.

about the endowments of universities, for example, as this information is not always accessible. However, the endowment of a university may be reflected in how often the university is mentioned in the newspaper. Since the newspaper is accessible, it is an example of a mediator. The more often a name occurs in the newspaper, the more likely it is that a person will recognize this name. For instance, Stanford University is more often mentioned in the national press than Miniscule State. Thanks to the mediator of the newspaper, a person can now make an inference about which of these two universities has a larger endowment. Three variables that describe the relationship between the criterion, mediator, and mind are the *recognition validity*, the *ecological correlation*, and the *surrogate correlation*.

The ecological correlation describes the relation between the criterion and the mediator. In the case of university endowments, the criterion is the endowment and the mediator variable is simply the number of times the university is mentioned in the paper (and not any information about its endowment). In the case of the Norway rats, the criterion is the toxicity of a food and the mediator variable could be the number of rats with that food on their breath (and not any other information concerning the health of these rats). The surrogate correlation is that between the mediator (which acts as a surrogate for the inaccessible criterion) and the contents of recognition memory. In our university example, the surrogate correlation is the number of times names are mentioned in the newspaper correlated against recognition of these names. Surrogate correlations can be measured against the recognition memory of one person (in which case the data will be binary), or against the collective recognition of a group, which we will demonstrate later.

The strength of the relationship between recognition and the criterion is the recognition validity, which we define as the proportion of times a recognized object has a higher criterion value than an unrecognized object in a given reference class. The recognition validity α is thus:

$$\alpha = R/(R + W)$$

where R is the number of correct (right) inferences made by the recognition heuristic computed across all pairs where one object is recognized and the other is not, and W is the number of incorrect (wrong) inferences under the same circumstances.

Could It Ever Be Smart to Reason by Recognition?

Food choice in rats may be guided by recognition, but what about inferences made by *Homo sapiens*? Won't inferences based on recognition (or more fittingly, on ignorance) be little more than guesses? Consider two examples of people using the recognition heuristic.

Which U.S. City Has More Inhabitants: San Diego or San Antonio?   We posed this question to students at the University of Chicago and the University of Munich. Sixty-two percent of the University of Chicago students, who have a reputation for being among the most knowledgeable in the United States, chose the correct answer. However, 100% of the German students chose correctly. How did the Germans infer that San Diego was larger? All of the German students had heard of San Diego, but many of them did not recognize San Antonio. They were thus able to apply the recognition heuristic and make a correct inference. The American students, recognizing both cities, were not *ignorant* enough to be able to apply the recognition heuristic.

Which English Soccer Team Will Win?   Fifty Turkish students and 54 British students made forecasts for all 32 English F.A. Cup third-round soccer matches (Ayton & Önkal, 1997). The Turkish participants had very little knowledge about English soccer teams, while the British participants knew quite a bit. Nevertheless, the Turkish group made predictions that were nearly as accurate as those of the English group (63% versus 66% correct). English soccer teams are usually named after English cities (for example, Manchester United), and people who are ignorant of the quality of English soccer teams can still use city recognition as a cue for soccer team performance. Cities with successful soccer teams are likely to be large, and large cities are likely to be recognized. Empirical evidence indicates the Turkish students indeed used the recognition heuristic: Among the pairs where one team was recognized (familiar to some degree) but the other was not, the former team was chosen in 627 out of 662 cases (95%). As before, the recognition heuristic can turn partial ignorance into reasonable inferences.

Both studies illustrate the ecological rationality of the recognition heuristic. The recognition heuristic is ecologically rational in the sense that it exploits the structure of information in natural environments: Lack of recognition in these environments is systematic and not random. Ignorance is beneficial if it is correlated with what one wishes to infer. The heuristic is not a general-purpose strategy because this correlation holds in some situations, but not in all. In many environments involving competition, such as inferring which of two colleges is more highly ranked, or which of two teams will win a match, the recognition heuristic works well. However, there are tasks in which recognition is not a good predictor. Let us look more closely at when the recognition heuristic succeeds and fails.

Accuracy of the Recognition Heuristic

What is the proportion of correct answers one can expect to achieve using the recognition heuristic on two-alternative choice tasks? Suppose there is a reference class of N objects and a test consisting of pairs of randomly drawn objects. When drawing pairs of objects, there are three ways they can turn out: one recognized and one unrecognized, both unrecognized, or both recognized. Suppose there are n recognized objects and thus $N - n$ unrecognized objects. This means that there are $n(N - n)$ pairs where one object is recognized and the other is unrecognized. A similar calculation shows that there are $(N - n)(N - n - 1)/2$ pairs in which neither object is recognized. Finally, there are $n(n - 1)/2$ pairs where both objects are recognized. To transform each of these absolute numbers into a proportion of cases, it is necessary to divide each of them by the total number of possible pairs, $N(N - 1)/2$.

To compute the proportion correct on such a test, it is necessary to know the probability of a correct answer for each type of pair. Recall that the recognition validity α is the probability of getting a correct answer when one object is recognized and the other is not. The probability of getting a correct answer when neither object is recognized (and a guess must be made) is .5. Finally, let β be the *knowledge validity*, the probability of getting a correct answer when both objects are recognized. Combining all these terms together, the expected proportion of correct inferences, $f(n)$, on an exhaustive pairing of objects is:

$$f(n) = 2\left(\frac{n}{N}\right)\left(\frac{N-n}{N-1}\right)\alpha + \left(\frac{N-n}{N}\right)\left(\frac{N-n-1}{N-1}\right)\frac{1}{2} + \left(\frac{n}{N}\right)\left(\frac{n-1}{N-1}\right)\beta \quad (1)$$

The right side of the equation breaks into three parts: the leftmost term equals the proportion of correct inferences made by the recognition heuristic; the middle term equals the proportion of correct inferences resulting from guessing; the rightmost term equals the proportion of correct inferences made when knowledge beyond mere recognition can be used. Inspecting this equation, we see that if the number of cities recognized, n, is 0, then all questions will lead to guesses and the proportion correct will be .5. If $n = N$, then the leftmost two terms become zero and the proportion correct will be β. We can also see that the recognition heuristic will come into play most when the participant is operating under "half ignorance," that is, when half of the objects are recognized ($n = N - n$), because this condition maximizes the number of pairs $n(N - n)$ in which one object is recognized and the other is unrecognized.

To summarize, based on the recognition validity α, the knowledge validity β, and the degree of ignorance, that is, n compared to N, Equation (1) specifies the proportion of correct inferences made by someone who uses the recognition heuristic. Now we will look at the most counterintuitive property of the recognition heuristic: the less-is-more effect.

The Less-Is-More Effect

Imagine that MacAlister's three sons have to take a quiz at school about German cities. The quiz consists of randomly drawn, two-alternative questions about population sizes of the 50 largest German cities. The youngest brother is ignorant, and has never even heard of Germany (not to speak of German cities) before. The middle brother is savvy, and recognizes 25 of the 50 largest cities from what he has overheard from day to day. The cities this middle brother recognizes are larger than the cities he does not recognize in 80% of all comparisons, that is, his recognition validity α is .8. The eldest brother is quite the scholar and has heard of all of the 50 largest cities in Germany. When any of the brothers recognizes both cities in a pair, he has a 60% chance of making the correct choice, that is, β is .6.

Suppose that all brothers use the recognition heuristic whenever they can. Which one will score the highest on the quiz? Figure 2-3, calculated from Equation (1), shows the performance of the three brothers. The smooth line connecting the points graphs the continuous version of Equation (1).

The youngest brother performs at chance level, and the eldest does better with 60% correct. Remarkably, the middle brother, who knows less than the eldest, makes the most accurate inferences. He is the only brother who can use the recognition heuristic. Moreover, he can make the best of his ignorance because he happens to recognize half of the cities, and this allows him to use the recognition heuristic most often. The recognition

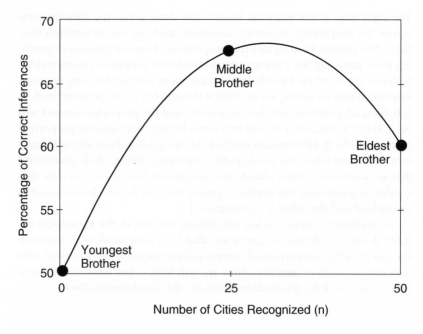

Figure 2-3: An illustration of a less-is-more effect. The youngest brother has never heard of any German city, and performs at chance level. The middle brother recognizes half of the 50 cities, and thus can apply the recognition heuristic in about half of the questions. This allows for 67.5% correct inferences (calculated from Equation (1); $\alpha = .8$ and $\beta = .6$). The oldest brother, who has heard of all the cities and thus knows more than the middle brother, gets only 60% correct inferences—a less-is-more effect. The curve also shows the performance for intermediate states of lack of recognition (calculated from Equation (1)). Note that the curve does not peak over the middle brother, but rather has its maximum slightly to the right of him. The reason for this is that β is .6 rather than .5.

heuristic can thus lead to a paradoxical situation where those who know more exhibit lower inferential accuracy than those who know less.

When Will the Less-Is-More Effect Occur?

The situation in which the less-is-more effect occurs can be stated in general terms. In the type of two-alternative tests described here where the recognition heuristic is consistently applied, *a less-is-more effect occurs when the recognition validity α is greater than the knowledge validity β.*

If this condition does not hold, then inferential accuracy will increase as more and more objects become recognized. We derive this result mathematically in Goldstein and Gigerenzer (1998).

A mathematical demonstration, however, is always based on simplifying assumptions. Here, for example, we have supposed that the recognition validity α remains constant across the x-axis in figure 2-3. In contrast to this figure, which represents individuals (the brothers) with different knowledge states and fixed α, the recognition validity usually varies when one individual comes to recognize more and more objects. The intuition for this result is as follows. When there are many different individuals with various levels of recognition, it is possible that each individual has the same recognition validity (that is, the objects they recognize are larger than the objects they do not recognize a certain proportion of the time, which we call α). However, when one individual comes to recognize more and more objects, the recognition validity changes because each newly recognized object, depending on how large it is, will increase or decrease the recognition validity. That is, coming to recognize smaller objects decreases recognition validity, and coming to recognize larger objects increases it.

Thus, the question must be posed: Can we demonstrate a less-is-more effect using realistic sequences of learning that do not satisfy the simplifying assumption that α is constant as n varies?

We created a computer program that learns about German cities in order of how well-known they are. To estimate this order, we surveyed 66 University of Chicago students and asked them to select the cities in Germany they recognized from a list, and then we ranked the cities by the number of people who recognized them. With this data, we hoped to approximate the order in which an American might learn about cities in Germany. The computer program first learned to recognize only Munich, the most well-known city, and was then given an exhaustive quiz consisting of all pairs of German cities. Next, already knowing Munich, it learned to recognize Berlin, the second most well-known city, and was tested again. It learned to recognize city after city until it recognized them all. In one condition, the program learned *only* the names of cities and made all inferences by the recognition heuristic alone. This result is shown by the bottom line on figure 2-4 labeled "no cues." When all objects were unrecognized, performance was at a chance level. Over the course of learning about cities, an inverse "U" shape appears, as in figure 2-3. Here the less-is-more curve is very jagged because, as mentioned, the recognition validity was not set to be a constant, but was allowed to vary freely as cities became recognized.

Would the less-is-more effect disappear if the computer program learned not just the *names* of cities, but information useful for predicting city populations as well? In a series of conditions with increasing information, the program learned the name of each city, along with one, two, or nine predictive cues for inferring population (the same cues as in Gigerenzer & Goldstein, 1996a). In the "one cue" condition, as the program learned to recognize a city, it also learned if it was once an exposition

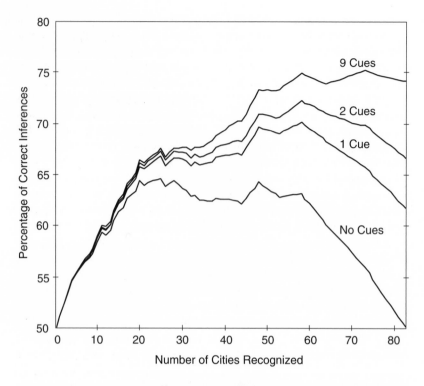

Figure 2-4: Less-is-more effects as cities become recognized in an order indicated by actual recognition data. Inferences are made on recognition alone (no cues), or with the aid of 1, 2, or 9 predictive cues.

site. Being an exposition site is a strong predictor of population with a high ecological validity of .91 (see Gigerenzer & Goldstein, 1996a).[1] The program then used a decision strategy called Take The Best (see chapters 4 and 5) to make inferences about which city is larger. All that is necessary to know for now is that Take The Best is an accurate strategy (as accurate as multiple regression for this task) for drawing inferences from cues, and it uses the recognition heuristic as its first step.

1. An ecological validity of .91 means that in 91% of the cases where one city has an exposition site and the other does not, the first is also the larger city. An ecological validity is a relation between a cue and a criterion, independent of a particular person. It is not the same as the knowledge validity β, which is the proportion of correct answers a person achieves when both objects are recognized, no matter what the values on the various cues are. Ecological validity is defined for the subset of pairs where both objects are recognized *and* one has an exposition site and the other does not. Both α and β are characteristics of a particular person.

Does adding predictive information about exposition sites wash out the less-is-more effect? It does not. The peak of the curve shifts slightly to the right, but it maintains its inverse "U" shape. When the program recognizes more than 58 cities, including information about exposition sites, the accuracy still goes down. In the "two cue" condition, the program learned if each city was an exposition site *and* if it had a soccer team in the major league—another cue with high validity (.87). The less-is-more effect was lessened—to be expected when adding knowledge—but still pronounced. Recognizing all cities and knowing all the information contained in two cues (the far right-hand point) resulted in fewer correct inferences than recognizing only 23 cities. Finally, in the "nine cues" condition, the program had all information about all nine cues available to it. This is surely more information for predicting German city populations than most German citizens know. This degree of knowledge must be enough finally to overcome the benefits of ignorance, right? Figure 2-4 shows the less-is-more effect finally flattening out. However, it does not go away completely: Even when all 747 (9×83) cue values are known and all cities are recognized, the point on the far right is still lower than more than a quarter of the points on that curve. A beneficial amount of ignorance can enable even higher accuracy than extensive knowledge.

The simulation can be summarized by two main results. The simplifying assumption that the recognition validity α remains constant is not a necessary precondition for the less-is-more effect. Moreover, the counterintuitive effect holds in this example even when complete knowledge about nine predictors is present.

A less-is-more effect can be observed in at least three different situations. First, it can occur between two groups of people, where the more knowledgeable group makes systematically fewer accurate inferences than a less knowledgeable group in a given domain. An example of this was the performance of the American and German students on the question about whether San Diego or San Antonio is larger. Second, a less-is-more effect can occur between domains, that is, where the same group of people makes a greater number of accurate inferences in a domain where they know little than in a domain where they know a lot. An empirical example will soon follow. Third, a less-is-more effect can occur over time, that is, where the same group makes increasingly worse inferences as they learn about a domain. For instance, the simulation results in figure 2-4 show how accuracy first increases and then decreases as knowledge is acquired.

So far, we have specified mathematically when the less-is-more effect occurs and shown that it also appears in realistic learning situations that violate the assumptions of the mathematical model. But can the effect be observed in real people? It could be that evolution has overlooked the inferential ease and accuracy the recognition heuristic affords. In the following section, we study whether people's judgments actually follow the recognition heuristic, and whether a less-is-more effect can be demonstrated empirically.

Empirical Evidence

Do People Use the Recognition Heuristic?

This simple test asks how often unprompted people will use the recognition heuristic. We quizzed Americans on all pairs of cities drawn from the 25 ($n = 6$) or 30 ($n = 16$) largest in Germany (300 or 435 questions) and asked them to choose the more populous city in each case. We had the participants check off from a list which of these cities they recognized, either before or after the test (this order, however, had no effect). From this recognition information, we could calculate how often participants had an opportunity to choose in accordance with the recognition heuristic and compare it to how often they actually did. Figure 2-5 shows the results for 22 individual participants. Note that the recognition heuristic predicts individual differences. Depending on the particular cities people recognize, their inferences about the population should systematically vary.

For each participant, two bars are shown. The darker bar shows how many opportunities the person had to apply the recognition heuristic, and the lighter bar shows how often that person's judgments agreed with the heuristic. For example, the person represented by the leftmost pair of bars had 156 opportunities to choose according to the recognition heuristic, and did so every time. The next person did so 216 out of 221 times and so on. The proportions of recognition heuristic adherence ranged between 100% and 73%. The median proportion of inferences following the recognition heuristic was 93% (mean 90%).

This simple test of the recognition heuristic showed that people adhere to it the vast majority of the time. Let us put the heuristic to a tougher test. Would people still rely on it when given information that suggests doing otherwise?

Do People Use the Recognition Heuristic Despite Conflicting Information?

In this experiment, we taught participants useful information that offered an alternative to following the recognition heuristic. The information was about the presence of major league soccer teams, powerful predictors of city population in Germany. We wanted to see which people would choose as larger: an unrecognized city, or a recognized city that they just learned has *no* soccer team. To get an idea of which German cities our participants might recognize, we ran a pilot survey of 26 participants and had them check off from a list those cities they had heard of before.

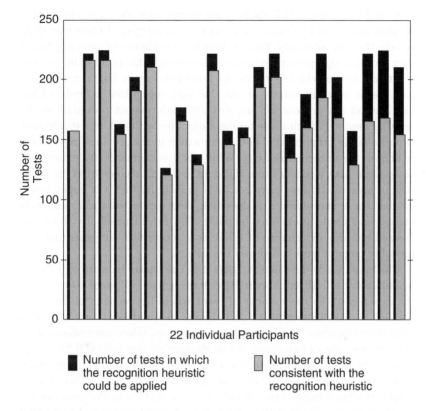

Figure 2-5: Recognition heuristic opportunities and usage by 22 individual participants. The individuals are ordered from left to right according to how closely their judgment agrees with the recognition heuristic. The darker bars are of different heights because individual participants recognized different numbers of cities.

The experiment began with a training session during which participants were instructed to write down all the information that would follow. They were first told that they would be quizzed on the populations of the 30 largest cities in Germany. Next they were taught that 9 of the 30 largest cities have soccer teams, and that the 9 cities with teams are larger than the 21 cities without teams in 78% of all possible pairs. Next, participants were allowed to draw eight cities at random and learn whether each has a soccer team or not. This drawing was rigged so that each participant chose the same four well-known cities that have soccer teams and four well-known cities that do not. Participants were then tested to make sure they could reproduce all of this information exactly, and could not proceed with the experiment until they did so. Either before or after the main task, participants were shown a list of German cities and asked to mark those that they had heard of before coming to the experiment.

With their notes beside them, participants were then presented pairs of cities and asked to choose the larger city in each pair. To motivate them to take the task seriously, they were offered a chance of winning $15 if they scored a high percentage correct. To reiterate, the point of the experiment was to see which participants would choose as larger: a city they have never heard of before, or one that they recognized beforehand but just learned has no soccer team. From the information presented in the training session (which made no mention of recognition), one would now expect a larger proportion of participants than in the previous experiment to choose the unrecognized city. Why? An unrecognized city either does or does not have a soccer team. If it does (a 5 in 22 chance from the information presented), then there is a 78% probability that it is larger, based on the soccer cue alone. If it does not, then soccer team information is useless and a wild guess must be made. The unrecognized city should be favored because any chance of it having a soccer team suggests that it is probably larger. Figure 2-6 shows the results.

The graph reads the same as figure 2-5. The darker bars are of different heights because individual participants recognized different cities before the experiment, so the number of cases where the recognition heuristic applied varied. Twelve of 21 participants made choices in accordance with the recognition heuristic without exception, while most others deviated on only one or two items. All in all, participants followed the recognition rule in 273 of the 296 total critical pairs. The median proportion of inferences agreeing with the heuristic was 100% (mean 92%), despite conflicting knowledge. These numbers are as high as in the previous experiment. It appears that the additional information was not integrated into the inferences, consistent with the recognition heuristic.

Does the Less-Is-More Effect Occur in Human Reasoning?

We have documented that the recognition heuristic can describe how humans make inferences in certain tasks. This result provides empirical support to the theoretical prediction that the less-is-more effect will appear. But we have yet to see this effect in the reasoning of real people. We administered two quizzes to 52 University of Chicago students. One quiz was on the 22 largest cities in the United States, cities about which they knew a lifetime of facts useful for inferring population. The other was on the 22 largest cities in Germany, about which they knew little or nothing beyond mere recognition—and they did not even recognize about half of them (Goldstein & Gigerenzer, 1998). Each question consisted of two randomly drawn cities, and the task was to pick the larger. One would expect American students to score substantially better on their native cities than on the foreign ones because of their lifelong acquaintance with their country. We considered this a tough test of the less-is-more effect. The curious phenomenon of a less-is-more effect is harder to demonstrate with real people than on paper, because the theory and simulation work we pre-

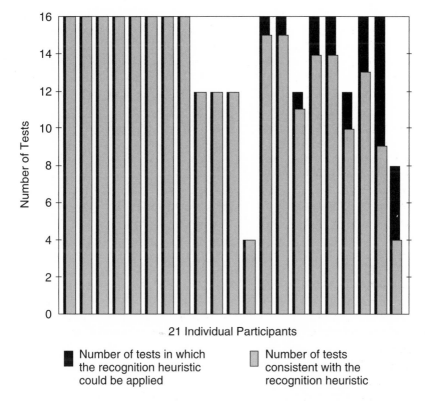

Figure 2-6: Recognition heuristic adherence despite training to encourage use of information other than recognition. The individuals are ordered from left to right according to how closely their judgment agrees with the recognition heuristic. The darker bars are of different heights because individual participants recognized different numbers of cities.

sented is about inference under uncertainty, but real people often have definite knowledge of the criterion. For instance, many Americans, and nearly all University of Chicago students, can name the three largest U.S. cities in order. This alone gives them the correct answer for 26% of the questions. Those who know the top five cities will get a free 41% correct. This definite knowledge of the rankings of the largest cities, combined with the lifetime of knowledge Americans have about their own cities, should make their scores on the domestic test hard to match.

The result was that the Americans scored a median 71% correct (mean 71.1%) on their own cities. On the less-familiar German cities, the median was a surprising 73% correct (mean 71.4%). Despite the presence of substantial knowledge about American cities, including some definite knowledge of which are the largest, the recognition heuristic resulted in a slight less-is-more effect. For half of the subjects, we kept track of which German cities they recognized, as in previous experiments. For this group, the median proportion of inferences according with the recognition heuristic was 91% (mean 89%). Furthermore, participants could apply the recognition heuristic nearly as often as possible, as they recognized a mean of 12 German cities, roughly half of the total. In a study that is somewhat the reverse of this one, a similar less-is-more effect was demonstrated with Austrian students who scored more accurate inferences on American cities than on German ones (Hoffrage, 1995; see also Gigerenzer, 1993).

Where Does Recognition Originate?

For some important adaptive tasks, such as avoiding food poisoning and identifying kin, organisms seem to be genetically prepared to act in accordance with the recognition heuristic. Wild Norway rats do not need to be taught to prefer recognized foods over novel ones. If a choice has life-threatening consequences, organisms that have to learn to use the recognition heuristic would likely die before they got the chance. Kin identification is an important adaptive task whose function seems to be avoiding incest and promoting nepotism (inclusive fitness) (Holmes & Sherman, 1983). Paper wasp females, for instance, use odor recognition (the odor they learned in their nest) to infer whether another wasp is a sister or nonsister. One can fool this mechanism by transferring newly emerged queens to a foreign nest, where they learn the odor of their (unrelated) nestmates (Pfennig et al., 1983). On the other hand, there are many domains in which organisms learn the predictive power of recognition through experience. Let us have a closer look at a source of name recognition in the realm of geography.

To what degree is the media responsible for the proper names we recognize? If the degree is high, the number of times a city is mentioned in the newspapers should correlate strongly with the proportion of the readers who recognize the city. The *Chicago Tribune* has a Sunday circulation of more than 1 million in the state of Illinois alone. We counted the number of articles published in the *Chicago Tribune* between 1985 and July 1997 in which the words "Berlin" and "Germany" were mentioned together. There were 3,484. We did the same for all cities in Germany with more than 100,000 inhabitants. The folks at the *Chicago Tribune* are not the world's most consistent spellers. We found Nuremberg spelled as Nurn-berg, Nurnburg, Nuernberg, and Nuremburg (the database contained no umlauts). We searched under all the spellings we could imagine for all the cities. Table 2-1 illustrates that, for the top 12 German cities, the number of newspaper articles mentioning a city is a good predictor of whether its name will be recognized. What we call the surrogate correlation in figure 2-2, that is, the Spearman correlation (over all cities) between the number of newspaper articles mentioning a city and number of people recognizing it, is .79. But what about the actual populations? The ecologi-

Table 2-1: Recognition of German and American Cities

City	Articles	Recognition (%)	City	Articles	Recognition (%)
Berlin	3484	99	New York	493	100
Hamburg	1009	96	Los Angeles	300	100
Munich	1240	100	Chicago	175	97
Cologne	461	82	Houston	73	80
Frankfurt	1804	96	Philadelphia	67	63
Essen	93	28	San Diego	78	47
Dortmund	84	19	Phoenix	56	53
Stuttgart	632	63	Dallas	39	100
Düsseldorf	381	81	San Antonio	4	23
Bremen	140	44	Detroit	66	80
Duisburg	53	7	San Jose	13	17
Hannover	260	88	Indianapolis	20	50

Left side: Number of articles in 12 years of the *Chicago Tribune* mentioning the 12 largest German cities and the percentage of 67 University of Chicago students who recognized each city. Cities are ranked according to their actual size. *Right side:* Number of articles in 2 years of *Die Zeit* mentioning the 12 largest U.S. cities and the percentage of 30 University of Salzburg students who recognized each city.

cal correlation, that is, the correlation between the number of newspaper articles and population, is .70. Finally, the correlation between the number of people recognizing the city's name and population is .60.[2]

These results suggest that individual recognition is more in tune with the media than with the actual environment, which indicates that city name recognition may come largely from the media. True population size is unknown to most people, but they can rely on mere recognition to make a fairly accurate guess.

But do these results stand up in a different culture? We looked at a major German-language newspaper, *Die Zeit*, and recorded the number of articles in which each of the U.S. cities with more than 100,000 inhabitants was mentioned. We compared this to the number of University of Salzburg students surveyed who recognized each city (Hoffrage, 1995). Table 2-1 shows again that the media references predict the number of people recognizing cities quite accurately. The surrogate correlation over all the cities between the number of newspaper articles and recognition is .86. The ecological correlation between the number of articles and population is .72, and that between recognition and the rank order of cities is .66. These results are quite consistent with those from the American participants, with slightly higher correlations. In all cases, the surrogate correlation is the

2. This correlation reflects the average recognition validity. It is calculated across persons, whereas the recognition validity is a characteristic of a particular person. The relation between validities and correlations is analyzed in chapter 6.

strongest, the ecological is the next strongest, and the correlation between recognition and the criterion is the weakest. In the next section, we see how institutions can exploit this relationship via advertising.

Institutions That Take Advantage of the Recognition Heuristic

Oliviero Toscani, the man behind the notorious Benetton advertising campaign, effectively bet his career on a series of advertisements that conveyed nothing about the product, but only sought to induce name recognition with shocking images such a corpse in a pool of blood, or a dying AIDS patient. In his book, Toscani (1997) reports that the campaign was a smashing success, which vaulted Benetton's name recognition higher than Chanel's and placed it among the top five brands in the world. Is recognition, regardless of how it is achieved, good for business? In the social world, name recognition is often correlated with wealth, resources, quality, power, and the like. Advertisers pay great sums for a place in the recognition memory of the general public. We have grown accustomed to seeing advertisements like Benetton's that communicate no product information besides proper names (this becomes especially clear visiting a foreign country where one has no idea to what the proper names refer). Less-known politicians, universities, cities, and even small nations go on crusades for name recognition. They all operate on the principle that if we recognize them, we will favor them.

There is evidence that one can induce name recognition furtively, and even unconsciously. The "overnight fame" experiments by Jacoby and colleagues (Jacoby, Kelley, Brown, & Jasechko, 1989; Jacoby, Woloshyn, & Kelley, 1989) demonstrate that people can be made confused about whether they have been shown a name in an experimental session or if they had encountered it before they came to the experiment. Jacoby's experiments have shown that exposing people to nonfamous names, waiting overnight, and then having them make fame judgments on these and other actually famous names causes them to confuse nonfamous names with famous ones. This demonstrates how a feeling of recognition can fool us into believing ordinary names are famous.

Mere Recognition Versus Degrees of Knowledge

We treat recognition as a binary phenomenon: one either recognizes or does not. How often one has been exposed to something is both hard to assess subjectively and irrelevant for the frugal recognition heuristic. These two features, the binary quality of recognition and the inconsequentiality of further knowledge, set the recognition heuristic apart from notions such as availability (Tversky & Kahneman, 1974), familiarity (Griggs

& Cox, 1982), or the feeling of knowing (Koriat, 1993). The terms "avail-ability" and "familiarity" are often used as common-sense explanations rather than as process models. Availability applies to items in memory and is often measured by the order or speed with which items come to mind, or the number of instances of a category that can be generated (see chapter 10). In contrast, as figure 2-1 shows, recognition concerns the dif-ference between items in and out of memory (Goldstein, 1997). Availabil-ity is about recall, not about recognition. The term "familiarity" is typi-cally used to denote a *degree* of knowledge or experience a person has with respect to a task or object. It does not pick up on the most important distinction for the recognition heuristic—that between recognized and un-recognized objects. As intuitive as notions such as availability and famil-iarity may be, there is a need to bring them from one-word explanations to precise models for heuristics (Gigerenzer, 1996). If this is done, then one could hope for a deeper, detailed understanding that can lead to unex-pected consequences including the less-is-more effect.

A feeling of knowing, in Koriat's usage, is a person's assessment of the likelihood of being able to retrieve something from memory in the future. For example, the probe question "Who is the prime minister of Canada?" may put many non-Canadians into a tip-of-the-tongue state in which they may have a feeling about whether they will be able to retrieve the answer that is eluding them. Unlike the recognition heuristic, feelings of knowing presuppose knowledge beyond recognition, namely, the information held in the probe question. Another key difference is that the recognition heu-ristic can use recognition to predict some criterion in the world, whereas the feeling of knowing only predicts future memory performance.

The Recognition Heuristic as a Prototype of Fast and Frugal Heuristics

In this book, we study the architecture and performance of fast and frugal heuristics. The recognition heuristic is the simplest of these adaptive tools. It uses a capacity that evolution has shaped over millions of years, recognition, to allow organisms to benefit from their own ignorance. The heuristic works quickly and with limited knowledge—and even requires a certain amount of ignorance. The building blocks it uses for search, stop-ping, and decision are astoundingly simple. Search is limited to recogni-tion memory—no recall of knowledge beyond recognition is attempted. Since search is limited in this way, the stopping rule is constrained— search terminates as soon as recognition has been assessed for both ob-jects. The decision is consequently based on only one piece of informa-tion, recognition. Because a lack of recognition is essential for enabling a decision, we call this heuristic principle *ignorance-based decision mak-ing*. These heuristic principles add up to a conflict-avoiding strategy that eliminates the need for making trade-offs between cues pointing in different directions (as in the case where one recognizes a city but knows that it has no soccer team).

Fast and frugal heuristics, including the recognition heuristic, are based on psychological capacities such as recognition and heuristic principles such as ignorance-based decision making and one-reason decision making (relying on just one piece of information instead of aggregating several). The observation that people often try to avoid trade-offs and focus on one good reason has been documented numerous times (e.g., Baron, 1990; Hogarth, 1987; Payne et al., 1993). However, many scholars, psychologists included, have mistrusted the power of these heuristic principles, and saw in them single-mindedness and irrationality. This is not our view. The recognition heuristic is not only a reasonable cognitive adaptation because there are situations of limited knowledge in which there is little else one can do. It is also adaptive because there are situations, including those defined in this chapter, in which missing information results in more accurate inferences than a considerable amount of knowledge can achieve. In these situations, the recognition heuristic can be said to be ecologically rational, having the capacity to exploit structures of information in the environment in a simple and elegant way.

3

Can Ignorance Beat the Stock Market?

Bernhard Borges
Daniel G. Goldstein
Andreas Ortmann
Gerd Gigerenzer

A good name is better than riches.
Cervantes (Don Quixote)

How complex a decision tool does an investor need to construct a successful stock portfolio? How much privileged information must one obtain to accomplish this goal? The tools and information professional investment firms use for investment decisions are far beyond the ordinary person's reach. Furthermore, the value of expert advice has been questioned; in the words of billionaire Warren Buffet, "the only value of stock forecasters is to make fortune tellers look good" (1987, p. 40). In this chapter, we propose a fast and frugal heuristic that exploits a lack of knowledge, rather than using market-specific information or tools, to construct stock portfolios. In particular, we test whether an ignorance-based decision-making mechanism we call the recognition heuristic (described in chapter 2) can make money on the stock market. This heuristic relies on only one piece of information to make investment decisions: company name recognition. No privileged company information needs to be researched, no sophisticated analytical or numerical tools need to be employed; the only thing one needs is a beneficial degree of ignorance.

This chapter reports a competition between the recognition heuristic and five benchmarks for stock selection: mutual funds, market indices, chance or "dartboard" portfolios, individual investment decisions, and portfolios of unrecognized stocks. In this chapter more than any other in this book, we attempted a daring and financially perilous undertaking—throwing a lowly fast and frugal heuristic into the highly volatile, ostensibly lucrative, and notoriously technical world of stock market investment. Will it survive? And will our money?

Investment Theory and Practice

Financial markets are notoriously unpredictable, and pose a challenge for a strategy as simple as the recognition heuristic. Given the tremendous rewards the stock market has to offer, theorists and practitioners have poured millions of hours and dollars into its prediction. Some have concluded that consistent success beating the market is not possible. Neoclassical economists, for instance, portray investors as unboundedly rational entities capable of forming rational expectations. This stance is captured in the efficient market hypothesis[1] (EMH), which maintains that agents cannot attain above-average returns in the long run (e.g., Lucas, 1980; Muth, 1961). In the words of Cootner (1967):

> If any group of investors was consistently better than average in forecasting stock price, they would bring the present price closer to the true value. Conversely, investors who were worse than average in forecasting ability would carry less and less weight. If this process worked well enough, the present price would reflect the best information about the future. (p. 80)

Despite early empirical challenges (e.g., Rozef & Kinney, 1976; Special Issue, *Journal of Financial Economics*, 1978), the EMH has been fully incorporated in the leading normative models, such as the widespread Capital Asset Pricing Model (e.g., Sharpe, 1964)—itself constituting the basis for modern portfolio (management) theory.

Many professional investment analysts, such as Soros (1994), have long doubted the realism and relevance of the efficient market hypothesis and have turned instead to technical trading models to exploit speculative opportunities. In fact, recent evidence suggests that technical trading models have been shown to yield small but significant returns (e.g., Brock et al., 1991). Furthermore, modern finance, based on the insights gained by behavioral economists (e.g., Arthur et al., 1997; DeBondt & Thaler, 1985; Shleifer & Summers, 1990; Thaler, 1992, 1993), has also started to recognize the limited usefulness of the EMH and begun to focus on how it is undermined by psychological expectations under bounded rationality.

Regardless of the shift in academic research, the actual performance of professionally managed investment funds indicates how difficult it is in the long(er) run to match or beat the market consistently. The track record of major U.S. investment management and mutual companies, for example, indicates that the vast majority of sophisticated experts perform

---

1. Specifically, EMH not only assumes that agents are fully rational but also that each agent knows that the other agents behave in such a manner.

worse than the market.[2] This sobering fact is a slap in the face of the sophisticated modeling employed by the financial industry. Indeed, almost 75% of the professionally managed U.S. stock funds performed below the Standard & Poor's 500 (S&P 500) performance criterion in 1996 (Kadlec, 1997).

The investment strategies of experts, despite their efforts to acquire and process the best possible information using the best financial modeling tools available, provide only average returns on a theoretical basis—and often worse ones in practice. In view of this evidence, is it possible, or even desirable, for "Joe Six-Pack" to invest his limited cognitive and financial resources in financial markets?

Ignorance-Based Investment Decisions

Since knowledge and expertise seem to be of less use in predicting the stock market than is commonly presumed and asserted, one has to wonder how an investment heuristic based on ignorance would fare. The recognition heuristic feeds on ignorance when it is systematically, rather than randomly, distributed. Originally, Goldstein and Gigerenzer (chapter 2) studied the recognition heuristic as a mechanism for two-alternative choice, and its formulation was simple: When choosing between two objects, and only one is recognized, choose the recognized object. A generalization of the recognition heuristic for choosing a subset of objects from a larger set, which can be applied to investment decisions, is: *When choosing a subset of objects from a larger set, choose the subset of recognized objects.*

For one individual, the recognition heuristic dictates choosing only the stocks he or she recognizes. When looking at the collective recognition of a group, as in our study, the strategy is to choose all the stocks recognized by a given percentage (e.g., 90%) of the group.

Putting the recognition heuristic to work requires a degree of ignorance (that is, a lack of recognition). For example, financial experts who recognize the names of all the major stocks cannot use the recognition heuristic to choose among those stocks. Entirely ignorant people who have not heard of any stocks at all, on the other hand, also cannot use the heuristic. Between these two extremes, a large contingent of people display what we call a "beneficial degree of ignorance."

To dare to pit the recognition heuristic against the challenges of the stock market is not necessarily a ruinous notion. We had two reasons to hope that the recognition heuristic would not fail utterly. First, consumers

---

2. Of course, this dismal performance is at least partly attributable to two recurring "cost" factors. First, funds need to be liquid, and not all money received for investment is invested in stocks but parked in cash accounts yielding few, if any, returns. Second, expert advice comes at a price, and many of the management fees levied are not at all, or only loosely, coupled to the success of the investment fund.

tend to choose products they have heard of—a behavior exploited by advertisers—and stocks are essentially "products" whose prices are determined by human choice. Second, several successful investment experts, such as Peter Lynch, have suggested that a lack of name recognition is grounds for eliminating a stock from consideration (Lynch, 1994). Can the recognition heuristic compete with the tools and knowledge of rational ivy-tower theorists and expensive Wall Street professionals in the hunt for stock market profits? More specifically, can stock portfolios be constructed that perform at least at the market level?

Company Recognition

We asked Germans and Americans to indicate which companies they recognized from those listed on the New York Stock Exchange (NYSE) and several German stock exchanges. A total of 480 people were surveyed concerning 798 companies, including the 500 companies of the American S&P 500 index (with the Dow 30 companies) and 298 German companies (with the Dax 30 companies). These people were grouped into one of four categories: American laypeople, American experts, German laypeople, and German experts. Laypeople were 360 pedestrians surveyed in downtown Chicago or Munich, each of whom provided recognition information for one-sixth of the total number of companies. Experts were 120 finance or economics graduate students interviewed at the University of Chicago or the University of Munich, each of whom provided recognition information for one half of the total set of companies. Table 3-1 shows the names of the companies that were recognized unanimously, for all groups. Figure 3-1 shows the number of companies recognized by a given percentage or more of the population. For instance, 8 German companies were recognized by 100% of the German laypeople, and 25 German companies were recognized by at least 90% of the German laypeople. One German company—Lufthansa—was recognized by 100% of the American experts, and only five by at least 90% of the American experts.

Which group recognized the most companies and which was most ignorant? American experts recognized the most company names, followed by American laypeople, German experts, and German laypeople. The fact that German experts recognized fewer companies than pedestrians in downtown Chicago may come as a surprise. Two possible reasons are the higher active participation of the American public in the stock market, and a larger number of American stocks than German stocks. The international recognition rates were the lowest: The American pedestrians surveyed, for instance, did not recognize a single German firm unanimously.

Can the Recognition Heuristic Make Money?

To test the performance of the recognition heuristic on the stock market, we constructed two investment portfolios consisting of highly recognized

Table 3-1: Companies Recognized by All Participants. (G = German companies; US = U.S. companies)

German Laypeople		U.S. Laypeople		German Experts		U.S. Experts	
Allianz AG	G	Amoco	US	Adidas AG	G	Allstate Corp.	US
Bayerische Vereinsbank	G	Chrysler Corp.	US	American Express	US	American Express	US
Commerzbank AG	G	Coca-Cola Co.	US	BASF AG	G	Ameritech	US
Daimler Benz	G	Ford Motor Co.	US	Bayer AG	G	Avon Products	US
Dresdner Bank AG	G	General Mills	US	HypoBank	G	Bell Atlantic	US
Lufthansa	G	Hilton Hotels	US	Bayerische Vereinsbank	G	Black & Decker Corp.	US
Porsche AG	G	Maytag Corp.	US	Daimler Benz	G	Citicorp	US
Siemens AG	G	Sears Roebuck & Co.	US	Dresdner Bank AG	G	Coca-Cola Co.	US
				Escada AG	G	Dow Jones & Co.	US
				Karstadt AG	G	Eastman Kodak	US
				Kaufhof AG	G	Ford Motor Co.	US
				Lufthansa	G	Intel Corp.	US
				Microsoft Corp.	US	J.P. Morgan & Co.	US
				Münchener Rück.	G	Kmart	US
				Telekom AG	G	Lufthansa	G
				Volkswagen AG (VW)	G	Merck & Co.	US
						Merrill Lynch	US
						Morgan Stanley	US
						Procter & Gamble	US
						Southwest Airlines	US
						Whirlpool Corp.	US

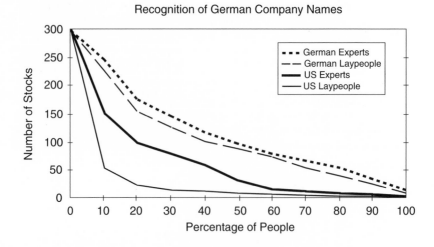

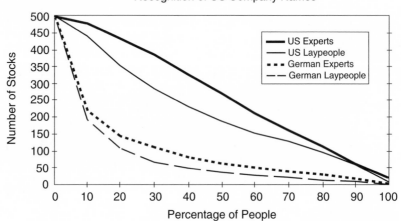

Figure 3-1: Recognition of stocks, in terms of the proportion of people recognizing the corresponding company names. For instance, 14 German company names were recognized by 100% of German experts, 33 company names were recognized by at least 90% of German experts, and so on.

companies, for each of the four groups. One portfolio consisted of highly recognized companies within the group's home country ("domestic recognition"), where we defined highly recognized companies as those recognized by 90% or more of the participants in a group. The other portfolio contained the 10 companies that each group recognized most often from the other country ("international recognition"). Thus there were a total of eight recognition-based portfolios, as shown in figure 3-2. Recall that the recognition heuristic dictates investing in highly recognized stocks.

We analyzed the performance of recognition-based portfolios for 6 months from the completion date of the recognition test, December 13, 1996. The returns of the recognition-based portfolios were compared with the performance of (a) the stocks of unrecognized companies, that is, companies recognized by fewer than 10% of the participants, (b) market indices, (c) mutual funds, (d) chance portfolios, and (e) individuals' investment choices. Well before these results became known, two of us decided to put our money where our heuristic was, and bet a nontrivial amount of our savings on German stocks recognized by Munich pedestrians. Would we regret, for the rest of our days, betting our hard-earned money on the ignorance of laypeople?

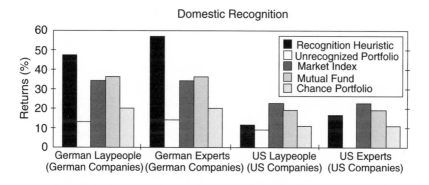

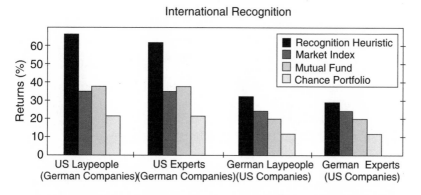

Figure 3-2: Performance of the recognition heuristic for the recognition of domestic and international stocks. Results are for the 6 months following the date of the recognition test, December 1996 to June 1997. For comparison, the performance of unrecognized stocks (0% to 10% recognition rates), market indices (Dow 30 or Dax 30), mutual funds (Fidelity Growth Fund or Hypobank Equity Fund), and chance portfolios (average returns of 5,000 randomly drawn portfolios) are shown.

How Does the Recognition Heuristic Compare with Choosing Unrecognized Companies?

The investment portfolio of German stocks based on the collective recognition of the 180 German laypeople resulted in a gain of 47% in the 6 months of the study.[3] The portfolio based on the unrecognized companies yielded a gain of only 13%. Figure 3-2 shows that this superior performance of domestic recognition holds in each of the four groups, laypeople and experts, German and American. The performance of the recognition heuristic was particularly strong in the two most ignorant groups, German laypeople and experts. For German experts, it reached a return of 57%, compared to 14% for the unrecognized stocks. Across all domestic tests, the average return of the portfolios built using the recognition heuristic was more than three times higher than those built from unrecognized stocks.

How Does the Recognition Heuristic Compare with Market Indices?

Recognized stocks outperformed unrecognized ones, but this may be of little interest to the investor whose main interest is beating the market. Performance of the overall market is commonly measured by indices such as the Dow 30 for American stocks and the Dax 30 for German ones. During our 6-month investigation, the Dax increased 34%. However, the sum of the prices of the 30 stocks constituting the Dax rose 41% over the same period. Hence, the stocks making up the Dax 30 index actually performed better than the Dax index; this is possible because the index is weighted to reflect the overall market development. The stock prices for the 298 German companies increased 24%. In the same period the Dow 30 increased by 23%, whereas the 30 companies in the Dow rose 8% and all 500 American stocks in our study increased by 10%. It appears that the Dow index may be difficult to attain.

Can the recognition heuristic come close to the Dow and Dax market indices? We tested this by tracking the performance of domestic recognition and international recognition. As figure 3-1 illustrates, domestic recognition rates are higher than their international counterparts.

Domestic Recognition   The investment portfolio of German stocks based on the recognition of the German laypeople outperformed the Dax 30 market index by 10%, based on a raw yield of 47% (figure 3-2). The portfolio

---

3. The portfolio returns were calculated as follows: raw score = (portfolio value t_1/portfolio value t_0) − 1 and the normalized score = ((portfolio value t_1/portfolio value t_0)/(market index t_1/market index t_0)) − 1. The price development for a handful of companies could not be tracked over the evaluation period and was therefore dropped from the analysis.

of German stocks based on the recognition of the German experts outperformed the market by 17%, with a stunning raw return of 57%.

How did the recognition portfolios for the two less-ignorant groups perform? The portfolio of highly recognized U.S. stocks based on U.S. laypeople's recognition made money, but fell 10% below the Dow 30 market
index. The unrecognized stocks lost 12% in relation to the market. Similarly, the American experts' recognized stocks yielded a 16% return, 6%
below the Dow 30, while the unrecognized stocks were a worthless investment, returning nothing.

International Recognition   Since the recognition of company names varied widely among participants in the international comparison, we constructed portfolios with the 10 most recognized stocks, that is, on the basis
of fixed numbers of stocks. We used the 10 most recognized companies
instead of the 90% criterion because, as figure 3-1 shows, international
recognition is so low that under some conditions there are no companies
that 90% of the group recognized.

How well did the 10 most recognized American stocks chosen on the
basis of German recognition do? The recognition heuristic, using international recognition, actually beat the Dow 30—a feat none of the other portfolios accomplished. The same result was obtained for the stocks recognized by German experts. The portfolio from the less knowledgeable
German laypeople even did better than that of the German experts.

Was international ignorance beneficial when going the other way
across the Atlantic? The 10 German stocks most recognized by American
laypeople outperformed the market by 23%. Similarly, the top 10 portfolio
based on U.S. experts' recognition greatly outperformed the market.

In all four cases of international recognition, the recognition heuristic
beat the relevant market index. Furthermore, in all four cases the international recognition led to higher returns than domestic recognition, and the
recognition of laypeople led to slightly more profitable portfolios than
that of experts. In general it seems that the greater the degree of ignorance,
the better it is for picking stocks.

As a control, we also calculated the performance of portfolios based on
the top 20 and top 30 recognized stocks, for the four international tests.
Figure 3-3 shows that in each of these four groups, stocks with higher
recognition rates lead to higher returns.

How Does the Recognition Heuristic Compare with Managed Funds?

We have tested the recognition heuristic against the market and unrecognized stocks, and so far it has done well, winning in all of four comparisons against unrecognized stocks, and in six out of eight comparisons to
market indices. How will a heuristic based on a lack of recognition fare
when compared to the tools and knowledge of professional portfolio man-

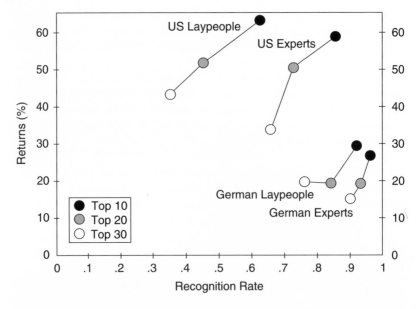

Figure 3-3: International recognition rates vs. returns. There is a direct relationship between the recognition rate and the returns, in each of the four groups. The top 10 are the 10 most recognized stocks from the international perspective (see figure 3-2). When this set is expanded to include the top 20 or 30 most recognized stocks, recognition rates necessarily decrease, and returns follow.

agers? Two major mutual funds, the American-based Fidelity Blue Chip Growth Fund and the German Hypobank Investment Capital Fund, served as benchmarks for the recognition heuristic. The Fidelity fund increased by 19% and the Hypobank fund increased by 36% over the December-to-June period.

Figure 3-2 shows that the recognition heuristic beats managed funds in six of the eight possible tests. For instance, the collective ignorance of 180 pedestrians in downtown Munich was more predictive than the knowledge and expertise of American and German fund managers. Again we see that international ignorance was even more powerful than domestic ignorance. In addition, the two most ignorant groups, German laypeople and experts, gained the most from their beneficial ignorance.

How Does the Recognition Heuristic Compare With Random Stock Portfolios?

Recall that according to the efficient market hypothesis, one should not be able to beat consistently a portfolio of randomly drawn stocks. For instance, the *Wall Street Journal*'s renowned investment column has suggested repeatedly that random stock picks, operationalized via a highly sophisticated dartboard mechanism, often outperform expert picks. We constructed 5,000 random portfolios consisting of 10 stocks from both the American and German markets and valued them for the December-to-June period. Figure 3-2 shows the average returns of the random portfolios: 22% for German stocks and 11% for American ones. The recognition heuristic beats the random portfolio performance in seven of the eight possible tests, and matches it in the remaining one. The recognition heuristic turned out to be far better at stock selection than chance.

How Does the Recognition Heuristic Compare With Individuals' Investment Choices?

How good are experts and laypeople at picking stocks in which to invest? Who will assemble the better portfolios, laypeople or experts? We asked the German experts and laypeople to identify up to 10 stocks that they would pick for investment purposes from the lists of companies in the recognition test. We assembled portfolios of the 10 most often selected German and American stocks chosen by German experts and laypeople.

The German laypeople tended to pick highly recognized German stocks for investment; the average recognition rate of their 10 most selected stocks was .80. Experts, however, opted for less recognized German stocks, with an average recognition rate of .48. The recognition heuristic makes a clear prediction here: The group that picks more highly recognized stocks should enjoy the greater return. Indeed, the laypeople's stock picks achieved a staggering return, whereas the experts' picks actually lost money (figure 3-4).

For the Germans' picks of 10 American stocks, the average recognition rate was lower (.27) and did not differ between experts and laypeople. Consequently, both portfolios of international picks performed much worse than the portfolios of recognized stocks in figure 3-2. Again, the stock picks of the laypeople outperformed those of the experts by a wide margin (figure 3-4).

From Recognition to Riches?

Can a fast and frugal heuristic that exploits patterns of ignorance rather than substantial knowledge make money on the stock market? For the period investigated, we have obtained the following results:

1. Portfolios of highly recognized stocks outperformed the portfolios of unrecognized stocks. This result was replicated in all four domestic tests (figure 3-2) and in all four international tests, where portfolio returns increased with their average recognition rates (figure 3-3).

2. In tests of international recognition, the recognition heuristic per-

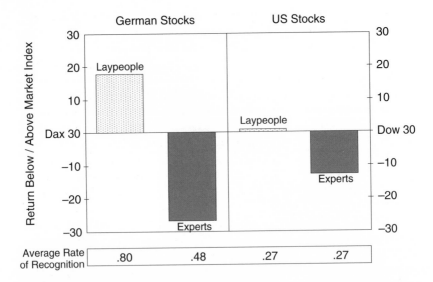

Figure 3-4: Stock-picking performance of German laypeople and experts on the two markets. The returns above or below the corresponding market index were calculated by (1 + raw change in portfolio)/(1 + raw change in market index) − 1.

formed above the market indices for each of the four conditions: American stock recognition by German laypeople and experts and German stock recognition by American laypeople and experts. These international tests indicate that the fewer companies a group recognizes, the better the recognition heuristic performs. Domestic recognition in Germany outperformed the Dax, but in the United States domestic recognition did not beat the Dow. Thus, in six out of eight tests, the recognition heuristic outperformed the market indices, often by a large margin.

3. In comparison with two major managed funds, the American Fidelity Blue Chip Growth Fund and the German Hypobank Investment Capital Fund, the recognition heuristic performed better in six out of eight tests.

4. The average return of random stock portfolios was consistently below the returns achieved by the recognition heuristic. This result held in seven out of eight tests (with the remaining one matching).

5. When people's investment choices followed the recognition heuristic, their portfolio earned a very impressive return above the Dax. In the three other cases, where the stocks picked had a low average recognition, returns were much lower. Experts picked stocks with low recognition rates, which performed dismally.

The predictive power of the recognition heuristic corroborates the notion that a lack of recognition can contain implicit knowledge as powerful as explicit knowledge. The superiority of international over domestic recognition and the superiority of laypeople over experts in stock picking supports the notion that a certain degree of ignorance can be a virtue.

How does the recognition heuristic do so well in the stock market? Strategic management and marketing research suggests a positive correlation between market share and firm profitability (e.g., Buzzell et al., 1975, and for a review, Ramanujam & Venkatraman, 1984). Thus, companies with the dominant market share are most likely to become both recognized and profitable. Another link to profitability is core competence, that is, "the collective learning in the organization, especially how to coordinate diverse production skills and integrate multiple streams of technologies" (Hamel & Prahalad, 1994, p. 82). Honda, for example, is generally portrayed as possessing a core competence in engines, which are featured in a variety of products, such as cars, lawn mowers, boat engines, and power generators. There seems to be evidence that core competence is linked to above-average performance (e.g., Hamel & Prahalad, 1994; Prahalad & Hamel, 1990). If there is a further link between core competence and company name recognition, an issue itself worthy of further research, it may explain why recognized companies are more profitable.

Another link between recognition and stock performance may exist. Professional fund managers seem to employ name recognition as if it were a fundamental indicator for stock valuation. Joerg-Viggo Mueller, investment relations manager at Hugo Boss AG, for example, is quoted as saying, "Boss shares are not blue chips [i.e., stocks from the most well-established corporations]—yet analysts often position us as if we were" (Deutsche Börse, 1997, p. 35). That is, members of the investment community attribute a higher quality to Hugo Boss shares than is warranted by strict fundamental analysis. Similarly, Manfred Ayasse, information relations manager at Porsche, suggests that "like consumers, investors cannot resist the 'good vibes' associated with a car like Porsche" (Deutsche Börse, 1997, p. 35). So, although investment professionals may not be able to apply the recognition heuristic themselves (since they recognize virtually all market firms), they may consider public name recognition as part of a stock's value. Names have value, as reflected in the explicit pricing of good will and evidenced by countless court cases over corporate name ownership.

The impressive performance of recognition-based portfolios was obtained in a strong bull market. We do not yet know how well these results would generalize to other periods, such as a decreasing bear market. One explanation for the recognition heuristic's good performance is that it is picking "big" firms, which are known to do well in up markets. This hypothesis can be tested in a down market, where big firms generally do more poorly than the market indices. If recognized stocks perform above big firms in upswings, and do not suffer as much in downturns, then we will have evidence distinguishing recognition effects from big-firm effects.

At least in the upswing period we have considered, the recognition-based portfolios outperformed the summed returns of the big firms of the Dax and Dow, giving us partial indication that these effects are distinct.

Would the logic of the recognition heuristic be spoiled when companies become recognized because of bad press, such as when the public learns of an oil company from news of an oil spill? One might expect such a stock to perform poorly. However, financial markets are fast and stock prices quickly adjust for expected losses in earning power. Once the bad news hits the mass media outlets, share prices may even increase because the bad news has been taken into account by insiders and the uncertainties with respect to future earnings have been reduced or even eliminated. Hence, "ignorant" investors recognizing a company by way of adverse news may in fact disproportionally benefit.

Ignorance Can Be Informative

In this chapter, we have taken a bold step into the unknown, throwing a heuristic fueled by ignorance onto the trading floor. The striking returns generated by recognition-based portfolios substantiate evidence in the previous chapter that the recognition heuristic can make accurate inferences in real-world domains. For the period considered here, at least, the recognition knowledge of pedestrians turned out to be more profitable than the considered opinions of mutual fund experts. The stock market may be a complex real-world environment in which lack of recognition is not completely random, but rather systematic and informative. In investments, there may be wisdom in ignorance.

Part III

ONE-REASON DECISION MAKING

4

Betting on One Good Reason

The Take The Best Heuristic

Gerd Gigerenzer
Daniel G. Goldstein

> Bounded rationality is what cognitive psychology is all
> about. And the study of bounded rationality is not the study
> of optimization in relation to task environments.
>
> *Herbert A. Simon*

God, as John Locke (1690/1959) asserted, "has afforded us only the twilight of probability; suitable, I presume, to the state of mediocrity and probationership he has been pleased to place us in here. . . . " In the two preceding chapters, we argued that humans can make the best of this mediocre uncertainty. Ignorance about real-world environments, luckily, is often systematically rather than randomly distributed and thus allows organisms to navigate through the twilight with the recognition heuristic. In this chapter, we analyze heuristics that draw inferences from information beyond mere recognition. The source of this information can be direct observation, recall from memory, firsthand experience, or rumor. Darwin (1872/1965), for instance, observed that people use facial cues, such as eyes that waver and lids that hang low, to infer a person's guilt. Male toads, roaming through swamps at night, use the pitch of a rival's croak to infer its size when deciding whether to fight (Krebs & Davies, 1991). Inferences about the world are typically based on cues that are uncertain indicators: The eyes can deceive, and so can a medium-sized ethologist mimicking a large toad with a deep croak in the darkness. As Benjamin Franklin remarked in a letter in 1789: "In this world nothing is certain but death and taxes" (Smyth, 1907, p. 69).

How do people make inferences, predictions, and decisions from a bundle of imperfect cues and signals? The classical view of rational judgment under uncertainty is illustrated by Benjamin Franklin's *moral alge-*

bra. In an often-cited letter to the British scientist Joseph Priestley, Franklin (1772/1987) explained how to decide which of two options to take, based on uncertain cues (which he calls "reasons"):

> [M]y Way is, to divide half a Sheet of Paper by a Line into two Columns, writing over the one *Pro*, and over the other *Con*. Then during three or four Days Consideration I put down under the different Heads short Hints of the different Motives that at different Times occur to me for or against the Measure. When I have thus got them all together in one View, I endeavor to estimate their respective Weights; and where I find two, one on each side, that seem equal, I strike them both out: If I find a Reason *pro* equal to some two Reasons *con*, I strike out the three. If I judge some two Reasons *con* equal to some three Reasons *pro*, I strike out the five; and thus proceeding I find at length where the Ballance lies; and if after a Day or two of farther Consideration nothing new that is of Importance occurs on either side, I come to a Determination accordingly. And tho' the Weight of Reasons cannot be taken with the Precision of Algebraic Quantities, yet when each is thus considered separately and comparatively, and the whole lies before me, I think I can judge better, and am less likely to make a rash Step; and in fact I have found great Advantage from this kind of Equation, in what may be called *Moral* or *Prudential Algebra*. (p. 878)

Franklin's moral algebra, or what we will call *Franklin's rule*, is to search for all reasons, positive or negative, weigh each carefully, and add them up to see where the balance lies. This linear combination of reasons carries the moral sentiment of rational behavior: carefully look up every bit of information, weigh each bit in your hand, and combine them into a judgment. Franklin's method is a variant of the classical view of rationality which emerged in the Enlightenment (see chapter 1), a view that is not bound to linear combinations of reasons. Classical rationality assumes that the laws of probability are the laws of human minds, at least of the educated ones (the *hommes éclairés*, see Daston, 1988). As Pierre-Simon Laplace (1814/1951, p. 196) put it, "the theory of probabilities is at bottom only common sense reduced to calculus."

But in real-world situations with sufficient complexity, the knowledge, time, and computation necessary to realize the classical ideal of unbounded rationality can be prohibitive—too much for humble humans, and often also too much for the most powerful computers. For instance, if one updates Franklin's weighted linear combination of reasons into its modern and improved version, multiple linear regression, then a human would have to estimate the weights that minimize the error in the "least squares" sense for all the reasons before combining them linearly—a task most of us could not do without a computer. If one were to further update Franklin's method to (nonlinear) Bayesian networks, then the task could become too computationally complex to be solved by a computer.

Despite their psychological implausibility, the preferred models of cognitive processes since the cognitive revolution of the 1960s were those assuming demons: subjective expected utility maximizing models of choice, exemplar models of categorization, multiple regression models of judgment, Bayesian models of problem solving, and neural-network models of almost everything. Demons that can perform amazing computations have not only swamped cognitive psychology, but also economics, optimal foraging theory, artificial intelligence, and other fields. Herbert Simon has countered, "there is a complete lack of evidence that, in actual human choice situations of any complexity, these computations can be, or are in fact, performed" (1955a, p. 104).

Simon proposed to build models of bounded rationality rather than of optimizing. But how? What else could mental processes be, if not the latest statistical techniques?

Simple Stopping Rules

In this chapter, we deal with the same type of task as in chapter 2: determining which of two objects scores higher on a criterion. This task is a special case of the more general problem of estimating which subclass of a class of objects has the highest values on a criterion (as in chapter 3). Examples are treatment allocation (e.g., which of two patients to treat first in the emergency room, with life expectancy after treatment as the criterion), financial investment (e.g., which of two securities to buy, with profit as criterion), and demographic predictions (e.g., which of two cities has higher pollution, crime, mortality rates, and so on).

To illustrate the heuristics, consider the following two-alternative choice task:

Which of the two cities has a larger population?
(a) Hannover
(b) Bielefeld

Assume that a person has heard of both cities, so cannot use the recognition heuristic. This person needs to search for cues that indicate larger population. Search can be internal (in memory) or external (e.g., in libraries). Limited search is a central feature of fast and frugal heuristics: not all available information is looked up, and consequently, only a fraction of this information influences judgment. (In contrast, laboratory experiments in which the information is already conveniently packaged and laid out in front of the participants eliminate search, and in line with this experimental approach, many theories of cognitive processes do not even deal with search.)

Limited search implies a stopping rule. Fast and frugal heuristics use *simple* stopping rules. They do not follow the classical prescription to search as long as the perceived marginal benefits of acquiring additional information exceed the perceived marginal costs (Stigler, 1961). That minds could and would routinely calculate this optimal cost-benefit trade-off is a dominant, yet implausible, assumption in models of information search (see the epigram introducing this chapter).

We demonstrate a simple stopping rule with figure 4-1. This figure represents a person's knowledge about four objects *a, b, c,* and *d* (cities, for example) with respect to five cues (such as whether the city has a big-league soccer team, is a state capital, and so forth) and recognition (whether or not the person has heard of the city before). For instance, if one city has a soccer team in the major league and the other does not, then the city with the team is likely, but not certain, to have the larger population. Suppose we wish to decide which of city *a* and city *b* is larger. Both *a* and *b* are recognized, so the recognition heuristic cannot be used. Search for further knowledge in memory brings to mind information about Cue 1, the soccer team cue. City *a* has a soccer team in the major league, but city *b* does not (these cue values are represented by "1" and

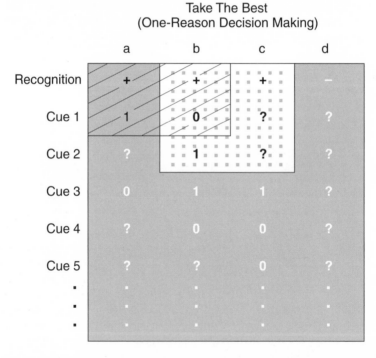

Figure 4-1: Illustration of bounded search through limited knowledge. Objects *a, b,* and *c* are recognized (+), *d* is not (–). Cue values are binary (0 or 1); missing knowledge is shown by a question mark. For instance, to infer whether *a > b*, Take The Best looks up only the values in the lined space. To infer whether *b > c*, search is bounded to the dotted space. The other cue values are not looked up and so are shown within the diagram as shrouded in the fog of memory.

"0" in figure 4-1). Therefore, the cue discriminates between the two cities. Search is terminated, and the inference is made that city a is the larger city. More generally, for binary (or dichotomous) cues, the simple stopping rule is:

> If one object has a positive cue value ("1") and the other does not (i.e., either "0" or unknown) then stop search.

For convenience, we use "1" for *positive* cue values, those that indicate higher criterion values (e.g., a larger population) and "0" for *negative* cue values, which indicate lower criterion values. If the condition of the stopping rule is not met, then search is continued for another cue, and so on. For instance, when deciding between b and c in figure 4-1, Cue 1 does not discriminate, but Cue 2 does. Object b is inferred to be larger on the basis of this single cue. Limited search works in a step-by-step way; cues are looked up one by one, until the stopping rule is satisfied (similar to the Test Operate Test Exit procedures of Miller et al., 1960). If no cue is found that satisfies the stopping rule, a random guess is made. No costs or benefits need to be computed to stop search. The following heuristics—Minimalist, Take The Last, and Take The Best—use this simple stopping rule. They also use the same heuristic principle for decision, one-reason decision making, that is, they base an inference on only one reason or cue. They differ in how they search for cues.

Heuristics

The Minimalist

The minimal intuition needed for cue-based inference is the direction in which a cue points, for instance, whether having a soccer team in the major league indicates a large or a small population. This direction can, for instance, be estimated from a small learning sample (and the estimated direction may sometimes be wrong, see below). The Minimalist has only this minimal intuition. Nothing more is known, for instance, about which cues are better predictors than others. Consequently, the heuristic for search that the Minimalist uses is to look up cues in random order. Whenever the Minimalist can, it will take advantage of the recognition heuristic (see chapter 2). However, there are situations where the recognition heuristic cannot be used, that is, when both objects are recognized, or when recognition is not correlated with the criterion.

The Minimalist heuristic can be expressed in the following steps:

> Step 0. If applicable, use the recognition heuristic; that is, if only one object is recognized, predict that it has the higher value on the criterion. If neither is recognized, then guess. If both are recognized, go on to Step 1.
>
> Step 1. Random search: Draw a cue randomly (without replacement) and look up the cue values of the two objects.

Step 2. Stopping rule: If one object has a positive cue value ("1") and the other does not (i.e., either "0" or unknown value) then stop search and go on to Step 3. Otherwise go back to Step 1 and search for another cue. If no further cue is found, then guess.

Step 3. Decision rule: Predict that the object with the positive cue value has the higher value on the criterion.

Take The Last

Like the Minimalist, Take The Last only has an intuition in which direction a cue points but not which cues are more valid than others. Take The Last differs from the Minimalist only in Step 1. It uses a heuristic principle for search that draws on a strategy known as an *Einstellung set*. Karl Duncker and other Gestalt psychologists demonstrated that when people work on a series of problems, they tend to start with the strategy that worked on the last problem when faced with a new, similar-looking problem (Duncker, 1935/1945; Luchins & Luchins, 1994), and thereby build up an Einstellung set of approaches to try. For the first problem, Take The Last tries cues randomly like the Minimalist, but from the second problem onward it starts with the cue that stopped search the last time. If this cue does not stop search, it tries the cue that stopped search the time before last, and so on. Because cues that recently stopped search tend to be more likely than others to stop search (i.e., they are cues with higher discrimination rates), Take The Last tends to search for fewer cues than the Minimalist. For instance, if the last decision was based on the soccer team cue, Take The Last would try the soccer team cue first on the next problem. In contrast to the Minimalist, Take The Last needs a memory for what cues discriminated in the past. Step 1 of Take The Last is:

Step 1. Einstellung search: If there is a record of which cues stopped search on previous problems, choose the cue that stopped search on the most recent problem and has not yet been tried. Look up the cue values of the two objects. Otherwise try a random cue and build up such a record.

Take The Best

There are environments for which humans or animals know (rightly or wrongly) not just the signs of cues, but also which cues are better than others. An order of cues can be genetically prepared (e.g., cues for mate choice in many animal species) or learned by observation. In the case of learning, the order of cues can be estimated from the relative frequency with which they predict the criterion. For example, the validity of the soccer team cue would be the relative frequency with which cities with soccer teams are larger than cities without teams. The validity is computed across all pairs in which one city has a team and the other does not. If people can order cues according to their perceived validities— whether or not this subjective order corresponds to the ecological order— then search can follow this order of cues. Take The Best first tries the cue with the highest validity, and if it does not discriminate, the next best cue, and so on. Its motto is "take the best, ignore the rest." Take The Best differs from the Minimalist only in Step 1, which becomes:

> Step 1. Ordered search: Choose the cue with the highest validity that has not yet been tried for this choice task. Look up the cue values of the two objects.

Note that the order that Take The Best uses is not an "optimal" one—it is, rather, a frugal ordering. It does not attempt to grasp the dependencies between cues, that is, to construct an order from conditional probabilities or partial correlations (see chapter 6). The frugal order can be estimated from a small sample of objects and cues (see chapter 5).

To summarize, the three fast and frugal heuristics just presented embody the following properties: limited search using step-by-step procedures, simple stopping rules, and one-reason decision making. One-reason decision making, basing inferences on just one cue, is implied by the specific stopping rule used here. It is not implied by all simple stopping rules. Furthermore, one-reason decision making does not necessarily imply the stopping rule used by the three heuristics. For instance, one could search for a large number of cues that discriminate between the two alternatives (such as in a situation where one has to justify one's decision) but still base the decision on only one cue.

Compare the spirit of these simple heuristics to Franklin's rule. One striking difference is that all three heuristics practice one-reason decision making. Franklin's moral algebra, in contrast, advises us to search for all reasons—at least during several days' consideration—and to weigh carefully each reason and add them all up to see where the balance lies. The three heuristics avoid conflicts between cues that may point in opposite directions. Avoiding conflicts makes the heuristics noncompensatory: No amount of contrary evidence from later (unseen) cues can compensate for or counteract the decision made by an earlier cue. An example is the inference that a is larger than b in figure 4-1; neither the two positive values for b nor the "0" value for a can reverse this inference. Basing an entire decision on just one reason is certainly bold, but is it smart?

Psychologically Plausible but Dumb?

Consider first a species that practices one-reason decision making closely resembling Take The Best. In populations of guppies, the important adaptive task of mate choice is undertaken by the females, which respond to both physical and social cues (Dugatkin, 1996). Among the physical cues they value are large body size and bright orange body color. The main social cue they use is whether they have observed the male in question mating with another female. The cues seem to be organized in a hierarchy, with the orange-color cue dominating the social cue. If a female has a choice between two males, one of which is *much* more orange than the other, she will choose the more orange one. If the males are close in orangeness, she prefers the one she has seen mating with another female. She prefers this one even if he has *slightly* less orange color. The stopping rule for the orangeness cue is that one male must be much (about 40%) more orange than the other. Mate choice in female guppies illustrates limited search, simple stopping rules, and one-reason decision making.

People, not just lower animals, often look up only one or two relevant cues, avoid searching for conflicting evidence, and use noncompensatory strategies (e.g., Einhorn, 1970; Einhorn & Hogarth, 1981, p. 71; Fishburn, 1988; Hogarth, 1987; Payne et al., 1993; Shepard, 1967a). For instance, Take The Best (unlike the Minimalist and Take the Last) is related to lexicographic strategies. The term *lexicographic* signifies that the cues are looked up in a fixed order of validity, like the alphabetic order used to arrange words in a dictionary. The Arabic (base 10) and Babylonian (base 12) number systems are lexicographic. To see which of two numbers with equal numbers of digits is larger, one has to look at the first digit: If this digit is larger, the whole number is larger. If they are equal, one has to look at the second digit, and so on. This simple method is not possible for Roman numbers, which are not lexicographic. In experimental studies, lexicographic strategies seem to be favored under time constraints (Payne et al., 1993; see also chapter 7). In addition, Take The Best and the more general framework of probabilistic mental models (Gigerenzer et al., 1991) have been successful in integrating various empirical phenomena (DiFonzo, 1994; Gigerenzer et al., 1991; Juslin, 1993; McClelland & Bolger, 1994).

However, simple heuristics that embody one-reason decision making, avoid conflicts, and are noncompensatory were often discredited as irrational, because they look stupid in comparison to traditional norms of rationality that focus on coherence rather than on performance in real-world environments. For instance, when Keeney and Raiffa (1993) discuss lexicographic strategies, they repeatedly insert warnings that this strategy "is more widely adopted in practice than it deserves to be" because "it is naively simple" and "will rarely pass a test of 'reasonableness'" (pp. 77–78). They did not actually perform such a test. We shall.

Can Fast and Frugal Heuristics Be Accurate?

Heuristics are often evaluated by principles of internal coherence, rather than by criteria that measure their performance in the external world: accuracy, frugality, and speed, among others. The major exception in judgment and decision-making research is the work by Payne et al. (1993), who have systematically compared the "effort-accuracy" trade-off of simple strategies to the performance of the weighted additive rule (Franklin's rule), which is often taken as normative for preferences (see also Beach & Mitchell, 1978; Beach et al., 1986). In contrast to our research, Payne and his colleagues studied preferences in artificial problems rather than inferences about the real world. One consequence is that there is no external criterion for accuracy (e.g., the actual population of a city), so norms must be constructed. In their studies, the weighted additive rule is taken as the gold standard, and accuracy is defined as how close a strategy comes to this rule. Therefore, no strategy can ever be more accurate than the norm.[1] When making inferences about the real world, however, it does not necessarily hold that the weighted additive rule is the best one can do.

How accurate can heuristics be that violate the following two commandments that are often taken as characteristic of rational judgment?

Complete search. Thou shalt find all the information available. If thou cannot because of time or computational constraints, then compute the point where the cost of further searching exceeds the benefits of doing so, and search until this point.

Compensation. Thou shalt combine all pieces of information. Thou shalt not rely on just one piece.

While Franklin's rule respects both commandments, the Minimalist, Take The Last, and Take The Best heuristics violate them. They do not look up all cue values (limited search) and do use a simple stopping rule. They do not combine cue values (noncompensation). The Minimalist, in addition, can violate transitivity, a sacred principle of internal coherence.[2]

To answer the question of how accurate fast and frugal heuristics are, we evaluated their performance in a competition that pitted three standard statistical strategies against the three fast and frugal heuristics introduced above. The goal was to see which strategy would yield the most accurate inferences while looking up the fewest cue values.

The Competitors

To provide standards of comparison, we introduce three competitors that do not violate these commandments of rational judgment. The first is a weighted linear combination of cues, which we call Franklin's rule, because it applies Franklin's principles to the two-alternative choice tasks considered here. It is actually a more empirical method than Franklin's

---

1. An exception is when the weighted additive rule is modified to use only limited information.

2. Intransitivity can result from the fact that the Minimalist picks cues in random order, as is illustrated by figure 4-1. For instance, if Cue 1 happens to be applied to objects a and b, Cue 2 to b and c, and Cue 3 to a and c, we get the intransitive judgment $a > b$, $b > c$, and $c > a$.

original moral algebra because the weights are not subjective but computed from the data. In the present simulation, the cue weights are ecological validities, to be defined shortly. Franklin's rule multiplies each cue value by its weight and sums the total, inferring that the object with the larger sum is the larger object. In the simulation, positive and negative cue values are coded as 1 and 0, respectively.

The other two competitors are linear combinations of cues, like Franklin's rule. One of them demands considerably more knowledge and computation, and one demands less. The more demanding algorithm is *multiple linear regression*. Multiple regression takes care of the dependencies between cues by calculating weights that minimize the error in the least-squares sense. Variants of weighted linear models have been proposed as descriptive or prescriptive models of cognitive processes, for instance, in N. H. Anderson's (e.g., 1981) information integration theory and in social judgment research (Brehmer, 1994; Brunswik, 1955). As descriptions of psychological processes, weighted linear models, and particularly multiple linear regression, are questionable given the complex computations they assume (Brehmer & Brehmer, 1988; Einhorn & Hogarth, 1975; Hogarth, 1987). A more psychologically plausible version of a linear strategy employs unit weights, as suggested by Robyn Dawes (e.g., 1979). This strategy simply adds up the number of positive cue values (or ones) and subtracts the number of negative cue values (or zeroes). Thus it is fast (it does not involve much computation), but not frugal (it looks up all cues). For short, we call this strategy *Dawes's rule*.

In the simulations we report, these three linear models serve as benchmarks against which to evaluate the performance of the fast and frugal heuristics. Note that Franklin's rule and multiple linear regression use all the information the three heuristics use, and more. They also carry out more sophisticated computations on this information.

The Environment

After Germany was reunified in 1990, the country had 83 cities with more than 100,000 inhabitants. These cities and nine cues for population size constituted the environment for the simulation. The cues were chosen from people's reported cues in experiments (Gigerenzer et al., 1991; Gigerenzer & Goldstein, 1996a). The task was to infer which of two cities has a larger population. Each cue has two important characteristics: its *ecological validity* and its *discrimination rate*. The ecological validity of a cue is the relative frequency with which the cue correctly predicts the criterion, defined with respect to the reference class (here, all German cities with more than 100,000 inhabitants). For instance, if one checks all pairs in which one city has a soccer team but the other city does not, one finds that in about 87% of these cases the city with the team also has the higher population. This .87 value is the ecological validity of the soccer team cue. In general, the ecological validity v_i of the ith cue is:

v_i = number of correct predictions/number of predictions

where the number of predictions is the number of pairs in which one object has a positive and the other a negative value. The ecological validities of the cues varied over the whole range (table 4-1).

A cue with a high ecological validity, however, is not very useful if its discrimination rate is small. The discrimination rate of a cue is the relative frequency with which a cue discriminates between pairs of objects from the reference class. The discrimination rate is a function of the distribution of the cue values and the number N of objects in the reference class. Let the relative frequencies of the *positive* and *negative* cue values be x and y respectively. Then the discrimination rate d_i of the ith cue is:

$$d_i = \frac{2x_i y_i}{1 - \frac{1}{N}}$$

as an elementary calculation shows. Thus, if N is very large, the discrimination rate is approximately $2x_i y_i$.

The larger the ecological validity of a cue, the better the inferences. The larger the discrimination rate, the more often a cue can be used to make an inference. The pairwise correlations between the nine cues ranged between −.25 and .54, with an average absolute value of .19.

Different strategies extract different information from the environment. The Minimalist, for instance, does not extract information about which

Table 4-1: Cues, Ecological Validities, and Discrimination Rates

Cue	Ecological Validity	Discrimination Rate
National capital (Is the city the national capital?)	1.0	.02
Exposition site (Was the city once an exposition site?)	.91	.25
Soccer team (Does the city have a team in the major leagues?)	.87	.30
Intercity train (Is the city on the Intercity line?)	.78	.38
State capital (Is the city a state capital?)	.77	.30
License plate (Is the abbreviation only one letter long?)	.75	.34
University (Is the city home to a university?)	.71	.51
Industrial belt (Is the city in the industrial belt?)	.56	.30
East Germany (Was the city formerly in East Germany?)	.51	.27

cues are better than others; it only needs to estimate in which direction a cue points. Take The Best extracts information about the order in which cues should be tried. All competitors made use of the actual cue values from the complete environment to calculate parameters such as ecological validities or regression coefficients.

Limited Knowledge

We simulated subjects with varying degrees of knowledge about this environment. Limited knowledge can take two forms. One is limited recognition of objects. The other is limited knowledge about the cue values of recognized objects. To model limited recognition knowledge, we simulated subjects who recognized between 0 and all (83) German cities (i.e., 84 different levels of recognition). To model limited knowledge of cue values, we simulated six classes of subjects, who knew 0, 10, 20, 50, 75, or 100% of the cue values associated with the objects they recognized. Combining the two sources of limited knowledge resulted in 6 × 84 types of subjects, each having different degrees and kinds of limited knowledge. For each type of subject, we created 500 simulated individuals, who differed randomly from one another in the particular objects and cue values they knew.

The simulation needed to be realistic in the sense that the simulated subjects should be able to invoke the recognition heuristic. Therefore, the sets of cities the simulated subjects recognized had to be carefully chosen so that the recognized cities were larger than the unrecognized ones a certain percentage of the time. We performed a survey to get an empirical estimate of the actual relationship between the recognition of cities and city populations. In a survey of undergraduates at the University of Chicago, we found that the cities they recognized (within the 83 largest in Germany) were larger than the cities they did not recognize in about 80% of the cases. We incorporated this value into our simulations by choosing sets of cities (for each knowledge state, that is, for each number of cities recognized) where the known cities were larger than the unknown cities in about 80% of all cases. Thus, the cities known by the simulated subjects had the same relationship between recognition and population as did those of the human subjects. For details of the simulation see Gigerenzer and Goldstein (1996a).

Each simulated subject made inferences about which of two cities is larger, using each of six strategies: the three fast and frugal heuristics (Take The Best, Take The Last, and the Minimalist) and the three linear methods (regression, Franklin's rule, and Dawes's rule). The question of how well a fast and frugal heuristic performs in a real-world environment has rarely been posed in research on inductive inference. If the simple heuristics are adapted to environmental structures, then they should not fail outright.

How Frugal Are the Heuristics?

We measure frugality by the number of cues a heuristic looks up. The three linear models always look up and integrate all 10 cues (9 ecological cues plus recognition). Across all states of limited knowledge, Take The Last looked up on average only 2.6 cues, the Minimalist 2.8 cues, and Take The Best 3.0 cues (table 4-2). Take The Last owes its frugality to the Einstellung set, which tends to collect the cues that discriminate most often. The reason why the Minimalist looked up fewer cues than Take The Best is that cue validities and cue discrimination rates are negatively correlated (table 4-1). Therefore, randomly chosen cues tend to have higher discrimination rates than cues chosen by cue validity. All in all, the three heuristics look up less than a third of the cues used by the linear models, on average.

How Accurate Are the Heuristics?

How accurate are the three heuristics, given that they look up only a fraction of the available information? Recall that the Minimalist looks up on average only 2.8 cues, uses one-reason decision making, does not know which cues are better than others, and can violate transitivity. It must be doomed to fail. Table 4-2, however, shows that the Minimalist achieves an average accuracy of 64.7%. This is slightly higher than Take The Last, but lower than Take The Best with 65.8%. But how much more accurate are Dawes's rule, Franklin's rule, and multiple regression, which use all cues' values and combine them? The result in table 4-2 is surprising. Dawes's rule is outperformed by each of the three heuristics, although

Table 4-2: A Tournament Between Three Fast and Frugal Heuristics (Minimalist, Take The Last, Take The Best) and Three Linear Strategies (Dawes's Rule, Franklin's Rule, and Multiple Regression)

Strategy	Knowledge About Cues	Frugality (Number of Cues Looked Up)	Accuracy (%)
Take The Last	direction	2.6	64.5
Minimalist	direction	2.8	64.7
Take The Best	order	3.0	65.8
Dawes's rule	direction	10.0	62.1
Franklin's rule	validities	10.0	62.3
Multiple regression	beta weights	10.0	65.7

Note. Results are averaged across all levels of limited knowledge, that is, limited recognition and limited number of cue values known (see text). For instance, the Minimalist looked up only 2.8 cues on the average and made 64.7% correct inferences.

Dawes's rule has all the information that the Minimalist and Take The Last have (only Take The Best knows about the order of cues, which is not available to Dawes's rule). Franklin's rule has all the information that each of the three heuristics has, and more. Still, it is outperformed by even the most frugal of the simple heuristics.

How do the heuristics compare to a more powerful competitor? Multiple regression calculates a set of weights considered optimal for linear prediction, and arriving at these weights requires considerable computational might. Though it makes more accurate inferences than both the Minimalist and Take The Last, regression is matched in accuracy by the fast and frugal Take The Best.

Figure 4-2 shows the accuracy of the six competitors as a function of the number of cities recognized. Here, the situation where all competitors perform best is shown, namely when knowledge of cue values is 100%. The figure shows that the Minimalist and Take The Last can compete well with the other algorithms in accuracy when the number of objects recognized is limited, but take a loss when all are known, that is, when complete information is available. Franklin's rule and Dawes's rule match Take The Best when no or all objects are recognized, but suffer with inter-

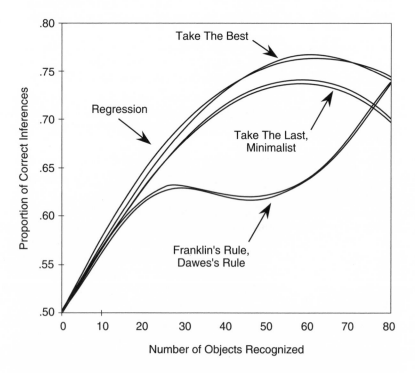

Figure 4-2: Results of the competition among decision strategies when knowledge of cue values is 100% but recognition rate varies.

mediate levels of recognition. Why is this? The reason is that these two strategies violate the wisdom of the recognition heuristic. They sometimes choose unrecognized cities as larger than recognized ones. In this environment, most cities have more negative cue values than positive ones: for example, the average city is not a state capital, does not have a major league soccer team, and so on. Dawes's rule, which subtracts the number of negative cue values from the number of positive ones, often arrives at a negative total for a recognized city that exceeds that of an unrecognized city (which is always −1, because of one negative reason: no recognition). The same holds for Franklin's rule, which weights the reasons (Gigerenzer & Goldstein, 1996a). Therefore, an unrecognized city is often inferred to be larger than a recognized one, which turns out to be a bad idea in this environment where the recognized cities were larger than the unrecognized cities 80% of the time. When one helps the linear strategies by endowing them with the recognition heuristic, their performance roughly matches that of Take The Best and multiple regression.

Figure 4-2 also illustrates a less-is-more effect (see chapter 2) in four of the six strategies. In contrast to figure 2-4, which shows a noisy less-is-more effect obtained by Take The Best in a simulation where the recognition validity was determined empirically at each level of recognition, here we see it in a smooth, refined form—a result of holding the recognition validity constant at our estimate of its empirical average.

Trade-Off Between Accuracy and Frugality

Within the three heuristics, the expected trade-off holds: the more frugal (the fewer cue values looked up), the less accurate. However, when we compare the family of heuristics to the three linear strategies, things get very interesting. Compared to multiple regression, Take The Best did not sacrifice accuracy for frugality—it achieved both. Compared to Dawes's and Franklin's rules, all three heuristics managed to be more accurate and yet more frugal at the same time.

When we first obtained these results, we could not believe them. We hired independent programmers in the United States and Germany to rerun the simulations to exclude possible wishful thinking on our part. When we finally published the results, we also included the data on the environment so that everyone could perform their own replications, and many did (Gigerenzer & Goldstein, 1996a). Fast and frugal heuristics do not necessarily have to trade accuracy for simplicity.

Can Frugality and Accuracy Both Be Possible?

Fast and frugal heuristics can make accurate inferences about unknown properties of the world, that is, inferences that are equal to or more accurate than the three linear strategies. In designing these simulations, we wondered if the heuristics would fail dismally. Before we reported the results, three eminent researchers in judgment and decision making predicted that Take The Best might perform 10 or 5 percentage points worse than the linear strategies. Each of the three heuristics, however, exceeded these expectations, and even outperformed some of the linear strategies. Take The Best matched or outperformed them all. At that juncture we did not understand how the competition could come out that way. The answer—in the form of what we call ecological rationality—only emerged after some further struggling, and will be developed in chapter 6. Here we summarize a few insights.

The observation of a flat maximum for linear models is one insight. If many sets of weights can perform about as well as the optimal set of weights in a linear model, this is called a flat maximum. The work by Robyn Dawes and others (e.g., Dawes & Corrigan, 1974) made this phenomenon known to decision researchers, but has actually been known longer. Since Wilks (1938) wrote about the robustness of equal weights, many have argued that weights are irrelevant both for making predictions by an artificial system (such as an IQ test) and for describing actual human inferences. In psychometrics, weighting the components of a test battery is rare because various weighting schemes result in surprisingly similar composite scores, that is, in flat maxima (e.g., Gulliksen, 1950). Flat maxima seem to occur when cues are strongly positively correlated. The performance of fast and frugal heuristics indicates that a flat maximum can extend beyond the issue of weights to decision strategies themselves: inferences based solely on the best cue can be as accurate as those based on a weighted linear combination of all cues.

There is also scattered earlier evidence that simple, noncompensatory heuristics can perform well. However, because much of the earlier work concentrated on preferences (rather than inferences) and on artificial stimuli (rather than real-world environments), external criteria of performance were often hard to come by. As mentioned before, the closest relatives of Take The Best are lexicographic strategies. Payne et al. (1993) showed that lexicographic judgments can sometimes be close to those of a weighted linear model, but they had no external criteria for accuracy. A second class of close relatives are simple algorithms in machine learning, which can perform highly accurate classifications (Holte, 1993; Rivest, 1987). A more distant relative to Take The Best is Elimination By Aspects (Tversky, 1972), which also employs limited search and a stopping rule, but deals with preference rather than inference, does not use the order of cues but a probabilistic criterion for search that requires knowledge of the quantitative validities of each cue, has no recognition heuristic built in, and does not employ one-reason decision making. Another more distant class of relatives are classification and regression trees (CARTs), which use a simple decision tree and one-reason decision making, but differ in the knowledge and computational power they use for setting up the simple tree. For instance, Breiman et al. (1993) reported a simple CART algorithm with only three binary, ordered cues that classified heart-attack patients into "high" and "low" risk groups. This noncompensatory tree was more accurate than standard statistical classification methods, which used up to 19 variables (see chapter 1). The practical relevance is obvious: In the emergency room, the physician can quickly obtain the measures on one, two, or three variables, and does not need to perform any computations since there is no integration. For theories that postulate mechanisms that resemble Take The Best see relevance theory (Sperber et al., 1995) and optimality theory (Legendre et al., 1993; Prince & Smolensky, 1991).

All in all, the observation of flat maxima, the performance of simple machine learning rules and CART trees, and the work by Payne, Bettman, and Johnson gave us hope that there was something larger to discover behind this first surprising finding.

Matching Stopping Rules to Environments

What structures of information in real-world environments can fast and frugal heuristics exploit in order to perform as accurately as they did? Where would they fail? Chapters 5 and 6 will address these questions. Here, we will illustrate this idea of ecological rationality—the match between mind and environment—by the *positive bias* of the stopping rule. Recall that the combination of a positive value and an unknown value stop search, but a negative and an unknown value do not. This asymmetry is what we mean by a positive bias. Positive biases of various kinds have been observed in humans (e.g., Klayman & Ha, 1987) and can result in both more frugal and more accurate inferences than an unbiased stopping rule. Consider first an unbiased stopping rule that demands a positive and a negative cue value (as proposed by Gigerenzer et al., 1991). This stopping rule would be less frugal, because search would take longer when there is limited knowledge (i.e., unknown cue values) than it would with a positive bias. Now consider a faster, unbiased stopping rule that always terminates search when the positive bias rule does, but in addition when a negative and an unknown value are obtained. Compared to this second unbiased stopping rule, a positive bias can be shown to achieve more accurate judgments in environments where negative cue values are more frequent than positive ones. The intuition for this result is that the unknown value is most likely negative. If the unknown value is negative, however, this will lead to fewer accurate judgments when one stops with a negative and an unknown value, because this would often mean that there were actually two negative values. Thus, a stopping rule with positive bias is ecologically rational in environments where negative cue values outnumber positive ones. An example is the environment studied in this chapter, where only relatively few cities have soccer teams in the major league, and only a few are state capitals (see also the "rarity" assumption of Oaksford & Chater, 1994). More generally, in environments where positive indicators are few and scattered—a rare symptom that signals a disease, an unusual feature that hints competence—a stopping rule with positive bias will prove ecologically rational.

Generalization

How does Take The Best estimate the order of cues? How do Take The Last and the Minimalist learn in which direction a cue points? There are several ways cues and their ranking may be learned. Cues, or the preparedness to learn cues, may be genetically coded through evolution. Cues for distance perception, mate choice, and food avoidance have been proposed as examples (e.g., Buss, 1992). Cues can also be learned through cultural transmission. For example, the cues needed for expertise can be learned from apprenticeship and the exchange of trade secrets. Finally, cues can be learned from direct observation. For instance, a person who knows some cue values for just 10 German cities, and knows for some pairs of these cities which has a higher population, could use this knowledge to estimate the rank order and direction of cues for the entire set. In contrast, in the simulations reported in this chapter, each strategy computed the parameters needed (direction of cue, cue order, cue validities, regression coefficients) from the entire data set.

How well would Take The Best do if it were to learn cues from a small sample? Recall that Take The Best extracts from a learning sample only the order and sign of the cues, a very small amount of information compared to the real-valued weights, regression coefficients, or conditional probabilities extracted by more complex statistical procedures. Thus, in a learning situation, Take The Best takes away only a small amount of information from a small sample. Regression, in contrast, extracts considerably more information from a small sample. Which is the better policy?

Figure 4-3 shows Take The Best, Take The Last, and the Minimalist competing with multiple regression at making generalizations from a training set to a test set. Each strategy estimated its respective parameters from a proportion (between 10% and 90%) of the German cities and made predictions about the complement. The process of dividing the environment into training and test sets, learning the parameters from the training set, and making predictions about the test set was repeated 500 times. In these simulations recognition was not a factor, that is, all objects were assumed to be recognized. Let us first consider the situation in which all cue values are known for all objects in the training and test sets (figure 4-3a). At the point where the training set is 50% of the total environment, for instance, Take The Best reaches 72% correct predictions, whereas multiple regression achieves 71%. More generally, throughout the entire range of training set sizes, Take The Best outperforms multiple regression, especially when the training set is small. Figure 4-3b shows a more difficult

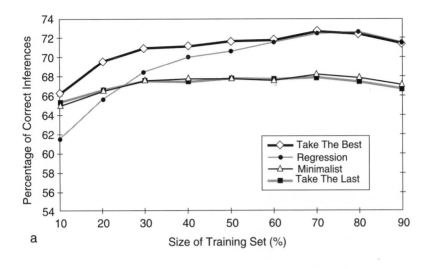

a

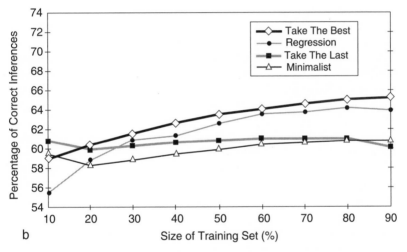

b

Figure 4-3: Generalizing from a training set to a test set. Results are shown for training sets with between 10% and 90% of the objects. Competitors were tested on the complement of the training set, so for instance in the 10% condition, the test set included the remaining 90% of the objects. We also varied the amount of missing knowledge in the environment. Figure 4-3a shows the cases where the training and test sets had no missing cue values. Figure 4-3b shows the case where 50% of the cue values, selected at random, were eliminated (replaced with question marks) from the overall environment before dividing it into training and test sets.

situation where half of the cue values were eliminated from the environment before the training and test sets were created. Here, the advantage of Take The Best is slightly more pronounced. Furthermore, when the training set is very small, the two most simple heuristics, Take The Last and Minimalist, perform as well as or better than the other strategies. These results indicate that Take The Best is more robust than multiple regression on this data set, and less prone to overfit a training set. Under situations of limited knowledge, simpler strategies may be more robust.

What about the generalization ability of strategies that are more computationally expensive than multiple regression? Using the German cities environment, Chater et al. (1997) tested Take The Best against complex strategies, including neural networks and exemplar models of categorization. Like multiple regression, none of these strategies has a stopping rule, but rather use all available cues. When the training set was less than 40% of the test set, Take The Best outperformed all other competitors. This advantage was largest (10 percentage points) when the size of the training set was smallest. Only when the training set grew beyond 40% of the German cities environment (which is actually more knowledge than most anybody has about German demographics, Germans included) did the competitors' performance increase above that of Take The Best, at most attaining a margin of about five percentage points. Note however that the simulations of Chater et al. have only dealt with the case where there were no unknown cue values (as represented by the question marks in figure 4-1).

These results, which came as a surprise to us, show how very simple heuristics can excel in situations where knowledge is limited, and where generalizations must be made from one sample to another. Chapters 5 and 6 will address the robustness of fast and frugal heuristics in more detail.

The Adaptive Toolbox

The Minimalist, Take The Last, and Take The Best are candidates for the collection of heuristics in what we call the adaptive toolbox. The emphasis is on "collection." None of these three strategies can perform all possible inferences under uncertainty—for instance, all three are designed to make estimates about which of two objects is larger, more effective, more dangerous, and so on. They cannot, for instance, estimate the quantitative values of one object. However, some of the building blocks—simple stopping rules, one-reason decision making—can be recombined to make heuristics for quantitative estimation, classification, and other tasks, as we will see in later chapters.

One may think of a collection of heuristics as a body made up of organs that have evolved over time rather than being designed in a grand plan. Thus, the adaptive toolbox may have evolved by adding features to already existing tools, rather than by replacing one generation of tools with a completely new generation. The three heuristics studied in this chapter, for instance, are built around the recognition heuristic. If the recognition heuristic can be used, search for further knowledge is not needed. If it cannot, the inference is made by the additional tools. Here, the order in which these two layers of heuristics are invoked follows their likely developmental and evolutionary order: Recognition and recognition memory are the more fundamental adaptive functions, less able to be damaged by age and brain injury (see chapter 2) than the recall memory used by Take The Best and its relatives.

The single most important result in this chapter is: Fast and frugal heuristics that embody simple psychological mechanisms can yield inferences about a real-world environment that are at least as accurate as standard linear statistical strategies embodying classical properties of rational judgment. This result liberates us from the widespread view that only "rational" algorithms, from Franklin's rule to multiple regression, can be accurate. Human inference does not have to forsake accuracy for simplicity. *The mind can have it both ways.*

When we concluded our first report of these results (Gigerenzer & Goldstein, 1996a) with the previous sentence, deep in our hearts we still had nagging doubts. Can heuristics really be fast, frugal, and accurate at the same time? Maybe there is something peculiar to city populations, or to German cities. Does the power of these heuristics to combine simplicity and frugality with accuracy generalize to other domains? What structures of information in natural environments do these heuristics exploit? Where do they break down? The following chapters tell what we have learned, so far. More surprises are to come.

5

How Good Are Simple Heuristics?

Jean Czerlinski
Gerd Gigerenzer
Daniel G. Goldstein

Psychology has forgotten that it is a science of organism-environment relationships, and has become a science of the organism. . . . This . . . is somewhat reminiscent of the position taken by those inflatedly masculine medieval theologians who granted a soul to men but denied it to women.

Egon Brunswik

Steve Bauer won the first day of the 1991 Tour de France, but placed 97th out of 200 at the end of the three-week race (Abt, 1991). Every day of this grueling bicycle tour covers a different type of terrain, and winning on one day does not guarantee good performance on the others. Likewise, Take The Best's success in Gigerenzer and Goldstein's (chapter 4) competition inferring German city populations does not guarantee that it will do well in other competitions. So before selling your sophisticated multiple regression software and converting to fast and frugal ways, heed this chapter. The strategies will complete two tours of 20 environments and predict everything from fish fertility to fuel consumption. The first tour will be data fitting: Strategies will train on the same course on which the race will be held. The second tour will be harder because the strategies will not be allowed to see the actual course until they race on it; they must train off-location. The results of these tours will pave the way for deciding when it pays to be fast and frugal and when it is better to use a more complex strategy such as multiple linear regression.

Meet the Environments

The glamour of the Tour de France is that it covers a wide variety of terrains, from flat to hilly to mountainous. Steve Bauer won the first day because he excelled on the plains, but lost the tour because he could not keep up on the mountains. The winner must be an all-rounder. Our tour is no different, consisting of 20 diverse environments. An environment consists of objects, each associated with a criterion to be predicted and a number of cues that may be helpful in predicting it. The task in the competition is to infer which of two objects scores higher on the criterion, for example, inferring which of two high schools has a higher dropout rate. Cues useful for making this inference could include the percentage of low-income students at the high school, the average SAT score, and the degree of parental involvement in their children's schooling. Our environments cover disparate domains from the objective number of car accidents on a stretch of highway to the subjective ratings of the attractiveness of public figures (table 5-1). The environments vary in size from 11 objects (ozone levels in San Francisco measured on 11 occasions) to 395 objects (fertility of 395 fish), and from 3 cues (the minimum needed to distinguish among the strategies) to 18 cues. To win this tour, an inference strategy will have to perform well in a variety of environments. Most of the environments come from statistics textbooks and are used to teach statistics, usually as examples of good applications of multiple regression. This should make it less than easy for Take The Best to compete with regression.

Meet the Competitors

Gigerenzer and Goldstein's competition (chapter 4) pitted a wide range of inference strategies against each other. Below we briefly describe four of the strategies; for more details see the previous chapter.

Take The Best

Imagine a bicycle built from the favorite parts of several racers, one contributing a frame, another a brake, a third a crankshaft. Instead of bicycle parts, Take The Best is assembled from cognitive building blocks: simple heuristics for search, stopping, and decision (see chapters 1 and 4 for definitions of these terms).

The first step of Take The Best is the recognition heuristic. In both tours, we will test the competitors in prediction tasks where all objects are recognized and all cue values are known; thus Take The Best will not be able to take advantage of the recognition heuristic, as it could in the previous chapter. Recall that Take The Best tries cues in order, one at a time, searching for a cue that discriminates between the two objects in question. For example, when inferring two professors' salaries, the rank cue might be tried first. If both professors are of the same rank (say both associate professors), then the gender cue might be tried. If one of the professors is a woman and the other is a man, then we say that the gender cue "discriminates." Once a discriminating cue is found, it serves as the

Table 5-1: A Description of the 20 Environments Used in the Competition

Psychology

Attractiveness of men: Predict average attractiveness ratings of 32 famous men based on the subjects' average likeability ratings of each man, the percentage of subjects who recognized the man's name (subjects saw only the name, no photos), and whether the man was American. (Based on data from a study by Henss, 1996, using 115 male and 131 female Germans, aged 17–66 years.)

Attractiveness of women: Predict average attractiveness ratings of 30 famous women based on the subjects' average likeability ratings of each woman, the percentage of subjects who recognized the woman's name (subjects saw only the name, no photos), and whether the woman was American. (Based on data from a study by Henss, 1996, using 115 male and 131 female Germans, aged 17–66 years.)

Sociology

High school dropout rates: Predict dropout rate of the 57 Chicago public high schools, given the percentage of low-income students, percentage of nonwhite students, average SAT scores, etc. (Based on Morton, 1995, and Rodkin, 1995.)

Homelessness: Predict the rate of homelessness in 50 U.S. cities given the average temperature, unemployment rate, percentage of inhabitants with incomes below the poverty line, the vacancy rate, whether the city has rent control, and the percentage of public housing. (From Tucker, 1987.)

Demography

Mortality: Predict the mortality rate in 20 U.S. cities given the average January temperature, pollution level, the percentage of nonwhites, etc. (Based on McDonald & Schwing, 1973; reported in StatLib.)

City population: Predict populations of the 83 German cities with at least 100,000 inhabitants based on whether each city has a soccer team, university, intercity train line, exposition site, etc. (From *Fischer Welt Almanach*, 1993.)

Economics

House price: Predict the selling price of 22 houses in Erie, PA, based on current property taxes, number of bathrooms, number of bedrooms, lot size, total living space, garage space, age of house, etc. (Based on Narula & Wellington, 1977; reported in Weisberg, 1985.)

Land rent: Predict the rent per acre paid in 58 counties in Minnesota (in 1977 for agricultural land planted in alfalfa) based on the average rent for all tillable land, density of dairy cows, proportion of pasture land, and whether liming is required to grow alfalfa. (Alfalfa is often fed to dairy cows.) (Data provided by Douglas Tiffany; reported in Weisberg, 1985.)

Professors' salaries: Predict the salaries of 51 professors at a midwestern college given gender, rank, number of years in current rank, the highest degree earned, and number of years since highest degree earned. (Reported in Weisberg, 1985.)

(*continued*)

Table 5-1: Continued

Transportation

Car accidents: Predict the accident rate per million vehicle miles for 37 segments of highway, using the segment's length, average traffic count, percentage of truck volume, speed limit, number of lanes, lane width, shoulder width, number of intersections, etc. for Minnesota in 1973. (Based on an unpublished master's thesis in civil engineering by Carl Hoffstedt; reported in Weisberg, 1985.)

Fuel consumption: Predict the average motor fuel consumption per person for each of the 48 contiguous United States using the population of the state, number of licensed drivers, fuel tax, per capita income, miles of primary highways, etc. (Based on data collected by Christopher Bingham for the *American Almanac for 1974*, except fuel consumption, which was given in the 1974 *World Almanac*; reported in Weisberg, 1985.)

Health

Obesity at age 18: Predict fatness at age 18 of 46 children based on body measurements from age 2 to age 18. The body measurements included height, weight, leg circumference, and strength. (Based on the longitudinal monitoring of the Berkeley Guidance Study, Tuddenham & Snyder, 1954; reported in Weisberg, 1985.)

Body fat: Predict percentage of body fat determined by underwater weighing (a more accurate measure of body fat) using various body circumference measurements (which are more convenient measures than underwater weighing) for 218 men. (Data supplied by A. Garth Fisher from the study of Penrose et al., 1985; reported in StatLib.)

Biology

Fish fertility: Predict the number of eggs in 395 female Arctic charr based on each fish's weight, its age, and the average weight of its eggs. (Data courtesy of Christian Gillet, 1996.)

Mammals' sleep: Predict the average amount of time 35 species of mammals sleep, based on brain weight, body weight, life span, gestation time, and predation and danger indices. (From Allison & Cicchetti, 1976; reported in StatLib.)

Cow manure: Predict the amount of oxygen absorbed by dairy wastes given the biological oxygen demand, chemical oxygen demand, total Kjedahl nitrogen, total solids, and total volatile solids for 14 trials. (Moore, 1975; reported in Weisberg, 1985.)

Environmental Science

Biodiversity: Predict the number of species on 26 Galapagos islands, given their area, elevation, distance to the nearest island, area of the nearest island, distance from the coast, etc. (Based on Johnson & Raven, 1973; reported in Weisberg, 1985.)

Rainfall from cloud seeding: Predict the amount of rainfall on 24 days in Coral Gables, FL, given the types of clouds, the percentage of cloud cover, whether the clouds were seeded, number of days since the first day of the experiment, etc. (From Woodley et al., 1977; reported in Weisberg, 1985.)

Oxidant in Los Angeles: Predict the amount of oxidant in Los Angeles for 17 days given each day's wind speed, temperature, humidity, and insolation (a measure of the amount of sunlight). (Data provided by the Los Angeles Pollution Control District; reported in Rice, 1995.)

Table 5-1: Continued

Ozone in San Francisco: Predict the amount of ozone in San Francisco on 11 occasions based on the year, average winter precipitation for the past two years, and ozone level in San Jose, at the southern end of the Bay. (From Sandberg et al., 1978; reported in Weisberg, 1985.)

Note. For each environment we specify the criterion, a sample of the cues for predicting the criterion, and the source of the data. Recall that the cues are either binary or were dichotomized by a median split, and that the task is always to predict which of two objects scores higher at the criterion.

basis for an inference, and all other cues are ignored. For instance, if gender discriminates between two professors, the inference is made that the male earns a higher salary, and no other information about years of experience or highest degree earned is considered. Could such one-reason decision making be accurate? This chapter will answer this question.

Since Take The Best does not integrate information or require extensive computations, it is fast. Since it has a stopping rule to effect limited search for cues, it is frugal. In this competition, Take The Best looks up cues in the order of their validities, which it has to estimate from a training set. Recall that the validity of a cue is defined as the number of correct inferences divided by the number of correct and incorrect inferences made using the cue alone (chapter 4).

The Minimalist

The fast and frugal Minimalist looks up cues in a random order, stopping when it finds a cue that discriminates between the two objects. Otherwise, it is exactly the same as Take The Best. In the simulation, it will not be able to take advantage of the recognition heuristic, for the same reason as for Take The Best.

Multiple Regression

Multiple linear regression is the most thoroughly trained and well-equipped rider in the pack. It rides on sophisticated computations rather than on fast and frugal building blocks. Regression assumes the data can be approximated by a hyperplane plus independent, identically distributed errors with zero mean. It then finds the hyperplane that minimizes the squared vertical distance between the hyperplane and the data points. Finding an optimal fitting surface is not the kind of calculation that can be easily carried out with pencil and paper or a standard pocket calculator—a computer is called for. When regression is used to make a prediction, all of the available cues must be gathered and plugged into the model, so it is not frugal. Furthermore, since multiple regression requires extensive computations, it is not fast.

Dawes's Rule

Dawes's rule is a simplification of regression. The model is still linear, but instead of optimal weights, only unit weights (+1 or −1) are used (Dawes, 1979). That is, it adds up the number of pieces of positive evidence and subtracts the number of pieces of negative evidence. We operationalize the assignment of the unit weights by giving a cue a weight of +1 if a cue's validity is above chance (.5) and −1 if it is below chance. Since using Dawes's rule to make a prediction still requires all of the cues, it is not frugal. But unlike regression it is fast, since the weighting scheme is trivial.

We have defined athletes with four differing strategies. Who will win the 20-environment tour?

The First Tour: Fitting Known Environments

In our first tour, the riders were allowed to examine every detail of the race course before the competition. There were no missing cue values or unrecognized objects, unlike the scenarios in chapters 2, 3, and 4. All of the cue and criterion values were available for calculating cue validities or linear weights. The strategies then predicted the criterion values (which they had already seen). This type of contest is called data fitting. The first two environments that were fit, high school dropout rates and professorial salaries, will be described in detail to give a sense of how the strategies compete against one another. Then we will jump to the end of the race to see who won the overall tour and by how much.

Dropping Out

The first stage of the tour is important for American society: predicting dropout rates at Chicago public high schools. The 1995 rates were published in *Chicago* magazine (Morton, 1995; Rodkin, 1995), along with possible cues such as the socioeconomic and ethnic compositions of the student bodies, the sizes of the classes, the attendance rates of the students, the parent participation rates, and the scores of the students on various standardized tests.

We prepared the raw data from the magazine to suit the four inference strategies. We converted all cue values that were real numbers into ones and zeroes using the median as a cutoff. These ones and zeroes were assigned such that the ones corresponded to higher values on the criterion.

After the data were transformed into the appropriate format, their characteristics could be measured. Overall, the dropout environment looked fairly challenging. The average cue validity was only .63, compared to .76 for the German city population data. The maximum cue validity was also rather low, .72. These characteristics should create considerable difficulties for Take The Best, which relies on only the best cue that discriminates between two high schools. Furthermore, the environment comprised a total of 18 cues, double the number in the city population environment. Since Dawes's rule improves in accuracy with the addition of more cues (see chapter 6), this environment was a particularly tough test for Take The Best and the Minimalist.

Before revealing the accuracy of the strategies in predicting dropout rates, let us review the results on German city populations (figure 4-2; the values on the right of the graph where all objects are recognized). Recall that multiple regression made 74% correct inferences. Dawes's rule did very well in comparison, also earning 74% correct. The surprising finding was that Take The Best matched the 74% performance of these linear strategies. Finally, the exceedingly simple Minimalist scored a respectable 70% correct.

What happened on the more difficult high school dropout environment? Despite the lower cue validities, regression was still able to get 72% of the inferences correct (table 5-2, "fitting"). Perhaps the large number of cues made up for the low validities. Dawes's rule did not seem to be able to take as much advantage of the many cues, getting only 64% correct. Take The Best made 65% of the inferences correctly—slightly better than Dawes's rule but still seven percentage points behind the performance of linear regression. The Minimalist was again the weakest strategy, but not too far behind Take The Best with 61% correct. Take The Best and the Minimalist looked up on average only a few cues (table 5-2). Speed and frugality paid the price of seven percentage points in lost accuracy on the difficult high school dropout data.

Policy Implications   Discovering which strategy best fits the data can have important consequences for public policy. For example, Take The Best regarded attendance rate, writing test score, and social science test score

Table 5-2: Predicting High School Dropout Rates

| Strategy | Frugality | Accuracy (% Correct) | |
		Fitting	Generalization
Minimalist	2.7	61	58
Take The Best	3.4	65	60
Dawes's rule	18	64	62
Multiple regression	18	72	54

Note. Performance of two fast and frugal heuristics (Minimalist, Take The Best) and two linear strategies (Dawes's rule, multiple regression) in predicting which of two Chicago high schools has a higher dropout rate. There were 57 public high schools and 18 predictors (table 5-1). Performance is measured in terms of frugality (average number of cues looked up) and accuracy (% correct). Accuracy is measured both for fitting data (test set = training set), and for generalization (test set ≠ training set). The average number of cues looked up was about the same for both kinds of competition.

as the most valid cues for dropout rate, in that order. In contrast, linear regression's top three predictors were percentages of Hispanic students, students with limited English, and black students. Thus, each strategy led to different implications for how we can help schools lower dropout rates. While a user of Take The Best would recommend getting students to attend class and teaching them the basics more thoroughly, a regression user would recommend helping minorities assimilate and supporting English as a second language (ESL) programs. Because regression resulted in the best fit, it looked like the regression user would be able to give better advice for lowering dropout rates.

Professors' Income

Let us now consider how well the strategies predict individual professors' salaries from the following five cues: gender, rank (assistant, associate, full professor), number of years in current rank, highest degree earned, and number of years since degree earned. The data is from a midwestern college, which shall remain anonymous. Clearly, this environment already had one binary variable (gender); the rest were dichotomized at the median.

This environment had a maximum cue validity of .98 and its average cue validity was .79, similar to the city population environment. It had only five cues, about half as many as for predicting populations. How would this affect the accuracy of Take The Best and the Minimalist? One intuitive answer would be that high cue validities and few cues allow the two heuristics to keep up with the algorithms that integrate information across cues; let us see if this was true.

Crossing the finish line first was the rider on the fanciest and most expensive bicycle, multiple regression, with a stunning 83% correct (table 5-3, "fitting"). This was surprising since the environment seemed to be

Table 5-3: Predicting Professors' Salaries

Strategy	Frugality	Accuracy (% Correct)	
		Fitting	Generalization
Minimalist	2.1	73	72
Take The Best	2.3	80	80
Dawes's rule	5	75	75
Multiple regression	5	83	80

Note. Performance of two fast and frugal heuristics (Minimalist, Take The Best) and two linear strategies (Dawes's rule, multiple regression) in predicting which of two professors at a midwestern college has a higher salary. There were 51 professors and five predictors (table 5-1). Performance is measured in terms of frugality (average number of cues looked up) and accuracy (% correct). Accuracy is measured both for fitting data (test set = training set), and for generalization (test set ≠ training set). The average number of cues looked up was about the same for both kinds of competition.

about the same as the cities except with half as many cues. Taking one cue at a time, Take The Best somehow managed second place by scoring 80% correct. Dawes's rule, the leaner linear model, got 75% correct, not as far behind linear regression as it was with school dropout rates. The Minimalist finally pulled in at 73%, almost as good as Dawes's rule.

It turned out that the best cue for predicting professor salary was rank, with a cue validity of .98. It may not come entirely as a surprise that the second best cue was gender, with a validity of .88. In this environment, regression was mostly in agreement, giving rank the greatest weight, followed by highest degree earned and gender.

The Overall Winner of the First Tour

We now have a sense of how the competition works and how the characteristics of the environments might affect the strategies. Let us finally find out which strategy won on the complete range of environments, that is, fitting both the mountain roads and the plains closely enough to win the overall tour.

How frugal were the heuristics? The Minimalist searched for only 2.2 cues on average to make an inference. Take The Best needed slightly more cues, 2.4, whereas the two linear strategies always used all the available information, 7.7 cues on average (the linear strategies have no heuristics for search and stopping). Thus, the two heuristics looked up fewer than a third of the cues. If they are so frugal, how accurate can they be?

Perhaps it is no surprise that the first-place finisher was multiple linear regression, which used all information and subjected it to complex computation (table 5-4, "fitting"). Across the 20 environments, regression scored 77% correct. However, the second-place finisher may be a surprise. The

Table 5-4: Performance Across 20 Data Sets

Strategy	Frugality	Accuracy (% Correct)	
		Fitting	Generalization
Minimalist	2.2	69	65
Take The Best	2.4	75	71
Dawes's rule	7.7	73	69
Multiple regression	7.7	77	68

Note. Performance of two fast and frugal heuristics (Minimalist, Take The Best) and two linear strategies (Dawes's rule, multiple regression) across all 20 data sets. The average number of predictors was 7.7. Performance is measured in terms of frugality (average number of cues looked up) and accuracy (% correct). Accuracy is measured both for fitting data (test set = training set), and for generalization (test set ≠ training set). The average number of cues looked up was about the same for both kinds of competition. For a similar result with slightly different data sets, see Gigerenzer et al. (1999), and for the performance of various strategies on the 20 individual data sets, see table 8-1.

fast and frugal Take The Best finished the tour only two percentage points behind regression, with 75% correct. This is close to what Gigerenzer and Goldstein (chapter 4) found, suggesting that our set had more cases similar to the city population data than to the high-school dropout data. The fast but not frugal Dawes's rule scored two percentage points behind Take The Best with 73% correct. It was quite a surprise that Dawes's rule scored worse than Take The Best, given that Take The Best was even more frugal and did not integrate what little cue information it did gather. Finally, the Minimalist pulled in last with 69% accuracy, a respectable score considering its extreme simplicity. The price of using a fast and frugal heuristic was small, about two percentage points for Take The Best and about eight for the Minimalist. Furthermore, more cue information did not guarantee more accuracy, since Take The Best was slightly more accurate than Dawes's rule despite using fewer cues.

We Knew It All Along

One reaction to a novel claim is to say that it is impossible. Gigerenzer and Goldstein (1996a) showed that their claim—that fast and frugal heuristics can also be accurate—was possible; and this chapter has further shown that it is not only sometimes possible but is, in fact, often the case. Environments in which the price of simplicity is high, such as when predicting dropout rates in high schools, seem to be the exceptions and not the rule.

Another reaction when an "impossible" novel claim has finally been proven is to say one "knew it all along" (see chapter 9 on hindsight where this memory distortion is modeled by Take The Best). In this section, we review the psychological literature to find what actually was known all along about how well fast and frugal heuristics can perform relative to more complex strategies.

The comparison is not entirely straightforward because earlier research differs from ours in a number of ways. First, the range of strategies compared in earlier studies was mostly restricted to different weighting schemes for linear models. Second, the range of environments was typically restricted to artificially generated data sets with multivariate normal distributions for the cues and criteria. Finally, the type of competition differed, usually involving not just fitting given data, but generalizing to new data, that is, training an algorithm on one part of the data and then making predictions on another part. If both parts are of equal size, this is usually called cross-validation. In the next section we will rerun the whole competition using cross-validation. First let us consider the previous literature.

Research on simple strategies began in earnest in the mid-1970s. Through computer simulations and mathematical analysis, researchers such as Schmidt (1971), Dawes and Corrigan (1974), and Einhorn and Hogarth (1975) found that a unit-weighted linear model (which we call Dawes's rule) was on average almost as accurate as multiple linear regression—and far more robust to boot. (A "robust" strategy or model is one that remains accurate when generalizing to new data, such as in cross-validation.) For example, in predicting grade point averages, a unit-weighted linear model made predictions that correlated .60 with the actual values, while a cross-validated regression model scored .57. Note that because regression was cross-validated—making predictions on data different from that on which it was trained—its performance can be lower than the unit-weighted model (which was not cross-validated). In the three other tasks considered, unit weights had a higher accuracy than cross-validated regression in two (Dawes & Corrigan, 1974). As Paul Meehl put it, "in most practical situations an unweighted sum of a small number of 'big' variables will, on the average, be preferable to regression equations" (quoted in Dawes & Corrigan, 1974, p. 105).

In a related but more recent line of research, Ehrenberg (1982) analytically compared regression weights to other weights. He showed that for typical values of a one-cue prediction problem (e.g., with a correlation of .7 between the criterion and the cue), using a slope differing from the optimal by as much as plus or minus 30% results in only a 4% increase in unexplained error. Dawes and Corrigan (1974, citing an unpublished manuscript by Winterfeldt & Edwards, 1973) called this the phenomenon of the flat maximum: Weights even vaguely near the optimal lead to almost the same output as do optimal weights.

These studies seem to say that Dawes's rule is often almost as accurate as multiple regression. But life is not quite that simple. First of all, in those cases in which real environments were used, only a few such environments were checked. Second, this research cross-validated only for regression but not for Dawes's rule, with the argument that "it is the human judge who knows the directional relationship between the predictor variables and the criterion of interest" (Dawes, 1979, p. 573). But even experts must have some method by which they estimate the direction of cues, and so the cross-validated simulations in the next section test how well Dawes's rule performs when it must estimate the direction of the cue, too. We will wait until a later section to operationalize Meehl's suggestion of using only "a small number" of variables; we will continue to use all the cues for now. Our work goes beyond previous research by operationalizing all aspects of Dawes's rule—testing cross-validated Dawes's rule against cross-validated regression—and seeing if the old findings still hold up.

We also go beyond previous research in pursuing the trade-off question more intensively: Just how much simpler can inference strategies be without losing too much accuracy? Our simulations test not just Dawes's rule against regression but also against Take The Best and the Minimalist. There have been some scattered experiments also trying very simple heuristics (e.g., Hogarth & Makridakis, 1981; Kleinmuntz & Kleinmuntz, 1981), but only Payne, Bettman, and Johnson (1988, 1990) have launched a consistent program of study. Their program focuses on preferences (e.g., between gambles) rather than on cue-based inferences, and they measure performance by a correlation of choices with a weighted additive model (the expected payoff) rather than with an external criterion (since for subjective choice there is none). For example, in their competitions the simpler heuristics typically achieved from 60 to 70 percent of the performance of the weighted additive model benchmark, but by this measurement method, the simple heuristics cannot be more accurate than the "rational" answer of the weighted additive model. Only with an external standard for the number of correct inferences is it possible to show that simple heuristics can be more accurate than more complex strategies. Thus, previous research has focused on preferences rather than inferences, and on artificial rather than real-world environments. As a consequence, it has not shed much light on the accuracy of simple heuristics in making inferences about the real world.

In this chapter, we test heuristics on a wider range of empirical data environments than has been used before. We run the Tour de France of heuristic decision makers.

The Second Tour: Generalizing to New Objects

Imagine a bicycle rider who spent all his time training on the plains of the Midwest and then tried to race in the varied landscapes of the Tour de France. What would probably happen? He might fail completely on the mountains. This is not to say he would have to go to France to train; as long as he could find a mixture of Colorado mountains, midwestern plains, and winding New England streets, he could adequately prepare for the Tour. Training on a course and racing (testing) on another is generalization, as opposed to fitting.

More precisely, generalization means that the strategies build their models (i.e., calculate regression weights, determine cue orders or cue directions, etc.) on some subset of all objects, the training set. The strategies then make predictions about the remaining objects, the test set. Generalization is a more difficult and realistic test of the strategies than training and testing on the same objects. In our simulations, we tested generalization by breaking the environment into halves, with a random assignment of objects to one half or the other. This is called cross-validation. The performance is then the proportion correct in the test set. Each environment was split 1000 times into training and test sets, in order to average out any particularly helpful or harmful ways of dividing the data.

Dawes's rule and the Minimalist might not seem to be doing any estimation, but in fact they use the first half of the environment to estimate the direction in which the cues point. In our simulations, they did this by calculating whether the cue validity was above or below the chance level. (This is equivalent to testing whether the cue has a positive or negative Goodman-Kruskal rank correlation with the criterion, as shown in chapter

6.) Take The Best estimates the direction of the cues and then orders them from best to worst predictor. Multiple regression estimates the optimal beta weights, taking into account the relationships between the variables.

We will now race through each of the environments and consider how the strategies perform in generalization. In chapter 4, we saw one case of generalization, predicting city populations. When the algorithms were trained on half of the cities, as in our second tour, Take The Best was slightly more accurate (72%) than multiple regression and Dawes's rule (71% each). Does this result generalize? Could it be that one-reason decision making can be more accurate across the 20 environments?

Dropping Out Again

We first tested generalization when predicting high-school dropout rates. The simplest strategy, the Minimalist, fell from 61% to 58%; similarly, Dawes's rule dropped from 64% to 62%. Take The Best, which estimates both cue direction and cue order, took a slightly larger loss and dropped to 60% (table 5-2, "generalization"). Finally, multiple regression dropped a whopping 18 percentage points, from 72% to 54%, which also made it by far the least predictive strategy of the bunch. It seems the simpler strategies are the more robust ones in generalization. What explains regression's huge drop?

We believe the answer is overfitting. Imagine that a bicycle rider trains on a course beginning with a steep ascent, continuing with a long, flat plain, and ending with a final descent, having exactly the same proportion of uphill, flat, and downhill regions as the test course will have. Every day, the rider's body gets used to pumping hard and heavy at first, then cruising quickly, then relaxing on the way down. The danger is that the rider may get so used to this pattern that he can no longer deal well with other combinations of hills and plains: If the test course is a drop, then a flat plain, ending with a steep ascent, the rider might have difficulties adjusting. Such overfitting can happen to inference strategies, too: They can learn the particular quirks of their training data, such as details of cue orders and intercorrelations, too well. The more closely a strategy tries to fit the training landscape, the greater is the danger of overfitting.

In the case of the dropout environment, there were 18 cues. Such an abundance of cues offered ample opportunity for accidental correlations. If regression built these accidents into its model, then its predictions on the second half of the data, which need not have the same accidental correlations as the first half, would be inaccurate.

Public Policy   Again, consider possible policy implications. In the fitting tour, the regression user would have confidently recommended expanding ESL classes to help the dropout rate. Because regression had the best predictions, this would seem the best policy. However, in the generalization tour, Take The Best was more accurate than regression, and it appears that regression overfitted the training data. While regression put a heavier weight on the influence of ESL classes on dropout rates based on the training data, this may have been a fluke that will not generalize. On the other hand, Take The Best's recommendation, based on the training data, to encourage attendance and teach the basics may be more generalizable. Dawes's rule and the Minimalist do not suggest specific recommendations—just to improve on all fronts—because they weight all predictors equally.

Later in this chapter, we will argue that regression carries a lower risk of overfitting in larger environments with more objects (or fewer cues). There are, though, only 57 public high schools in Chicago, and if this number of objects does not suffice for regression, then regression simply should not be used. There is no more data to collect for it. One might try to train regression on dropout rates from other cities or from previous time periods in Chicago, but then one risks again overfitting, finding factors relevant to other places and times than to today's Chicago public high schools.

Professors' Income

Let us also briefly consider generalizing predictions of professors' salaries based on five cues. Regression's score dropped only slightly, from 83% to 80%. Dawes's rule and Take The Best held their ground at 75% and 80%, respectively (table 5-3, "generalization"). The Minimalist dropped one point to 72%. Compared with the task of predicting high school dropout rates, predicting income was based on a smaller number of cues and on cues with higher validity. It seemed that with these characteristics, the drop in accuracy also was less than was the case in predicting city populations.

We now have some idea of how generalization affects the strategies. Which of the strategies will make robust generalizations across the 20 environments?

The Winner of the Second Tour

On average, regression dropped a stunning nine percentage points in accuracy, from an average of 77% for the fitting task to 68% for generalization (table 5-4, "generalization"). Meanwhile, Dawes's rule fell four percentage points, from an average of 73% to 69%, as did the Minimalist, from 69% to 65%. The small size of these drops was probably due in part to the fact that these two strategies estimated very little—only the directions of the cues.

The overall winner was Take The Best at 71% accuracy, down five percentage points. Take The Best earned the highest accuracy in generalization among the four strategies, despite its fast and frugal nature. Across the 20 environments, regression and Dawes's rule used an average of 7.7 cues per inference, whereas Take The Best only used 2.4 cues, the same small number as for the fitting task. The fact that a heuristic can disobey the rational maxim of collecting all available information and yet be the most accurate is certainly food for thought.

Take The Best outperformed multiple regression by an average of three percentage points when making generalizations. Startling at this result is, it is not entirely inconsistent with the previous literature, which showed that in several types of environments regression generalized less well than the simpler Dawes's rule (without cross-validation). Our second tour, however, has shown that Dawes's rule is also in danger of overfitting. Moreover, simplicity and frugality, pushed to the extreme, can eventually have a price: The Minimalist placed last. But this price was not very high, for the Minimalist's average performance was a mere three percentage points behind multiple regression.

Tinkering With the Rules of the Tour

Some colleagues were skeptical about the possibility that one-reason decision making could be fast, frugal, and accurate at the same time. They suggested modified versions of the competition, predicting that the counterintuitive accuracy of Take The Best would quickly vanish. One early conjecture voiced against the results reported in Gigerenzer and Goldstein (1996a; see also chapter 4), was that the recognition heuristic, with its high empirical validity (.8) for population size, would be the main cause for the accuracy of Take The Best. We have taken care of this conjecture in this chapter: In both tours, all objects were recognized, so that the recognition heuristic could not operate. We will consider four further modifications and conjectures.

Use exact rather than dichotomized numbers. In the simulations reported, we have dichotomized all quantitative cues at the median (except for the binary cues, such as gender) rather than using the exact values. This procedure was assumed to mimic the limited knowledge about cue values that people typically have, and the potential unreliability of precise values. Each competitor, the linear strategies and the heuristics, based their predictions on these binary or dichotomized values. A reasonable conjecture is that part of the power of multiple regression is lost when it is applied to dichotomized data. Some colleagues suggested rerunning the tour and letting every strategy have the exact quantitative cue values. There are two major ways lexicographic strategies such as Take The Best can be extended to make inferences from quantitative values (Payne et al., 1988, 1990). In the first version, search continues until the first cue is found in which the two values are different; in the second, search continues until the difference between cue values exceeds a threshold or "just noticeable difference." To avoid the arbitrariness in defining how large the threshold should be, we went with the first version.

We reran Take The Best and multiple regression under the conditions of the second tour. Take The Best, when adapted to quantitative values, was even more frugal than its standard version. Search often stopped after the first or second cue, because even small quantitative differences were sufficient to halt search and prompt a decision. But how accurate were the inferences based on quantitative predictors? Our colleagues were right: Multiple regression did improve when given real numbers—but so did Take The Best. Across the 20 environments, Take The Best made 76% correct predictions, compared to regression, which also earned 76% correct. Thus, one-reason decision making in the form of Take The Best could still match multiple regression in accuracy, even with exact quantitative values. This counterintuitive result came as a surprise to us, but, by then, we were getting used to surprises.

Give Dawes's rule another chance by using only the "big" cues. Recall Paul Meehl's conjecture: "an unweighted sum of a small number of 'big' variables will, on the average, be preferable to regression equations." In the two tours, Dawes's rule had access to all of the cues. Meehl, however, suggested using only the "big" cues, that is, the most valid ones. When Dawes's rule estimates the direction of a cue in the training set, erroneous estimates of the direction occur most often with low-validity cues. We developed a version of Dawes's rule that ignored cues with an estimated validity of .7 or less. We reran this truncated version of Dawes's rule under the conditions of the second tour. The accuracy indeed increases from 69% with Dawes's rule (see table 5-4) to 71% with the truncated Dawes's rule, three percentage points above the accuracy of regression. Meehl's intuition turned out to be correct across the 20 environments. Using only a small number of "big" cues, without weighting them, is, on average, more accurate in *generalization* than a regression that weights all cues. But Meehl's intuition can be pushed even further. Take The Best, which uses only the "best" cue that discriminates between two objects, turns out to be as accurate.

But what if Take The Best does not have the order of cues (as in Tour 1), and needs to estimate it from a very small sample? Recall first that Take The Best does not try to estimate an optimal order of cues (as, for instance, classification trees attempt to do; see chapters 6 and 8). Instead, it uses a simple and frugal method to create an order (for binary cues, the cue order can be calculated with one simple pass through the objects; see Czerlinski, 1998 for details). Ordering cues by their cue validity, as Take The Best does, is not called "optimal" because this procedure ignores all dependencies between cues. We saw that, for estimating population size, Take The Best lost on accuracy when the training set was very small, but multiple regression lost even more (figure 4-3). These results suggest that Take The Best is relatively robust when making predictions from a small number of observations. But does this result generalize to other data sets? We tested the accuracy of Take The Best when it had to estimate the cue order from just 10 randomly chosen objects rather than from the full first half of the objects, as in the second tour. It then made predictions on the other half of the environment just as in the regular second tour.

This tour tested the degree to which Take The Best depends on copious information for assessing the order in which to try cues. The result across 20 environments was that Take The Best scored about 66% correct predictions, losing five percentage points from when it had access to half the environment for training. These numbers match the result in estimating city populations in chapter 4. This Sample-10 tour is similar to allowing bicycle riders only very limited training, say by announcing the layout of the race course only days ahead of the race. It seemed that even with very few observations, Take The Best could still make reasonably accurate predictions.

But Take The Best cannot estimate quantities, whereas multiple regression can. This conjecture addresses the generality of Take The Best, Take The Last, and the Minimalist. These three heuristics can make predictions about which object has a higher value on a criterion, such as which of two highways is more dangerous, but they cannot make quantitative predictions, such as how high the car accident rate on one of those two highways is. The heuristics are specialized for particular classes of tasks, whereas multiple regression is more general. In chapter 10, we will study a heuristic that can make quantitative predictions, and employs one-reason decision making like Take The Best. What we call the adaptive toolbox is a collection of different heuristics designed from the same kinds of building blocks. The building blocks, not the specific heuristics, have generality. The specificity of the individual heuristics enables them to be fast, frugal, and accurate—with little trade-off.

How Does Take The Best Do So Well?

What is the difference between the environments in which Take The Best performed poorly and those in which it did well? This question concerns the ecological rationality of Take The Best, that is, the fit between the structure of the heuristic and that of an environment (chapter 1). This question is the focus of the next chapter—here we will raise the question, review previous research, and test three of its predictions empirically.

Characterizing Environments: A Review

The literature suggests variables that matter in predicting whether cross-validated regression or Dawes's rule without cross-validation would win our competition. Our goal, however, was to understand the performance of fast and frugal heuristics, so it is unclear whether these earlier findings are relevant. Furthermore, previous research has used either simulation studies of hundreds of randomly generated environments, or mathematical analysis with numerous simplifying assumptions about the form of the data. There is cause to doubt whether such findings would generalize to our empirical environments. Let us nevertheless consider what has been discovered, but with these caveats in mind.

Schmidt's (1971) simulations on random data (multivariate normal distributions) showed that in cross-validation regression outperformed Dawes's rule on average only for large numbers of objects. For example, with four cues, one needs a sample size of at least 50 objects for regression to beat Dawes's rule. For six cues, one needs at least 75 objects. For 10 cues, 100 objects are required. As a rule of thumb, it seems one should not use regression with fewer than 10 objects per cue; otherwise, unit weights will outperform regression weights on average. Regression is likely to overfit the data when there are too few objects for the number of cues. That is, regression takes account of numerous intercorrelations that may be artifacts of the current sample. Similarly, the fewer kinds of training course a bicycle rider is exposed to, the more likely she is to overfit the ones she has seen.

Einhorn and Hogarth (1975; see also Hogarth, 1981) confirmed Schmidt's findings and added two other factors. Dawes's rule can be expected to perform about as well as multiple regression when (a) the coefficient of determination (R^2), from the regression model is in the moderate or low range (.5 or smaller) and (b) the cues are intercorrelated. The coefficient of determination measures the linear fit between the criterion and the cues.

If we take these three factors together, the literature indicates that regression models are slightly more accurate than Dawes's rule if there are many objects per cue, a high linear predictability of the criterion, and cues are not highly correlated. Under the opposite conditions, Dawes's rule is slightly better.

We shall now see if number of objects per cue, ease of linear predictability, or degree of cue intercorrelation can explain why Take The Best was so successful in the real-world environments of the two tours.

Is It the Number of Objects per Cue?

Figure 5-1 shows that the advantage of Take The Best over multiple regression (the difference in accuracy) depends on the ratio between the number of objects and cues. Take The Best won by more when there were fewer objects per cue. However, a large number of objects per cue, even more than 10, did not guarantee that regression would tie or outperform Take The Best. For instance, the largest ratio in figure 5-1 was obtained for predicting body fat, with 218 men measured on 14 cues, resulting in about 16 objects per cue. Even with this high ratio of objects per cue, Take The Best made a higher proportion of accurate inferences than multiple linear regression.

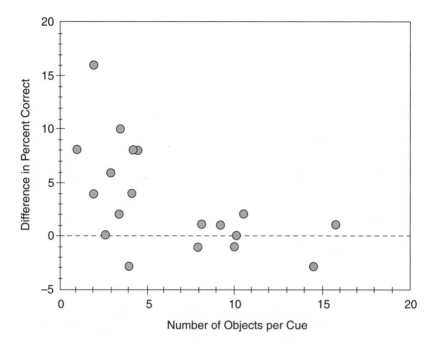

Figure 5-1: Take The Best's advantage over multiple regression (in percent correct) plotted against the number of objects per cue for 19 of the 20
environments (Tour 2). The missing environment is fish fertility, which is
well off the scale with 395 objects and 3 cues. Take The Best scored 1.8
percentage points behind regression on the fish fertility data.

The finding that the number of objects per cue was a good predictor of
Take The Best's advantage provides support to the hypothesis that regression was overfitting when there were few objects per cue. There is a more
direct test of this hypothesis: Compare cross-validated regression with regression that merely fits the data, as the number of objects per cue is varied (figure 5-2). The result shows a trend similar to that in figure 5-1: The
smaller the number of objects per cue, the larger the difference between
the performance of regression in the fitting and generalization tasks. In
both figures, the plots have nonconstant variance and appear curved.

Is It the Ease of Linear Predictability?

The second characteristic of environments is the coefficient of determination (R^2). The idea is that in environments with a high coefficient of determination, multiple regression results in better predictions than Dawes's
rule, while the exact weighting scheme does not matter much for data that
is not very linear anyway. We measured R^2 by running regression on the
full environment. However, there appeared to be no relation between R^2

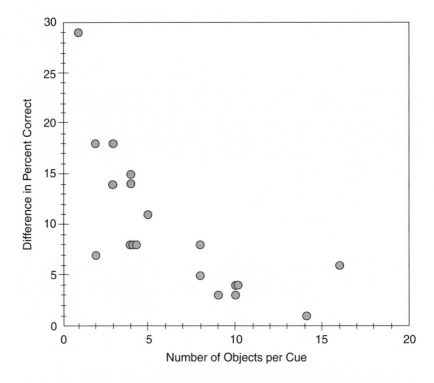

Figure 5-2: The accuracy of multiple regression in the fitting task (Tour 1) minus its accuracy in the generalization task (Tour 2) plotted against the number of objects per cue for 19 of the 20 environments. The fish fertility environment is again omitted. In data fitting, regression scored 0.4 percentage points higher than in cross-validation on this data set.

and the difference in accuracy between Take The Best and multiple regression.

Is It the Cue Intercorrelation?

If all cues were perfectly correlated ($r = 1.0$), then one-reason decision making would be as accurate as a linear combination of all cues. Therefore, several of our colleagues have suggested that the higher the intercorrelation between cues, the greater the advantage Take The Best has over regression. (Some others proposed the opposite relationship.) To test this hypothesis, we measured the correlations between each pair of cues in each environment, took the absolute values, and then averaged them. Will environments with high average absolute correlations give Take The Best more of an advantage over regression? We found no trend, so this variable does not seem to explain Take The Best's success. Nor did one of the following variables: the maximum cue intercorrelation, the minimum cue intercorrelation, and the variance of the correlations.

What structures of real-world environments does Take The Best exploit in order to perform so well? From the three characteristics reported in studies that compared Dawes's rule with regression, only one, the ratio between the number of objects and the number of cues, was related to the advantage Take The Best had over regression. Thus, the hypotheses derived from previous work comparing Dawes's rule with regression only partially shed light on the question of which environment structures can be exploited by fast and frugal heuristics. The following chapter offers more insight into this question, based on mathematical intuition and proof.

What We Have Learned

To control for the natural reaction to all new results, the "I knew it all along" reflex, we had asked several prominent researchers in judgment and decision making to predict how close Take The Best would come to multiple regression in accuracy. These researchers were expert on non-compensatory strategies and multiple regression. Their predictions were consistent: They bet on between 5 and 10 percentage points more accuracy for multiple regression. Our results surprised them as much as us.

In this chapter, we have considered those surprises:

1. The original results obtained by Gigerenzer and Goldstein (1996a) and summarized in chapter 4 generalized to 20 environments and to situations where the recognition heuristic played no role. This undermines the conjecture that there is something peculiar or wrong with the original domain of population sizes of German cities.

2. When one replaces the fitting task used by Gigerenzer and Goldstein with a generalization task, the fast and frugal Take The Best was even more accurate across 20 real-world environments than multiple regression. Take The Best achieved this accuracy despite using less than one third of all cues. Also, the myopic Minimalist came close to multiple regression in accuracy. Extending earlier findings, Dawes's rule slightly outperformed regression even when both were cross-validated.

3. Several variants of the competition did not change these results much. For instance, even with quantitative rather than binary predictors, Take The Best still matched and slightly outperformed the accuracy of multiple regression.

An important issue that we could not resolve in this chapter is the *how* question. How can one-reason decision making be as accurate, and sometimes even more accurate, than linear strategies—despite the latter's use of all cues and, in some cases, complex matrix computations? The result in figure 5-1 indicates that the relation between the number of cues and objects plays a role in the answer. But this does not explain the cause nor provide a proof. The next chapter will give several analytical answers and proofs. What structures of information in environments can Take The Best exploit, that is, what structures make a heuristic ecologically rational?

We began this chapter with a Darwinian message from Egon Brunswik: To understand the mind one needs to analyze the texture of its environment, past and present. Brunswik, however, also tentatively suggested that multiple regression could provide a model for how the mind infers its environment, and many neo-Brunswikians since have relied exclusively on these linear models. Our results indicate instead that mental strategies need not be like multiple regression to make accurate inferences about their environments. In the situations we studied in this chapter, simple heuristics can achieve the same goal. One-reason decision making can win a whole Tour.

6

Why Does One-Reason Decision Making Work?

A Case Study in Ecological Rationality

Laura Martignon
Ulrich Hoffrage

Entia non sunt multiplicanda praeter necessitatem
(No more entities should be presumed to exist than are
absolutely necessary)

William of Occam

Occam's Razor, originally formulated as a maxim against the proliferation of nominal entities, has become a methodological principle dictating a bias toward simplicity in theory construction. In today's scientific jargon Occam's Razor has become this: Prefer the simplest model that explains the data. The need for such a maxim suggests that scientific theories often exhibit the opposite tendency and, in striving for optimality, become exceedingly intricate. Is natural, unaided, human inference similarly elaborate and tortuous? A well-established trend in cognitive psychology has been to project scientific tools into mental theories: As Gigerenzer (1991a) has suggested, models of the mind's function have often reflected the computationally expensive statistical tools used in scientific induction. This book has a different viewpoint, revealing the simple heuristics the mind can use without necessarily sacrificing accuracy.

Can a simple heuristic for pair comparison be fast, frugal, *and* accurate? We were surprised by the performance of Take The Best in 20 varied environments as discussed in chapter 5, and wondered why it did not trade accuracy for simplicity. In that chapter we found, with extensive data analysis, that the relationship between the number of objects and the number of cues influences the performance of Take The Best. In this chapter, we add analytic methods to help explain Take The Best. As outlined in chapter 1, the reason for the success of a heuristic can be found in its ecological rationality, more precisely, in the fit between the structural properties of the heuristic and the structure of the environment it is applied to.

In the first section of this chapter, we identify structures that favor Take The Best and structures that favor its competitors. In the second section, we examine the robustness of Take The Best, in particular the robustness of its frugal principles for search and its stopping rule. We conclude by looking at Take The Best from three perspectives, viewing it first as a special case of a linear model, second as a lexicographic method, and third as a classification tree.

Structures of Environments

Before describing the structures of environment that favor Take The Best we must formalize what we mean by environment. An environment consists of a set of objects, where each object is characterized by a criterion value and a cue profile (see table 6-1 for an example of an environment consisting of eight objects listed in criterion order, and each characterized by a profile of three cues). We only deal with cases in which all cue values are known and all objects are recognized. In the words "structure of the environment," we are using a shorthand for the structure of information that is known about an environment. We analyze Take The Best in three information structures, for noncompensatory, scarce, and abundant information.

Noncompensatory Information

Take The Best is based on one-reason decision making: The decision which of two objects scores higher on the criterion is made solely on the

Table 6-1: An Environment Consisting of Eight Objects Listed in Criterion Order Where a Scores Highest

Object	Cue 1	Cue 2	Cue 3
a	1	1	1
b	1	1	0
c	1	0	1
d	1	0	0
e	0	1	1
f	0	1	0
g	0	0	1
h	0	0	0

Note. Each object is characterized by a profile of three cues. This is a perfect environment for Take The Best, because this heuristic achieves 100% performance across all pair comparisons when using the cues to infer which object scores higher.

basis of the most valid cue that discriminates between the two objects. The decision may be wrong, yet none of the remaining cues, nor any combination of them, will change it. In other words, Take The Best is a noncompensatory strategy. Such a strategy works best if the environment has a similar structure, where each cue is more important than any combination of less valid cues. The alphabetical order of words, for example, is clearly noncompensatory; the first letter that is different in two words is the only one that matters in ordering them alphabetically. This is what makes looking up a word in a dictionary so easy. Another example is number comparison. If two large numbers have the same number of digits, then one can determine which is larger by comparing first their leftmost digits. If both digits are equal, one proceeds to compare the next two digits, and so on, until two corresponding digits differ. This procedure is similar to Take The Best's search through cues. Noncompensatory number systems (e.g., the Indo-Arabic system) make calculations and comparisons easy. This is one reason why they were preferred to other systems such as Roman numerals.

Consider an example of noncompensatory cues in vision, illustrated in figure 6-1. Are the left fencer's legs outside or inside the ring? And which is further away from the viewer—the referee or the foil? Here, the criterion is distance, and we are confronted with the kind of task examined in chapters 4 and 5, namely, comparing objects by a criterion. There is a vast literature on how cues are processed for depth perception. A large amount of experimental evidence suggests that several cues are used (e.g., Bruno &

Figure 6-1: A visual illusion (Petter's illusion) that can be attributed to noncompensatoriness (from Metzger, 1975, with permission of the publisher).

Cutting, 1988; Massaro, 1988a), although there is little agreement on how they are combined. There exist phenomena, however, that suggest that cues for depth perception are sometimes noncompensatory. In figure 6-1 many people "see" the foil behind (or through) the referee, and the legs of the left fencer in front of the fence. Because this is a two-dimensional picture, some of the important cues for depth perception, such as stereo-motion and binocular disparity, are absent and cannot be used to discriminate between objects. There are several cues that can still be used—object overlap (closer objects partially obscure ones that are further away), object size (larger objects are closer than smaller objects), perspective, height in the plane (the referee's feet are closer to the horizon than the foil), and common sense, which suggests that the foil is not behind or through the referee.

The mechanism behind the illusion is the noncompensatory processing of cues. If object overlap could be used to judge the distance of foil and referee, it alone would allow a decision, but since both are black in the picture, this cue does not discriminate. The next cue, object size, does discriminate, and its inference (that the referee is closer than the foil) cannot be overruled by the combination of all the other cues.

If cue weights are noncompensatory, then linearly combining cues gives the same performance as processing cues in lexicographic fashion, one cue at a time (see Result 1, below). In this situation the performance, not the process, of a lexicographic strategy is identical to that of a linear model. The typical claim is that cues are combined linearly (Bruno & Cutting, 1988; Jameson & Hurvich, 1959; see also Julesz, 1971). Yet cues may appear to be combined linearly although they are processed lexicographically. This view is consistent with the arguments of Runeson (1977) and Runeson and Costall (1991), who have repeatedly stressed that models that assume linearity may not capture the subtleties of cue processing for depth perception. The noncompensatory order of cues seems to be part of the process. The idea that one cue may dominate all others was present, although not thoroughly worked out, in Brunswik's (1956) view of cognition, which was motivated by models of cue processing in perception.

As another real-world example of a noncompensatory process let us recall the mating strategies of female guppies mentioned in chapter 4. A female guppy places orangeness above other cues for mate choice (Dugatkin, 1996). If a possible mate is significantly more orange than another, the female guppy will choose the more orange mate. But if the difference in orangeness is not significant then a social cue is used: The female guppy will mate with the male that she has previously seen mating with another female.

These are illustrations of strategies that use cues in a noncompensatory way. We now define, in general terms, what a noncompensatory strategy is. Consider an ordered set of M binary cues, $C_1, \ldots C_M$. These cues are noncompensatory for a given strategy if every cue C_j outweighs any possible combination of cues after C_j, that is, C_{j+1} to C_M. In the special case of a weighted linear model with a set of weights $W = \{w_1, w_2, w_3, \ldots, w_M\}$ a strategy is noncompensatory if for every $1 \le j \le M$ we have $W_j > \sum_{k>j} W_k$. In other words, a linear model is noncompensatory if, for a given ordering of the weights, each weight is larger than the sum of all weights to come. A simple example is the set $\{1, 1/2, 1/4, 1/8, 1/16\}$.

A linear model with a noncompensatory set of weights ends up making exactly the same inferences as Take The Best. The converse is also true (Martignon & Hoffrage, 1999).

Result 1: Noncompensatory information. The performance of Take The Best is equivalent to that of a linear model with a noncompensatory set of weights (decaying in the same order as Take The Best's hierarchy). If an environment consists of cues that are noncompensatory when ordered by decreasing validity, then the corresponding weighted linear model cannot outperform the faster and more frugal Take The Best.

Loosely speaking, Take The Best embodies a noncompensatory structure, and if the environment has the same structure then there is a fit. The degree to which this fit exists contributes to the ecological rationality of Take The Best. Three of the 20 data sets discussed in chapter 5 have noncompensatory regression weights decreasing in the same order as do the validities of the cues; and, as predicted by Result 1, the performance of regression and Take The Best coincide. If the fit is not perfect, but approximate, then Take The Best will still be about as accurate as the corresponding linear model.

The equivalence of Take The Best and multiple regression can be seen in the artificial environment in table 6-1, which consists of eight objects $\{a, b, c, d, e, f, g, h\}$ and their values described by three binary cues. Assume that a scores highest on the criterion, b next, and so on. This is an ideal environment, not a real-world one: The cue profiles correspond to the numbers from 7 to 0 expressed in base two. The validity and discrimination rate (see chapter 4) of each cue is optimal given the preceding one. How does multiple regression perform? We have to imagine some criterion with values, say 8 for a, 7 for b, 6 for c, and so on until 1 for h. In this case the beta weights for the first, second, and third cues are .873, .436, and .218, respectively. (All intercue correlations are 0.) This is a noncompensatory set of cue weights, and consequently Result 1 predicts a perfect match between Take The Best and multiple regression. Indeed, both algorithms achieve the same performance, namely 100% correct inferences. How accurate is Dawes's rule, the simplest linear model, in this environment? Recall that Dawes's rule simply sets all weights equal to 1. For the specific task of score comparison the scores of Dawes's rule can be computed by adding the number of 1s in each cue profile, rather than

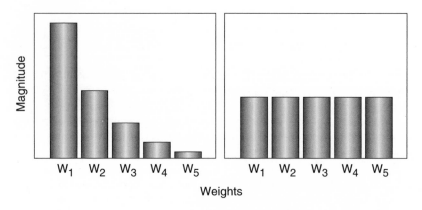

Figure 6-2: Examples of noncompensatory (left) and compensatory (right) weights.

adding the number of 1s and subtracting the number of 0s.[1] Dawes's rule makes one wrong inference for one pair, *de*, and it is forced to flip a coin in the case of six pairs (*bc, be, ce, df, dg,* and *fg*), resulting in a performance of 86%.

Take The Best "bets" that the environment is skewed as in figure 6-2 (left), whereas Dawes's rule treats information in the world as if it were levelled as in figure 6-2 (right). It is likely that there is more skewness than equality in the world (see chapter 10), so that betting on skewness may turn out to be a better strategy. Multiple regression, in contrast, does not make blind bets but computes its parameters to fit the structure. The price for this is more computation and less robustness (see below).

Scarce Information

Skewness is not the only environmental property that benefits Take The Best. In many real-world situations, we have to make decisions based on scarce information. We will now give a formal definition of what we mean by "scarce information" and then show how it affects the accuracy of Take The Best.

How much information is needed to differentiate between N objects? Think of the yes-no parlor game. Imagine you and another person are in a room where there are 64 toys. Suppose that you have to determine

---

1. The scores for Dawes's rule (chapters 4 and 5) are usually defined as the number of 1s in the cue profile minus the number of 0s. For the comparison task treated here, Dawes's rule is equivalent to comparing the scores obtained by counting the number of 1s in each profile. Twice the number of 1s minus the number of cues is equal to the number of 1s minus the number of 0s. Therefore, the orderings defined by both scores coincide.

which of these toys has been mentally selected by the other person. You are allowed to ask only questions requiring a yes or no answer. What is the smallest number of questions you have to ask to determine the selected object? The answer is $\log_2 64 = 6$. More generally, according to information theory (Shannon, 1948), a class of N objects contains $\log_2 N$ bits of information. The environment shown in table 6-1 has eight objects that are perfectly coded by three (i.e., $\log_2 8$) binary cues. Observe that these cues are very specially tuned to each other: The cue profiles represent the objects uniquely and unambiguously. In most environments with eight objects and three cues perfect coding is not achieved. If there were only two cues, perfect coding is impossible. This motivates the following:

Definition: An environment with M binary cues and N objects provides scarce information if $M < \log_2 N$.

In the environment of table 6-1, as mentioned above, Dawes's rule has a performance of 86% whereas Take The Best makes 100% correct inferences. Furthermore, if only the first two cues are considered, Take The Best would achieve 93% correct inferences and Dawes's rule would again achieve 86%. The environment consisting of the first two cues provides scarce information. Here, as observed, Take The Best outperforms Dawes's rule. Is this still true when the set is generalized to contain more objects? The following result has been shown to be true for "small" environments—those with up to 500 objects—by exhaustive counting (Martignon & Hoffrage, 1999):

Result 2: Scarce information. In the majority of small environments with scarce information, Take The Best is more accurate than Dawes's rule.

Here we are looking at the performance of both algorithms across environments with a fixed number of objects and a fixed number of cues providing scarce information. An intuitive explanation of this result is that when using a large number of cues, Dawes's rule can compensate for possible errors in the first ones and seldom has to guess. With scarce information, these advantages are lost: Dawes's rule cannot really exploit compensation and is forced to make many guesses.

The comparison with multiple linear regression in scarce environments is more difficult. Extensive simulations for up to 30 objects and five cues suggest that in scarce environments multiple linear regression is, on average, more accurate (in fitting) than the fast and frugal Take The Best. There are exceptions, as table 6-2 shows. Here, assuming again that the criterion values are 8, 7, . . . , 1, the performance of Take The Best is 91%, whereas that of multiple linear regression is 87.5%. We do not have a theorem characterizing all situations in which Take The Best wins. But we do know that when the regression weights are noncompensatory and

Table 6-2: An Environment Where Take
The Best Outperforms Multiple Regression

Object	Cue 1	Cue 2	Cue 3
a	1	1	1
b	1	0	0
c	1	1	1
d	1	1	0
e	0	1	1
f	0	1	0
g	0	0	1
h	0	0	0

Note. Performance is 91% for Take The Best and 87.5%
for multiple regression.

they decrease in the same order as cue validities, then Take The Best and
regression always make the same inferences.

Abundant Information

In general, adding information to a scarce environment will do little for
Take The Best, while it can compensate for mistakes Dawes's rule makes
when based on the first cues only.

An environment provides *abundant information* when all possible uncertain, yet valid, cues are present. In an environment with N objects and
binary cues, the number of possible cues is the number of different 1-0
sequences of length N. Note that the expression "all possible uncertain,
yet valid, cues" does not refer to all possible real-world cues but to the
different 1-0 sequences. Whereas the number of real-world cues is infinite
(because different real-world cues may have the same value for each object), the number of different 1-0 sequences is finite. As an example of
abundant information, consider five objects {*a, b, c, d, e*} where, as usual,
a scores highest on the criterion, *b* next highest, and so on. Table 6-3
shows the eight uncertain and valid binary cues (i.e., with validity larger
than .5 but less than 1) that exist for five objects.

Dawes's rule computes the score of each object by counting the number
of 1s, and achieves a performance of 100% correct inferences. Eight cues
are sufficient for guaranteeing perfect inferences on five objects. (In an
environment consisting only of the first seven cues, Dawes's rule would
have to make one guess, for pair *bc*, and give a performance of 95%.)
Franklin's rule (see chapter 4), which multiplies each cue value by its
validity, adds these numbers, and infers that the object with the larger
sum ranks higher on the criterion, also achieves a performance of 100%
in this environment. Are these results true in general?

The following result is true for environments with five or more objects
(an analytical proof is given in Martignon & Hoffrage, 1999):

Table 6-3: An Environment With Five Objects Ordered According to
the Criterion, and With Abundant Information

Object	Cue 1	Cue 2	Cue 3	Cue 4	Cue 5	Cue 6	Cue 7	Cue 8	Score
a	1	1	1	0	1	1	0	1	6
b	0	1	1	1	0	0	1	1	5
c	1	0	1	0	1	0	1	0	4
d	0	1	0	0	1	1	0	0	3
e	0	0	1	0	0	0	0	1	2
$v =$	5/6	5/6	3/4	3/4	4/6	4/6	4/6	4/6	

Note. Abundant information refers to all nonredundant binary cues that have a validity v
of more than .5 and less than 1. Both Dawes's rule and Franklin's rule are perfect on this
environment.

Result 3: Abundant information. When information in an environment is abundant, Dawes's rule makes a correct inference for each
possible pair of objects. The same is true of Franklin's rule.

In contrast, the more frugal Take The Best cannot achieve perfection in
such environments, because its errors cannot be compensated by later
cues. For instance, in the environment of table 6-3, Take The Best's performance is fully determined by the first three cues, and the values of the
other cues are not consulted. Based on the three most valid cues (regardless of whether Cue 1 or Cue 2 is checked first, or whether Cue 3 or Cue
4 is checked third), Take The Best's performance is 90%.

Table 6-3 reveals a counterintuitive fact about Take The Best. One
might believe that the performance of Take The Best can never be higher
than the validity of the most valid cue. But this is wrong. For instance, in
table 6-3, Take The Best's accuracy (9/10 = 90%) exceeds the validity of
the most valid cue (5/6 = 83%). In fact, four pairs of objects are left undiscriminated by the most valid cue and on these pairs the remaining cues
make only correct inferences (the concept of conditional validity, which
helps to understand this phenomenon, will be introduced below).

To summarize, we analyzed three information structures—noncompensatory, scarce, and abundant—and examined how Take The Best performs
in each context as compared with standard linear models. This demonstrated three aspects of Take The Best's ecological rationality, and there
are probably more. The fit between fast and frugal heuristics and the
structure of environments explains why there need not always be a trade-
off between simplicity and accuracy—a heuristic can have it both ways.

The Robustness of Take The Best

So far, we have investigated the fit between a heuristic and the structure
of a known environment. The next step is into unknown territory: How

will a fast and frugal heuristic perform when making inferences about new objects, based on information acquired on a training set? Does frugality provide a sound basis for generalization beyond the training data? According to decision theory, costless additional information is never harmful to the decision maker (e.g., Clemen, 1996). In practice, the problem is to distinguish real information from noise. This is not a problem when fitting known data, in which case the optimal strategy can, in general, be specified. In the comparison task analyzed in this chapter, the profile memorization method (see chapter 8) captures all information the data contains.[2]

However, when generalizing from known to unknown data there is no provably optimal model. A strategy that attempts to squeeze too much information out of a training set may fail dismally on a test set. The danger lies in overfitting the training set. The phenomenon of overfitting is easily explained. Consider a large data set from which we extract a smaller training set. We train models on the smaller set, and look at how well they generalize to make decisions about the entire data set. A model overfits the training set if an alternative model exists that, even though it does not do as well on the training set, nonetheless is more accurate when it generalizes to the entire data set. To understand why overfitting occurs, it helps to appreciate that the training set has both inherent structure and noise. It is the inherent structure that generalizes beyond the training set, and this is what a model should capture. If a model is too flexible (as is often the case with complex models that have a large number of free parameters) it will go beyond the inherent structure to fit the noise in the training set. This can cause significant degradation in performance when the model is applied to cases outside the training set (i.e., when it is generalized). The simple models—those obeying Occam's Razor—are less prone to overfitting, because they are parsimonious, using a minimum number of parameters and thus avoiding fitting noise. (For instance, the simple Dawes's rule is well-known for its robustness.) But there is a limit to simplicity. The opposite danger is to underfit. A model can fail in two

---

2. Following this method, one starts by memorizing all cue profiles and how they score on the criterion. Then, this information is used for inferring whether object *a* scores higher than object *b*. If a pair of profiles appears only once in the list of all possible pairs, one remembers which profile scored higher and makes that inference. If some cue profiles occur more than once and, consequently, several pairs of objects have the same pair of cue profiles, the probabilistic recipe is to count how often the first profile scores higher than the second one. The profile memorization method will pick the profile that has the greatest chance of scoring higher. When fitting the training set, this method is closely related to Persson's (1996) exemplar-based model. In environments where each cue profile appears exactly once, as in the one described in table 6-1, the profile memorization method always achieves 100% correct inferences. If there are repeated profiles—and therefore also repeated pairs of profiles—this method will score less than 100% correct inferences and so will any other algorithm.

ways: by having too many free parameters and overfitting, or by being too simple and underfitting.

The art is to strike a balance between these two extremes. Two opposite approaches can achieve this. One is to minimize overfitting by selecting a "near-optimal" strategy from the vast number of all possible—simple and complex—models. In the last decade a flurry of paradigms have been designed to control overfitting and the associated high variance in performance when generalizing (e.g., Geman et al., 1992). Among them is the Bayesian paradigm, which has become widely used for searching across classes of models—be they decision trees, regression models, or neural networks (Chipman et al., 1996; Friedman & Goldszmit, 1996; MacKay, 1995)—and which provides a unified approach to developing robust estimates of both structure and parameters (see chapter 8). These techniques are far from being boundedly rational.

The second approach, promoted in this book, is to use a fast and frugal heuristic that "bets" on the structure of the environment, without trying to compute the optimal model. For instance, Take The Best bets that the structure of information is skewed in a noncompensatory fashion and its success depends on how well this assumption is fulfilled by the environment.

As discussed in chapter 1, a heuristic can be characterized by three principles: search, stopping, and decision. Search principles direct how the information is searched, stopping principles define when to terminate a search, and decision principles specify how the information searched for is used to make a decision.

Both the search and stopping parameters determine whether the heuristic strikes a balance. As we shall see, the search process of Take The Best is neither too complex nor too simple, and its stopping rule has the adequate flexibility.

The Robustness of Search Principles

So far we have compared Take The Best with linear models, which have no heuristic principles of search and stopping (although they may have heuristic principles of decision; for example, Dawes's rule bases its decision on the simplest linear combination of all cues). Take The Best is a lexicographic strategy—therefore principles of search and stopping need to be specified. A heuristic principle of search determines which cue to look up first, second, third, and so on. A lexicographic strategy can use various methods to determine this cue hierarchy. Take The Best uses a frugal method, but there are many others, for instance, finding the "optimal" ordering. This section first relates this frugal method to other known principles for determining order, and then analyzes the robustness of frugal search.

Take The Best fixes its cue hierarchy by ranking cues according to their validities. Whereas a human may directly estimate the cue order, a computer needs to compute the validities first and then use them to sort the cues. The concept of cue validity therefore deserves a closer look. Following Gigerenzer and Goldstein (1996a) we define the ecological validity of a cue as the proportion of right inferences:

$$v = \frac{R}{R + W} \tag{1a}$$

where R denotes the number of right inferences and W denotes the number of wrong inferences. We call a cue *neutral* or uninformative if $v = .5$, and *valid* if $v > .5$. Note that Take The Best operates only with valid cues: If the validity of a cue is less than .5, the values of this cue are inverted by changing 1s into 0s and vice versa. Equation (1a) can be quickly computed if one displays the objects in decreasing order as we have done in all the tables in this chapter. One simply counts how many times a 1 precedes a 0 to obtain R and how many times a 0 precedes a 1 to obtain W. To calculate the number of discriminated pairs (i.e., the denominator), one can even do something simpler than computing W: One can also multiply the number of 1s by the number of 0s. Another, quite different but practical way of computing the ecological validity is the following:

$$v = \frac{R_0 - \dfrac{N_0(N_0 + 1)}{2}}{N_0 N_1} \tag{1b}$$

where R_0 denotes the sum of all ranks of 0 entries, N_0 is the number of 0 entries, and N_1 the number of 1 entries. The advantage of (1b) is that cue validity can be computed without generating all pairs. Note that the numerator corresponds to the well-known U value for the Mann-Whitney test, and the denominator corresponds to $R + W$ (for the equivalence between (1a) and (1b), see Martignon & Hoffrage, 1999).

The ecological validity v is a positive rescaling of the well-known Goodman-Kruskal rank correlation γ defined by:

$$\gamma = \frac{R - W}{R + W} \tag{2}$$

A simple calculation shows that $\gamma = 2v - 1$. Thus, both notions of validity, v and γ, define the same hierarchy when used as a criterion to order cues, and both can be used as alternatives.[3] Choosing the Goodman-Kruskal

3. Cue validities can also be used as weights in a linear model, as in Franklin's rule. Provided with the Goodman-Kruskal rank correlation in the perfect environment of table 6-1, Franklin's rule has noncompensatory weights, namely, 1, .5, and .25. In contrast, provided with v, Franklin's rule has compensatory weights, namely 1, .75, .625. This demonstrates that—within the framework of linear models—

rank correlation as a validity criterion can have advantages: A neutral or uninformative cue satisfies $\gamma = 0$, and a valid cue satisfies $0 < \gamma \leq 1$.

Another approach to defining the validity of a cue is to look at the performance of Take The Best when the cue in question is the only one that can be used. Each time the cue does not discriminate between two objects, we flip a coin. The performance of a Take-The-Best-type algorithm based only on this cue is what we call the *success* (*s*) of the cue:

$$s = \frac{R + 0.5(P - R - W)}{P} \tag{3}$$

where P is the total number of pairs. This criterion is the expected proportion of correct inferences and was chosen, for instance, as the validity definition for the heuristic Categorization by Elimination, described in chapter 10. The ecological validity v is also related to success: It is the probability of the success of a cue, conditional on discrimination.

Our list of relevant candidate definitions for validity would be incomplete without Kendall's τ, which is given by a slight modification of γ, namely:

$$\tau = \frac{R - W}{\sqrt{P(R + W)}} \tag{4}$$

where P again denotes the number of pairs, R the number of right inferences, and W the number of wrong inferences (for details on γ and τ see Gigerenzer, 1981).

A sophisticated heuristic for search is to operate with a *conditional validity* (*cv*). The conditional validity is computed for each cue on the set of pairs not discriminated by the cues already used. The first cue used by this type of search is the most valid, as for Take The Best. The second cue is the most valid for the set of pairs that the first cue did not discriminate, and so on; if the validity of a cue on the remaining pairs turns out to be below .5, the values of this cue are inverted by changing 1s into 0s and vice versa. The following is a straightforward result.

> *Result 4:* When training set and test coincide, the accuracy of a lexicographic strategy with conditional validity is larger than or equal to that of Take The Best.

---

it is not only the environment that determines whether compensation can occur, but also how validity is measured (for the constructive nature of measurement, see Gigerenzer, 1981). In table 6-3, the Goodman-Kruskal validities form a noncompensatory set. Multiple regression also has a noncompensatory set of weights, but in a different order. Thus, Result 1 does not apply.

A lexicographic strategy can employ a frugal heuristic for search (such as using ecological validity), a sophisticated heuristic for search (such as using conditional validity), or it can even try to optimize search. Table 6-4 shows a simple example of a case where the search by ecological validity (v) is not optimal. Let us compute the ecological validity of Cue 1. As we already mentioned, a simple method is to count how many times a 1 precedes a 0. This number, which is the number of correct inferences, is then divided by the product of the number of 1s and the number of 0s. Cue 1 has a higher validity than Cue 2 ($5/7 = 15/21$ and $10/15 = 14/21$, respectively). Actually, all other definitions of cue validity, except Kendall's τ, rank Cue 1 higher than Cue 2. Yet consulting Cue 1 before Cue 2 leads to only 13 correct inferences while consulting Cue 2 first leads to 14 correct inferences!

Thus, Take The Best does not necessarily choose the optimal ordering. How can this optimal ordering be found? Schmitt and Martignon (1999) prove that there is no simpler procedure than testing all possible permutations of cues and comparing the performance of a lexicographic strategy for each of these orderings. This procedure is anything but fast and frugal, because in an environment with M cues, $M!$ orderings have to be checked. The problem of finding the optimal order is NP-complete ($M!$ exceeds $2^{(M-1)}$; for an explanation of NP-completeness see chapter 8).

How do different search principles influence the performance of lexicographic strategies? We answer this question for the task of comparing German cities (see chapter 4). Figure 6-3 shows the accuracy distribution of all possible orderings. The optimal ordering achieves a performance of 75.8% (the right extremity in this distribution). The mean of this distribution (70.0%) corresponds to the expected performance of the Minimalist, which uses the simplest search principle by picking cues in random order (see chapter 4). All other search principles have a performance between

Table 6-4: A Puzzling Environment

Object	Cue 1	Cue 2
a	1	0
b	1	1
c	1	1
d	1	1
e	1	1
f	0	1
g	1	0
h	1	0

Note. Although Cue 1 has a higher validity than Cue 2, a lexicographic algorithm can achieve a higher performance if Cue 2 is looked up first.

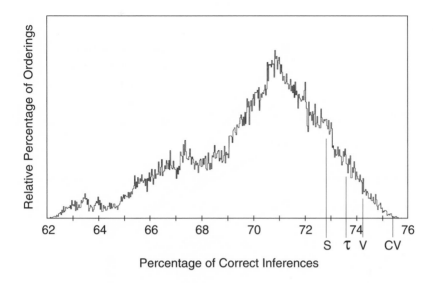

Figure 6-3: Distribution of performances for all possible cue orderings in the German city environment. The mean of the distribution (70%) corresponds to the expected performance of the Minimalist (random ordering). The performance of lexicographic strategies, which search for cues according to ecological validity (i.e., Take The Best), success validity, Kendall's τ, and conditional validity are denoted by *v, s, τ,* and *cv,* respectively.

these two values: Conditional validity (*cv*) achieves 75.6%; ecological validity (*v*), as used by Take The Best, achieves 74.2%; Kendall's τ achieves 73.5%; and success (*s*) achieves 72.7%. Only 1.8% of the orderings allow a higher performance than the ordering of Take The Best. Thus, the search principle of Take The Best achieves a satisficing performance, in that improving this performance involves paying too high a price in terms of computational complexity; to determine the optimal ordering for the German city environment takes a fast computer almost four days!

How robust is Take The Best's search principle compared with those of the other strategies? To answer this question, we need to compare the accuracy when fitting known data with the accuracy obtained when generalizing to unknown data. Usually generalization is performed within a homogeneous population—from a subset to either the whole population or another subset.[4] The cross-validation results of chapter 5 belong to the latter category. Here we check the robustness of search principles by the

4. In another scenario, there is no population containing training and test set, or if there is one, it is vague and heterogeneous, such as professors' salaries all over the world. Dawes (1979) showed examples of medical diagnosis data where Dawes's rule remained fairly robust even under change across time.

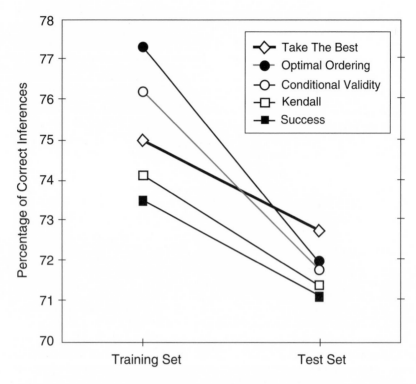

Figure 6-4: Robustness of lexicographic strategies with different orderings for cue search in the German city environment. The training set consisted of half of the cities randomly drawn from the environment, the test set the remaining half. Performance is averaged across 100 trials.

same procedure: We randomly take a subset of half of the German cities for which we determine the orderings depicted in figure 6-3, check the performance first in the subset (i.e., the training set) and then in the other half of the cities (i.e., the test set). This procedure is repeated 100 times for randomly chosen subsets. The results are shown in figure 6-4. As expected, for all orderings, the performance in the test set is lower than that in the training set. Surprisingly, Take The Best uses the most robust search principle. The complex search principles (optimal ordering and *cv*) dropped the most, proving that they fitted noise in the training set.

The Robustness of Stopping Rules

The stopping rule used by Take The Best allows it to search through all retrieved cues when necessary. Of course, there are other possibilities. One could, for instance, think of stopping right after the first or the second most valid cue, flipping a coin for undiscriminated objects. The other extreme is to have no stopping rule at all. This is the case for linear models, which consult and use all the available cues. Take The Best falls between these two extremes. An important feature of its stopping rule is its flexibility: For a particular pair of objects Take The Best may stop its search after the first cue (because this cue discriminates between the objects), and for another pair it may look up all information (because no discriminating cue has been found). To explore the robustness of this flexible stopping rule, we cross-validated various strategies in the 20 data sets introduced in chapter 5. Figure 6-5 shows the performance of these strategies in training and test sets averaged across all these data sets.

Again, performance drops for all strategies from training to test set. The strategy that fits the training set best is multiple regression, whereas the most robust is Take The Best, since it achieves the highest performance in the test set. Multiple regression clearly overfits. Dawes's rule is more robust than multiple regression. The two truncated versions of Take The Best, one of which restricts its search to the first cue (TTB-Truncated #1),

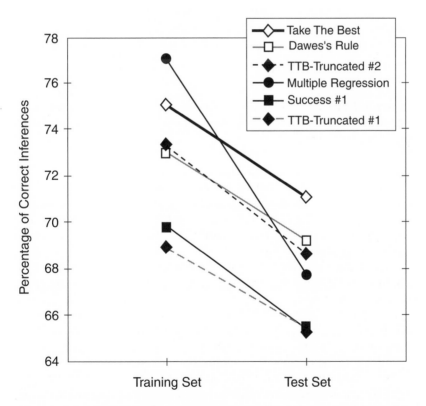

Figure 6-5: Robustness of various strategies with different stopping rules averaged across 20 environments (100 trials in each). Multiple regression overfits, while Take The Best is fairly robust.

the other to the first two cues (TTB-Truncated #2), underfit. When truncating the search after one cue, ecological validity is not the best criterion for selection, because it does not take discrimination rate into account. But even the most successful cue when used alone (success #1) underfits.

Take The Best's stopping rule is ecologically rational: When to stop is not constant and fixed but depends on the available information. In our 20 data sets the average number of cues used by Take The Best is 2.4 (see chapter 5). A rationale for the robustness of Take The Best is that these few most valid cues are likely to remain highly valid in generalization. This also explains why the truncated Dawes's rule, as discussed in chapter 5, is more robust than the normal (untruncated) Dawes's rule.

Three Perspectives on Take The Best

We claim that Take The Best is a mental process, which can be represented mathematically as an algorithm. This algorithm can be seen as embedded in more than one mathematical structure. Since different perspectives may enrich the understanding of the algorithm, let us describe at least three of them.

The Linear Model Perspective

Linear models are among the most widely used tools for inference. As mentioned in chapter 4, the weighing and adding of cues for decision making reflects the moral ideal of rational choice that has been prevalent since the Enlightenment. Linearizing the world has become a basic tool in the realm of statistical inference in general. Historically, a peak was reached in the use of linear models for statistical inference with the advent of linear regression, which solves an important optimization problem: It minimizes the sum of squares of deviations between predicted and observed criteria. The rapid diffusion of the linear regression method and its acceptance in practically all scientific fields is one of the great success stories in the history of statistics (Stigler, 1986).

From the point of view of accuracy, linear models can be outperformed by other procedures, for example, the Bayesian networks discussed in chapter 8. But if several pieces of evidence have to be taken into account, more complex models such as these networks can soon become intractable. In fact, linear models, in spite of their structural simplicity, still perform remarkably well; linearizing the world has not lost its position as a sound, transparent, and simple approach to decision making.

One limitation of linear computations is that they can only be performed mentally if they involve few terms. Franklin himself needed paper and pencil to balance positive and negative reasons. Dawes's rule, which counts up the number of confirmatory cues and subtracts the number of disconfirmatory cues, can be computed mentally if the number of cues is not too large. For real-world decisions, there is rarely time to add or sub-tract each item of information in turn, let alone to perform paper and pencil computations. If all of the useful information were simultaneously available and could be processed in parallel—by assessing it in a single moment—these time constraints would vanish. However, in the kind of inference tasks we are concerned with, cues have to be searched for, and the mind operates sequentially, step by step and cue by cue. Linear mod-els can be processed either in parallel or sequentially: The weighted cue values can be added one by one by a sequential mechanism or in a single shot. For linear models with noncompensatory weights, sequential pro-cessing that stops after the first cue that discriminates leads to exactly the same performance as parallel processing of all cues. It is these linear mod-els that are equivalent to Take The Best (Result 1).

Lexicographic Algorithms for Comparison

Natural environments are rich in order structures, rankings, and hierar-chies. Nevertheless, as the Bourbaki group so insistently pointed out (Bourbaki, 1963), order theory was neglected in the history of mathemat-ics. It was the merit of nineteenth-century mathematicians (mainly Dede-kind, 1887/1987) to perceive that order theory is at least as profound and far-reaching as algebra and topology. In the Bourbaki compendium of mathematics, its three realms are, in fact, the three disciplines—algebra, topology, and order—from which everything else is derived (Bourbaki, 1963). From the point of view of order theory, Take The Best has a perfor-mance of 100% if (and only if) the mapping that assigns a cue profile to an object is an order *homomorphism* of the set of all objects ordered by the criterion into the set of natural numbers expressed in binary form. This means that if object a is larger than object b according to the crite-rion, then the profile of a represents a natural number that is larger than the number represented by the profile of b.

Classification Trees

Another candidate method for the comparison task dealt with in this chapter is the classification tree. It is no exaggeration to say that classifica-tion trees have been used for millennia. As early as the third century, the Greek philosopher Porphyrius Malchus classified species by the method called "per genus et differentiam" (collecting items of the same genus and separating them according to specific differences), which corresponds to using a simple classification tree.

A classification tree for these problems is a tree-structured graph. The nodes are cues and the arcs between nodes indicate the values of the cue at the tail of the arc. Each path from root to leaf consists of a possible combination of cue values, and the leaf node indicates the decision to be made (e.g., $a > b$ or $b > a$). To classify an object, one begins at the root, examines the root cue, proceeds along the arcs corresponding to the cues' values, examines the cue at the head of each arc, and continues in this way to reach the decision at the leaf of the tree. Take The Best corresponds to a simple classification tree, as illustrated in figure 6-6. The root node is the cue with the highest validity. If the objects differ on the first cue, then a decision is made; otherwise the second cue is looked up, and so on.

The problem of constructing the adequate classification tree for a given data set can be extremely difficult. In the past 20 years, learning classification trees from data has become an important research topic in both statistics and machine learning. Much interest has been focused on the development and evaluation of efficient heuristics for constructing classification trees that perform well and that generalize well to new data sets. CARTs (classification and regression trees, introduced by Breiman et al., 1993) have been extremely successful as tree construction mechanisms that guarantee high accuracy. The Bayesian paradigm also provides efficient search methods for good classification trees (see chapter 10).

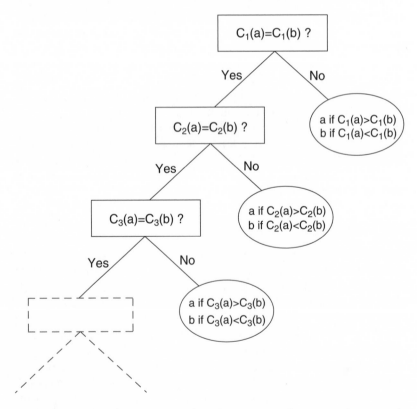

Figure 6-6: Take The Best as a classification tree for comparing two objects, a and b, on the basis of cues C_i.

The step toward fast and frugal strategies for tree construction has been undertaken only recently in machine learning. Similarly to Take The Best, the 1-R classification tree algorithm introduced by Holte (1993) is based on one-reason decision making. In the specific case of classification for comparison, 1-R chooses the cue with the highest validity and acts—like Take The Best—on the basis of this cue alone. That is, if the cue discriminates between the objects, it chooses the object with the higher cue value. However, unlike Take The Best, 1-R does not proceed to the next cue if the first does not discriminate, but chooses at random. Thus, 1-R is identical to Take The Best truncated after the first cue. With binary cues, 1-R has a disadvantage compared to standard Take The Best (both when fitting known data and when generalizing to new data, see figure 6-5), because it necessarily involves an excessive number of random decisions.

The algorithm 1-R was actually conceived for classification based on real-valued cues and various categories. Holte tested 1-R on a large number of data sets (in particular, several data sets from the UC Irvine repository—see Merz & Murphy, 1996); he obtained an excellent performance (Holte, 1993), only slightly less accurate than C-4, the tree construction algorithm introduced by Quinlan (1986). (For more details, see chapter 11.) The success of the best cue can be surpassed if the rest of the cues perform better than chance on the pairs left undiscriminated by the best one, which is generally the case.

Concluding Remarks

Whereas an all-purpose integration algorithm clumps information together to make inferences, a smart heuristic subtly exploits those properties of the available information that are essential for the specific task. Evolution has frequently provided us with the ability to capture the relevant features of environmental information and adjust our tools according to them.

Lexicographic models based on binary cues yield the same performance as linear models with noncompensatory weights. How, then, can one distinguish which model a person used to arrive at a choice? Our conjecture is that a lexicographic model is more natural than a linear one. Linearity is an often artificial simplification device that permits us to model the world in ways understandable to our minds. Order is not only in our minds—it is "out there"; the world is crowded with order structures. Lexicographic models provide a powerful way to generate inferences, by taking into account structures more explicitly present in the environment. They exploit skewness. Sometimes they exaggerate: They skew the world more than the world is skewed. But often enough the skewness of the environment is noncompensatory. In this case, Take The Best and more sophisticated linear models show equal performance when known data are fitted for inferences on the same data.

However, there are also some (extreme) environments that sharpen differences: Scarce environments favor Take The Best, while abundant information favors Dawes's rule. These theoretical results fit with empirical results obtained by Payne, Bettman, and Johnson (1988, 1993), who found that people choose their strategies according to the conditions the environment imposes on them. For instance, the algorithms people choose depend on how much time they have for making a choice or an inference, and what the decision might cost. If time is short they will make inferences by means of lexicographic models (see chapter 7). The same holds if they have a very good cue. In contrast, people will integrate information if the penalties for errors are high, or if they have more time at their disposal. It could be a verse in Salomon's Kohelet: There is a time to use Take The Best and a time to use Dawes's rule. Through the last millennia, evolution may have given us a good intuition for these fundamental differences between strategies and thus taught us when to use which strategy. The next chapter will be devoted to the problem of identifying the policy used by subjects in different tasks and in different environments.

7

When Do People Use Simple Heuristics, and How Can We Tell?

Jörg Rieskamp
Ulrich Hoffrage

> Possibly our feeling that we can take account of a host of different factors comes about because, although we remember that at some time or other we have attended to each of the different factors, we fail to notice that it is seldom more than one or two that we consider at any one time.
>
> *Roger N. Shepard*

Mr. K., who just came into a substantial sum of money, is considering how to invest it for maximum profit. Two friends of his who invest in stocks and shares keep themselves informed of all the relevant facts. One of them, Ms. Speed, is a broker; she often has to decide within seconds which shares to buy. For the other friend, Mr. Slow, buying shares is more of a hobby, but nevertheless he takes his investments very seriously and often takes the whole weekend to make up his mind about new purchases. In this chapter we will put ourselves in the position of Mr. K., who is trying to figure out how his friends make decisions; like Mr. K. we want to find out what kind of decision strategies people use when they have to make choices. Do people use simple heuristics? How can we know? These are the two questions we address.

First, we ask whether people use simple heuristics. Previous chapters of this book have demonstrated that fast and frugal heuristics can be highly accurate. The fact that these simple heuristics not only are accurate but also require little cognitive effort makes it plausible that people actually use them. We assume that people have a repertoire of different strategies—an adaptive toolbox—and that they use different strategies from this toolbox under different conditions. Which conditions may have an impact on strategy selection? One possibility is time pressure. Ms. Speed, who makes decisions under time pressure, will probably apply a different strategy than Mr. Slow. The fast and frugal heuristics proposed in this book are highly adapted to situations in which time and knowledge are limited. They are fast, easy to use, and require little information—nevertheless, they perform quite well. Chapter 4 dealt with limited knowledge. In the present chapter we will deal with limited time, asking: Does time pressure foster the use of simple heuristics?

Second, we consider the important question of how one can identify what strategy a person is using. Two main research approaches have been developed to investigate and identify people's strategies. One, the process-oriented approach, focuses on the predecisional process by looking, for instance, at the order of information acquisition; the other, the outcome-oriented approach, focuses on the outcomes of the decision process and builds models that predict these outcomes.

This chapter is structured as follows. We start with a description of various decision strategies. We then outline an experiment in which participants had to choose among alternatives under low and high time pressure. Next, the process- and outcome-oriented approaches are described, and our experiment is used as an illustration for the methodological problems in identifying strategies. Finally, we review some studies that have investigated conditions that should have an impact on decision strategies, including time pressure.

Simple Heuristics for Making Decisions

Heuristics provide a description of the successive stages of a decision process. (But keep in mind that individuals' actual decision processes may differ from a heuristic if they carry out supplementary operations not described by the heuristic.) In box 7-1, we present a short summary of various decision strategies that have been proposed in the literature. They all choose one out of several alternatives, where each alternative is characterized by cue (or attribute) values, and where the importance of a cue is specified by its weight (or validity). The list in box 7-1 is far from complete, partly because we are studying inferences rather than preferences (which often involve making a choice between gambles). Strategies that are more suitable for preferences are not included. Moreover, our purpose in this chapter is not to give a complete overview of candidate strategies. We believe that our main conclusions do not depend on the selection of strategies listed in box 7-1 but rather hold for a wide range of strategies.

One general problem is how a strategy deals with incompatible value ranges for different cues (or attributes). For instance, if the values of one cue range from 0 to 100 and those of another from 30,000 to 100,000, what should a strategy do? In chapter 5, continuous cue values were split at their medians, resulting in binary values. For the experiment reported below, the continuous cue values were mapped onto a categorical scale, always with the values 1, 2, 3, 4, and 5. Original values between the lowest value and the 20th percentile were transformed into the value 1, between

Box 7-1: Decision Strategies

Franklin's rule calculates for each alternative the sum of the cue values multiplied by the corresponding cue weights (validities) and selects the alternative with the highest score.

Dawes's rule calculates for each alternative the sum of the cue values (multiplied by a unit weight of 1) and selects the alternative with the highest score.

Good Features (Alba & Marmorstein, 1987) selects the alternative with the highest number of good features. A good feature is a cue value that exceeds a specified cutoff.

Weighted Pros (Huber, 1979) selects the alternative with the highest sum of weighted "pros." A cue that has a higher value for one alternative than for the others is considered a pro for this alternative. The weight of each pro is defined by the validity of the particular cue.

LEX or lexicographic (Fishburn, 1974) selects the alternative with the highest cue value on the cue with the highest validity. If more than one alternative has the same highest cue value, then for these alternatives the cue with the second highest validity is considered, and so on. Lex is a generalization of Take The Best (see text).

LEX-Semi or lexicographic semiorder (Luce, 1956) works like LEX, with the additional assumption of a negligible difference. Pairs of alternatives with a negligible difference between the cue values are not discriminated.

EBA or Elimination by Aspects (Tversky, 1972) eliminates all alternatives that do not exceed a specified value on the first cue examined. If more than one alternative remains, another cue is selected. This procedure is repeated until only one alternative is left. Each cue is selected with a probability proportional to its weight. In contrast to this probabilistic selection, in the present chapter the order in which EBA examines cues is determined by their validity, so that in every case the cue with the highest validity is used first.

LEX-ADD or lexicographic additive combination is a combination of two strategies. It first uses LEX-Semi to choose two alternatives as favorites, then evaluates them by Dawes's rule and selects the one with the highest sum.

the 21st and 40th percentile into the value 2, and so on. All the strategies listed in box 7-1 can take these categorical cue values as input. For simplicity, so far we have not examined how the strategies would operate with limited knowledge, that is, unknown cue values.

Chapter 1 distinguished among a heuristic's principles of search, stopping, and decision. Principles of search direct how information is searched, principles of stopping define when search is terminated, and principles of decision specify how the information searched for is used to make a decision. These principles can be used to characterize any specific strategy. For each of these principles, we introduce one distinction. First, a strategy can search for information in either an *alternative-wise* or a *cue-wise* manner. Alternative-wise search seeks all cue values for one alternative before the next alternative is considered, whereas cue-wise search seeks all the cue values for one cue before another cue is checked. For instance, Mr. K. could use the relevant cues one after another to compare shares (cue-wise search) or evaluate each share on all the cues one after another (alternative-wise search). Second, a strategy may or may not have a stopping rule for deciding when to stop information search and to make a choice. While in many experiments the number of cues is limited, outside those experimental settings, stopping rules become essential. Third, a strategy may or may not allow for compensation. A strategy is compensatory if there is at least one cue that can be outweighed by other cues; a strategy is noncompensatory if a cue cannot be outweighed by any combination of less important cues (see chapter 6). A compensatory strategy integrates (at least some of) the available information and makes trade-offs between the relevant cues to form an overall evaluation of each alternative.

The principles of search, stopping, and decision are connected to each other. For instance, when a heuristic searches for only one (discriminating) cue, this constrains the possible decision rules to those that do not integrate information. Thus, if an individual does little search, then the process-oriented approach has strong implications for the possible character of the heuristic principle of decision. On the other hand, if search extends to many cues, this does not constrain the decision rule. The cues may be weighted and integrated, or only the best of them may determine the decision. The latter case illustrates the limits of the process-oriented approach, which focuses on search. If an individual acquires a large amount of information, this does not necessarily imply that the person also would base the decision on all of this information. Nevertheless, the underlying assumption of the process-oriented approach is that information search is related to the decision strategy, and hence, characteristics of the search reveal important aspects of the decision strategy actually used by a person.

We now use the three principles to classify the decision strategies in box 7-1. Franklin's rule, Dawes's rule, Good Features, Weighted Pros, and LEX-ADD are compensatory strategies, none has a stopping rule, and for all of them (except Weighted Pros and LEX-ADD), alternative-wise search is most appropriate. LEX, LEX-Semi, and EBA are noncompensatory strategies, have a stopping rule, and use cue-wise information search.

Compensatory strategies do not always entail compensation; whether it occurs depends on the number of cues, on the variability of cue values and validities, and on exactly how this information is processed. Franklin's rule processes all available information, whereas Dawes's rule replaces the validities with (positive or negative) unit weights. (In this chapter we consider only positive unit weights, because in our experiment higher cue values always indicate higher criterion values.) Good Features is similar to Dawes's rule but does not require addition of the cue values. One advantage of these three strategies is that an additional alternative in a decision task does not require a totally new evaluation of all alternatives. This is not true for all compensatory strategies: In contrast to the others, the score that Weighted Pros computes for an alternative depends on the cue values of the other alternatives. This is because a "pro" is defined by a comparison between the cue values for all alternatives. This feature also explains another peculiarity of Weighted Pros: It is the only compensatory strategy that searches for information cue-wise. LEX-ADD combines compensatory and noncompensatory elements, as well as alternative- and cue-wise search. Thus, Weighted Pros and LEX-ADD form a bridge between the compensatory strategies with alternative-wise search and the noncompensatory heuristics with cue-wise search.

LEX, LEX-Semi, and EBA are noncompensatory, which means that a cue supporting one alternative cannot be outweighed by any combination of less important cues, even if they all support a different alternative. This is because these three heuristics do not necessarily use all the information available. LEX is similar to the Take The Best heuristic (except that there is no recognition heuristic as the initial step, see chapter 4). In fact, it is one possible generalization of it from two-alternative to multialternative choice tasks. If two or more alternatives are tied, that is, they have the same value on the cue with the highest validity, and no other alternative has an even higher one, then there are two possible ways of continuing the procedure. The first way of generalizing Take The Best, which we have chosen in this chapter, is to consider the cue with the second highest validity only for those alternatives with the highest cue value. By emphasizing the idea of a lexicographic ordering of alternatives, it leads to selective information search, because alternatives are often eliminated by the heuristic in earlier steps of the decision process. The second method of generalizing Take The Best would lead to the procedure of reconsidering the cue with the second (and—possibly—third, fourth, and so on) highest validity for *all* alternatives. This second way emphasizes the concept of one-reason decision making, whereby at each step of the decision process all the alternatives are compared with respect to one particular cue, and this cue alone can determine which alternative is chosen.[1] Because of its

---

1. To illustrate, one can use each of these ways to decide which of three companies, *a, b,* and *c* has the highest profit. Suppose that two different cues (e.g., assets and number of employees) are positively correlated with the company profit. Companies *a* and *b* have large assets, while company *c* has low assets. However, company *a* has few employees, company *b* a medium number of employees, and company *c* many employees. If the most important cue is assets, then one cannot discriminate between companies *a* and *b*, so one would next use the number of employees as a cue. Taking the lexicographic route, one would then choose company *b*. The other way of generalizing Take The Best would lead one to select company *c*.

highly selective and cue-wise information search, LEX can be considered very simple to use. By comparison, LEX-Semi is less frugal, because more cue values (and also more cues) must usually be checked (see also Payne et al., 1988). EBA's information search is similar to that of LEX and LEX-Semi, but there is an important difference: With EBA, elimination of alternatives depends on a cutoff, whereas with LEX and LEX-Semi no cutoff needs to be specified and elimination is solely determined by the cue values of the alternatives.

All that is needed to make a choice is to identify the alternative that scores highest with respect to the criterion; it is not necessary to know either the exact criterion values or the rank order of the inferior alternatives. In this respect, cue-wise search is advantageous because it enables individuals to identify inferior alternatives at an early stage of search and then concentrate on the superior alternatives. By contrast, in an alternative-wise search it is necessary to evaluate each alternative in turn; only when all the alternatives have been considered does it become clear which one is superior. Hence, if Mr. K. wants to choose between different shares, it might be simpler for him to use one cue after another to compare the shares and concentrate on the most promising ones.

How do strategies compare in terms of the amount of processing required to execute them? Because compensatory strategies usually have no stopping rule, they look up all cues and are therefore less frugal than noncompensatory strategies. For instance, Franklin's rule, which uses all cue values and weights, is neither frugal nor computationally simple (see also Payne et al., 1988, 1993). Compensatory strategies evaluate each alternative on its own by computing scores, which then have to be stored in memory so that they can be compared. The limited capacity of human working memory (Miller, 1956) poses a problem for strategies requiring short-term information storage that makes high demands on memory. For a choice task in which the information is supplied simultaneously, a cue-wise information search can involve less memory and fewer computations than an alternative-wise search. A cue-wise search makes it possible to use each cue step-by-step in order to compare the alternatives. This step-by-step procedure can be used to establish alternatives as favorites. The individual simply has to keep in memory the alternatives regarded as favorites, but does not need to remember any cue values. The favorites can be examined in the light of newly acquired information. In contrast, an alternative-wise search has the advantage of forming a more precise view of a specific alternative, but it does make it more difficult to see differences between specific aspects of the alternatives.

Could a difference in the "effort" required to use the strategies help us to predict which of them will provide a better model of what people actually do? Payne, Bettman, and Johnson (1988, 1993) believe so, and have proposed an "effort-accuracy" framework based on the assumption that people have a repertoire of different decision strategies that can be evaluated in terms of their costs and benefits. The costs are related to the cognitive effort needed to process the strategy; the benefits are related to accuracy. Payne et al. (1993) state that "the decision maker assesses the various benefits and costs of the different strategies that are available and then chooses the strategy that is best for the problem" (p. 91). According to this view, the decision maker anticipates the effort and the accuracy of a strategy and uses these as criteria to select the "best" strategy. Payne et al. concede that such selections among strategies are not necessarily conscious and that the trade-off between effort and accuracy of strategies may have been learned by experience. In some situations particular decision strategies may not be examined with regard to effort and accuracy at all because they exceed the critical threshold of effort that an individual can expend. In their framework, the assessment of effort may serve two different functions: either as an additional criterion besides accuracy for evaluating decision strategies, or as a constraint to eliminate strategies from consideration.

Consistent with Payne et al. (1993), we assume that the constraints under which people have to make their decisions, such as limited time and limited knowledge, are important determinants of judgment and decision making. The view of Payne et al. leaves open the possibility that these constraints are supplementary criteria that have to be evaluated during a particular decision process. In contrast to this view, we consider limited time and limited knowledge as constraints under which people have already developed or learned their smart heuristics. This implies that an individual's repertoire of strategies includes some that take the constraints into account. We do not assume that a trade-off between effort and accuracy or an evaluation of strategies is computed during the decision process. Based on an individual's prior experience of decision making, a particular situation could prompt her or him to use a particular decision strategy.

Payne et al.'s framework and our view lead to similar assumptions: Under particular conditions, especially under time pressure, individuals use simple strategies. We assume that people are equipped with simple strategies for situations of severe time pressure, and that these strategies require little effort. Thus, simple heuristics that need less information, do not require integration of information, and use cue-wise search should be good at modeling people's decision strategies under time pressure.

One plausible assumption is that individuals will acquire less information under high time pressure than under low time pressure. If they shift their decision strategy toward a noncompensatory strategy, where the order of the information search is determined by the importance of the cues, they will focus their attention on the more important cues. This leads to the following hypotheses: (1) Under high time pressure, the proportion of participants whose decision strategies can best be described with a simple, noncompensatory heuristic will be larger than under low time pressure; and (2) participants will show more selective information search and acquire relatively more information about the important cues under high time pressure than under low time pressure.

To test these hypotheses, we conducted an experiment in which we investigated people's decision strategies under low and high time pressure (see box 7-2). In the next two sections, this experiment will be used as an illustration of the two main approaches for investigating people's decision strategies.

Box 7-2: Experimental Task

From four publicly held companies, participants had to select the one with the highest yearly profit (reference year was 1994). Each set of companies was selected from a sample of 70 real companies, forming the environment. Six company variables were used as cues. The importance of each cue is given by its cue validity. The cues (and their validities) were: the amount of *investments* (.78), the amount of the company's *share capital* (.68), the number of *employees* (.64), the *recognition rate* (.50), the *share price* on the stock market at the end of 1994 (.48), and the *dividend* for the share (.37). Note that a validity of .25 reflects chance performance. To determine the validities, every possible set of four out of the sample of 70 companies was examined; the proportion of sets in which the company with the highest cue value was also the company with the highest profit determined the validity. (The recognition rate is the rate at which the company was recognized by participants in a survey.) The information was presented on a computerized information board.

The experiment began with a training phase of seven choices, in which the participants received feedback about the correct choice. (The main purpose was to get the participants used to the task, rather than to get them to learn the cue validities. The concept of the cue validities was explained to the participants before the experiment and the validities were presented on a card next to the monitor.) After the training phase, participants had to make 15 choices under low time pressure (50 seconds for each choice), and then 15 choices under high time pressure (20 seconds). A clock in the top left corner of the screen showed the passing time. To open an information box the participants had to click on that box, and had to click again to close it before they could open another box. When the time had expired, the participants could not acquire additional information and had to make the choice. For each correct choice the participants earned one German mark (approximately 60 U.S. cents).

Looking at the Decision Process

One way in which Mr. K. could find out more about his friends' decision strategies is to observe their activities before they finally make their decisions. What kind of information do they seek and in what order do they collect it? More generally, what happens before the decision is made? What are the processes that lead to the final decision? Many researchers employ such a process-oriented approach and important contributions have been made, for instance, by Payne et al. (1988, 1993), Beach and Mitchell (1978), and Svenson (1979). Of special interest is the order in which information is acquired by participants, how the information is cognitively represented, and how this representation is transformed to reach a decision. The investigatory methods used include asking participants to describe the process by which they arrived at their decisions, as well as monitoring the information search.

The first method involves collecting verbal descriptions of the decision process—either during decision making with the "think-aloud" technique (e.g., Timmermans, 1993), or retrospectively after the decision has been made. These descriptions can provide information about the cognitive operations and decision strategies. The retrospective technique has often been criticized with the argument that people do not have access to their cognitive operations and cannot accurately describe their decision processes (Nisbett & Wilson, 1977). Some authors support protocol analysis instead (Ericsson & Simon, 1993; Montgomery & Svenson, 1989; Payne et al., 1978). A modification of the think-aloud technique is the "write-aloud" technique, which was used by Gigerenzer and Hoffrage (1995) in a study on Bayesian reasoning. In this study participants were instructed to make notes while working on reasoning problems; afterward the researchers used these notes to interview the participants about their reasoning.

The second method monitors the decision maker's information search. The information is presented on a (computerized) information board in the form of an alternative-by-attribute (cue) matrix. The information is usually not visible and participants have to ask or perform some action to acquire the attribute values. A similar method is the eye-movement recording technique, which infers the information search from participants' eye movements (Russo & Dosher, 1983). The results obtained by applying such techniques are interpreted on the basis of the assumption that the order of information search depends on the individual's decision strategy. For a comparison between verbal protocol techniques and methods that monitor information search, see Biggs, Rosman, and Sergenian (1993).

One widely used method of monitoring information search is a computer program called Mouselab (Johnson et al., 1991). In our experiment this program was used to present the four companies and the six cues in the form of an information board (figure 7-1). The cue values were hidden

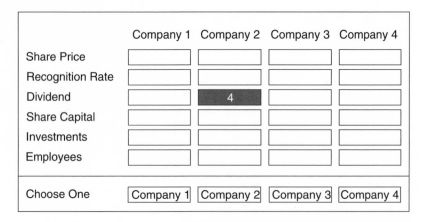

Figure 7-1: Computerized information board (generated by Mouselab) showing four companies and their six (hidden) cues, which can be revealed one at a time. Here, Company 2's dividend value is looked up by the participant.

in boxes, but could be revealed by clicking on the boxes. Only one box could be opened at a time. The final company choice was made by selecting a box at the bottom of the screen.

How can monitoring information search be used to identify strategies? The Mouselab program gives two types of information: the sequence in which a participant opened the boxes and the period of time a participant kept each box open. These types of information allow one to calculate several process variables that describe the search process. Most of the variables discussed next were also used by Payne, Bettman, and Johnson (1988).

One obvious characteristic of search is the amount of information looked up. For example, in our experiment the participants performed 33 box openings on average under the condition of low time pressure. Since the information board only consists of 24 different boxes, this means that some participants opened some of the boxes more than once. For none of the decision strategies listed in box 7-1 is it necessary to examine information more than once. The reason people do so is probably that they simply forget the cue values due to limits in their working memory (Miller, 1956). Another reason might be that they seek information twice in order to be more confident with their choice; they might start with a particular heuristic to establish a first favorite choice and acquire information repeatedly to support this favorite as their final choice (for a similar view, see Svenson, 1992). Nevertheless, the number of box openings tells us that the search process is not accurately described by any of the strategies under discussion. Under the condition of high time pressure the average number of box openings was 19. This lower figure is not surprising, but it does indicate that, at least for some participants, the use of a strategy that requires all available information was no longer possible. From a broader perspective, the average number of box openings prompts the question of how an individual's information search is related to the decision strategy applied. Even if someone acquires a large amount of information, this does not necessarily mean that all of this information is used to make the decision. Rather, the decision may only rest on those pieces of acquired information that are required by a particular strategy.

The search process can also be characterized by the average period of time each box was kept open. We might expect that high time pressure accelerates the rate of information acquisition. A reduced average time for each box allows more information to be acquired within the same total time. The information boxes were on average kept open for 430 ms under low time pressure and for 325 ms under high time pressure. A more specific interpretation can be made if we calculate the lengths of time the boxes remained open for each particular cue or alternative. What proportion of the total time boxes were kept open did the participants spend on the most important cue? Under low time pressure this proportion was 21% across participants; under high time pressure it increased to 25%. (Since six cues were used in the experiment, one cue corresponds to 16.6% of all the available information.) The increase from 21% to 25% indicates greater attention to the cue with the highest validity. In contrast, the proportion of time spent for the cue with the lowest validity slightly decreased from 13.5% to 11%. More generally, under high time pressure the time spent on each cue was more closely associated with the validities of the cues than under low time pressure. This can be shown by the correlation between the validities of the cues and the time spent on each cue. Under low and high time pressure this correlation was .69 and .82, respectively, which demonstrates that the attention paid to each cue is largely determined by the validities of the cues and—to a lesser extent—by the amount of time pressure. One interpretation of these results is that people change their decision strategy under high time pressure in favor of non-compensatory strategies.

Did the standard deviation of the proportion of time spent on each cue vary with time pressure? Under low time pressure, the standard deviation was on average 80 ms; it increased under high time pressure to 100 ms. Thus, individuals did not spend equal time on each cue and under high time pressure their attention was more unequally dispersed among the different cues. A similar variable is the standard deviation of the proportion of time spent on each alternative. Under low and high time pressure this standard deviation was 130 and 120 ms, respectively. The unequal attention to the alternatives did not increase under high time pressure. This result is in contrast to the expectation that unequal attention to the alternatives would increase as a consequence of the more frequent use of noncompensatory strategies under high time pressure. One explanation for this result could be that participants under low time pressure used the remaining time to consolidate their favorite choice.

The next variable, "pattern," was proposed by Payne (1976) to characterize the type of information search used. After closing one particular box, a decision maker can open either another box for the same alternative (which is called a transition within alternative) or one for the same cue (a transition within cue). Pattern equals the number of transitions within alternatives minus the number of transitions within cues, divided by the total number of both transition types. (Moves to a box that is for both another alternative and another cue are not considered when calculating this variable.) The values for this variable range from −1 to +1; positive values indicate more alternative-wise information search, while negative values indicate a more cue-wise information search. In our experiment, the average value for "pattern" was −0.13 under low time pressure and −0.28 under high time pressure. These values reveal an information search that is more often cue-wise, especially under high time pressure. Cue-wise search is consistent with the use of any noncompensatory heuristic or the Weighted Pros heuristic.

Awkwardly, the values for the variable pattern are affected by asymmetric information matrices, which means that if the number of cues is larger than the number of alternatives (as is the case in our experiment), a positive value for the variable can be expected even if the information search is random. Therefore, a correction for the bias of asymmetric matrices would yield even more evidence of cue-wise search in the experiment.[2]

Although the differences between the values of the process variables under low and high time pressure are small, most of them express relevant effect sizes. The value differences under low and high time pressure for the number of opened boxes, the average time a box was open, the proportion of time spent on the most important cue and that spent on the least important one, and the standard deviation of the proportion of time

---

2. Also, even heuristics such as Weighted Pros or LEX, which are characterized by a cue-wise information search, could include transitions within alternatives. If someone applies Weighted Pros and acquires the information of one cue over all alternatives and then moves to another cue, this move from one cue to another could be a transition within the same alternative. This information search seems to be possible for someone who applies Weighted Pros, but for the information board used in the experiment this search could yield a value of only −0.57 (which is far above the possible minimum of −1) for the variable "pattern." If, for instance, another person uses LEX and cannot discriminate between two of four alternatives after examining the cue with the highest validity, this person will compare the two remaining alternatives on the cue with the second highest validity. This information search could lead to the value of only −0.6 for "pattern." Thus, even for heuristics characterized by cue-wise information search, the negative maximum of the variable pattern is often unattainable and values such as those reported for our experiment are even more consistent with cue-wise information search (see also Böckenholt & Hynan, 1994).

spent on each cue have large effect sizes, while the differences for "pattern" and the correlation between the time spent on each cue and the cue validities have medium effect sizes (calculated and classified following Cohen, 1988).

The process variables are useful for revealing different decision processes, but can they also be used to identify specific strategies? Some authors suggest that a combination of process variables permit such identification (Billings & Marcus, 1983; Westenberg & Koele, 1992). Westenberg and Koele assumed that the EBA heuristic could be identified by the combination of a negative value for the variable "pattern" (indicating cue-wise information search) and a different amount of information acquired for different alternatives (indicating that some received more attention than others). One drawback of this identification method is that EBA cannot be distinguished from other noncompensatory heuristics, such as LEX and LEX-Semi (which were not considered in Westenberg and Koele's study). Another drawback is that a decision strategy is classified as noncompensatory if the amount of information acquired differs even slightly for different alternatives. But this can often occur, especially in tasks in which more than two alternatives are available, and it seems reasonable to assume that even if people use a compensatory strategy, they will sometimes not acquire or ignore information for particular alternatives. Therefore, we do not feel that the process variables allow us to identify uniquely the decision strategy of an individual participant.

In sum, the process analysis of our experiment shows that the participants predominantly used a cue-wise information search; this could be concluded from the variable pattern. This type of information search is consistent with LEX, LEX-Semi, EBA, Weighted Pros, or LEX-ADD. However, it is difficult to differentiate among these heuristics. In evaluating the process-oriented approach, we conclude that while it is useful for showing different decision processes under different conditions, it is problematic when used as a method of identifying particular decision strategies. Furthermore, although it can be assumed that people who use a compensatory strategy acquire more information than people who use a noncompensatory strategy, it is difficult to determine a critical value that can discriminate between these strategies. Nevertheless, it is reasonable to assume that process data can be used to reduce the number of plausible strategies. Table 7-1 shows the relationship between compensatory and noncompensatory strategies with respect to the process variables. Weighted Pros, which is not included in table 7-1, could have been assigned to the compensatory group except that for the variable pattern a negative value would be expected. The compensatory heuristic LEX-ADD is not included in table 7-1 either, because the expected values of the process variables are a mixture of the expected values for the strategies LEX and Dawes's rule.

Although various authors have proposed investigating both the participants' choices and the predecision process (e.g., Einhorn & Hogarth, 1981;

Table 7-1: Process Variables That Distinguish Compensatory From
Noncompensatory Strategies

	Strategies	
	Compensatory	Non-compensatory
Process Variables	Franklin's Rule, Dawes's Rule, Good Features	LEX, LEX-Semi, EBA
Number of information box openings	>	
Average time a box was open	<	
Proportion of time spent on the most important cue	<	
Standard deviation of the proportion of time spent on the alternatives	<	
Standard deviation of the proportion of time spent on the cues	<	
Pattern	positive values	> negative values
Correlation between time spent on each cue and cue validities	<	

Note. Strategies are explained in box 7-1.

Einhorn et al., 1979), most process-oriented studies do not consider
choices (e.g., Payne et al., 1988). If process data suggest cue-wise information processing, but do not discriminate among different strategies, an
analysis of the actual choices might be valuable in filling in this gap.

Looking at the Outcome

Mr. K. could also try to model his friends' choices by working out the
relationship between the information about alternative shares (the input)
and their final decisions about which shares to buy (the output). Many
researchers have in fact adopted such a research strategy. The most prominent representative of this approach is the neo-Brunswikian "social judgment theory" proposed by Ken Hammond (1955; for overviews see also
Brehmer & Joyce, 1988; Cooksey, 1996; Doherty, 1996). As a framework
for describing people's judgment policies, social judgment theory mainly
uses linear models, particularly multiple regression. In a technique called
"judgment analysis" or "policy capturing," this statistical model is used
to describe how participants utilize available cues to arrive at their judgments. A person's "policy" is described as a vector of weights in a regression equation, making the judgment a linear function of the cues. Al-

though neo-Brunswikians have mostly restricted themselves to using multiple regression as a tool for describing judgments, this analysis is in principle open to testing other candidate models. Indeed, in Egon Brunswik's work one cannot find this restriction, and Kenneth Hammond (1996b) recently pointed out that focusing on regression was a regrettable error.

In the outcome analysis reported below, each of the strategies listed in box 7-1 was used to predict participants' choices.[3] In contrast to the standard policy-capturing technique, whereby the model is made to fit by deriving the multiple regression weights from the participants' data, we formulated the strategies a priori with weights specified by the cue validities (see box 7-2). This can result in lower fits to participants' choices than the standard technique, which would have resulted in different weights for different participants.

Before we proceed, we want to point out one limitation of this approach. Different strategies frequently lead to identical prediction so that an individual's decision cannot be assigned unambiguously to one strategy. To illustrate this problem, we determined the overlap between the predictions of the Take The Best heuristic (which is similar to LEX) and those of multiple regression for the city environment in chapter 4. Take The Best and multiple regression were used to predict which of two cities has the larger population. The environment consisted of 83 cities and nine cues with binary cue values. The overlap of predictions was determined for all possible paired comparisons of two cities. If Take The Best and multiple regression made the same prediction for a particular comparison, the match was counted as "1." If not, it was counted as "0," and if one or both of them had to guess, this was counted as ".5." The results indicate that for most of the cases the predictions made by Take The Best and by multiple regression coincided: Averaged across all possible comparisons, the match was 92%. After excluding all cases where either Take The Best or multiple regression had to guess, this value increased to 96%.

Such a large overlap has implications for policy capturing. Suppose that a participant consistently uses Take The Best to make inferences for 100 paired comparisons randomly drawn from this city environment and that another participant consistently uses multiple regression for the same set. Would a neo-Brunswikian who applies the policy-capturing technique detect any difference between these two participants? The answer is no. The multiple correlations and the weights in the regression equation that describe the policies of these two fictitious participants do not differ from

---

3. These predictions were then compared to the actual choices. Each strategy's prediction was based on the information in all 24 boxes. This may be considered problematic because—especially under time pressure—not all of this information may be looked up by participants. However, basing the predictions only on those pieces of information that have actually been looked up would be more problematic: It is not clear how to determine the prediction of a strategy when a participant does not look up the information that it requires.

each other (Hoffrage et al., 1997). Thus, one should be aware that linear models are hardly more than what Hoffman (1960) called a "paramorphical" representation, that is, a mathematical representation that may not necessarily be a valid description of the actual reasoning process (see also chapter 6, on noncompensatory sets of weights). This problem is not restricted to linear models, but also arises for other models used to describe human judgments or decisions. Moreover, linear models can still be very useful for predicting outcomes or examining individual differences.

In sum, outcome analysis faces the same problem as process analysis: separability, that is, the difficulty of discriminating between strategies. One solution to this problem is to select the alternatives presented to participants in a way that forces the strategies to make different predictions. However, selecting alternatives to minimize the overlap of the strategies' predictions often makes the item set unrepresentative and the results difficult to generalize. There seems to be a dilemma here: Either the item set is representative, with generalizable results but barely distinguishable strategies, or the item set is selective, with distinguishable strategies but possibly limited generalizability.

In the experiment, we used an environment of 70 randomly drawn publicly held companies. Each item consisted of a set of four companies, and the task was to choose the one with the highest profit. We constructed two different item sets. The first, "representative" set had 30 items, each consisting of four randomly selected companies. Here, the overlap of identical predictions of the strategies listed in box 7-1 was very high: For 23 of the 30 items all the strategies chose the same company. The percentage of identical predictions for each pair of strategies was about 92% (averaged across all possible pairs of strategies).

For this reason, the second, "selected" item set of 30 items was constructed to reduce the overlap between Dawes's rule and LEX, chosen as representatives of compensatory and noncompensatory strategies, respectively. Our procedure for assembling the selected item set was to generate items randomly one after another and keep mainly those where Dawes's rule and LEX differed in their chosen alternative.[4] In the selected item set, the same prediction was made by all the strategies for only 2 of the 30 items. In contrast to the representative item set, the average percentage of identical predictions for a pair of strategies was only 50%. The alternatives in the selected item set were slightly more similar to each other than those in the representative set: The average standard deviation of the cue

---

4. Also, we tried to avoid a large deviation between the cue validities in the selected set and the validities in the set of all possible items. To this end, items that led to distorted cue validities were excluded from the selected item set, and in addition, two further items with an identical prediction for Dawes's rule and LEX were included. Note that all items of the selected item set did occur in the environment, and the performance of the strategies was not considered at all in the selection procedure.

values between the alternatives was higher for the representative set than for the selected set (mean standard deviation of 1.3 versus 1.2), which means that the choices in the selected set should be perceived as more difficult. In the experiment, 50 participants worked on the selected set and 25 on the representative set.

What is the performance of the strategies for the two item sets, again defined as the proportion of times the highest-profit company is picked? As can be seen in table 7-2, in the representative set the strategies make on average 73% correct predictions. In the selected set, the performance of the strategies is not only on average poorer, but the variance between strategies is also larger. In both item sets, the performance of simple heuristics is on average comparable to the performance of Franklin's rule, which looks up all cue values and requires considerable computations. In particular, Weighted Pros and LEX-Semi make more correct choices in the selected set than Franklin's rule. In the representative set, LEX and Good Features make as many correct choices as Franklin's rule.

These results are interesting and deserve some attention in light of the results of research on preferences. The fact that heuristics can perform as well or better than Franklin's rule could only be obtained because we used an external criterion (the profit of the company) to determine whether or not a strategy's prediction was correct. In research on preferences, such a criterion does not exist. Here the normative proposition is often made that the expected value model (which is similar to Franklin's rule) is the best method for making a choice among different alternatives, and used as a norm against which all strategies are evaluated (e.g., Payne et al., 1988). As a consequence, the performance of other heuristics in the preference literature can only be as good as the performance of Franklin's rule, but never better, as they were here.

How frugal are the strategies for the two item sets? Here frugality is defined as the percentage of information boxes (out of all 24 boxes) that had to be opened by each strategy to come to a decision. Table 7-3 shows these percentages averaged across all items. For most of the compensatory strategies, all information is necessary to reach a decision. LEX is most frugal, using only a quarter of the information.

Finally, how well do the heuristics describe participants' choices? We first considered all correctly predicted choices across all participants and all items. As can be seen in figure 7-2, the proportion of correctly predicted choices is much higher in the representative than the selected item set. However, the differences between the proportions of correctly predicted choices for the different strategies are also much smaller in the representative set. This result can be explained by the high overlap of identical predictions between strategies in this set.

Figure 7-3 shows the results in terms of the participants' strategies. The strategy that predicted the largest number of choices for each individual participant was assigned to that participant. If two or more strategies predicted the same number of a participant's choices, the participant was

Table 7-2: Performance of the Strategies for the Representative and the Selected Item Set

	Franklin's Rule	Dawes's Rule	Good Features	Weighted Pros	LEX-ADD	LEX	LEX-Semi	EBA
Representative item set	77	75	77	73	70	77	73	73
Selected item set	57	37	43	60	53	53	63	47

Note. Performance is expressed as percentage of items in which the most profitable company was correctly predicted (strategies are explained in box 7-1).

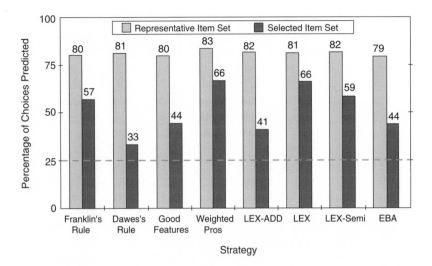

Figure 7-2: Accuracy of different decision strategies in predicting participants' choices on representative and selected item sets. The horizontal
line indicates the accuracy that can be expected by chance (25%).

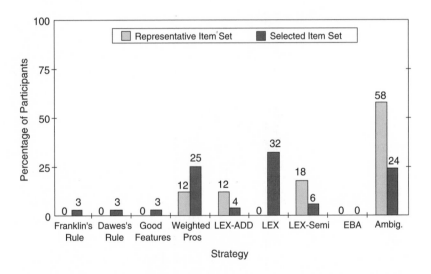

Figure 7-3: Percentage of participants who were assigned to each of the
strategies on the basis of both item sets, aggregated over both time pressure conditions.

Table 7-3: Frugality of the Strategies for the Representative and the Selected Item Sets

	Franklin's Rule	Dawes's Rule	Good Features	Weighted Pros	LEX-ADD	LEX	LEX-Semi	EBA
Representative item set	100	100	100	100	60	26	49	60
Selected item set	100	100	100	100	63	24	47	63

Note. Frugality is shown as percentage of cue values used when predicting the company with the highest profit (lower values indicate more frugal strategies; strategies are explained in box 7-1).

classified as "ambiguous." The heuristics that could be assigned to the participants most frequently were LEX-Semi, Weighted Pros, and LEX-ADD for the representative set, and LEX, Weighted Pros, and LEX-Semi for the selected set. The proportion of participants who could not be assigned unambiguously to one strategy was relatively high, especially for the representative set.

The results underline the importance of constructing item sets that allow one to distinguish among different strategies. For this reason, the analysis of the influence of time pressure was only conducted for the 50 participants who worked on the selected set. In addition, the category "ambiguous" was resolved by dividing each ambiguous participant among all the strategies that tied for first place in predicting his or her choices (e.g., if two strategies tied for first, each was increased by .5). Figure 7-4 shows the participant-strategy match under low and high time pressure. The strategies that could be assigned to the participants most often were LEX and Weighted Pros. LEX describes more participants' strategies under high time pressure, while Weighted Pros accounts for more under low time pressure. This indicates a shift from the compensatory heuristic (Weighted Pros) under low time pressure to a more simple and noncompensatory heuristic (LEX) under high time pressure, consistent with our first hypothesis that the proportion of participants whose decisions can

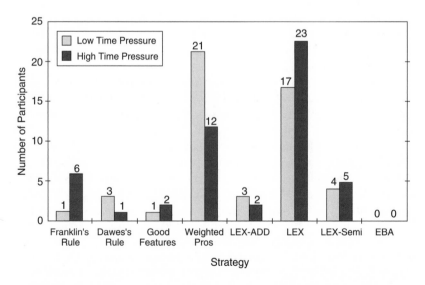

Figure 7-4: Number of participants who were assigned to the strategies, separated for low time pressure (50 seconds) and high time pressure (20 seconds). (This data is restricted to the 50 participants who worked on the selected item set.)

be described best with a noncompensatory heuristic is greater under high time pressure than under low time pressure.

Out of all decision strategies, LEX and Weighted Pros were identified as the best at describing participants' choices. What is the result if only these two heuristics are compared? We compared LEX with Weighted Pros in the selected item set and again assigned the participants to the heuristic that predicted the highest number of their choices. In this direct comparison, under low time pressure 26 participants were assigned to Weighted Pros and 15 participants to LEX, while under high time pressure 15 participants were assigned to Weighted Pros and 27 to LEX. (For the other 9 participants under low time pressure and 8 participants under high time pressure, both heuristics predicted an identical number of choices.) To summarize, this direct comparison leads to an interpretation similar to that of the outcome analysis for all strategies reported above: Under high time pressure, the noncompensatory heuristic LEX is more useful for predicting the participants' choices than the compensatory Weighted Pros.

We can now try to integrate variables from the process-oriented approach into our outcome analysis to yield a clearer interpretation of the results. Table 7-4 depicts the process measurements for those participants who were assigned to Weighted Pros and LEX. If the classification of participants' strategies is valid, different participants should differ on the process variables. The process measurements are consistent with this expectation, especially under high time pressure. Participants assigned to LEX looked up, on average, less information. They also showed higher selectivity in their information search. For instance, they showed a higher correlation between the time spent on each cue and the validities of the cues. However, these differences are small, and some of them are contrary to expectations, especially under low time pressure.

To sum up, we applied an outcome analysis to find out which of several strategies is the most suitable for predicting individuals' choices. We emphasized an important methodological point: If the alternatives of a decision task have been chosen randomly, it is likely that different strategies perform about equally well in predicting the choices of the participants. If two strategies always predict identical choices, it is impossible using outcome analysis to determine which strategy was used by an individual. As Wallsten (1980) pointed out, a good fit between a model and a decision does not necessarily mean that the cognitive process behind the decision adhered to that model. Even if a model can predict an individual's choices, it is not certain that the individual used that model as a strategy to make his or her decisions, and the process underlying a decision can remain unclear (Luce, 1995). One way of tackling this problem is to construct an item set with a low overlap between the strategies' predictions. We followed this procedure in our experiment, and it enabled us to identify two heuristics—LEX and Weighted Pros—as the most accurate models of the participants' strategies.

Table 7-4: Process Measurements for Participants Who Were Assigned to Either the LEX or Weighted Pros Strategy, Under Low and High Time Pressure (Selected Data Set)

| | Outcome Analysis | | | |
| | Low Time Pressure | | High Time Pressure | |
Process Variables	LEX (n = 14)*	Weighted Pros (n = 18)	LEX (n = 18)	Weighted Pros (n = 7)
Number of opened information boxes	32.9 boxes	33.3 boxes	18.5 boxes	20.5 boxes
Average time a box was open	0.45 seconds	0.35 seconds	0.32 seconds	0.28 seconds
Proportion of time spent on the most important cue	20%	21%	28%	23%
Standard deviation of the proportion of time spent on the alternatives	sd = 0.12	sd = 0.12	sd = 0.13	sd = 0.10
Standard deviation of the proportion of time spent on the cues	sd = 0.08	sd = 0.07	sd = 0.11	sd = 0.09
Pattern	−0.38	−0.01	−0.53	−0.13
Correlation between time spent on each cue and cue validities	r = 0.70	r = 0.73	r = 0.91	r = 0.80

*E.g., 14 participants were assigned to LEX under low time pressure.

When Do People Use Simple Heuristics?

Mr. K., who has become fascinated by decision-making research in general and simple decision heuristics in particular, broadens his initial question. He now wonders what conditions lead to more frequent use of simple heuristics. As we have shown, one such condition is time pressure. What can we predict with respect to time pressure, and what do we know from other studies?

It can be assumed that people react to time constraints either by applying the same decision strategy more quickly by considering the information faster, or by shifting their strategy (e.g., by cutting the information search short or by using a totally different strategy), in order to conduct a more selective information search. The first reaction leads to accelerated information acquisition. Many studies have demonstrated such an acceleration under time pressure (Ben Zur & Breznitz, 1981; Edland, 1994; Kerstholt, 1995; Payne et al., 1988); the evidence usually consists of a larger amount of information being acquired in the same period of time. There is also evidence for the second reaction, shifting the decision strategy. For instance, some authors have demonstrated an increased attention to the more important attributes, and hence higher selectivity in information search (Ben Zur & Breznitz, 1981; Böckenholt & Kroeger, 1993; Kerstholt, 1995; Payne et al., 1988; Wallsten & Barton, 1982). Others have shown that individuals under high time pressure employ a more cue-wise information search (Maule, 1994; Payne et al., 1988). In a study by Edland (1994), people responded to time constraints by more frequently using simple decision strategies. In a study by Payne, Bettman, and Luce (1996), the effect of time pressure was investigated with the additional aspect of opportunity costs. The authors address the question of whether people change their strategy when delay in making a decision leads to decrement in a benefit. Participants' reactions to opportunity cost were similar to the reactions to time pressure, resulting in the use of simpler strategies. For an overview of research on the effect of time pressure on judgment and decision making, see Svenson and Maule (1993).

What other conditions foster more frequent use of simple decision strategies? Most studies on strategies are concerned with the influence of task characteristics (for a discussion see Einhorn, 1970). One important characteristic is the type of decision task, such as choice versus judgment. Judgments often require an estimation of a particular value. Several authors assume that the use of noncompensatory heuristics is more frequent for choice tasks (Billings & Marcus, 1983; Hertwig & Chase, 1998; Montgomery et al., 1990). Westenberg and Koele (1992) found that information search differs for choice and for ranking tasks and concluded that noncompensatory heuristics are more often used for choice tasks.

It is important to interpret the results of a particular decision task in relation to the type of the task. While outcome-oriented studies mainly require judgments, the process-oriented approach usually studies choices.

In a review of 45 process-oriented studies, Ford et al. (1989) found that 35 of the studies used a choice task, while a judgment was required in only 7 of them. Three of the studies used both choices and judgments. The divergent results of outcome- and process-oriented approaches in the literature may reflect this asymmetry.

What role does the number of alternatives and cues play? With more alternatives and cues, the complexity of the decision task probably increases. Ford et al. (1989) concluded that higher task complexity leads to more selective information search. A number of authors have shown that the use of simple, noncompensatory strategies increases when the number of alternatives increases (Billings & Marcus, 1983; Johnson & Meyer, 1984; Payne, 1976; Timmermans, 1993). Likewise, an increase in the number of cues leads to reduced information search (Shields, 1983). However, Payne (1976) found no evidence for a shift from compensatory to noncompensatory strategies when the number of cues increased, suggesting that its influence is less clear.

Does the range of the cue values, the correlation between the cues, and the different variability of the cue weights matter? A narrow range of cue values can lead to a higher subjective weight of that cue for a judgment than a wide range (Mellers & Cooke, 1994). Negative intercue correlation impels people to devote more effort to the task and to show less selective and more alternative-wise information search (Bettman et al., 1993). Under the condition of high variability of cue weights, people tend to use a more selective and cue-wise information search (Payne et al., 1988).

Social context can also influence the use of decision strategies. One important context characteristic is accountability, that is, pressure to justify one's view to others. Tetlock (1983) hypothesized that people who are accountable for their decisions try to achieve greater accuracy or better decision quality, unless they can avoid the increased effort of a more accurate decision by adapting the decision to others' expectations. This hypothesis is grounded in the assumption that people expect to make more accurate decisions with strategies that require more effort. Indeed, McAllister, Mitchell, and Beach (1979) demonstrated that participants who have to account for their decisions more frequently select strategies that require considerable effort but offer a higher probability of a correct decision. The same result was found for the effect of the importance of the decision task. In a study by Billings and Scherer (1988), participants responded to the greater importance of a task with increased information search, although this effect was found for a choice task but not for a judgment task.

The main individual characteristics that are reported to influence decision strategies are knowledge and experience, emotional and motivational factors, cognitive abilities, and gender. In a broader context, Shanteau (1988) summarized how experts' decision strategies differ from those of novices. Experts adjust their initial decisions more often, and they try to learn from the successes and failures of earlier decisions; they accept small errors but avoid large mistakes. Shanteau (1992) argued that the amount of information used is not connected with expertise. The assumption that experts make better judgments because they use more information does not appear to be true. Instead Shanteau assumed that the difference between novices and experts is the ability to discriminate between relevant and irrelevant cues. Experts seem to use the same number of cues but are more likely to use cues that are more useful for making appropriate decisions. Klayman (1985) examined the influence of cognitive capacity. He showed that children with high cognitive capacity acquire more information for important decisions where several alternatives are available.

What We Have Learned

This chapter has had two goals. The first was to examine the question of whether people use simple heuristics; the second was to discuss two possible approaches to identifying these strategies: process analysis and outcome analysis. Both approaches are useful for investigating decision making. Although neither of them is sufficient on its own to gain a precise view of people's decision strategies, the use of both approaches can increase the psychological insight into the decision process.

The process-oriented approach monitors the predecisional information search and records the length of time people spend examining particular pieces of information. The experiment reported in this chapter showed that this method indeed captures some aspects of the decision process. Most participants used a cue-wise information search to acquire information. Their attention in both low and high time-pressure conditions was focused on important cues. The time spent on each cue was highly correlated with the validities of the cues, particularly under high time pressure. These results lent support to the hypothesis that participants use noncompensatory heuristics. However, process data cannot identify which particular heuristic is the most adequate decision model; the noncompensatory heuristics we tested differ only slightly with respect to their expected information search and attention to particular information.

The main idea of the outcome-oriented approach is to build decision models that predict the choices of individuals. Usually linear models are used, although this approach is not restricted to such models. In our experiment we used various additional strategies to predict participants' choices. For a representative item set it was difficult to assign one particular strategy to an individual, due to the high overlap in predictions among the strategies. The heuristics that were best at modeling the choices in the selected item set, where this overlap problem was reduced, were Weighted Pros under low time pressure and LEX, a generalization of Take The Best, under high time pressure. This leads to the important interpretation that people change their decision strategy under severe time constraints, a result that was confirmed by process analysis.

Both Weighted Pros and LEX use the cues one after the other (cue-wise search) to compare the alternatives. Moreover, both only examine whether one alternative has a higher cue value than the other alternatives; the absolute difference between the cue values is ignored. These heuristics are therefore very sensitive to differences between cue values. However, whereas LEX is noncompensatory, Weighted Pros is compensatory, because it integrates information. On the other hand, compensation occurred less frequently with Weighted Pros than with Franklin's rule.

Keeping in mind that heuristics are only models of actual reasoning, we have presented evidence that heuristics with a cue-wise information search can describe individuals' decision strategies for choice tasks. Individuals seem to use a fast and frugal noncompensatory strategy (LEX) with a simple stopping rule. Although under particular conditions there has also been evidence for a strategy that integrates information (Weighted Pros), this integration is based on only a subset of the information available. This is in line with Shepard (1967a), who argued that people seldom consider more than one or two factors at any one time, although they feel that they can take a host of factors into account. Consistent with other research (Simon, 1990), our participants avoided strategies that use all available information and require a great deal of computation. Even if people use a large amount of information and do integrate it, they seem to use simple cognitive operations. Taken together, the results reported in this chapter strongly indicate that people indeed use smart and simple decision strategies.

8

Bayesian Benchmarks for Fast and Frugal Heuristics

Laura Martignon
Kathryn Blackmond Laskey

> When your Daemon is in charge, do not try to think con-
> sciously.
>
> *Rudyard Kipling*

This chapter is devoted to the demonic beauty of Bayesian models for inference. First, we describe the changing relationship between Bayesian models and theories of human reasoning during the past three centuries. Second, we describe the Bayesian paradigm. Third, we propose three Bayesian models as competitors of both the less demonic linear regression model and the all-too-innocent Take The Best. We then discuss the subtle issue of how to measure the complexity of the inference strategies treated in this book, and the role of Bayesian models as benchmarks for fast and frugal heuristics. Throughout this chapter, we address the general question: What is the proper role of probability theory in the psychology of fast and frugal heuristics?

The Laws of Probability and the Laws of Reasoning

The first chapter of this book sketched the probabilistic revolution in Western thought and the ups and downs of the belief in probability as the cornerstone of reason. The identification of the rational ideal with probabilistic reasoning was first articulated during the Enlightenment, a time of heady enthusiasm for reason's potential to liberate humankind from the shackles of dogma and superstition. The Enlightenment thinkers saw themselves as discovering and formalizing fundamental laws of hu-

man reasoning. They viewed probability—an extension of the logical calculus—as the calculus of reason and an essential cornerstone of rational
choice. The laws of probability were viewed not just as normative, but
also as descriptive of enlightened human thinking. *L'homme éclairé*, that
is, the enlightened man (Daston, 1988), if not the man on the street,
would, according to Laplace, reason by means of the probability calculus.
The formal edifice of probability and decision theory erected by Thomas
Bayes, Jakob and Nikolas Bernoulli, Pierre Simon de Laplace, and others,
became *the* paradigm of human rationality. Yet the identification of the
laws of human reasoning with those of probability did not last.

After the horrors of the French Revolution, which some viewed as a
consequence of excessive rationality, probability theory ceased to be seen
as common sense reduced to a calculus. The focus slowly shifted, and
probability theory became another mathematical tool of the natural sciences. From the middle of the nineteenth century, probability gradually
gained ground in physical theories. It first appeared in the theory of heat.
In 1871, Ludwig Boltzmann (1909/1968) interpreted the irreversibility of
thermal processes as the tendency of molecules to evenly distribute their
energies, and his calculations relied on probability theory. In 1900, Max
Planck invoked probability in his theory of radiation (Planck, 1958). With
the further development of quantum theory, probability invaded atomic
theory. The emergence of quantum mechanics was crucial to the probabilistic revolution (Krüger et al., 1987), when the deterministic view of nature, held by Isaac Newton, René Descartes, and Laplace, gave way to a
probabilistic one.

As a description of human reasoning, probability had been rejected
from the early nineteenth century onward, but except for some inveterate
rationalists, this rejection only continued in the first half of the twentieth
century. The frequentist school of probability (Mises, 1957) attempted to
put probability on a firm foundation as an objective, measurable property
of random, repeatable events. It was not until well into the twentith century that the notion of probability as a calculus of rational deliberation
resurfaced (de Finetti, 1937; Savage, 1954). Yet the attempt to resurrect
the ideal of the rational probabilist was met with skepticism and even
outright hostility. The subjectivity of Savage's theory, which abandoned
the assumption that enlightened individuals with the same knowledge
would necessarily agree on the "correct" probabilities, was unsettling to
scientists trained to search for objectively verifiable truths about nature.
Modern experimental psychology opened up another front in the war
against the view of the rational human as probabilist, in a flurry of work
documenting the ways in which actual human reasoning differs from the
probabilistic norm. These deviations were regarded by many as cognitive
illusions, as proof that unaided human reasoning is riddled with fallacies
(e.g., Tversky & Kahneman, 1974).

However, it soon turned out that ordinary people's Bayesian reasoning
can be improved and cognitive illusions reduced when information is pre-

sented in frequency formats (Gigerenzer & Hoffrage, 1995). Yet, if there are many cues, applying the probabilistic (i.e., Bayesian) norm may not be feasible if the person making decisions does not have a calculator to hand. As the number of cues increases, the probabilistic paradigm based on Bayes's theorem soon becomes intractable even with a computer. It was the intractability of probabilistic strategies that created the most serious roadblock to their acceptance as models of human cognition and machine intelligence.

The heuristics used by humans, as we argue in this book, are adaptive strategies that have evolved in response to the need to draw inferences and make decisions with bounded knowledge and limited time. Cognitive resources being limited, good reasoning relies on a toolbox of ecologically rational fast and frugal strategies. The general, abstract methodologies scientists have developed as tools for inference probably have little in common with the psychologically plausible process of inference in human choice and decision making in everyday life.

Does this mean that formal theories of probabilistic rationality have become irrelevant and their study should be abandoned? There was definitely a time when it appeared that not only cognitive psychology, but also artificial intelligence and machine learning were moving in that direction. In the 1980s, Rivest (1987) had a major impact on artificial intelligence by introducing his decision lists, which are closely related to heuristics such as Take The Best and have become central to theoretical computer science. A few years later, Holte showed that very simple classification rules, even simpler than Take The Best, perform excellently (Holte, 1993).

But probabilistic inference has been enjoying a resurgence in recent years, albeit in a more limited, humble, and we believe, appropriate role. In spite of prophecies of the demise of probability, in spite of the assumption that computational intractability would doom probabilistic inference to become a theoretical oddity with little application to practical reasoning, there has been an unexpectedly vigorous renaissance in the last decade. The rapid and exuberant growth of Bayesian models and Bayesian techniques for inference, parameter learning, and even structure learning have caused enthusiasts to go so far as to declare that the twenty-first century will be the century of Bayes. Ward Edwards, one of the chief proponents of Bayesian decision making, is preparing a celebration in London, gathering all Bayesians around Bayes's tomb in the year 2001.

In the spirit of the recent resurgence of the probabilistic approach, this chapter explores the appropriate use of probability theory by cognitive scientists who promote fast and frugal heuristics. When performing a comparison, estimation, or categorization task, even the most committed Bayesian, if faced with computational constraints, will accept a fast and frugal strategy as a shortcut or approximation whenever it is certain that the loss in performance is not dramatic. The principles of decision theory (Clemen, 1996) dictate balancing the cost of computation against the accuracy gain. At the other end of the spectrum, even the strongest advocate of the bounded rationality approach can see the value of the Bayesian paradigm because it provides the best available benchmarks for evaluating the performance of fast and frugal heuristics. Thus at the meta level of algorithm evaluation, the Bayesian and the fast and frugal views meet in peace, each with different, yet compatible, objectives and expectations. The proponent of bounded rationality needs the help of the demon to provide a standard of comparison against which to evaluate the quality of fast and frugal heuristics.

Bayesian Demons

Chapter 1 distinguished between two visions of reasonableness: models of demons and models of bounded rationality. Demons do not have the infallible, universal knowledge of the superintelligence imagined by Laplace. Yet they behave like computationally unconstrained agents who throw frugality to the winds and are willing and able to apply the entire arsenal of lengthy deliberation and modern computing power to the problem at hand. Among the demons contemplated in this book, Bayesian models are the wildest type. They are the least frugal and definitely the slowest of the models we have considered. Yet—from the point of view of performance, theoretical consistency, and transparency—they are the most fascinating demons.

Previous chapters have shown that a simple fast and frugal heuristic such as Take The Best matches and often even outperforms tame versions of demons such as multiple regression. The strong performance of Take The Best occurs both within training samples and in generalizations to test samples. The aim of this chapter is to compare the performance of Bayesian demons with that of Take The Best. We examine first the unbounded Bayesian demon, whose capacities are beyond our reach, and then three workable Bayesian models: profile memorization, naive Bayes, and a special Bayesian network recently developed by Friedman.

Bayesian models start with a prior distribution for the relationship between cues and criterion, use the training sample to update the prior distribution and obtain a posterior distribution, and then apply this posterior distribution to evaluate the test set. The least frugal demon is a fully unbounded Bayesian strategy. The unbounded Bayesian demon is not sure which class of models—regression, logistic regression, CART, Bayesian network, or other—applies to a problem. Anything this demon is uncertain about is assigned a prior distribution, so a prior distribution is defined over the model classes. The next level of uncertainty applies to structural assumptions within a class of models—which regressors to include in the regression equation, where to make the splits in the classification tree, what arcs belong in the Bayesian network. Again, the demon assigns a prior distribution to these uncertainties. Finally, it assigns a prior distribution to the parameters for a given structure—regression weights, criterion probabilites at the leaf nodes of the classification tree, local conditional tables in the Bayesian network. Thus, this demon carries a staggering number of possible models. Each is assigned a prior probability, and each is updated to obtain a posterior probability. The final judgment is based on a weighted average of the conclusion of each of the models, where each model is weighted by its posterior probability. Clearly, the task faced by such a demon is far too daunting for even the fastest computers.

Profile Memorization Method

The first class of Bayesian models that actually can be applied to the real-world environments studied in chapter 5 is the *profile memorization method*. This is limited to situations where training and test sets coincide, where the goal is to fit a training sample and not to extrapolate to cases not yet seen. The method is to memorize every cue profile and its corresponding criterion value. For each pair of profiles the method will choose the one for which the memorized criterion is larger. If there are several pairs of objects with the same pair of cue profiles, the profile memorization method looks at all the pairs and determines the frequency with which an object with the first cue profile scores higher on the considered criterion than the object with the second profile. This proportion is the probability that the first object scores higher. If forced to find a deterministic answer, the method chooses the object that has the greater probability of a high value on the criterion. This Bayesian model has a frequentist attitude! The strategy is optimal from the probabilistic point of view.

The value of the profile memorization method is that it represents the optimal solution, that is, for a given data set it reaches the maximum performance that can be achieved. But when the training and test sets differ, that is, when we are generalizing from known to unknown data, there is no single provably optimal strategy.

In contrast to the profile memorization method, the following two types of Bayesian models can be used for both fitting and generalization tasks.

Naive Bayes

Naive Bayes (also known as "idiot Bayes") assumes that cues are independent of each other given the criterion. Naive Bayes is a special case of the more general class of Bayesian networks (Pearl, 1988). Let us explain how naive Bayes is applied in the context of the inferential task described in several other chapters, that is, to identify which of two objects has the larger criterion value, when presented with a set of cues related to the criterion. We assume a population of objects, each characterized by a criterion value and a set of M cues. The cues are assumed to take on one of two values (1 and 0). The criterion values are ordered either cardinally or ordinally.

Let us consider how a Bayesian network for this task could be constructed. Consider a population of objects. Each object is defined by a criterion value X, and a set of M cues, $C_1, \ldots, C_M$. Suppose a and b are two objects chosen at random from this set, with criterion values X_a and X_b, and cue values $C_j(a)$, $C_j(b)$, respectively, where j lies between 1 and M. The task is to infer from the cue profiles $(C_1(a), \ldots, C_M(a))$ and $(C_1(b), \ldots, C_M(b))$, whether X_a is larger or smaller than X_b. That is, the objective is to infer

$$\text{Prob}(X_a > X_b \mid a = (C_1(a), \ldots, C_M(a)), b = (C_1(b), \ldots, C_M(b))) \quad (1)$$

which is the probability of a scoring higher than b on the criterion X, given the cue profiles of a and b.

As a concrete example let us discuss the task investigated in chapter 4, where pairs of German cities were compared to determine which one had a larger population. There were nine cues: "Is the city the national capital?" (NC); "Is the city a state capital?" (SC); "Does the city have a soccer team in the major national league?" (SO); "Was the city once an exposition site?" (EX); "Is the city on the intercity train line?" (IT); "Is the abbreviation of the city on license plates only one letter long?" (LP); "Is the city home to a university?" (UN); "Is the city in the industrial belt?" (IB); "Is the city in former West Germany?" (WG).

Figure 8-1 shows one possible Bayesian network for the task of comparing two German cities to determine which is larger. A Bayesian network is a graphical representation of a probabilistic model of the relationships among a set of variables. Each node in the network represents a variable, taking values in a set of mutually exclusive possibilities. For instance, a

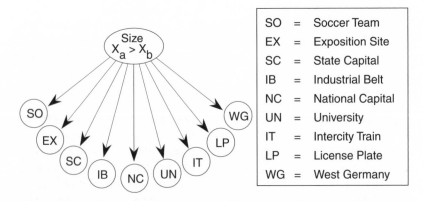

Figure 8-1: Naive Bayes network for comparing the sizes of German cities on the basis of nine cues.

city may or may not have an intercity train, and exactly one of these has to be true. The Bayesian network in figure 8-1 has 10 variables: one for the criterion and one for each of the nine cues. The criterion variable can take on two possible values: that the first city a is larger or that the second city b is larger. Each cue variable can take on four possible values:

- (0,0) Both cities have value 0 on the cue
- (1,0) City a has value 1 on the cue; city b has value 0
- (0,1) City a has value 0 on the cue; city b has value 1
- (1,1) Both cities have value 1 on the cue

Variables in a Bayesian network are represented by nodes connected by directed arcs (or arrows) that indicate probabilistic dependencies. If an arrow begins in node g and ends at node h, g is called a *parent* of h and h is called a *child* of g. A node j is called a *descendant* of g if there is a direct path of arrows connecting g to j. One can say that each variable is independent of its *nondescendants* if its parents are known, that is, the value of a variable is independent of the values of all nondescendant variables, given that one knows the values of the parent variables. Thus, in figure 8-1, all cues depend on the criterion variable, but conditional on the criterion variable, cues are independent of each other. For example, the probability that a city is a state capital (SC) or has a soccer team (SO) depends on the population size criterion (in this case, the probability is higher for the larger city). However, if we know which of the two cities is the larger, then in the network in figure 8-1, there is no relationship between whether it is a state capital and whether it has a soccer team.

The model of figure 8-1 is an example of naive Bayes. This particular network is the simplest Bayesian network relating these nine cues to all nine criteria. There is empirical evidence suggesting that people act as naive Bayesians, in that they tend to assume the independence of different pieces of evidence (Waldmann & Martignon, 1998) until they have evidence of interactions. However, people are poor at the quantitative estimation of conditional probabilities with two or more cues.

To form a complete probability model for the network in figure 8-1, one must specify 10 local probability tables (LPTs), one for each variable. Each LPT is a set of probability distributions: one distribution for the variable given each possible value of its parent variable(s). In figure 8-1, we need to specify a probability distribution for the criterion variable and two probability distributions for each cue: one for the case that the first city is larger and one for the case that the second city is larger. The distribution for the criterion is straightforward: If pairs are to be chosen at random then there is a 50% chance that the first city will be the larger one. To compute LPTs for the cues given the criterion, we use the training sample to update a uniform prior distribution (Cooper & Herskovits, 1992). This method is essentially the same as using sample frequencies when the sample size is large, but is more robust for small sample sizes.

Now, after training is done, suppose a pair of cities with a given cue profile is observed. The problem is to compute the conditional distribution on the criterion variable given these cue values. That is, we wish to compute the probability as in Equation 1. In general, this computation can be carried out by entering the network into any of a number of Bayesian network software packages, declaring the observed cue values as evidence, and querying the posterior distribution for the criterion node. For the naive Bayes network of figure 8-1, there is a simple expression for computing the probability distribution of the posterior distribution for the criterion variable:

$$
\begin{aligned}
\mathrm{Prob}(X_a > X_b \mid a = (C_1(a), \ldots, &C_M(a)), \, b = (C_1(b), \ldots, C_M(b))) \\
&= \alpha \times \mathrm{Prob}(C_1(a), C_1(b) \mid X_a > X_b) \ldots \\
&\times \mathrm{Prob}(C_M(a), C_M(b) \mid X_a > X_b) \times \mathrm{Prob}(X_a > X_b)
\end{aligned}
\tag{2}
$$

where α is a normalizing constant chosen to ensure that the probabilities add up to 1. Here we have merely used Bayes's inversion rule, assuming all cues are independent of each other given the criterion as dictated by our naive Bayes network. Since $\mathrm{Prob}(X_a > X_b \mid C_i(a), C_i(b))$ is the ecological validity (see chapter 6) v_i of C_i if $C_i(a) = 1$, $C_i(b) = 0$ and $1 - v_i$ if $C_i(a) = 0$, $C_i(b) = 1$, it turns out that in the case of naive Bayes the probabilities become simple expressions involving exclusively the validities of the cues.

A Savvy Bayesian Network

Naive Bayes has something in common with Take The Best and Dawes's rule (see chapter 6): It "bets" on the structure of the environment. It blindly assumes that cues are conditionally independent. If there are strong dependencies between cues given the criterion, naive Bayes may lose in accuracy. Our aim is now to extract information on cue-conditional interdependencies from the data. We apply an approach of *learning* Bayesian networks, from data originally developed by Cooper and Herskovits (1992), of which a more efficient version was developed by Friedman and Goldszmit (1996). These algorithms, although far simpler than the unbounded Bayesian demon described above, are more complex, more expressive, and potentially more accurate than the other demons we have considered.

A more general Bayesian network (see, for example, the network of figure 8-2) may contain more complex dependencies among the nodes. The more highly connected the network, the more complex the dependency structure it can represent. More complex networks in general require more complex computations for computing the conditional distribution of one node given others. More complex networks also have larger LPTs, and therefore require more data to obtain reliable estimates of the probability tables. In the extreme of a fully connected network with an arc between every pair of nodes, computing Equation (1) amounts to applying the profile memorization method, which will result in poor esti-

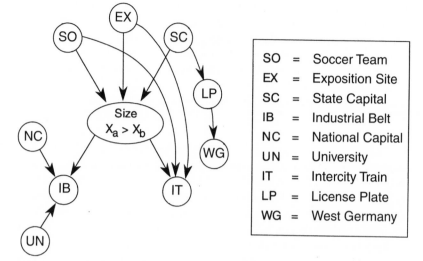

Figure 8-2: Full Bayes network for the German city data. The Markov blanket of the Size node in this network (obtained by Friedman's search method) includes all other nodes with the exception of LP and WG, which become irrelevant to computing city size, given the other cues.

mates of probabilities unless the sample size is large enough that there are many observations for each cue profile. In general, accurate estimation of the probability tables requires samples with many observations. Thus for this type of inference problem there is a trade-off: greater generality of representation (i.e., greater number of links between nodes representing possible dependencies) versus computational tractability and robust inference with smaller sample sizes.

Of course, some dependencies are stronger, and therefore more important to include, than others. Ignoring the weaker dependencies may help to avoid overfitting. As discussed more fully in chapter 6, the term "over-fitting" describes a general phenomenon that occurs when fitting a model for generalization: One may fit many more parameters than are required to capture the inherent structure of the data. The excess parameters fit the noise rather than the structure, and can cause poor performance on previously unseen data. The Bayesian needs a way to decide which dependencies to include and which to ignore. Methods have been developed by the artificial intelligence and statistics communities for searching through a large space of possible Bayesian networks to find one that is a good model, that is, one capturing the relevant, strong probabilistic dependencies among objects of the training set.

One class of search methods views the problem of finding a good Bayesian network as a problem in Bayesian inference (Cooper & Hersko-vits, 1992). This approach identifies networks in which variables are connected. Weak dependencies tend to be ignored because of the "natural Occam's Razor" associated with Bayesian model selection (Kass & Raftery, 1995). The prior distribution amounts to a bias toward frugality, in that a more complex model will achieve a higher posterior probability than a simpler model only when the improvement in performance is unlikely to be due to chance alone. These Bayesian search methods find a "good" network and then determine the conditional probabilities associated with the links in the network. In other words, they are methods for learning both structure and parameters.

We applied a Bayesian network search algorithm developed by Fried-man and Goldszmit (1996) to the comparison task presented in previous chapters for the 20 data sets discussed in chapter 5. This algorithm extends the approach of Cooper and Herskovits (1992) to exploit not only the global structure of a Bayesian network, but also local structure (called asymmetric independencies) within LPTs, thus increasing efficiency of learning (i.e., permitting more complex global structures to be learned with smaller sample sizes). Figure 8-2 shows the network obtained with Friedman's search method, for the task of comparing German cities according to their population size.

To use the network of figure 8-2 to infer which city is larger given the cue values requires solving Equation (1). There are standard software packages to do this. But it is useful to note that in the case in which all cues are known, Equation (1) can be solved with the following:

> *Theorem* (Pearl, 1988): The conditional probability of a node *j* being in a certain state given knowledge on the state of all other nodes in the network, is the product of the conditional probability of the node given its parents multiplied by the conditional probability of each one of its children given its parents, where all this is multiplied by a normalizing constant.

In symbols:

Prob(node *j* | all other nodes)
$= \alpha \times$ Prob(node *j* | parents of *j*)

$$\times \prod_k \text{Prob(child } k \text{ of } j \mid \text{parents of } k)$$
(3)

where α is the normalizing constant.

The set—consisting of a node, its parents, its children, and the other parents of its children—is called the *Markov blanket* of that node. What the theorem states is that a node's probability depends on all other nodes in the network only through its Markov blanket. Given its Markov blanket, it is independent of all other nodes in the network.

Figure 8-2 shows the Markov blanket of the node Size, which represents the criterion variable for the German cities task. This node has two possible states: "city *a* has more inhabitants than city *b*" and "city *b* has more inhabitants than city a." The Markov blanket of this node consists of all cues except license plate (LP) and West Germany (WG), which are neither parents, nor children, nor parents of children, of node Size. This means that these two cues are irrelevant to the criterion when the other seven cue values are known. To compute the probability distribution for the criterion node, we use the theorem presented in Equation (3).

Prob(Size | UN,NC,IB,SO,EX,SC,IT,WG,LP)
= $\alpha \times$ Prob(Size | SO,EX,SC) $\times$ Prob(IB | Size,UN,NC)
$\times$ Prob(IT | Size,SO,EX)   (4)

where α is a constant chosen so that the probability of the two states of the size variable add up to 1.

The probabilities on the right-hand side of Equation (4) are taken from the LPTs of the network of figure 8-2. This represents an enormous computational reduction in the calculation of probability distributions. There are 2^{19} probabilities to estimate for a general probability distribution, one for each combination of cue/criterion values. The complexity is far less when the conditional independencies are taken into account. The probability distribution for Size given the cues is the product of three factors, one for each of the LPTs that mentions the Size variable. Each of these has 2^7 entries, so 3×2^7 probabilities must be estimated for the task of inferring the probability for Size given its Markov blanket. The more conditional independence, the greater the potential reduction in the number of probabilities to be computed. It is precisely this kind of reduction in computational complexity that has led to the popularity of Bayesian networks in both statistics and artificial intelligence in the last decade.

The number of probabilities to be estimated is still exponential in the number of parents per node, because each node stores a probability distribution for each combination of values for its parents. Again, the complexity of the problem may be reduced by making structural assumptions constraining the probabilities. The algorithm we applied uses a decision tree to estimate the local probability tables. The decision tree greatly reduces the number of computations. Here the problem of finding a good tree was solved with the same type of approach used to determine the network describing dependencies between cues, described above.

Figure 8-3 illustrates the decision tree produced by the program for Prob(Size | SO,EX,SC). The probability distribution for the Size variable is obtained by tracing the arcs of this tree. From figure 8-3 we see that the first step is to check the exposition (EX) cue. If neither city is an exposition site, the probability is determined by whether the city has a soccer team (SO), and the state capital (SC) cue is irrelevant. Conversely, when one or both cities are exposition sites, then the probability distribution is determined by the state capital (SC) cue, and the soccer team (SO) cue is irrelevant. Thus, instead of requiring $2^7 = 128$ probability distributions for

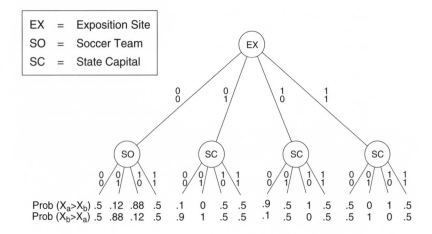

Figure 8-3: Tree for computing the local probability table for the Size node of figure 8-2. For instance, if neither of the two cities a and b is an exposition site (symbolized by the two zeros in the left branch), then the only relevant cue is SO, that is, whether a city has a soccer team in the major league (cue SC is irrelevant). If a has a soccer team but b does not ("1" for a and "0" for b) then $\text{Prob}(X_a > X_b \mid \text{SO,EX,SC}) = .88$.

the Size node, the decision tree representation of figure 8-3 requires only $2^4 = 16$.

To summarize, the method we used to find a probability model for the relationship between cue and criterion involves:

1. Searching over a large space of directed graphs representing Bayesian networks on cue and criterion variables
2. Searching over decision-tree models for the within-node LPT structure
3. Estimating probability distributions for LPTs
4. Computing the posterior distribution of the criterion variable given cue values using Equation (4)

This method is much more computationally intensive than multiple regression, not to mention Take The Best. In fact, the complexity of searching the entire space of Bayesian networks and within-node decision trees—computed in terms of elementary operations as a function of M cues and N objects—contains an exponential term in M. This space is far too large to search exhaustively even for a relatively small problem such as predicting the population sizes of German cities. Thus, the demon actually makes use of heuristic search. We have also unabashedly used the highest-probability network identified by the algorithm (such as the one for the cities data reproduced in figure 8-2), rather than, in true demonic fashion, trying to compute the full posterior distribution for the criterion variable. The full posterior distribution is an average in which the result given by each network is weighed by its posterior probability—clearly an infeasible calculation.

The Competition

Can the performance of the fast and frugal Take The Best ever come close to that of a demon, the Bayesian network? We tested the performance of four competitors—Take The Best, naive Bayes, Bayesian network, and multiple regression—for two tasks: fitting given data (training set is equal to test set) and generalization to new data (training set is not equal to test set, i.e., cross-validation). In the generalization task, 50% of the objects in the data set were chosen at random 10,000 times and the model obtained on the training set was then tested on the remaining 50%. These two tasks correspond to the two "tours" in chapter 5, and we ran the competition for the 20 environments used in chapter 5. In addition, the profile memorization method was used to determine the maximum performance when the test set is the training set. The conditions of the competition were the same as the two tours in chapter 5.

Each competitor was presented with a training sample to learn about the relationship between cues and criterion. For example, Take The Best uses the training sample to learn the ordering of the cue validities. Linear regression uses the training sample to estimate regression coefficients. After this opportunity to learn, the competitors are then tested on their ability to ascertain the ordering of criterion values on a set of test pairs. The inferences the competitors had to make included the following. Which of two German cities has the higher population? Which of two U.S. cities has the higher homelessness rate? Which of two individual Arctic female char fish produces more eggs? Which of two professors at a midwestern college has the higher salary? (For a complete description see chapter 5.)

Consider first the results when inferring city populations (table 8-1). When performance is tested on the training set (fitting), the accuracy of Take The Best is only two percentage points lower than that of the Bayesian network. The upper limit of correct inferences is computed by the profile memorization method as 80%, which is four percentage points above the performance of the Bayesian network. When the test set is different from the training set, there is no theoretically best solution, but the competitors can still be compared with each other. In this case, multiple regression takes a slightly larger cut in performance than Take The Best and the Bayesian network.

When evaluating homelessness, the Bayesian network performs eight percentage points better than Take The Best on the training set (table 8-1, "Fitting"). This difference is reduced to two percentage points when the test set is different from the training set (table 8-1, "Generalization").

Table 8-1: Performance of Different Algorithms in 20 Data Sets

Environment	# Objects	# Cues	Fitting					Generalization			
			PM	TTB	Reg	NB	BN	TTB	Reg	NB	BN
Ozone in San Francisco	11	3	85	84	85	84	84	79	77	80	78
Cow manure	14	6	83	79	79	79	80	76	72	78	79
Oxidant	17	4	93	84	84	84	84	80	76	81	82
Mortality	20	15	100	77	83	78	79	62	54	66	67
House price	22	10	96	86	86	87	87	84	68	86	86
Rainfall	24	6	71	67	71	68	68	53	56	57	59
Biodiversity	26	6	88	84	80	83	83	80	72	80	82
Attractiveness of women	30	3	80	71	71	71	71	66	67	68	59
Attractiveness of men	32	3	75	73	73	73	73	71	69	72	70
Mammals' sleep	35	9	95	78	79	77	83	75	65	76	80
Car accidents	37	13	93	71	79	75	75	64	64	71	71
Obesity at age 18	46	10	70	74	74	77	79	71	63	71	69
Fuel consumption	48	6	87	78	79	78	80	73	74	76	76
Homelessness	50	6	82	69	70	68	77	63	62	64	65
Professors' salaries	51	5	87	80	83	80	84	80	80	80	81
High school dropout rates	57	18	90	65	72	65	65	60	54	61	60
Land rent	58	4	82	80	81	80	81	77	80	77	78
City population	83	9	80	74	74	74	76	72	71	72	74
Body fat	218	14	87	59	61	80	82	56	55	79	80
Fish fertility	395	3	75	73	75	73	75	73	75	74	75
Average over the 20 data sets			85	75	77	77	79	71	68	73	74

Note. PM = profile memorization, TTB = Take The Best, Reg = Regression, NB = naive Bayes, BN = Bayesian network.

As a final example, consider predicting which of two professors at a midwestern college has the higher salary. When the task is fitting known data, the performance of Take The Best is four percentage points lower than the Bayesian network. When training and test sets differ, this difference decreases to one percentage point and Take The Best almost matches the Bayesian network.

The following observations can be made from examining the results across different data sets:

1. On average, Take The Best is only four percentage points less accurate than the Bayesian network when the test set is the same as the training set (fitting). Take The Best pays only a small price in accuracy for being fast and frugal.
2. On average, Take The Best is only three percentage points less accurate than the Bayesian network when the test set is different from the training set (generalization). The Bayesian network deals poorly with generalization in small data sets, whereas Take The Best is fairly robust through all the data sets.
3. Naive Bayes lives up to its reputation of being simple, fast, and robust. Like Take The Best (see chapter 6), naive Bayes bets on the structure of the environment: It bets that cues are independent conditional on their value on the criterion. The more frugal Take The Best almost matches naive Bayes on average on the 20 data sets.

The general result is surprising. Simple one-reason decision making, as employed by Take The Best, is almost as accurate as the computationally expensive Bayesian network. Even compared to a demon, Take The Best had to make little trade-off between being fast and frugal, and being accurate.

Complexity: Demons and Heuristics

It is wise to choose an approach to a task by balancing the need for accuracy against computational load. We should therefore compare different algorithms not just on their accuracy, but also the computational load involved in applying them. This computational load includes both the upfront effort required to learn a model and the run-time effort to apply the algorithm to specific cases.

We have formulated computational models of fast and frugal heuristics in the form of step-by-step algorithms, rather than in terms of parallel processing. Thus, when talking about the complexity of a cognitive algorithm, we are counting operations as they are performed consecutively. Let us take a look at the sequential complexity of the algorithms treated in this book from the point of view of computer science, where complexity is defined in terms of the time required to perform all operations necessary.

Theoretical computer science provides a number of methods for studying the complexity of algorithms. One possibility is to count the number of steps in an algorithm and then to express this number as a function of the parameters involved in the algorithm. One then determines the order of complexity of this function. One criterion is O( ) (called the Landau symbol), defined as follows: When we are given two functions F(N) and G(N) on the natural numbers, we say that F is of the order of G, and write $F = O(G)$, if there exists a constant K such that:

$$\frac{F(N)}{G(N)} < K$$

for all natural numbers N different from 0. Thus, for instance, the function $F(N) = 3N + 1$ is of the order of $G(N) = N$, but N^3 is not of the order of N^2. $O(1)$ means a constant time that is not a function of N. Every polynomial in N, that is, a linear combination of powers of N, is of the order of the highest power of N in it. Since what is being counted is the number of steps in a sequential process, it is common to view the resulting O( ) criterion as the "time complexity" of the algorithm. Landau's criterion O( ) admits a straightforward generalization when more than one variable is involved, as is the case in table 8-2. It is usual in computer science to

Table 8-2: Worst-Case Complexity of Algorithms

Algorithm	Setup	Decision
Bayesian network	$O(2^{M^2})$ for structure search	$O(2^M)$
Profile memorization	$O(MN)$ for storage	$O(1)$
Estimation tree	$O(2^M)$ for search	$O(N\log N)$
Naive Bayes	$O(MN\log N)$ for validities	$O(M)$
Exemplar model for categorization	$O(MN)$ for storage	$O(MN)$
Neural network	$O(M^3N)$	$O(N^2)$
Multiple regression	$O(M^2N)$	$O(M)$
Franklin's rule	$O(MN\log N)$	$O(M)$
Dawes's rule	$O(MN\log N)$ for validities	$O(M)$
Take The Best	$O(\max(MN\log N, M\log M))$ for validities and cue sorting	$O(M)$
QuickEst	$O(\max(MN\log N, M\log M))$ for validities and cue sorting	$O(M)$
Categorization by Elimination	$O(M\log M)$ for cue sorting	$O(M)$
Minimalist	$O(MN\log N)$ for validities	$O(M)$

Note. Here N denotes the number of objects and M the number of cues of a given environment. Computing the validity of each cue has a complexity of $N\log N$ if one uses Equation (1b) of chapter 6. Observe that, because there are usually many more objects than cues ($N > M$), $\log M$ is usually less than $N\log N$, so that the setup complexity of Take The Best and QuickEst is just $MN\log N$. The profile memorization method is a good example for the difference between machines and humans: What is of low complexity for a machine can be unattainable for a human mind (here, to memorize all MN cue values), and vice versa. (QuickEst is described in chapter 10, and Categorization by Elimination in chapter 11.)

consider worst-case complexity, as we shall do here. This provides a bound on how long an algorithm can take. We note that average-case *complexity* may be of more interest, but is more difficult to estimate and requires assumptions about the problem set.

For an inference algorithm that operates on a reference class of N objects and M cues, the order of the number of operations performed will depend on both parameters.

An intuitive way to determine the O( ) complexity of an algorithm is to ask how many times each input element must be manipulated during the course of the algorithm's execution. If, for example, each of the N elements needs to be seen once, as in the case of finding the mean of a list of numbers, the time complexity is $O(N)$. For the setup of Take The Best, M cues must be sorted according to their validity. Standard computer sorting algorithms require $M\log M$ steps. The actual time spent on each computation is a constant factor and does not affect the time complexity measure. This constant factor is important in determining practical performance as well as the problem size at which the "crossover" occurs between two algorithms of different complexity, so as to establish which would take more time in practice. However, no matter what the constant factor is, an algorithm of higher time complexity will eventually, for large enough problems, be slower than one of lower complexity.

Algorithms that have a complexity measure that is the sum of two or more measures have the time complexity of the larger of the two measures by definition. As examples, an algorithm that first finds the distances between every pair of a set of points with a time complexity of $O(N^2)$ and then prints out the list of points with a time complexity of $O(N)$ ends up having the time complexity of the more expensive part, namely $O(N^2)$.

Algorithms that are considered "simple" fall in the $O(N)$ to $O(N^3)$ range. For example, finding an item in a list is $O(N)$, the best sorting algorithms are $O(N\log N)$, and performing calculations using all pairs in a list is $O(N^2)$. Unfortunately, there is a large class of problems that require algorithms with the time complexity of $O(2^N)$ or even $O(N^N)$ for an optimal solution. Many scheduling and design optimization algorithms fall into this "exponential" category. These algorithms with a complexity of order larger than any power of N are clearly of order larger than any polynomial in N (because, by definition, a polynomial is of the order of its highest power of N) and are called *NP-complete*, which means "not (to be) complete(d) in polynomial time." In practice, these NP-complete algorithms are intractable for large Ns. Alternative algorithms that allow a trade-off of solution quality for time complexity are needed in these cases. The general problem of Bayesian inference is NP-complete (Cooper, 1990). That is, when there are no restrictions on the structure of the Bayesian network, the problem of inferring which criterion is larger given the cue values is not of polynomial order.

Table 8-2 summarizes time complexity measures for several of the algorithms and heuristics treated in this book. This table is useful for comparing the worst-case performance of the different algorithms. We have divided the overall time complexity in two phases: one for setup and one for decision. We note, however, that two algorithms may have the same worst-case complexity but perform very differently in practice (or vice versa). We note also that even when claims of cognitive plausibility are made, as for some of the algorithms studied in this book, the time complexity of a computer implementation may bear little relation to how long it takes a person to complete the task. What will be clear from our analysis of worst-case time complexity is that the class of fast and frugal heuristics proposed in this book deserve to be called fast even in the rigorous framework of worst-case complexity in theoretical computer science.

Conclusions

We think of our lives as consisting of a series of decisions, some large and significant, others smaller and less significant, but each confined to a relatively small and restricted domain. Savage (1954, p. 83) reminds us that in actuality we have but one decision to make: how we shall live our lives. In other words, we must choose a policy for drawing inferences and making decisions. All other decisions follow from that.

So how should we choose? Shall we adopt the normative Bayesian approach to inference and decision making, or shall we stick to simple heuristics such as the fast and frugal ones presented in this book?

This need not be an exclusive either/or decision: Fast and frugal heuristics can have their place in everyday affairs where time is limited and knowledge is scarce, and Bayesian tools can be the choice of someone who is in no hurry and has access to a computer (Winterfeldt & Edwards, 1986). Obtaining those extra percentage points of accuracy may be well worth the computational cost in high-stakes decisions such as those involving human lives or having serious long-term environmental or social impact. A Bayesian who tries to optimize under constraints must choose a strategy under a combination of criteria, such as computational cost, accuracy, and perhaps even transparency. Thus, it may happen that a Bayesian may choose to apply Take The Best, or another fast and frugal heuristic, over more expensive Bayesian networks for some classes of problems. Bayesian reasoning itself may tell us when to choose.

The results reported in this chapter were obtained with real-world data. However, it is important to note the restricted applicability of our results. First, we studied situations in which the *problem representation* was given to us, and that representation was one of comparison using a set of cues given a priori. We did not study situations in which the task is to construct a representation (i.e., to determine the appropriate cues). A second limit on the applicability of our results is that we studied inferences only under complete knowledge, unlike Gigerenzer and Goldstein

(1996a; see chapter 4), who studied the performance of heuristics under limited knowledge. Limited knowledge (e.g., knowing only a fraction of all cue values) is a realistic condition that applies to many situations in which predictions must be made. It is important to note that Bayesian networks can be applied when not all cue values are known. The simple formula given in Equation (3) must be replaced by a more complex belief propagation algorithm (Jensen, 1996), but the distribution of the criterion may be obtained, conditional on whatever cue values are known. Finally, the Bayesian network model we put forward as a paragon of rationality is itself only a heuristic approximation to a full Bayesian model. It uses heuristic search rather than enumerating all possible Bayesian networks and it chooses a single best model rather than averaging over all models with nonnegligible posterior probability. Moreover, the algorithm assumes the use of independent observations, and our data does not fulfill this condition. This is because the data we used consist of pairs of objects, where each object participates in multiple pairs in the data set, introducing dependency. We used an easily available algorithm that we expected to provide a good benchmark. More sophisticated Bayesian algorithms will soon be proliferating in the literature—how will they compare?

In summary, this chapter has argued several related points. First, a major, important role for Bayesian models is as a benchmark for evaluating fast and frugal heuristics. Second, given a heuristic algorithm and a benchmark algorithm, one can examine the trade-off between computational cost and accuracy. This enables the development of policies to determine which solution methods are most appropriate for particular classes of problems. One could even argue for the application of the Bayesian ideal of rationality at the meta level, at the level of selecting policies for which approach to use on given classes of problems. Therefore, a decision-theoretic argument can be developed for the use of fast and frugal heuristics in place of optimizing strategies in situations in which computational time and cost are important considerations. In making predictions about 20 real-world environments, we found that Take The Best was almost as accurate as a Bayesian network. The trade-off between simplicity and accuracy turned out to be almost negligible. Take The Best is a fast and frugal strategy that is quite useful in situations in which a few points of accuracy can be sacrificed to save considerable computational cost.

Appendix

Ward Edwards, who had posed the challenge of comparing Take The Best with Bayes, had a creative reaction to the results in table 8-1, responding with the following limerick:

To Bayes or not to Bayes?
A Limerick

Gerd and his joyful friends all had visions:
Take The Best can make ideal decisions.
    "Let us put Take The Best
    to a rigorous test
To avoid all collegial derisions."

So they ran Take The Best against Bayes.
Their finding leaves me in a daze.
    If you are a go-getter
    You know Bayes did better
Because we all know that Bayes pays.

But TTB did quite well too
Although it uses only one cue.
    If the felt need to work
    Tends to drive you berserk
Bayes and TTB just about drew.

TTB brought straight lines to their knees
And even put Bayes in a squeeze
    The moral's quite clear:
    You can act without fear,
Guided by whichever you please.

Ward Edwards
September 1997

Part IV

BEYOND CHOICE:
MEMORY, ESTIMATION,
AND CATEGORIZATION

9

Hindsight Bias

A Price Worth Paying for Fast and Frugal Memory

Ulrich Hoffrage
Ralph Hertwig

Remembering is not the re-excitation of innumerable fixed, lifeless and fragmentary traces. It is an imaginative reconstruction, or construction . . .

Sir Frederic Bartlett

Frustration about a fallible memory is familiar to most of us: "But men are men; the best sometimes forget" (Shakespeare, *Othello*). Remembering past events is not merely retrieving them from storage like books from a library. Memories can be lost or distorted, and memories for events that never even happened can be induced (e.g., Loftus, 1997; Schacter, 1995). Our memory is not like that of a Laplacean demon—we cannot perfectly recall everything we have ever thought, said, or experienced. Other chapters in this book deal with constraints of limited time and knowledge; in this chapter we focus on the constraints imposed by the limited capacity of human memory. How can memory work given its limitations? Our answer is, by *reconstruction*: When retrieval fails, inferential heuristics are employed. This answer is by no means new. It was already proposed by Sir Frederic Bartlett, one of the pioneers of modern memory research. In his classic *Remembering* (1932/1995, p. 213), Bartlett proposed that memory is a process of reconstruction (see—or recall if you can—the epigram that opened this chapter).

Reconstruction, however, has its price. We focus on one, the well-known hindsight bias, and propose a computational model for this effect based on a fast and frugal heuristic. Hindsight bias has often been regarded as just another error of human information processing. We argue, instead, that it is a by-product of two generally adaptive processes: first, updating knowledge after receiving new information; and second, draw-

ing fast and frugal inferences from this updated knowledge. Before speci-
fying the model, we illustrate hindsight bias by exploring a topic that concerns every citizen of a modern democracy: public polling and electoral
outcomes.

Public Polling, Elections, and Hindsight Bias

The history of American political polling is closely linked to the name of
George Gallup. Gallup believed that his ideal of direct democracy called
for public information and policy evaluation not filtered through the economic elite (Hamilton, 1995). In the early 1930s, he realized his vision
of going directly to the voter by polling for a local election in Iowa
in which his mother was a candidate. Shortly afterward, he began to
apply this technique to predicting election results for dissemination by
the public media. Since Gallup's early polls, polling has "moved to the
epicenter of American campaigns" (Hamilton, 1995). For instance, Gallup
and Harris, giants of the polling industry, attracted Richard Nixon's interest and became prime candidates for attack and manipulation by his
administration (Jacobs & Shapiro, 1996). The acceptance of polling as a
political tool did not go unchallenged. Indeed, it has been contended that
opinion polls do not lead to political responsiveness, but are used by
elites to manufacture the public attitudes they desire (see Jacobs & Shapiro, 1996).

The Achilles heel of polling companies is that the public can retrospectively check their predictions' accuracy. This is fine as long as they were
accurate. In fact, for the Gallup company, the 1997 British parliamentary
elections were just such a success story. In a poll sponsored by *The Daily
Telegraph*, Gallup predicted the results almost perfectly. Based on inter-
views conducted a day before the elections with a randomly selected national sample of 1,810 citizens eligible to vote, Gallup forecast a 13%
margin of victory for the Labour Party over the Conservative Party. The
actual results of these historic elections, which ended the Conservatives'
18 years in power, put the final difference at 14%.

Such a post hoc reality check can, however, also be highly embarrass-
ing. A famous "miss" by Gallup and others was Truman's victory in the
1948 presidential elections. In those first days of November, 1948, everyone knew that Thomas Dewey would defeat Harry Truman in the upcoming presidential elections. Pollsters and professional politicians alike predicted it. Daily newspapers came out eight to one in favor of Dewey. In
its desire to get a scoop, the *Chicago Daily Tribune* jumped the gun in its
November 4 edition and, relying on the seemingly reasonable predictions
of Gallup and other polling companies, reported that Dewey would be the
next president (Hamilton, 1995). (You may recall the photo of the smiling

president-elect, Harry Truman, holding aloft the newspaper with the now famous headline, DEWEY DEFEATS TRUMAN.)

What pollsters would like to do to save face in such situations is to say: "We knew it all along—that's what we really predicted." But the public memory represented in newspapers, videotapes, and other physical media make this ploy impossible—the pollsters must stand by their past predictions. Individuals speaking (or just thinking) in everyday life, however, usually have only their fallible internal memory to go on—and no external records to embarrass or contradict them. This can lead to situations in which an individual inaccurately remembers a prediction or statement he or she made in the past. For instance, Uncle Joe might contend that he knew Truman would win all along, even though he had earlier believed that Dewey would make it to the White House. This tendency to believe falsely—after the fact—that one would have predicted the outcome of an event is known as *hindsight bias* (for other systematic distortions in reconstructing the past, see Johnson & Sherman, 1990).

Recent laboratory research in psychology shows that hindsight bias is common in laypeople and experts (e.g., voters, physicians, businesspeople), and that it is manifest across a variety of judgments (e.g., confidence judgment, choice, categorization, or quantitative estimation; for a review, see Hawkins & Hastie, 1990). Not surprisingly, it also occurs in predictions of political election outcomes. For instance, before the 1982 Hawaiian gubernatorial election, Synodinos (1986) asked participants in a study to indicate the probability of each of the canditates winning the election. After the election, another group of participants was asked to make these predictions as if they had been asked before the election. As expected, the participants showed a "knew-it-all-along" tendency: The postelection probability estimates for the winner were higher than those made before the election, whereas the postelection estimates for the two losers were lower than the preelection estimates.

Synodinos (1986) demonstrated the effect of outcome knowledge by comparing two different groups of participants. Hindsight bias can also be found within a single participant. Fischhoff and Beyth (1975), for instance, had a group of student participants judge a variety of possible outcomes of President Nixon's visits to Peking and Moscow *before* they occurred in 1972. The possible outcomes were presented as assertions, such as: "The United States will establish a permanent diplomatic mission in Peking, but not grant diplomatic recognition" and "President Nixon will meet Mao at least once." Participants rated their confidence in the truth of the assertions on a 0% to 100% scale. *After* the visits, the assertions were repeated, and the participants were asked to recall their original confidence. The participants exhibited hindsight bias: Recalled confidence for events they thought had happened was higher than original confidence, while recalled confidence for events they thought had not happened was lower.

Views of Hindsight Bias

Hindsight bias has been interpreted in various ways. We distinguish two types of interpretations and add a third one. Fischhoff (1975), whose early experimental studies carved out this new topic for memory researchers, stressed that hindsight bias is not only robust and difficult to eliminate (Fischhoff, 1982a), but also has potentially harmful consequences:

> When we attempt to understand past events, we implicitly test the hypotheses or rules we use both to interpret and to anticipate the world around us. If, in hindsight, we systematically underestimate the surprises that the past held and holds for us, we are subjecting those hypotheses to inordinately weak tests and, presumably, finding little reason to change them. Thus, the very outcome knowledge which gives us the feeling that we understand what the past was all about may prevent us from learning anything from it. (Fischhoff, 1982b, p. 343)

Rather than stressing the harmful consequences of hindsight bias, others (e.g., Campbell & Tesser, 1983) have pointed out its potentially adaptive aspects. Presenting ourselves as wiser after the fact may enable us to appear intelligent, knowledgeable, or perspicacious. In fact, as long as no record of our previous judgments is available (which, unlike for pollsters, is generally the case), the immediate benefits of presenting oneself as knowledgeable outweigh the unlikely costs of being revealed as an imposter. In addition to hindsight's potential benefits in social interaction, hindsight bias may play an important role in creating and maintaining a coherent conception of oneself. Take, for instance, the situation of people who suddenly find themselves in a society whose value system has completely changed. The 1990s have seen an unusual number of such rapid societal transformations, from the fall of the apartheid regime in South Africa to the end of the socialist regimes in the Soviet Union and East Germany, among other countries. Many of those who held a responsible position in the old regimes are now being asked by their families and friends, or interrogated by official bodies (e.g., the Commission for Truth and Reconciliation in South Africa), to account for their previous behavior. Under these circumstances, hindsight bias—here the belief that one's past convictions and behavior are compatible with what the new regime considers to be right—can be an effective way of preserving the integrity of one's personality (and perhaps one's skin).

We propose a third view (which does not exclude the two views outlined above). According to this view, hindsight bias is a by-product of an adaptive process rather than being an adaptation itself (for a general version of this argument, see Campbell, 1959). To introduce this view, we first address the question: What are the alternatives to the assumption that human memory is unbounded in its capacity?

Consider the following situation. Mr. Loman is a salesman who visits his clients by car. Every day, he repeatedly decides where to park his car, then stores this information in memory, and finally, after completing his business appointment, retrieves the car's location from memory. He does this very many times in the course of weeks, months, and years. How could a memory system be designed that allows Mr. Loman quickly and reliably to retrieve the knowledge about where he parked his car most recently? Is a system that maintains access to the knowledge of all past parking locations efficient? Some current conceptions of human memory seem to assume that we do in fact keep a record of every discrete event we have experienced and that, when we retrieve information or classify an object, we compare a probe with all our existing memory traces. For instance, exemplar models (e.g., Estes, 1986; Hintzman, 1988; Medin & Schaffer, 1978; Nosofsky, 1986; Ratcliff, 1978) are based on such an assumption. Although these models have provided impressive accounts of a wide array of memory phenomena, their psychological plausibility has been questioned, both for the extensive similarity computation, as well as for the vast memory resources they require (Nosofsky et al., 1994; see also chapter 11 for an alternative).

Sharing these doubts, we concur with Anderson and Schooler's (1991) argument that "it is just too expensive to maintain access to an unbounded number of items" (p. 396). In addition, a stockpile of memories (e.g., the memories of all the previous locations of Mr. Loman's car) may interfere with the only information that is relevant right now (e.g., where his car is currently parked). In this sense, forgetting may be necessary for memory to maintain its function, insofar as it prevents us from using old and possibly outdated information (Bjork, 1978; Ginzburg et al., 1996). A well-known phenomenon that reflects the adaptive nature of forgetting is the Zeigarnic effect. Zeigarnic (1927) showed that memory for tasks that have been completed declines rapidly compared to those tasks that have not yet been completed (e.g., a waiter's memory of the amount of the bill, depending on whether or not the customer has already paid). Thus, forgetting should most likely occur once the usefulness of some information has passed.

An alternative to a memory system that includes an immense, continuously expanding long-term storage is a system that maintains access primarily to the information most likely to be needed and most likely to be correct. For such a memory system, it is crucial to update information constantly and automatically. This process would avoid the problems of an exploding number of items, and the increasing retrieval time required if memory probes were compared with stored traces in a serial manner. It would make possible a boundedly rational memory system, which keeps available only those items that are most likely to be needed. Such a process of information updating is consistent with Bartlett's (1932/1995) classical finding that schemata are constantly changing and being updated.

Besides the fact that for most experiences there is no need for later recall (Anderson & Schooler, 1991), there is another reason why it is not necessary to maintain a memory trace for everything we have thought, said, or experienced in the past: When something needs to be recalled, there are alternatives to memory retrieval. For example, imagine that you own 25 shares of stock in a company, which are listed in the newspaper as being worth $378.50 each. To calculate their total value, you multiply 25 times 378.5. A couple of days later, you want to know this value again. Can you remember $9,462.50? Probably not. However, this is not a problem, because you can compensate for your failure to retrieve it from memory by performing the same calculation again: Recall can be replaced by recalculation. We posit that the same sort of recalculation can be done— and, in fact, is done—when a past judgment, such as the prediction of the outcome of an election, needs to be recalled. If it cannot be recalled, going through the same process that led to the original judgment can provide a good approximation, and perhaps even a perfect substitute. There is, however, an important difference between a multiplication and a judgment. Performing arithmetic computations is a technical skill and we are trained to do it reliably. Therefore, performing the same multiplication a second time should yield the same result. In contrast, making a judgment often implies drawing knowledge-based inferences. If knowledge is constantly updated, as suggested above, inferences based on the updated knowledge may be different from those based on past knowledge.

Updating knowledge is the key assumption underlying the model of hindsight bias proposed below. It applies to situations where the original judgment was a knowledge-based inference. If the attempt to remember this original judgment directly fails, it will be reconstructed by repeating the same process that led to this judgment. However, knowledge about the outcome of an event, or feedback on whether an inference was correct, leads to an updating of relevant knowledge. As a consequence, the reconstruction based on the updated knowledge can be systematically different from the construction based on the original knowledge. This difference is what is known as hindsight bias. Thus, in our view, the so-called bias is a by-product of an adaptive process, namely knowledge updating.

Previously, we proposed a model that accounts for a puzzling effect in research on hindsight bias, namely the observation that hindsight bias is larger for assertions where the feedback is "true" than for assertions where the feedback is "false" (Hertwig et al., 1997). That model explained this finding as a result of the co-occurrence of hindsight bias and the reiteration effect, that is, the phenomenon that mere repetition of an assertion increases confidence in its correctness. However, that model does not explain why there is hindsight bias in the first place. The present model does. Although it is not the only account of hindsight bias where a hindsight judgment is seen as a "reconstruction of the prior judgment by 're-judging' the outcome" (Hawkins & Hastie, 1990, p. 321), it seems fair to say that ours is the only account that has specified a process model for knowledge-based inferences. It allows us to explain, at the level of individual responses from individual participants, why hindsight bias occurred, did not occur, or even was reversed.

Inferring Past Judgments Fast and Frugally

What processes do people go through when they try to reconstruct their original judgment? We suggest that asking this question is the same as asking what processes underlie the original judgment. The theory of *probabilistic mental models* (PMM theory; Gigerenzer et al., 1991) provides one answer. The PMM framework applies to tasks in which a choice must be made between two alternatives according to a quantitative criterion, together with a judgment of confidence that the chosen alternative is correct. (In one such task, participants are asked: "Which city has more inhabitants, Heidelberg or Bonn?" "What is your confidence that the alternative you have chosen is the correct one?") We now extend the PMM framework to a context in which feedback about the correct answer is given, and the mind reconstructs the original response (both the choice and confidence). We call this model RAFT (for Reconstruction After Feedback with Take The Best).

Original Response

A concrete example will help to illustrate the task and the proposed mechanism: A friend of ours from southern California, Patricia, is trying to reduce her consumption of cholesterol. However, she has a sweet tooth and at a restaurant wants to order a dessert, either chocolate fudge cake or pumpkin custard pie. She asks herself which of the two foods has more cholesterol (in order to choose the one having less). Because Patricia does not know the correct answer, she tries to infer it from what she knows about the two foods. We hypothesize that to make this inference she will construct a probabilistic mental model. Such a PMM consists of a reference class, probability cues, knowledge about the objects of the reference class with respect to these cues, and a heuristic for processing this knowledge.

Knowledge About Cues   According to PMM theory, knowledge is conceptualized as a set of cues (e.g., amount of saturated fat), and the values these cues have regarding the alternatives (henceforth, foods). When comparing the cue values of two foods, there are—in the case of a quantitative cue—four possible relations: "larger" (e.g., cake contains more saturated fat than pie), "smaller," "equal," or "unknown." Henceforth, we refer to these relations as *object relations*. (Note that it is sufficient to have an intuition, right or wrong, concerning the object relations; whether these relations are directly retrieved or deduced from absolute cue values is left open.)

PMM theory also assumes that people have intuitions about the predictive power of a cue. The predictive power of a cue can be measured by its ecological validity. Ecological validity is defined as the relative frequency with which the cue correctly predicts which object scores higher on the criterion in a defined reference class (chapter 4). It is determined by considering only those comparisons where the cue discriminates (i.e., the object relation is "larger" or "smaller"). Let us assume that Patricia's reference class consists of foods sampled from her local supermarket, and let us consider saturated fat as a quantitative cue for cholesterol. When we took a random sample of 36 food items from a supermarket and checked all possible pairs, we found that in about 80% of these pairs, the food item with more saturated fat (cue) also has more cholesterol (criterion). This value is the ecological validity of the saturated fat cue (in our supermarket sample).

Heuristic   How can Patricia use this knowledge to infer which food has more cholesterol? We account for her inference with a heuristic in the PMM framework called "Take The Best" (Gigerenzer & Goldstein, 1996a; see also chapter 4). If both foods are known, Take The Best starts with an estimated rank order of cues according to their validities and makes the inference on the basis of the highest ranking ("best") cue that discriminates between the two foods. Suppose that Patricia's PMM consists of three cues, amount of saturated fat, calories, and protein, which are already ordered according to their validities (80%, 70%, and 60%, respectively). Her original mental model about the relations between cake and pie on these cues is depicted in figure 9-1 (in the original response column). The highest ranking cue, saturated fat, does not discriminate; therefore Take The Best will try the next cue, calories. Because the cake has more calories than the pie, the heuristic stops searching and chooses cake as the alternative with more cholesterol. Confidence in the correctness of the decision is the validity of the cue that determined that decision (here, 70% as the validity of the calorie cue).

A defining characteristic of this fast and frugal heuristic is its simple stopping rule: Terminate search when the first good reason is found that speaks for one alternative over the other. No other cues are looked up after this point, and no cost-benefit computations are made in an attempt to determine the "optimal" stopping point for memory search. Such a simple stopping rule is crucial for memory-based inferences where much time and effort could be spent searching for information in the fog of memory. In the study reported below, we taught participants about only three cues (those listed in figure 9-1) and thus have artificially limited the search. In real-world inferences about food, there would typically be many more cues available and search would continue beyond such a small number of cues unless a stopping rule terminated it.

	Hindsight bias at the level of confidence			
	Original response		Recalled response	
	Cake	Pie	Cake	Pie
Saturated fat (80%)	? →		>	
Calories (70%)	>		>	
Protein (60%)	>		>	
Choice	*Cake*		*Cake*	
Confidence	*70%*		*80%*	

Figure 9-1: Hindsight bias at the level of confidence. The probabilistic mental model contains three cues ranked according to their validity (specified in parentheses). The symbols ">" and "?" denote the relations between objects on these cues. For instance, in the left column, which describes the knowledge underlying the original response, the object relation on the saturated fat cue is unknown. As indicated by the arrow ("→"), this object relation changes after feedback that cake has more cholesterol than pie. The relation shifts toward feedback, that is, from "?" to ">" in the updated mental model (right column). As a consequence, hindsight bias occurs. Note that Take The Best stops cue search before reaching the shaded object relations.

Feedback and Reconstruction

Some weeks after having dinner at the restaurant, Patricia goes to the market and finds out that chocolate fudge cake has more cholesterol than pumpkin custard pie. She tries to remember her past choice. What is the mechanism of recalling the original response? Figure 9-2 illustrates the cognitive processes as assumed by the RAFT model. First, an attempt is made to retrieve the original response directly from memory. The chance of doing this successfully depends on factors such as time delay between original judgment and recollection (Fischhoff & Beyth, 1975; Hertwig, 1996), and depth of encoding of the original response (Hell et al., 1988). If the original response is directly (and veridically) recalled from memory, no hindsight bias is obtained (upper left box in figure 9-2).

If the original response cannot be retrieved from memory, an attempt is made to reconstruct the original PMM that led to this response. An identical reconstruction will be obtained if (a) the type of strategy (e.g., lexicographic strategy, linear model, neural net, or Bayesian net) is the

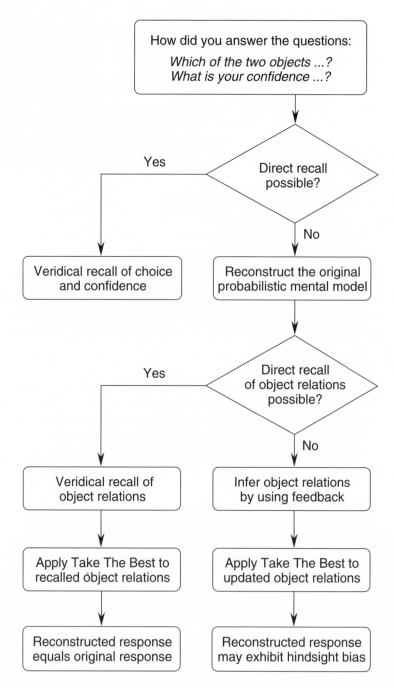

Figure 9-2: Flowchart of the RAFT model for hindsight bias.

same for the original response and its reconstruction; (b) this strategy operates with the same parameters (e.g., the same cue order, weights, or
probabilities); (c) the strategy uses the same cues; and (d) the values that
are retrieved on these cues are the same. A violation of any of these requirements may lead to differences between the original and the reconstructed response. In fact, RAFT posits a violation of requirement (d), that
is, a systematic difference between the cue values underlying the original
response and the reconstructed response. RAFT does not exclude the possibility that requirements (a), (b), and (c) may also be violated, and there
are indeed such accounts of hindsight bias (e.g., Hawkins & Hastie, 1990).
Nevertheless, we argue and provide evidence that the violation of requirement (d) is sufficient to account for hindsight bias.

Knowledge Updating   Why should there be a change in object relations
on the cues after feedback? Usually there is more than one cue that can
be used to infer a criterion. Thus, if information on one cue is not available, this cue can be replaced by another. Egon Brunswik (1952) called
this "vicarious functioning." Further, it is not only cues that are inter-
changeable, but also a cue and the criterion: For many cases, the possibility of drawing inferences from a cue to a criterion can also be reversed.
For instance, not only can the amount of saturated fat be used to infer the
amount of cholesterol, but the reverse is also true. Suppose you know
neither how much saturated fat nor how much cholesterol is in chocolate
fudge cake. If you now learn that cake has a lot of saturated fat, you can
use this as a cue to infer that it also has a lot of cholesterol. Similarly, if
you are told that cake has a lot of cholesterol, you can use this as a cue to
infer a high saturated fat value. Thus, new information about the criterion
can be used to update related knowledge in semantic memory—similarly
to the updating of outdated information in episodic memory (as in Mr.
Loman's car-parking case, see also Bjork, 1978). Updating is adaptive: It
increases the coherence of our knowledge and the accuracy of our inferences (since more recent information is typically more valid and more
relevant).

  Thus, our conjecture is that knowledge stored in memory is in a state
of flux, constantly changing, in part because new information is acquired,
and in part because knowledge related to this new information is updated.
Next, we show how such changes in knowledge over time lead us to predict and account for hindsight bias (as depicted in the branch at the bottom right of figure 9-2).

Predictions

The fact that the same variable may serve as either a criterion or a cue
offers an interesting perspective. In the restaurant, Patricia worried about
cholesterol, and her original mental model contained saturated fat as a
cue (to infer cholesterol). In an attempt to reconstruct her original mental

model, saturated fat—or more precisely, the knowledge she had about saturated fat when she was in the restaurant—becomes the criterion. In some cases veridical retrieval of this past cue and current criterion may be possible; in others it may not. As a substitute for such a gap in memory, Patricia could use the knowledge she has now. However, in the meantime she found out which of the two foods has more cholesterol, and this new information might have led to an updating of related knowledge, such as saturated fat. As a consequence of this cue-criterion switch, the knowledge in the updated mental model will show systematic shifts toward feedback (Prediction 1). Because RAFT assumes that updating only occurs with some probability, this prediction does not necessarily hold for each single item.

According to RAFT, systematic changes in knowledge about cues can explain systematic changes in recollection of choice and confidence. That is, the occurrence of hindsight bias is contingent on the reconstructed knowledge. After excluding cases where original and recalled responses are identical (and thus can be attributed to direct memory), RAFT should be able to account for individual recollections: Regardless of whether hindsight bias or reversed hindsight bias is observed, this observation should match RAFT's prediction, which is derived from the recalled object relations for this item (Prediction 2).

Illustrations of the RAFT Model

We now illustrate how RAFT accounts for recollections made with hindsight. When Patricia tried to infer at the restaurant which of the two foods has more cholesterol, she did not know the value on the saturated fat cue (i.e., the most valid cue, see figure 9-1). After she found out that cake has more cholesterol than pie, this value was updated. The consequence is that in hindsight, when Patricia tries to remember her *original* judgment, the saturated fat cue—which was not available to her at the restaurant—discriminates, and Patricia infers that she thought that cake is the one with more cholesterol. She also infers that her confidence in this choice was 80% (the cue validity of saturated fat). Thus, her reconstructed choice is identical to her original choice. Her reconstructed confidence, however, increased relative to her original confidence. This is an example of hindsight bias. More generally, hindsight bias at the level of confidence occurs if a choice is correctly recalled, but recalled confidence increases after feedback indicating the originally selected alternative was correct (or decreases after feedback that it was wrong).

Not only can recalled *confidence* differ from original confidence, but recalled *choice* can differ from original choice as well. Hindsight bias at the level of choice occurs when feedback indicates that the originally chosen alternative was wrong and the recalled choice is the correct alternative (e.g., original choice is pie, feedback is cake, and recalled choice is cake). RAFT can account for hindsight bias at the level of choice as well.

Figure 9-3 (panel A) provides an example: At the restaurant, only the protein cue discriminated, pointing to the pie. After feedback, however, the saturated fat cue discriminates, pointing to the cake. If the original choice is reconstructed from this updated knowlegde, RAFT predicts hindsight bias at the level of choice.

It is also conceivable for hindsight bias to be reversed. Reversed hindsight bias at the level of choice occurs when the original choice is correct according to feedback, but recalled choice is wrong. Reversed hindsight bias at the level of confidence occurs if recalled choice equals original choice, but recalled confidence decreases after feedback confirming—or increases after feedback does not confirm—the originally selected alternative. How does RAFT account for reversed hindsight bias? It does so by allowing for random shifts in the object relations. That is, beyond systematic shifts due to feedback, RAFT posits unsystematic shifts due to the imperfect reliability of one's knowledge. Such random shifts are assumed to be independent of feedback. For this reason they may either coincide with the direction of feedback, or be counter to it. In figure 9-3 (panel B), a random shift changed the object relation on the saturated fat cue counter to the direction of the feedback. This random shift leads to reversed hindsight bias at the level of confidence.

To summarize, our starting point was the observation that human memory is bounded in its capacity. An alternative to unbounded memory is a system that maintains access to the information that is most likely to be needed and most likely to be correct. For such a memory system, it is

| | Panel A: Hindsight bias at the level of choice | | | | Panel B: Reversed hindsight bias at the level of confidence | | | |
| | Original response | | Recalled response | | Original response | | Recalled response | |
	Cake	Pie	Cake	Pie	Cake	Pie	Cake	Pie
Saturated fat (80%)	?	→	>		>	→	?	
Calories (70%)	?		?		>		>	
Protein (60%)	<	→	?		>		>	
Choice	Pie		Cake		Cake		Cake	
Confidence	60%		80%		80%		70%	

Figure 9-3: Hindsight bias at the level of choice (panel A), and reversed hindsight bias at the level of confidence (panel B). For an explanation of the symbols, see figure 9-1.

crucial to update information constantly and automatically. We suggest that hindsight bias is a by-product of this adaptive updating. Assuming a fast and frugal heuristic for reconstructing past judgments based on updated knowledge, RAFT explains this so-called bias.

Empirical Evidence

We conducted a study that was designed to test Predictions 1 and 2 (see Hoffrage et al., 1999). The experiment started with a phase in which participants learned the values of the saturated fat, calorie, and protein cues for various food items. They were also taught the validities of these cues (80%, 70%, and 60%) for inferring which of the food items has the higher amount of cholesterol. Immediately after this learning phase, the participants were given a list of food pairs and asked two questions about each pair: "Which food do you think has more cholesterol?" and "How confident are you that your choice is correct?" (The confidence rating scale ranged from 50% to 100%.) After they had given their responses, we asked them to recall the amounts of saturated fat, calories, and protein they had learned for each food item or to indicate for each food pair the relation between the food items on each cue (this is their knowledge before feedback).

In the second session, participants in the experiment first received the correct answer (feedback) for each of the questions they had answered in the first session. In the control condition, no feedback was provided. Then all participants were asked to recall (a) which food they had originally chosen as having more cholesterol, (b) how confident they were that their choice was correct, and—in a new questionnaire—(c) the originally learned cue values or the foods' relations on the cues (this is their knowledge after feedback). Recording participants' knowledge was important here because, according to RAFT, the occurrence of hindsight bias depends on this knowledge.

We first investigated whether participants showed any hindsight bias. For correct choices, hindsight bias occurred if recalled confidence increased, and for wrong choices hindsight bias occurred if recalled confidence decreased. In order to be able to include confidence judgments for correct and wrong choices in a single analysis, we mapped original and recalled confidences for wrong choices on a full-range scale. For example, a confidence judgment of 70% that the wrong alternative was the correct one was coded as 30% (confidence in the correct alternative). On this full-range scale, hindsight bias would always appear as an increase in confidence. Confidence increased in the feedback condition by an average of 3.4 percentage points, whereas in the no-feedback condition, it decreased by 0.6 percentage points. The effect of the difference is of medium size ($d = 0.54$, Cohen, 1988, p. 20) and is larger than the average effect size reported in Christensen-Szalanski and Fobian Willham's (1991) meta-analysis.

Did relations on cues shift systematically after feedback (Prediction 1)? Shifts can occur toward or away from feedback. A shift toward feedback occurred when the cue originally pointed to the wrong alternative and now points to the correct alternative, or does not discriminate anymore. A shift toward feedback also occurred when the cue originally did not discriminate but now points to the correct alternative. The same logic defines shifts away from feedback. A cue does not discriminate if a participant did not specify the object relation on this cue (or the values for the two objects). In the feedback condition, 66.0% of the relations remained unchanged after feedback (across all participants, items, and cues). Did the remaining relations shift systematically toward feedback? Figure 9-4 shows the percentages of shifts toward and away from feedback. Consistent with Prediction 1, in the feedback condition, shifts toward feedback outnumbered those away from it, whereas in the no-feedback condition, both kinds of shifts occurred equally often.

Can we specify more precisely when shifts toward feedback occur? We suggest that updating after feedback should occur most likely when a cue did not discriminate at the time of the original response. To illustrate this rationale, let us first consider those cues that discriminated. The fact that a cue discriminated implies that knowledge was available in the original

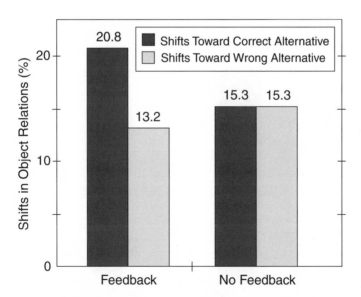

Figure 9-4: Proportion of object relations shifting toward and away from feedback. Shifts toward the correct or wrong alternative are equivalent to shifts toward or away from feedback, respectively, when feedback is given.

mental model. The mere existence of knowledge provides the chance that it can be accessed again at some later point and that the object relation is veridically retrieved—even after feedback. In contrast, if the relation was unknown, then feedback does not need to overcome preexisting knowledge to become manifest. A similar implication holds for "equal" relations. Here, a shift in one cue value is sufficient to change the relation. For a discriminating relation, a shift may reduce the difference between the two values but not necessarily cause a change in the relation.

Is updating after feedback most likely when a cue did not discriminate at the time of the original response? To answer this question, we calculated the differences in the proportions of shifts toward and away from feedback (across all participants, items, and cues). Figure 9-5 displays the results. In 38.7% of the cases in which cues originally did not discriminate, cues disciminate after feedback: in 27.7% of the cases, they point to the correct alternative, and in 11.0% to the wrong alternative. This difference of 16.7 percentage points is depicted by the leftmost bar in figure 9-5. In contrast, when cues originally discriminated, shifts were almost symmetrical—the difference between shifts toward and away from feedback decreased to 2.8 percentage points. In the no-feedback condition, the difference between shifts was miniscule for both discriminating and nondiscriminating cues. These results strongly confirm the prediction that the impact of feedback is most pronounced when a cue did not discriminate at the time of the original response.

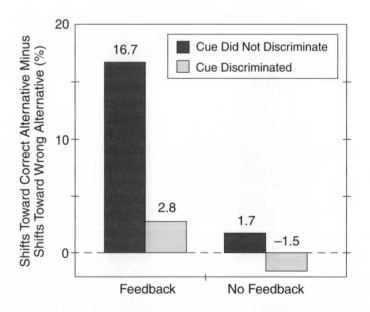

Figure 9-5: Proportion of object relations shifting toward the correct alternative minus those shifting toward the wrong alternative, depending on whether a cue discriminated when the original response was given.

Can hindsight bias and reversed hindsight bias be predicted from re-called object relations (Prediction 2)? To test this prediction, we first ex-cluded cases where original and recalled response are identical, because they can be attributed to accurate memory (and are thus not subject to reconstruction). Next, we determined RAFT's prediction for each partici-pant as follows. For each food pair, we applied Take The Best to the up-dated knowledge and compared the resulting choices and confidences with the original choices and confidences. This comparison determined whether RAFT would predict hindsight bias, reversed hindsight bias, or no hindsight bias (predicted outcome). The predicted outcome was then compared with observed outcomes (hindsight bias or reversed hindsight bias), and for each participant, we finally determined the percentage of correct predictions across items.

Averaged across all participants, the percentage of correct predictions was 76.3%. RAFT correctly explains nearly as many of the observed out-comes in the feedback and the no-feedback conditions: 76.6% and 75.9%, respectively. This is not surprising as RAFT can also account for recon-structed judgments based on cue values that were *not* updated (e.g., be-cause *no* feedback was provided). To see how good the performance of RAFT is we compared it with a chance model (for details, see Hoffrage et al., 1999). Averaged across all participants in the feedback and the no-feedback conditions the performance of this chance model was 67.9% (i.e., 8.4 percentage points worse than RAFT's performance; $t = 5.0$, $p = .001$).

Looking Back

We proposed a model of the cognitive processes underlying hindsight bias. This model assumes that information about the correct answer leads to an updating of elusive cue values. If the original response is inaccessi-ble, it will be reconstructed based on cue values that may have been up-dated. As a consequence, the reconstructed response may exhibit hind-sight bias. Consistent with Prediction 1, we found that feedback on the criterion systematically influenced participants' recollection of their knowledge about cues. Consistent with Prediction 2, a majority of the cases in which either hindsight bias or reversed hindsight bias occurred was accurately predicted by applying Take The Best to the recalled (and updated) cue values. In Hoffrage et al. (1998), we report a further study that replicated the present results, report evidence for a third prediction (that assisting the recall of cue values reduces hindsight bias), and discuss how RAFT explains other findings obtained in research on hindsight bias.

Fast and Frugal Inferences

The model of hindsight bias we have proposed integrates ideas from Sir Frederic Bartlett, Egon Brunswik, and Herbert Simon. Like Bartlett, we see remembering as a process of reconstruction. Bartlett himself did not go on to specify how this reconstruction can be modeled. In our view, consistent with Brunswik's (1952, 1957) framework, reconstruction is based on uncertain cues. However, in contrast to the neo-Brunswikian idea that cues are weighted and integrated by multiple regression (Cooksey, 1996; Doherty, 1996; Hammond, 1955), our assumption is that the nature of the inferential mechanism is fast and frugal. Take The Best is such a fast and frugal mechanism. Because it has a stopping rule, it does not seek all the available information, and it is computationally simple compared with multiple regression. Thus, RAFT's inferential mechanism is a bounded rational one (Simon, 1982; chapter 1).

As many of the results reported in this book suggest, Take The Best can compete impressively with more complex strategies. Because of its psychological plausibility, we chose to model people's recollections with this simple heuristic. Would we have achieved a better fit of the predicted and actual responses if we had used computationally more powerful but psychologically less plausible strategies? To answer this question, we reanalyzed the data and tested Prediction 2 with several other strategies, including a unit-weight linear model (Dawes's rule, chapter 4), a linear model with cue validities as the weights (Franklin's rule, chapter 4), and naive Bayes (chapter 8). None of the alternative strategies modeled actual responses better than Take The Best; they all performed similarly well. One reason for this is that the strategies' responses were generated from only three cues, and thus for most constellations of cue values they made the same inference (see chapters 6 and 7). As it is psychologically more plausible, and in light of the evidence that people's choices can best be modeled by heuristics that only process some of the available information (chapter 7), we suggest Take The Best as the more likely candidate strategy of people's memory inferences.

Conclusion

The adaptive process of knowledge updating relieves us of the need to store everything we have thought, said, or experienced in the past. Updating makes us smart by preventing us from using information that may be outdated due to changes in the environment. As Bartlett put it: "In a world of constantly changing environment, literal recall is extraordinarily unimportant" (1932/1995, p. 204). Adaptive updating has an uninvited byproduct: hindsight bias. But this by-product may be a relatively low price to pay for a memory that works fast and frugally.

10

Quick Estimation

Letting the Environment Do the Work

Ralph Hertwig
Ulrich Hoffrage
Laura Martignon

> We may look into that window [on the mind] as through a glass darkly, but what we are beginning to discern there looks very much like a reflection of the world.
>
> *Roger N. Shepard*

"*September 30, 1659*. I, poor, miserable Robinson Crusoe, being shipwrecked, during a dreadful storm in the offing, came on shore on this dismal unfortunate island, which I called 'the Island of Despair,' all the rest of the ship's company being drowned, and myself almost dead" (Defoe, 1719/1980, p. 74). Thus begins *Robinson Crusoe*. Daniel Defoe's classic novel has been interpreted as everything from a saga about human conquest over nature to an allegory about capitalism. At a much more mundane level, however, Crusoe's adventures illustrate the crucial importance of being able to estimate the frequency of recurrent natural events accurately. Of his first attempt to sow grain, he wrote in his journal: "Not one grain of that I sowed this time came to anything; for the dry months following, the earth having had no rain after the seed was sown" (p. 106). From then on, Crusoe kept track of the rainy and dry days in each month, and subsequently sowed seed only when rainfall was highest. He reaped the rewards of this strategy, later reporting: "I was made master of my business, and knew exactly when the proper season was to sow; and that I might expect two seed times, and two harvests, every year" (p. 107).[1]

---

1. Crusoe's story may not be completely fictitious. Before the publication of *Robinson Crusoe*, Defoe might have read about Alexander Selkirk, a sailor who survived five years on a desert island—Juan Fernandez Island off the coast of

Defoe equipped the fictional Crusoe with a journal, which helped him to predict rainfall. Are real humans equipped to estimate environmental quantities even without the benefit of written records? One domain where we would expect to find evidence of such an ability—if it exists—is in foraging for food. Humans have spent most of their evolutionary history in hunter-gatherer foraging economies in which they have had to decide what to hunt. The Inujjuamiut, a group of Eskimos who live in Canada, afford us an opportunity to observe how contemporary human hunter-gatherers select strategies for obtaining food (Smith, 1991). One of the In-ujjuamiuts' food sources is the beluga whale. When hunting belugas, the Inujjuamiut encircle a group of them and drive them into shallow water. Exploiting the whales' sensitivity to noise, the hunters then "herd" them by pounding on the gunwales of their canoes and shooting in a semicircle around them. While the whales are being killed with high-powered rifles and secured with floats, the pursuit of the next group of belugas gets underway.

Inujjuamiut foraging strategies—their strategies for choosing prey and hunting methods—can be modeled by the *contingency prey model*. According to the anthropologist Eric Alden Smith (1991, p. 237), this model is the best tool yet devised for explaining hunter-gatherer prey choice. It suggests why the Inujjuamiut undertake time-consuming and dangerous whale hunts rather than pursuing easier prey, such as ducks, geese, and seals. Its basic intuition, shared by other foraging models, is that a forager who has encountered a food item (prey or patch) will only attempt to capture it if the return per unit time for doing so is greater than the return that could be obtained by continuing to search for another item. Hence prey choice depends on rankings of food items in terms of return rates (see chapter 15). Setting aside the details of this model (see Smith, 1991), one of its crucial assumptions is that to be ranked according to their net return, food items (from prey) must be classified according to their statistically distinct *return rates* (per-unit handling time, i.e., time spent in pursuit, capture, and processing) and *encounter rates* (per-unit search time). Thus, just as Defoe equipped Crusoe with journal entries from which to estimate rainfall, the contingency prey model endows humans with the cognitive abilities necessary to estimate environmental quantities (e.g., the rate at which they encounter a certain type of prey).

But literary devices and theoretical assumptions aside, the question remains: Do humans actually have this ability, and how can it be modeled? According to Brown and Siegler (1993), psychological research on real-world quantitative estimation "has not culminated in any theory of esti-

---

Chile. Selkirk was left there at his own request after quarreling with his captain. When it was published, Selkirk's story was a sensation. The public was fascinated by the way this man had survived—as was Defoe, who may even have met him, as some scholars believe (see Swados's Afterword in Defoe, 1719/1980).

mation, not even in a coherent framework for thinking about the process. This gap is reflected in the strangely bifurcated nature of research in the area. Research on heuristics does not indicate when, if ever, estimation is also influenced by domain-specific knowledge; research on domain-specific knowledge does not indicate when, if ever, estimation is also influenced by heuristics" (p. 511). In this chapter, we attempt to bridge this gap by designing a heuristic adapted to make fast and frugal estimates in environments with a particular statistical structure. Before describing this heuristic, we review previous research on quantitative estimation, focusing on how people estimate numbers of events (both types and tokens); the events in question may be objects, people, or episodes.[2] We review two classes of estimation mechanisms: estimation by direct retrieval and estimation by inference.

Estimation by Direct Retrieval

The Scottish Enlightenment philosopher David Hume believed that the mind unconsciously and automatically tallies event frequencies and apportions degrees of belief in events accordingly. Hume (1739/1975) claimed that the psychological mechanism for converting observed frequency into belief was extremely finely tuned: "When the chances or experiments on one side amount to ten thousand, and on the other to ten thousand and one, the judgment gives the preference to the latter, upon account of that superiority" (p. 141).

Recent research on human monitoring of event frequencies (Hasher & Zacks, 1979, 1984) supports Hume's position by suggesting that memory is extremely sensitive to frequency of occurrence information (Hasher & Zacks, 1984, p. 1379), although not as finely tuned as Hume suggested. People's sensitivity to natural frequency of occurrence has been demonstrated using a variety of stimuli. For instance, several authors have documented that people's judgments of the frequency with which letters and words occur generally show a remarkable sensitivity to their actual frequencies (e.g., Attneave, 1953; Hock et al., 1986; Johnson et al., 1989).[3]

Hasher and Zacks (1979, 1984) assumed that people automatically encode the occurrences of an event, store a fine-grained count of its frequency, and when required to estimate its frequency, access this count. They proposed that people can estimate frequencies accurately because

2. This chapter does not review research on estimation of psychophysical stimuli (e.g., Haubensack, 1992; Mellers & Birnbaum, 1982; Parducci, 1965), probabilities (e.g., Kahneman et al., 1982; Peterson & Beach, 1967), or statistical parameters, such as central tendency, variability, and correlation (e.g., Busemeyer, 1990).

3. For instance, Attneave (1953) asked participants to judge the relative frequencies of all the letters in the alphabet and found a correlation of .79 between actual relative frequencies and the medians of the judged frequencies.

registering event occurrences is a fairly automatic process, that is, it requires little to no attentional capacity. In this view, frequency is one of the few attributes of stimuli that seems to be encoded automatically (others being spatial location, temporal information, and word meaning). Although the claim that event frequencies are automatically encoded may be too strong and has been seriously criticized (see Barsalou, 1992, chap. 4), there seems to be broad agreement with the conclusion that Jonides and Jones (1992) summarized as follows: "Ask about the relative numbers of many kinds of events, and you are likely to get answers that reflect the actual relative frequencies of the events with great fidelity" (p. 368). A similar conclusion has also been drawn in research on probability learning, about which Estes (1976) remarked: "The subjects clearly are extremely efficient at acquiring information concerning relative frequencies of events" (p. 51).

Estimation by Inference

Where Hasher and Zacks assume that people have access to a count of the event, the advocates of a rival approach contend that people infer this value from cues correlated with it. The researchers who advocate this approach may be divided into two groups according to their postulate of the nature of these cues: ecological versus subjective.

Inference by Ecological Cues

According to Brunswik (1952, 1955), the perceptual system estimates a distal variable (e.g., distance) by using proximal cues that are probabilistically related to it (e.g., perceived size of an object, converging lines). For the system to respond successfully, Brunswik argued that cues should be utilized according to their ecological validity (see discussion in Hammond, 1966, p. 33), and that this concept is best measured by correlational statistics. Thus, ecological validity was defined as the correlation between a proximal cue and a distal criterion (Brunswik, 1952).

Unlike Hasher and Zacks's theory, Brunswikian theories of human judgment (e.g., Gigerenzer et al., 1991; Hammond et al., 1975) assume that the criterion—for instance, the frequency of sunny days in Rome in May—will typically *not* be directly retrieved from memory. Instead, it will be inferred based on proximal cues—for instance, the fact that Rome is located in southern Europe. Nevertheless, the Brunswikian research shares an interesting link with that of Hasher and Zacks (1984): While the latter assumes and provides evidence that people store accurate records of event frequencies, the former assumes and provides evidence that people keep fairly accurate records of ecological cue validities (e.g., Arkes & Hammond, 1986; Brehmer & Joyce, 1988). Learning cue validities, however, requires the ability to register event frequencies and their co-occurrences accurately, except when knowledge of the validities is evolutionarily built in (e.g., in depth perception).

Inference by Subjective Cues: Availability

In a classic study by Tversky and Kahneman (1973), people had to judge whether each of five consonants (K, L, N, R, V) appears more frequently in the first or the third position in English words. Although all five consonants are more frequent in the third position, two-thirds of the participants judged the first position to be more likely for a majority of the letters.[4]

Tversky and Kahneman (1973) proposed the *availability heuristic* as a mechanism of real-world quantitative estimation that can account for systematic biases in people's estimates. According to the availability explanation, assessments of frequency (or probability) are based on the number of instances of the event that "could be brought to mind" (p. 207). That is, its basic assumptions are that people draw a sample of the event in question (e.g., by retrieving words that have the letter "R" in the first and third position, respectively) or assess the ease with which such a sample could be drawn, and then use the sample statistics to estimate the criterion. However, sample parameters may systematically deviate from population parameters (e.g., if it is easier to retrieve words with a certain letter in the first than in the third position, the sample will not be representative of the population). In this way, use of the availability cue may lead to systematic biases. Because the ability of a sample to predict the criterion can only be evaluated with respect to the sample drawn by a specific person, the availability cue is subjective rather than ecological.

Since Tversky and Kahneman (1973) proposed availability and other heuristics as important mechanisms underlying judgments of (relative) frequency and probability, their findings and the proposed heuristics have stimulated a tremendous amount of research and have raised serious concerns about people's ability to estimate event frequencies and probabilities accurately. At this point, the operation of availability is "one of the

4. In discussing Tversky and Kahneman's study, Lopes and Oden (1991) observed that 12 of the 20 English consonants are more frequent in the first position than in the third position, possibly explaining their results. In contrast, if one assumes that people have experienced a representative sample of letters and their positional frequencies (e.g., during reading), then their mental models should be well adapted to a representative sample presented by the experimenter. Sedlmeier et al. (1998) gave participants a representative sample of consonants (i.e., some that are more and some that are less frequent in the second position) and vowels. In each of three studies, they found that the estimated relative frequencies in the first versus the second position closely agreed with the actual rank ordering, except for an overestimation of low and underestimation of high values. Neither of the two versions of the availability heuristic that Sedlmeier et al. tested was able to account for these results.

most widely shared assumptions in decision making as well as in social judgment research" (Schwartz et al., 1991, p. 195). For example, it has been suggested that availability may account for people's tendency to exaggerate the frequency of some specific causes of death such as tornadoes (Lichtenstein et al., 1978) and for their performance in estimating demographic parameters such as countries' population size (Brown & Siegler, 1992, 1993).

Paradoxical Assumptions and Contradictory Findings

Here is the puzzle. Hasher and Zacks (1984) argued that people encode occurrences of an event, store a count of its frequency, and when required to estimate its frequency, access this count. Tversky and Kahneman (1973), in contrast, seemed to assume that people do not keep a record of event frequencies but construct a sample of the event in question and then infer event frequencies from the ease with which the sample could be constructed. Hasher and Zacks (1984) concluded that their experiments "reliably and unequivocally [sic] demonstrate remarkable knowledge of the frequency of occurrence of all events so far tested" (p. 1373), whereas Tversky and Kahneman (1973) took their results as evidence that the use of the availability heuristic leads to "systematic biases" (p. 209).

These contradictory assumptions and findings have been reported side by side in scientific journals and textbooks, without much discussion about how each line of research qualifies the other's findings (for exceptions, see Ayton & Wright, 1994; Holyoak & Spellman, 1993; Williams & Durso, 1986).[5] Suppose one tried to resolve the conflict by assuming that the two accounts—accurate judgments based on memorized experienced frequencies and (in)accurate judgments based on subjective cues—apply to different situations: The former holds whenever humans have experienced and encoded events one by one before making judgments, and the latter holds whenever humans have not directly experienced the criterion and thus have to rely on (subjective) cues correlated with it to derive a judgment.

This resolution, however, cannot work. Tversky and Kahneman's experiments also included situations where participants actually experienced the events sequentially. In one study, for instance, participants were serially presented with names of well-known personalities of both sexes (e.g., Elizabeth Taylor), and one group was then asked to judge whether the list contained more names of men or women (Tversky & Kahneman, 1973). Another example is their classic study of positional letter frequen-

---

5. One reason why this conflict did not attract more attention may be that Hasher and Zacks (1984) seem to have downplayed it. In a footnote they wrote: "The conflict between our view and that of Tversky and Kahneman is more apparent than real" (p. 1383; see their arguments in their footnote 9).

cies, mentioned above, in which they asked participants to judge events they had previously experienced sequentially. Both studies illustrate that availability is also intended to apply to experienced events.

In our view, the conflicting findings about the accuracy of people's frequency judgments and the conflicting claims about the underlying mechanisms cannot be reconciled simply by running more experiments in which people's estimates are observed to be either correct or incorrect. Contexts that elicit both biased and unbiased estimates can no doubt be found. The more interesting issue is how we can make theoretical progress in modeling the cognitive processes underlying quantitative estimation. Toward this goal, we pose two interrelated questions that are pertinent to both Hasher and Zacks's and Tversky and Kahneman's approaches. First, what do humans need to count in order to meet their adaptive goals? Second, what is the structure of the environments in which quantification occurs, and what heuristics can exploit that structure?

What Needs Counting?

The world can be carved up into an infinite number of discrete events or objects. Which of them deserve monitoring? Hasher and Zacks (1984, p. 1373) did not explicitly address this question, but proposed that for the frequency of a stimulus to be encoded and stored, it must at a minimum be "attended" to. The notion of "attention" was not precisely explicated.[6] How plausible is such a domain-general encoding mechanism, that is, a mechanism constrained only insofar that it requires attention (or "conscious" attention, as later proposed by Zacks et al., 1986)?

Consider, for instance, the processing that might occur when we walk down the street engaged in an engrossing conversation. We are generally successful at avoiding collisions with objects and other people, thus indicating that we take note of their locations. But later, would we be able to judge the relative frequency of their locations in relation to us (e.g., how many objects to the right and how many to the left of us), or the relative frequency of men and women who were wearing hats? Why should we be able to make such judgments retrospectively if we did not consider them useful at the time? More generally, do we encode every event and keep track of its frequency of occurrence, just because we have experienced it?

This is a question that neither the British empiricists nor Hasher and Zacks (1984) seriously addressed. For instance, David Hartley (1749) suggested a domain-general physiological mechanism of frequency counting

---

6. However, we can exclude one possible definition: intentional monitoring. Hasher and Zacks (1984) argued that a stimulus can be automatically encoded even if it is not intentionally monitored, which implies that intentional monitoring was not part of their definition of attention.

designed in analogy to Newton's theory of vibrations (Daston, 1988, p. 203). According to this mechanism, repeated occurrences of an object create cerebral vibrations until "grooves of mental habit" are etched into the brain. Hartley's is a content-general mechanism, insofar as it does not put any constraints on the type of objects to be counted. One can also find modern "cognitive" relatives of Hartley's physiological mechanism that are similarly unconstrained. Take, for instance, MINERVA 2 (e.g., Hintzman, 1984, 1988), which has been used to model frequency judgments. This model keeps copies (in terms of memory traces) of all events we have experienced over a lifetime (although one may bring content-specific considerations in through the back door by way of learning parameters, as Hintzman, 1988, does).

Should we be able to judge the relative frequency of men and women wearing hats? Marcia Johnson and her colleagues (Johnson et al., 1989) suggested that this is unlikely. On the basis of a series of ingenious studies, they demonstrated that, for frequency judgments to reflect presentation frequency accurately, two conditions must be met: The exposure time must be ≥ 2 seconds, and processing must involve directing attention to the identity of objects as well as their spatial location. Although their findings imposed an initial constraint on the mechanism, it remains essentially unconstrained with respect to what is counted.

Brase, Cosmides, and Tooby (1998) have proposed a more stringent constraint. They argued that another way to restrict the counting mechanism is to consider the nature of what is counted; there are aspects of the world that one would not expect a human inference mechanism to count spontaneously. According to their account, individuated whole objects rather than arbitrarily parsed objects (i.e., random chunks, nonfunctional fragments, etc.) are the natural unit of analysis: Toddlers may spontaneously count teddy bears, but not teddy bears' ears (as long as they have not been broken off the parent object).

A variation on Brase et al.'s approach is to consider the adaptive value of what is counted: Keeping track of event frequencies is most likely to occur in domains where knowing frequency counts has a plausible adaptive value for the organism. It is easy to see the value of monitoring the frequencies of specific events in the domains of mating and foraging (e.g., among the Inujjuamiut). But can considerations of adaptive value help us to derive counterintuitive predictions in other domains? We think so. Despite Tversky and Kahneman's (1973) seemingly unsupportive results (in their letter study), there is good reason to predict that people can quantify the statistical structure of language because of its adaptive value.

What Is Adaptive About Knowing the Statistical Structure of Language?

In any specific language certain sound sequences are more likely to occur within some words than in others. For instance, consider the sound sequence "pretty baby": The transition probability from "pre" to "ty" is greater than that from "ty" to "ba." Thus we would be more likely to expect a word break between the latter two syllables. For babies acquiring language, keeping track of these transition probabilities may have an important function, because these probabilities help them to identify boundaries between words (a problem that continues to hamper attempts to build a computer that "understands" spoken language). Recent results reported by Saffran, Aslin, and Newport (1996) indicate that babies are indeed sensitive to such transition probabilities.

To test whether babies have access to this kind of statistical information, Saffran et al. tested infants' ability to distinguish between "words" and "part-words" (using nonsensical stimuli in both cases). The stimulus words included sound sequences such as "bidaku" and "padoti" and a sample of the speech stream is "bidakupadotigolabubidaku. . . . " The babies listened to a two-minute tape of a continuous speech stream consisting of three-syllable words repeated in random order. A synthesized woman's voice spoke the sound stream with no inflection or noticeable pauses between words, removing the word boundary cues contained in normal speech. The only possible cues were the relative frequencies of co-occurrence of syllable pairs, where relatively low relative frequencies signal word boundaries.

After listening to the speech stream, the infants heard four three-syllable test words one at a time. Two words were from the speech stream and two were part-words. The part-words consisted of the final syllable of a word and the first two syllables of another word. Thus, a part-word contained sounds that the infant had heard, but it did not correspond to a word. Infants would be able to recognize part-words as novel only if the words from the original speech stream were so familiar to them that new sequences crossing word boundaries (i.e., the part-words) would sound relatively unfamiliar. In fact, the infants did listen longer to part-words than to words, indicating that they found them more novel than the words.

This example illustrates the importance of asking what information is adaptive to encode, store, and quantify. With this question in mind, one can derive interesting and counterintuitive predictions, for instance, that language learners will learn the statistical structure of language quickly. We now turn to the second important question: What is the structure of the environments in which quantities need to be estimated?

The Importance of "Ecological Texture"

"Although errors of judgments are but a method by which some cognitive processes are studied, the method has become a significant part of the message" (Kahneman & Tversky, 1982, p. 124). This quotation illustrates Kahneman and Tversky's awareness that the heuristics-and-biases program came to focus on humans' cognitive errors at the expense of their cognitive successes. In fact, their initial framing of the availability heuristic stressed an ecological perspective that was later largely abandoned. Of the availability heuristic Tversky and Kahneman (1973) wrote:

> Availability is an ecologically valid clue for the judgment of frequency because, in general, frequent events are easier to recall or imagine than infrequent ones. However, availability is also affected by various factors which are unrelated to actual frequency. If the availability heuristic is applied, then such factors will affect the perceived frequency of classes and the subjective probability of events. Consequently, the use of the availability heuristic leads to systematic biases. (p. 209)

Not only did Tversky and Kahneman (1973) conceptualize availability as an "ecologically valid clue" to frequency, but they also stressed that it exploits the structure of the environment in the sense that objectively frequent events have stronger representations because these are strengthened by event repetitions, and thus, ceteris paribus, are easier to recall than infrequent ones. In light of its beginnings, the availability heuristic could have been developed into a cognitive strategy that reflects the texture of the environment as well as the mind, but was not.

Several decades ago, Egon Brunswik (1957) already emphasized the importance of studying the fit between cognition and the environment: "If there is anything that still ails psychology in general, and the psychology of cognition specifically, it is the neglect of investigation of environmental or ecological texture in favor of that of the texture of organismic structures and processes. Both historically and systematically psychology has forgotten that it is a science of organism-environment relationships, and has become a science of the organism" (p. 6).

In what follows, we propose an estimation heuristic that differs from those identified in the heuristics-and-biases program (e.g., availability) in several ways. First, how it exploits a particular environmental structure is specified. Second, it has a precise stopping rule that terminates memory search. Finally, it is formalized such that we can simulate its behavior. For these reasons, it exhibits bounded rationality. Before we analyze the structure of a specific class of environments in which various quantities have to be estimated, let us consider what adaptive value estimating one such quantity—population size—might have. We speculate that estimation of population demographics may be a descendant of an evolutionarily important task, specifically, estimation of social group size.

Estimation: Using Ecological Cues in a J-Shaped World

Because humans have always lived in groups (e.g., families, clans, tribes), it is very likely that social environments played a major role in shaping the human mind. Until recently, this possibility has largely been overlooked in research on human reasoning and decision making. Wang (1996a, 1996b), however, demonstrated how social cues can affect decision making in surprising ways. Using Tversky and Kahneman's (1981) famous Asian disease problem, he found preference reversals (often considered irrational because they violate the invariance axiom of expected utility theory) when the text indicated that the decision was to be made for a large group. When the text indicated that the decision would affect a smaller group, however, most participants favored the risky outcome in both the loss and the gain framing.

Wang's (1996a) finding suggests that humans are sensitive to group size when making decisions. One may speculate that this sensitivity rests on an evolved ability to estimate group sizes. In fact, the ability to estimate the size of social groups accurately might have been of value in a number of circumstances encountered by our evolutionary ancestors, for instance, when they had to make quick decisions about whether to threaten to fight over resources with other families, clans, or tribes. Humans' social structures have changed since the time when we lived in hunter-gatherer societies. Group size has been directly affected by the shift from nomadic bands to small agricultural and pastoral communities to large populations of many thousands of people whose economic and social center is the city (e.g., Reynolds, 1973). Interestingly, in samples of American and Chinese participants, Wang (1996a) found that decision making is sensitive to culturally specific features of social group structure. Evolutionary considerations aside, we assume that the estimation heuristic proposed here is adapted to modern group sizes. We now consider the statistical structure of the environment in which the heuristic operates.

Let us start to analyze the statistical structure of population demographics by considering the following question. What distribution results if one makes a scatterplot of people's performance on the following task? Name all the characters in Shakespeare's *Comedy of Errors*. If we plotted people's performance on this task (e.g., the number of people who can name no, one, two, three, etc. characters), we would probably find that many people would get a low score, and that only a few people can attain a high score. Thus, contrary to the typical assumption of educational researchers that knowledge, learning, and performance generally conform to a bell-shaped distribution across individuals, in which moderate values are most frequent, human performance is often best characterized by the "empirical law of the higher, the fewer" (Walberg et al., 1984, p. 90), or in other words, by positively skewed, *J-shaped* distributions (where the "J" is rotated clockwise by 90 degrees).[7]

7. These distributions are related to Zipf's law (Zipf, 1949), which is the observation that frequency of occurrence of some event (P) as a function of the rank (i) when the rank is determined by the frequency of occurrence, is a power-law function $P_i \sim 1/i^a$ with the exponent a close to unity. The most famous example of Zipf's law is the frequency of English words. Assume that "the," "to," and "of" are the

Athletic performance can also follow such J-shaped distributions. Take the final distribution of medals in the 1996 Summer Olympics in Atlanta as an example. A total of 197 nations competed for 842 medals in the Atlanta games. Figure 10-1 plots the total number of medals won (gold, silver, and bronze) by each nation, excluding those that won no medals. The average number of medals won was 4.3. At one extreme, the United States, Germany, and Russia won 101, 65, and 63 medals respectively; in other words, 1.5 percent of the participating nations (and 8.5% of the world population) won almost one-third of all medals. At the other extreme, 118 participating nations won no medals at all. Highly positively skewed distributions also characterize many processes and phenomena in biology (e.g., fluctuations in neural spikes plotted by amplitude), geography (e.g., earthquakes plotted by severity), psychology (e.g., distribution of memory traces plotted by the likelihood they are needed; Anderson & Schooler, 1991), and other fields.

Cities plotted by actual population also form J-shaped distributions. In any given region, there are a few large settlements and a large number of small settlements. Herbert Simon (1955b) argued that in the special case of city population size, such a distribution is expected if the population growth is due solely to the net excess of births over deaths, and if this net growth is proportional to the present population size. Urban growth models that use techniques originally developed to model clumping and motion of particles in liquids and gases also predict this city size distribution (Makse et al., 1995). Figure 10-1 also shows the populations of German cities with more than 100,000 inhabitants ranked by their size. This distribution reflects the empirical law of the higher, the fewer in three ways: the largest value (here Berlin) is an extreme outlier; the mean (309,000), which is strongly influenced by such extreme observations, is much higher than the median (180,000); and the standard deviation (428,000) is large relative to the mean.

To what extent is it plausible to assume that people actually know about the J shape of distributions such as that of German cities? We asked 74 German participants to estimate the number of German cities in 25 size categories (100,000–199,999; 200,000–299,999; etc.). Figure 10-2 shows the distribution of their mean frequency judgments in comparison with the actual frequency distribution. (Note that compared with figure 10-1 the axes are reversed.) Although participants underestimated the relative number of cities in the smallest category (100,000–199,999), the results

---

three most frequent words (i.e., receive ranks 1, 2, and 3); then, if the number of occurrences is plotted as the function of the rank, the form is a power-law function with exponent close to 1. There are several variants of Zipf's law, such as Pareto's law, which essentially form J-shaped distributions. More generally, Grüneis et al. (1989) proved that J-shaped distributions belong to a class of distributions that can be modeled in terms of an adjoint Poisson process.

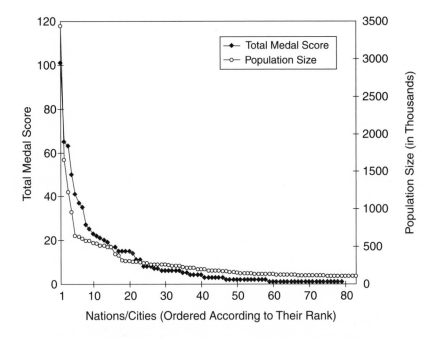

Figure 10-1: Distribution of medals won per nation at the 1996 Summer Olympics in Atlanta, and of the population size of the 83 largest German cities (*Fischer Welt Almanach*, 1993).

indicate that they were well aware of the skewness. Now that we have established that people have an intuition about the higher, the fewer characteristic of the German city size distribution, we turn to the next question: How might a heuristic exploit this J-shaped ecological structure so as to reduce the computational effort needed to make an estimate?

Fast and Frugal Estimation: The QuickEst Heuristic

Let us start by considering a technical problem, namely, sorting pieces of coal according to size. One way to sort them is to use a conveyor belt that carries the coal pieces across increasingly coarse sieves. The belt is designed so that first small pieces fall through the "small" sieve into the crusher below, then medium-sized pieces fall through the "medium" sieve, and so on. Pieces that make it across all the sieves are dumped into a catchall container. Let us assume that the sizes of the coal pieces follow a J-shaped distribution, that is, most pieces are small and only a few pieces are (very) large. The conveyor belt's design minimizes the time required for the sorting process by exploiting this fact, sorting out the large number of small pieces first, then the fewer larger ones, and finally the

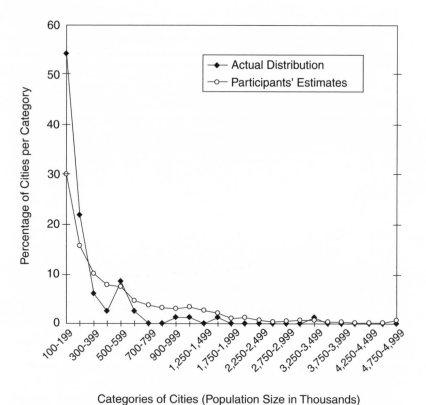

Categories of Cities (Population Size in Thousands)

Figure 10-2: Percentage of German cities in 25 size categories, along with estimates made by participants (percentage values derived from frequency estimates).

very few largest ones. Figure 10-3 illustrates the design features of such a conveyor belt. We now propose an estimation heuristic, the Quick Estimation heuristic (QuickEst), which exploits the J-shaped distribution in a way similar to the conveyor belt for sorting coal.

QuickEst's Design Properties

QuickEst's policy is to use environmental structure to make estimates for the most common objects (e.g., in the cities environment, the smallest cities) as quickly as possible. What design features of the heuristic enable it to implement this policy?

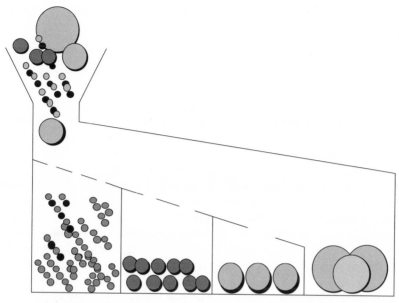

Small Objects   Medium Objects   Large Objects   Catchall Category

Figure 10-3: Illustration of a conveyor belt that sorts pieces of coal according to their size. (Although this is a fictitious example, its design resembles that of actual conveyor belts advertised at the Web sites of various manufacturers.)

How Are the Cues Ranked?   When a person is asked to estimate the population of a city, the fact that it is a state capital may come to mind as a
potential ecological cue. Cities that are state capitals (e.g., Munich, the
capital of the state Bavaria) are likely to have larger populations than
cities that are not state capitals, the major exceptions to this rule being in
the United States. For any binary cue i, one can calculate the average size
of cities that have this feature (s_j^+, e.g., the average size of all the German
cities that are state capitals) and the average size of those cities that do
not have this feature (s_j^-). Note that for the purpose of the simulations, we
calculated s_j^- (s_j^+) from the actual sizes of the German cities that do not (or
do) have the property. The input for this calculation, however, need not
be the actual values, but could instead be imprecise subjective values.

Because positive cue values by definition indicate larger cities, s_j^- is
smaller than s_j^+. For this reason, cues are ranked in the QuickEst heuristic
according to s^-, with the smallest s^- first. This design follows the coal-
sorting analogy, insofar as the cues (sieves) are ranked according to their
coarseness, with the smallest cue first. For this ranking, the heuristic does

not need to know s^- exactly; it only needs to estimate a relative ranking of cues according to s^-.

When Is Search Stopped?   Each cue asks for a property of a city, for instance, "Does the city have a university?" QuickEst has a simple stopping rule: Search is terminated when the first property is found that the city does not have (i.e., the response to the question is "no"). If a city has the property, then search continues, and its value on the cue with the next lowest s^- is retrieved from memory. This stopping rule has a *negative bias*, that is, a negative but not a positive value terminates search. This has an important consequence: As there are only a few cities with mainly positive cue values and many with mostly negative values, a stopping rule with such a negative bias generally enables the heuristic to stop earlier in the search and arrive at estimates quickly.[8]

Owing to its stopping rule, QuickEst's inference is based on the first property a city does not have. In contrast to computationally expensive strategies such as multiple regression, QuickEst does not integrate cue values. An important consequence of QuickEst's stopping rule is that the heuristic is noncompensatory. Further cue values (even if all of them are positive) do not change the estimate based on the first negative cue value encountered. By virtue of its simplicity, noncompensatory decision making avoids dealing with conflicting cues and the need to make trade-offs between cues.

How Coarse Are the Estimates?   The estimate of QuickEst is the s^- of the first property a city does not have, rounded to the nearest *spontaneous number*. According to Albers (1997), spontaneous numbers are multiples of powers of 10 $\{a\,10^i : a \in \{1, 1.5, 2, 3, 5, 7\}\}$, where i is a natural number. For instance, 300, 500, 700, and 1,000 are spontaneous numbers, but 900 is not. By building in spontaneous numbers, the heuristic takes into account two frequently observed properties of people's estimates. First, spontaneous numbers are related to what Albers (1997) described as number "prominence," that is, the phenomenon that in cultures that use the decimal system the powers of 10 "are the most prominent alternatives which have highest priority to be selected as responses, or terms by which given responses should be modified" (Albers, 1997, part I, p. 6). Second, spontaneous numbers relate to the phenomenon that, when asked for quantitative estimates (e.g., the price of a Porsche Carrera), people provide relatively coarse-grained estimates (e.g., $70,000, i.e. 7×10^4 rather than $75,342). This graininess of estimates, or crude levels of "relative exact-

---

8. For instance, in the reference class of all the German cities with more than 100,000 inhabitants and for the following *eight* ecological cues—soccer team, state capital, former East Germany, industrial belt, license plate, intercity train line, exposition site, and university (see chapter 4)—the German cities have on average about *six* (5.7) negative values.

ness" (Albers, 1997, part I, p. 12), reflects people's uncertainty about their judgments (see also Yaniv & Foster, 1995).[9]

The property that s^- is rounded to the nearest spontaneous number has two implications: First, for the numerical estimation the heuristic does not need to estimate s^-. It only needs to estimate which of two neighboring spontaneous numbers is nearer to s^-, and this spontaneous number is then given as the estimate.[10] Second, the heuristic's estimates can only achieve the precision and not exceed the graininess of spontaneous numbers.

How Can the Heuristic Deal With the Few Very Large Cities?   The present stopping rule speeds up estimation by terminating search as soon as a property is found that the city in question does not have. Still, there are a handful of very large "outlier" cities that do have most properties. To avoid an unnecessarily time-consuming search for a possible property they do not have, QuickEst has a "catchall" category in reserve. That is, the heuristic stops adding more cues to its cue order as soon as most cities (out of those the heuristic "knows," i.e., the training set) have been sifted out. For our simulations, we assume that searching cues is stopped as soon as four-fifths of all the cities have already been sifted out by the heuristic. The remaining fifth of the cities are put into a catchall category and automatically assigned an estimate of s_j^+ (where cue j is the cue by which these largest cities were "caught" last) rounded to the nearest spontaneous number.

How Is QuickEst Ecologically Rational?   QuickEst exploits the characteristics of the city population domain in two ways. First, its stopping rule—stop when the first negative cue value is found—limits the search process effectively in an environment in which negative cue values predominate. Second, its rank ordering of cues according to s^-, with the smallest s^- first, gives QuickEst a bias to estimate any given city as relatively small. This is appropriate for objects that fall in J-shaped distributions, in which most

9. Because there are more of them in the range of small digits (1, 1.5, 2, 3) than in the range of large digits (5, 7), spontaneous numbers also seem to be predicated on Benford's law. Benford's law (1938; Raimi, 1976) states that if numerical data (e.g., atomic weights) are classified according to the first significant digit, the nine classes that result usually differ in size. Whereas in a randomly generated data set, each number would be the first significant digit with frequency 1/9, in many real-world data sets, this frequency is approximately equal to $\log_{10}(p+1)/p$. Thus, the digit "1" is first about 30% of the time, "2" somewhat less often, and so on, with "9" occurring as the first digit less than 5% of the time. Consistent with Benford's law, 57% of German cities with more than 100,000 inhabitants begin with "1," whereas only 1.2% begin with "9."

10. Suppose that s^- lies in the interval between the spontaneous numbers 300,000 and 500,000. To decide whether s^- is to be rounded up or down, the heuristic only needs to know whether s^- belongs to the right or to the left of the interval's midpoint (i.e., 400,000). This only requires a choice (i.e., is s^- larger or smaller than 400,000).

objects have small values on the criterion, and only a few objects have (very) large values. In addition to being ecologically rational, QuickEst is psychologically plausible in that it provides estimates with the precision and graininess of spontaneous numbers.

Illustration

An American colleague of ours, Valerie, knows the approximate population size of five German cities from previous trips to Germany (Munich, 1,000,000; Frankfurt, 700,000; Nuremberg, 500,000; Bonn, 300,000; and Heidelberg, 150,000). Valerie also knows the cities' values on three cues (exposition site, state capital, and university). Given her limited knowledge about the reference class, German cities, how accurately could she infer the size of, for instance, Leverkusen? To answer this question, we first describe how QuickEst, as a model for Valerie's inferences, learns its parameters.

Training   QuickEst ranks cues according to the average population size of cities that have negative values (s^-). Given Valerie's knowledge, the cue with the smallest s^- is "exposition site," which provides the estimate 200,000.[11] The next cue is "state capital," which yields the estimate 500,000. Based on these two cues, the heuristic can sift out most of the cities Valerie knows: four out the five (i.e., 80%) have a negative value on at least one of these two cues. Thus, the only city that has positive values on the exposition site and state capital cues, Munich, is put into the catch-all category. The estimate for this category is derived from the last cue in which Munich was "caught," here the state capital cue. The estimated size is 1,000,000 (which simply equals the size of Munich).

In sum, given Valerie's knowledge of German cities, the realization of the QuickEst heuristic includes two of the three cues she knows (exposition site and state capital), and a catchall category. This design allows QuickEst to derive one of three unique estimates for any given city in the reference class: 200,000, 500,000, and 1,000,000 inhabitants. How well does this realization of QuickEst perform when applied to new cities, for instance, Leverkusen and Hamburg?

Estimation   To estimate the size of Leverkusen, QuickEst first retrieves that city's values on the exposition site cue. Because it does not have an exposition site, search is stopped and Leverkusen is estimated to have a population of 200,000, close to the 160,000 inhabitants it actually has. To derive an estimate for Hamburg, QuickEst looks up its value for the expo-

---

11. This figure is calculated as follows: Two of the five cities Valerie knows, Heidelberg and Bonn, do not have an exposition site. That is, s_{expo}^- equals the average size of Heidelberg and Bonn (225,000) rounded to the nearest spontaneous number (200,000).

sition site cue; as the value is positive, it then retrieves the value for the state capital cue, which is also positive. As a result, Hamburg ends up in the catchall category and is estimated to have a population of 1,000,000, which is not very close to the 1,650,000 inhabitants it actually has.

How good—or bad—is this performance, and how frugal is QuickEst in comparison with other heuristics?

Test of Performance: Environment and Competitors

To test QuickEst's performance more generally, we computed its estimates for the real-world environment of German cities with more than 100,000 inhabitants. After its reunification in 1990, Germany had 83 such cities. All of these cities (except Berlin) and their values on eight ecological cues to population size (the same cues as were used in chapter 4, except the national capital cue) were included in the test. (Berlin was excluded because it is an outlier and an error in estimating its population dwarfs errors of proportionally comparable size.) To evaluate the performance of QuickEst, we compared it with two competitors that demand considerably more computation and/or knowledge: multiple regression and an estimation tree (for quantification of the heuristics' complexity, see chapter 8).

Multiple regression is a demanding benchmark insofar as it calculates least-squares minimizing weights that reflect the correlations between cues and criterion, and the covariances between cues. Multiple regression has been proposed as both a descriptive and a prescriptive cognitive model, although its descriptive status is debated, given the complex calculation it assumes (for references on this issue, see chapter 4).

The second benchmark is an estimation tree (for more on tree-based procedures, see Breiman et al., 1993). With the aid of a computationally expensive Bayesian search process (e.g., chapter 8; Chipman et al., 1998), this tree was identified as one with a high probability of good performance.[12] It collapses cities with the same cue profile—that is, the same cue value on each of the eight ecological cues—into a class. The estimated size for each city equals the average size of all cities in that class. (The estimate for a city with a unique cue profile is just its actual size.) As long as the test set and training set are identical, this algorithm is optimal, and is equivalent to the exemplar-based algorithm model proposed by Persson (1996).[13] When the test set and training set are not identical the tree will

---

12. The Bayesian search was limited to the subset of trees that classified each new profile in the interval whose boundaries are defined by the cue profiles of known cities.

13. The optimal solution is to memorize all cue profiles and collapse cities with the same profile into the same size category. In statistics, this optimal solution is known as true regression and approximates the profile memorization method for optimal performance in choice tasks (see chapters 6 and 8).

encounter new cities with possibly new cue profiles. If a new city matches an old cue profile, its estimated size is the average size of those cities (in the training set) with that profile. If a new city has a new cue profile, then this profile is matched to the profile most similar to it. How is this done?

First, the cues are ordered within each profile according to their validity, with the one highest in validity first (for more on cue validity, see chapter 6). Second, the cue profiles are ordered lexicographically such that those with a positive value on the most valid cue are ranked first. Profiles that match on the first cue are then ordered according to their value on the second most valid cue, and so on. New cue profiles are filed with the lexicographically ordered old profiles according to the same logic. As an estimate of the size of a city with a new profile, the estimation tree takes the average size of those cities whose profile is above the new one in the lexicographical order. The estimation tree is an exemplar-based model that keeps track of all exemplars presented during learning as well as their cue values and sizes. Thus, when the training set is large, it requires vast memory resources (for the pros and cons of exemplar-based models, see Nosofsky et al., 1994).

We simulated population estimates, assuming varying degrees of knowledge about this environment. We tested a total of 10 sizes of training sets, in which 10, 20, 30, 40, 50, 60, 70, 80, 90, and 100 percent of the cities (and their respective sizes) were known. In the training phase, the three strategies—QuickEst, multiple regression, estimation tree—learned a model (or parameters) of the data (i.e., cities and their cue values; weights, s_j^+, s_j^-, etc.). To obtain reliable parameters, 1,000 random samples were drawn for each training set. For example, we drew 1,000 samples of 41 cities (50% training set) randomly from the reference class of 82 cities.

In the test phase, we applied the strategies to the complete reference class (i.e., test set, which includes the training set). The strategies' task was to estimate the populations of all the cities (assuming that the cities' values on the cues were known). To make the simulation psychologically more plausible, we assumed that the probability that a city belonged to the training set was proportional to its size. This assumption captures the fact that people are more likely to know about larger cities than smaller ones.

How Frugal Is QuickEst?

QuickEst is designed to make estimates quickly. How many cues must the heuristic consider before search is terminated? Figure 10-4 shows the number of cues that had to be retrieved by each strategy for various sizes of training sets. On average, QuickEst considers 2.3 cues per estimate—a figure that remains relatively stable across training sets. In contrast, multiple regression always uses all eight available cues. The estimation tree uses more and more cues as the size of the training set increases—across

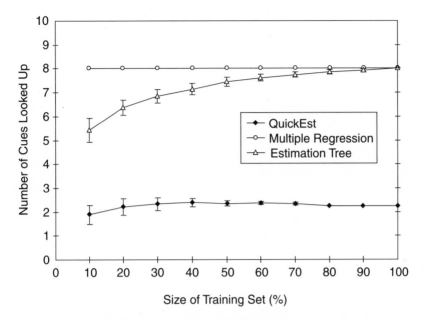

Figure 10-4: Number of cues looked up by QuickEst, multiple regression, and by the estimation tree as a function of size of training set. Vertical lines represent standard deviations.

all training sets, it uses an average of 7.2 cues. Thus, QuickEst bases its estimates on about 29% and 32% of the information used by multiple regression and the estimation tree, respectively.

How Accurate Is QuickEst?

How accurate is QuickEst, which involves simple averaging and rounding, compared with multiple regression, which involves complex calculations? We compared the three strategies' performance using two different measures of accuracy. First, we used the most common measure of estimation accuracy, according to Brown and Siegler (1993), that is, the (mean) absolute error (i.e., absolute deviation between actual and estimated size). Second, for the (82 × 81)/2 city pairs in the complete set of paired comparisons, we simulated choices ("Which of the two cities is larger?") based on the estimates generated, and then calculated the proportion of correct inferences drawn.

Absolute Error

What price does QuickEst pay, in terms of absolute error, for considering only a few cues? Figure 10-5 shows the absolute error as a function of the

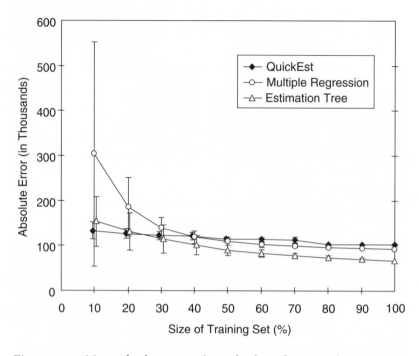

Figure 10-5: Mean absolute error (i.e., absolute deviation between predicted and actual size) as a function of size of training set. Vertical lines
represent standard deviations. Note that some of the points have been
offset slightly in the horizontal dimension to make the error bars easier to
distinguish, but they correspond to identical training set sizes.

amount of learning (i.e., sizes of the training set). The 10% training set
exemplifies a situation where knowledge is scarce (which is likely to be
the rule rather than the exception in most domains). For this set, Quick-
Est's estimates are incorrect by an average of about 132,000 inhabitants
(about half the size of the average German city in the simulated environment), compared with 303,000 for multiple regression, and 153,000 for
the estimation tree. That is, under the psychologically relevant circumstances of scarce knowledge, QuickEst outperforms multiple regression
clearly and the estimation tree by a small margin.

How does performance change as a function of learning (i.e., more
cities known)? When 50% of the cities are known, for example, QuickEst
and multiple regression perform about equally well, and the estimation
tree outperforms both by a small margin. When the strategies have complete knowledge (all cities are known), multiple regression outperforms
QuickEst by a relatively small margin—their respective absolute errors are
about 93,000 and 103,000—and the estimation tree outperforms both competitors (absolute error is about 65,000, which equals the optimal performance, see footnote 13). That is, under the psychologically rather unlikely

circumstances of complete knowledge, QuickEst falls only slightly below the performance of multiple regression but is clearly outperformed by the estimation tree. (Even when multiple regression uses only those cues whose weights are significantly different from zero—7.3 on average instead of 8—its absolute error improves so slightly that the difference could hardly be seen if plotted in figure 10-5, except for the 10% training set.)

This result is similar to that reported by Chater et al. (1997). They tested the fast and frugal choice heuristic Take The Best (chapter 4), of which QuickEst is a relative, against four computationally expensive strategies, including neural networks and exemplar models. The task was to determine which of two German cities had the larger population size. Chater et al. found that when the training set was less than 40% of the test set, Take The Best outperformed all other competitors. Only when the training set grew beyond 40% did the competitors' performance increase above that of Take The Best.

Where does QuickEst make substantial errors? Figure 10-6 shows the deviations between actual and estimated size (in the 100% training set) for each strategy as a function of population size. Each heuristic has a distinct error pattern. Whereas QuickEst estimates the sizes of the many small cities quite accurately, it makes substantial errors on the few large

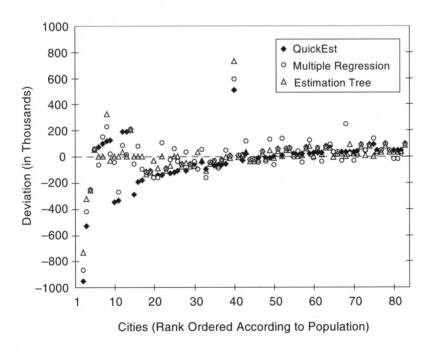

Figure 10-6: Deviation between actual and estimated size (in the 100% training set) for the three estimation methods on all cities, rank ordered according to population size.

cities because it puts them in its catchall category. Multiple regression, in contrast, makes substantial errors along the whole range of population size. The estimation tree makes relatively small errors for both small and large cities.

Another aspect of figure 10-6 deserves attention. More than the estimates made by the estimation tree and multiple regression, QuickEst's estimates are regressed toward the mean: On average, it underestimates the size of large cities and overestimates the size of small cities. Such a regression effect is typical in human quantitative estimation (e.g., Attneave, 1953; Lichtenstein et al., 1978; Sedlmeier et al., 1998; Varey et al., 1990). In figure 10-6, the overestimation of small city sizes appears miniscule compared to the underestimation of large city sizes. However, if the deviations between predicted and actual size are divided by actual size, then the regression effect for small cities is larger than for large cities. In the 100% training set, the median regression across all cities is 56%, 45%, and 23% for QuickEst, multiple regression, and the estimation tree, respectively (we applied the analysis described in Sedlmeier et al., 1998, footnote 1). Thus, QuickEst comes closest to showing the regression of about 70% observed in people's estimates in other tasks (Sedlmeier et al., 1998).

QuickEst uses only spontaneous numbers as estimates. What price will multiple regression pay if it has to work with the same psychological constraint? Recall that under complete knowledge (i.e., when all cities are known), multiple regression outperformed QuickEst (absolute errors of 93,000 vs. 103,000). If multiple regression also rounds its estimates to the nearest spontaneous number, however, it performs worse than QuickEst (absolute errors of 114,000 vs. 103,000).

To summarize, although the QuickEst heuristic involves only about a third of the information available to its competitors and fewer complex calculations than multiple regression, it outperforms multiple regression and the estimation tree when knowledge is scarce. In addition, QuickEst's performance is relatively stable across different amounts of learning: The absolute error is only 1.3 times higher for the 10% training set than for the complete knowledge case. In contrast, the absolute errors of multiple regression and the estimation tree in the 10% training set are 3.3 and 2.3 times higher than the absolute errors for complete knowledge, respectively. Only in the psychologically less plausible situation of abundant knowledge (i.e., 50% or more of the cities are known) is QuickEst (slightly) outperformed by its competitors.

Proportion of Correct Inferences

How many correct inferences do the heuristics make when comparing pairs of cities? Figure 10-7a shows the results for the proportion of correct inferences excluding cases of guessing (i.e., city pairs for which the heuristics chose randomly because the predicted sizes were identical), and

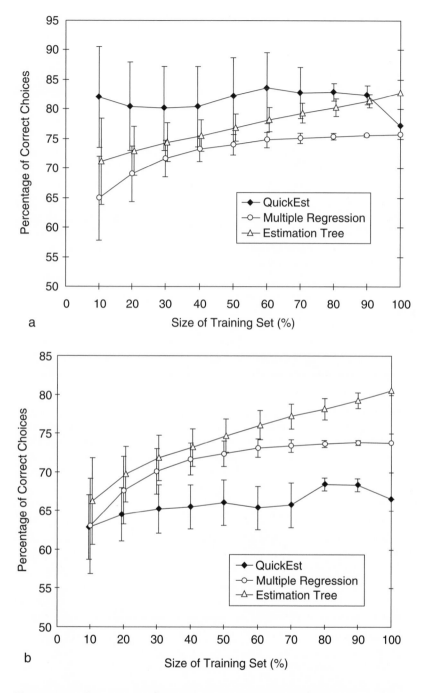

Figure 10-7: Percentage of correct city comparison inferences as a function of the size of training set, both excluding guessing (a) and including guessing (b). Vertical lines represent standard deviations. Note that some of the points have been offset slightly in the horizontal dimension to make the error bars easier to distinguish, but they correspond to identical training set sizes.

figure 10-7b shows the results including guesses. QuickEst's performance is excellent when it does not have to guess: Across all training sets, its proportion of correct inferences is 81%, whereas those of multiple regression and the estimation tree are 73% and 77%, respectively.

In cases in which the predicted sizes are identical, each of the strategies guesses randomly between the two cities, and thus, the proportion of correct inferences in such cases is expected to be 50%. Because this value is lower than the performance of the strategies without guessing, we can predict that overall performance decreases when guessing is included (see figure 10-7b). QuickEst suffers most because it falls back on guessing more because it has a smaller set of numerically distinct estimates available: Across all training sets, its proportion of correct inferences with guessing is 66%, whereas those of multiple regression and the estimation tree are 71% and 75%, respectively.

Conclusion

Let us conclude, as we began, with one of Robinson Crusoe's journal entries. Once Crusoe realized that his island was regularly visited by savages, he prepared himself for a possible confrontation with them. One early morning, he was surprised by

> seeing no less than five canoes all on shore together on my side of the island; and the people who belonged to them all landed, and out of my sight. The number of them broke all my measures; for seeing so many and knowing that they always came four, or six, or sometimes more, in a boat, I could not tell what to think of it, or how to take my measures, to attack twenty or thirty men single-handed; so I lay still in my castle, perplexed and discomforted. (Defoe, 1719/1980, p. 198)

For many evolutionarily important tasks, from choosing where to forage to deciding whether to fight, adaptive behavior hinges partly on organisms' ability to estimate quantities. Such decisions often have to be made quickly and on the basis of incomplete information. What structure of information in real-world environments can fast and frugal heuristics for estimation exploit to perform accurately? We presented a heuristic, QuickEst, that exploits a particular environmental structure, namely, J-shaped distributions. We demonstrated by simulation that where knowledge is scarce—as it typically is in natural decision-making settings (e.g., Klein, 1998)—the fast and frugal QuickEst outperforms or at least matches the performance of more expensive methods such as multiple regression and estimation trees. QuickEst is an ecologically rational strategy whose success highlights the importance of studying environmental structures.

11

Categorization by Elimination

Using Few Cues to Choose

Patricia M. Berretty
Peter M. Todd
Laura Martignon

Categorize or die.

F. Gregory Ashby

Hiking through the Bavarian Alps, you come across a large bird perched on a fence. You pull out your European bird guidebook to identify it. From the shape of its head, you assume that this is a bird of prey, so you turn to the section on raptors in the guide. You next use size to narrow down your search to a few kinds of hawks; then you use color to limit the possibilities further. When you consider the bird's tail length, you finally have enough information to determine the exact species. Using only four features (cues), you correctly identify this bird as a sparrow hawk.

Now imagine that rather than observing a bird on a fence, you spot one flying overhead. The bird is moving rather rapidly and is backlit by the sun so you are only able to perceive a few of its attributes. The first thing you notice is the bird's size, followed by the shape of its silhouette, and lastly its fluid gliding motion. Again, with limited information you are able to categorize the bird as a sparrow hawk, but this time using a different (and smaller) set of cues than when the bird was stationary.

How would this categorization process proceed if a rabbit rather than a human were watching the bird? The rabbit would not be interested in knowing the exact species of bird flying overhead, but instead would want to categorize it as predator or not, as quickly as possible—the *Rabbit's Guide to Birds* has only two short sections. While the rabbit could also use several cues to make its category assignment, as soon as it finds enough cues to decide on the category "predator"—for instance, if this bird is gliding—it should not bother gathering any more information, and just head for shelter. Obviously, for a rabbit, speed is of the essence when it comes to categorizing birds as predators or nonpredators.

Humans and animals alike face circumstances where rapid categorization, making use only of immediately available information, is called for. Quickly categorizing the intention of another approaching creature as either hostile or courting, for instance, enables the proper reaction in enough time to ensure a happy outcome. Indeed, the function of categorization itself can be regarded as a means for making speedy snap judgments about things in our environment: Correctly placing an object into a category after observing only a few of its features allows one to generalize beyond those features and make predictions about other properties of that object (Anderson, 1991; Medin et al., 1987; Rosch, 1978). If the purpose of categorization is to allow rapid predictions, a process of categorization that required an exhaustive search of all relevant features before reaching a conclusion would defeat this goal. That is, if each feature takes time to acquire or observe, a process that uses all features will be slower than a process that does not require all features. Rapid categorization thus best supports rapid category-based prediction—but how can it be accomplished? A fast and frugal algorithm that stops looking for features as soon as there is sufficient information to make a decision would satisfy our goal.

In this chapter, we consider the case for just such a fast and frugal model of categorization, akin to the categorization process based on ordered cues described in the first paragraph. This model, which we call Categorization by Elimination (or CBE; see Berretty et al., 1997), uses only as many of the available cues or features as are necessary to first make a specific categorization. As a consequence, it often uses far fewer cues in categorizing a given object than do standard models that integrate cues— hence its fast frugality. Despite its frugality, the accuracy of this approach typically rivals that of more computationally involved algorithms, as we will show. We therefore propose Categorization by Elimination as a parsimonious psychological model, as well as a useful candidate for some applied categorization tasks.

We describe competing psychological and machine-learning models of categorization in the next section. Because Categorization by Elimination is closely related to Tversky's Elimination by Aspects model of choice (Tversky, 1972), we proceed to a discussion of the main assumptions of elimination models. We next present the CBE model in detail. Most other recent models of human categorization have been tested in quite restricted (low-dimensionality) environments having only two or three cues, situations in which CBE can show little advantage. Therefore, we have experimentally investigated a multiple-cue categorization task in which we can compare our model with others in accounting for human performance. We describe this study, which involves categorizing animate motion trajectories into different behavioral intentions using seven cue dimensions, at the beginning of the fifth section on results (it is covered much more extensively in chapter 12). CBE performs there as well as linear categorization methods, and does not overfit the data as much as neural networks sometimes do. We continue in that section to look at how well our algorithm does alongside some of the cue-integrating categorization methods developed in psychology and machine learning on standard data sets from the latter field. This comparison shows that CBE competes in accuracy with more traditional methods in a variety of domains, even when using far fewer cues. Finally we consider some of the challenges still ahead for developing fast and frugal categorization algorithms. Throughout the remainder of the chapter we use the terms cues, aspects, dimensions, and features, as appropriate, all to mean roughly the same thing.

Existing Categorization Models

The proliferation of categorization models in both psychology and machine learning demands some categorization itself. Psychologists are primarily concerned with developing models that best describe human categorization performance, while in machine learning the goal is to develop models that attain the highest accuracy of categorization. These two goals are not necessarily mutually exclusive; indeed, one of the main findings so far in the field of human categorization is that people are often able to achieve near-perfect accuracy (that is, categorize a stimulus set with minimal errors; see Ashby & Maddox, 1992). As a consequence, some models (e.g., Miller & Laird's symbolic concept acquisition model, 1996) are aimed at filling both roles.

Categorization models can be analyzed according to the three heuristic building-block dimensions introduced in chapter 1: How does a particular model search for information to make a category judgment? When will the model stop searching for information? And what decision process will it use once it has all the information it requires? However, this sort of analysis does not always get us very far, because there has been little focus in the psychological literature in particular on how people acquire the information they need (the first two dimensions). The majority of psychological studies of categorization have used simple artificial stimuli (e.g., semicircles in two-dimensional space; Nosofsky, 1986) that vary on only a few (two to four) dimensions.[1] With all of the (limited) information presented to participants, there is no need for search, and so no need to stop search, either—only the decision rule needs to be specified. It remains to be demonstrated how accurate humans can be when categorizing objects

1. Posner and Keele (1968) have used multidimensional random dot stimuli to test human classification, but the exact number of dimensions is undeterminable.

that have many dimensions. This is in contrast to the more natural high-dimensional categorization applications used in machine learning, such as wine tasting (Aeberhard et al., 1994) or handwriting recognition (Martin & Pittman, 1991). In that field, appropriate information search can be very important. Here we briefly review some of the currently popular categorization models for human categorization and machine learning with the three heuristic building blocks in mind. In many cases, though, we must extrapolate or remain silent because an algorithm was not designed with the concerns for limited time, memory, or computational effort that the building blocks embody.

Theories of categorization in the psychology literature have been instantiated primarily in exemplar models (e.g., Kruschke, 1992; Nosofsky, 1986), decision-bound models (e.g., Ashby & Gott, 1988), and rule-based models (e.g., Miller & Laird, 1996; Nosofsky et al., 1994). These models assume that any object may be represented as a point in a multidimensional space of cue values (possibly with some uncertainty). Furthermore, these models all assume that humans integrate features in the categorization decision process—that is, we combine multiple cues to come to a final judgment. By relying on integration, these models can suffer greatly in performance when too few cues are available, as we will show later. Finally, these models imply that categorizers use all of the cues that are present—that is, there is no explicit stopping rule for information search, and we do not discard any available information. This can lead to time pressure when many cues are available. To point out these important aspects of psychological categorization models, we will now compare Nosofsky's generalized context model and Ashby's decision bound theory.

Exemplar models (Brooks, 1978; Estes, 1986; Kruschke, 1992; Medin & Schaffer, 1978; Nosofsky, 1986) assume that humans categorize novel objects by computing the similarity between an object and all exemplars in every category in which the novel object could be placed, using all the cues available. Thus there is no stopping rule for information search. Two main types of decision rules are used: The object can be identified with the category to which it is most similar according to the similarity metric, or it can be assigned a category probabilistically using normalized similarity values as probabilities (as in most exemplar models). Nosofsky's (1986) generalized context model (GCM) allows for variation in the amount of attention given to different features during categorization (see also Medin & Schaffer, 1978). Therefore, because some cues can be given attention weights of zero and thus ignored, it is possible that different cues can be used in different tasks. But the particular cues that are used and their weights remain the same for the entire stimulus set for each particular categorization task. (In contrast, as we will see, CBE can use a different set of cues to categorize each new object.) These weights could be used to order cues in search, if time pressure prevented an agent with this kind of model from accessing all available information—although not explicitly addressed by exemplar theorists, an underlying assumption is that cues with larger attention weights could be assessed and used before cues with smaller attention weights.

Decision bound theory (or DBT; see Ashby & Gott, 1988) assumes that there is a region in multidimensional space associated with each category, and therefore that categories are separated by bounds between regions. Decision bounds are determined by the mean, variance, and covariance of the stimulus points within each category. DBT uses a deterministic response rule to categorize an object according to the region of perceptual space in which it lies. If some cues are not available when categorization is to be performed, then a lower-dimensional projection of the original learned perceptual space (defined by all of the available cues) would be used. Again, there is no explicit search order or stopping rule, and the decision is made by combining cue values.

While these psychological models all categorize by integrating all the cues available (except in exemplar models if a cue has an attention weight of zero), their memory requirements do differ. GCM assumes that all exemplars ever encountered are stored and used when categorizing a novel object, while DBT only needs to store the bound-determining parameters of each category. We will return to the issue of memory and the trade-off with cue use in the final section.

A different approach to categorization is captured in rule-based models. Miller and Laird's (1996) symbolic concept acquisition (SCA) model incrementally builds up a set of rules for classifying stimuli according to specific discrete features. The first rules to be constructed are very general ones that only test a single feature. If the current set of rules cannot distinguish between categories, then more detailed rules will be added, which must match the stimuli on more features. After a set of rules has been learned in this way, new stimuli are categorized by first checking them against specific rules incorporating all the available features. If there is no exact match between all perceived features and a specific rule, then features are successively dropped until a more general rule that does match the remaining features is found. Thus cue search order, stopping condition, and final decision are all specified by the model's rules. There are similarities between this approach and Categorization by Elimination; in particular, the order in which features are processed can be related to our cue validity measure. But a major difference is that during categorization, CBE begins with a single feature (rather than all those available), and only adds new ones if necessary, thereby decreasing computation. Another model that tests rules in this more efficient general-to-specific order is Feigenbaum and Simon's EPAM symbolic discrimination-net model (Feigenbaum & Simon, 1984); however, our two approaches differ significantly beyond this point.

The quest for psychological plausibility and computational simplicity was taken up by Nosofsky, Palmeri, and McKinley (1994) in developing their rule-plus-exception (RULEX) model. In RULEX, simple logical rules are learned for binary-valued feature dimensions, mapping particular feature values onto particular categories. However, these rules can be imperfect, so exceptions must be memorized as well. Nosofsky et al. found that accurate categorization could be achieved in their data sets with very few stored rules plus exceptions. This simple approach can also account for individual differences in categorization performance. However, RULEX was designed for the limited case of two categories defined by binary-valued cues (though it is now being extended); we will aim for a more general model.

In machine learning, predominant categorization theories include neural networks, Bayesian models, and decision trees. The goal of these machine learning models is usually to maximize categorization accuracy on a given useful data set. Limiting algorithmic complexity is not typically the most important factor in developing machine learning models, which can sometimes lead to computation-intensive models that are not psychologically plausible.

Neural network-based categorization and classification models (see, e.g., Hertz et al., 1991) can learn hyperplane boundaries between categories, capturing this knowledge in their trainable weights. Values of all available cues in a particular stimulus are usually processed through a nonlinear decision (activation) rule to determine the region of multidimensional space, and hence the associated category, in which that stimulus falls, both during learning (training) and generalization (testing). Neural networks are usually conceived of as parallel processing systems, so that they expect to have all input data available simultaneously, without need for either search or stopping rules. Once a network has been trained with a particular set of cues, categorization performance will typically suffer if any of those cues are missing in stimuli during testing; however, one of the hallmarks of distributed models of this type is graceful degradation, in which performance declines gradually rather than catastrophically with decreasing input knowledge.

The Bayesian approach to categorization formulates the problem in a probabilistic framework: Find the category that maximizes the probability that a new (nontrained) object belongs to it, given the object's cue values and knowledge of the cue validities. The naive Bayes classifier assumes that all cues are independent of each other on the categories concerned, which greatly simplifies the calculations involved in setting it up. The structure of the created classifier determines which cues will be used, but their order is not specified. In some categorization domains the performance of the naive Bayes approach has been shown to be close to that of neural networks and decision trees (Blum & Langley, 1997; Domingos & Pazzani, 1996). Anderson (1991) has also proposed a naive Bayes method as a normative model for human behavior. He did not intend his Bayesian approach to be a model of a psychological mechanism, and indeed the computations involved are too complex: People have difficulty even handling conditional probabilities that involve more than one cue and one category at a time. But Anderson has analyzed a variety of experimental results and found that human categorization behavior can be close to that of the naive Bayes standard. While a naive Bayes model may not be psychologically plausible, the full Bayesian approach, that is, respecting all relevant dependencies, is even less so—see chapter 8 for a discussion of the complexities involved in these demonic methods.

In decision tree models of classification, a primary goal is to simplify the actual categorization process by reducing the number of dimensions needed to determine an object's category. But to achieve this decision-making simplification, quite complex methods are usually employed to select the dimensions used at various points in the tree. For example, the setup phase of Quinlan's (1986, 1993) ID3 decision tree calculates the attribute that provides the greatest information for determining the correct category and uses it as the root (i.e., first decision branch point) of the tree. The rest of the tree's branches are chosen recursively by again computing the most informative attribute at each successive decision point. Once a tree has been set up, its structure determines the exact number and sequence of cues that must be used to reach a final category decision, and all of the decision making itself is done at the successive branch points on any particular path through the tree.

Breiman et al.'s (1993) classification and regression tree (CART) models also require extensive calculations of statistical tests between pairs of features to determine which ones will be used where in the decision tree. For both ID3 and CART, the values of previously checked attributes can affect what attribute is looked at next, so that different objects may be categorized using different sets of attributes (see the patient classification example at the beginning of chapter 1). The large amount of computation required to set up these models before a single categorization decision can be made (even if each subsequent decision is itself simple) renders them rather unrealistic from a psychological perspective. Holte (1993) has greatly simplified the decision tree approach by considering only a single cue dimension, divided up into regions each corresponding to a particular category. With enough such divisions, this simple method can be very accurate, but the memory requirements become quite high.

One example of a model that does attempt psychological plausibility is Gennari's (1991) CLASSIT, which applies selective attention to unsupervised concept formation. This system makes an initial classification of an object by using as few of the most salient cues as necessary. However, all cues must still be considered before a final decision is settled on, to make sure that further information would not change the initial classification. This "worst case" stopping rule for checking cues is a form of constrained optimization as defined in chapter 1.

Even though many of the machine learning models (e.g., CART and CLASSIT) use only a few cues during a given categorization, the process of setting up the algorithm's decision mechanisms beforehand, including determining which cues to use, can be complex (e.g., CART's use of t-tests—see Breiman et al., 1993) or time consuming (e.g., neural network training iterations). Can we instead design a heuristic categorization method that is simple to set up, employs limited cue search and simple decision rules, and yet still produces high accuracy?

Elimination Models

Motivated by the psychological plausibility concerns introduced in the first section, that humans and other animals often must categorize objects based on few cues in little time, we wanted to develop a fast and frugal categorization method. Such a method can combine the best aspects of both the psychological and machine learning categorization models: simple decision processes and limited cue use. This combination of features is embodied in a class of psychological theories known as elimination models.

Elimination models were originally developed for choice and preference tasks (Restle, 1961; Tversky, 1972). In a sequential elimination choice model, one object is chosen from a set of objects by repeatedly eliminating subsets of objects from further consideration, thereby whittling down the set of remaining possibilities until a single choice remains. Objects in the set are defined by a number of features. To eliminate the first subset of objects, a feature is selected in some way, and all objects with that feature are removed from the set of possibilities. Subsequent subsets are chosen in the same manner with successive features, and are removed. The object remaining after this elimination process is the final choice. Thus elimination models must specify a search-order building block, and stop information search as soon as a single choice remains, so that their stopping rule and decision rule are intertwined (as in decision trees).

The most widely known elimination model in psychology is Tversky's (1972) Elimination by Aspects (EBA) model of probabilistic choice. One of the motivating factors in developing EBA as a descriptive model of choice was that there are often many relevant cues that may be used in choosing among complex alternatives (Tversky, 1972). Tversky therefore wanted his model to incorporate a psychologically plausible procedure to select and order the cues to use from among many alternatives. In EBA, the cues, or aspects, are selected in a probabilistic order based on their utility for making a particular decision (e.g., for choosing a restaurant from those nearby, the most important aspects might be what it serves and how much it charges). Remaining possibilities that do not match the current aspect being considered (e.g., restaurants that do not serve seafood) are eliminated from the choice set. Furthermore, only aspects that are present in the remaining choice set are considered (e.g., if all nearby seafood restaurants are equally inexpensive, then high price cannot be used as an aspect to distinguish further between them). Additional aspects are used to eliminate possibilities until a single choice is left. This use of only the necessary aspects is markedly different from the categorization models described in the previous section that use all available cues. (See chapter 7 for more on EBA and other elimination-based heuristics used for choice.)

Moving from choice toward categorization, elimination models have also been developed for identification. Townsend and Ashby's (1982) sequential feature testing algorithm is an elimination model of the decision process involved in letter recognition using visual features. As in Elimination by Aspects, each feature is weighted (here with values that best mimic human performance). However, rather than selecting the next aspect based on those present in the current subset of choices, the aspect with the next highest weight is picked. If this aspect was perceived in the letter shown, all remaining letters without that aspect are eliminated from the choice set (so for instance, if a curved part was seen in the letter "b," then all letters without curved parts, including "x" and "k," would be eliminated from further consideration). Likewise, if this aspect was not perceived, all letters with that aspect are eliminated. Aspects are checked until only one letter remains, or if all letters are eliminated, then a random choice is made.

To repeat, there are two main assumptions underlying elimination models, and thus CBE. First, the cues used must be ordered in some way (even if only probabilistically)—a search-order building block is required. Second, it is not always necessary to use all cues to reach a decision—the simple stopping rule is to halt search when a unique decision has been determined (or when no more cues are available). Although these assumptions have not been tested explicitly in a categorization task (to our knowledge), they have been tested in various studies on other forms of decision making.

Previous research has suggested that people process cues in order of their usefulness for a particular task. Studies of information search in hypothesis testing have shown that people prefer to use diagnostic cues over nondiagnostic cues (Skov & Sherman, 1986; Trope & Bassok, 1982). The diagnosticity of a binary cue for distinguishing between two hypotheses is defined as the likelihood ratio between the probability that the first hypothesis is true, given that the cue is present, and the probability that the second hypothesis is true, given that the cue is present. A cue's diagnosticity thus indicates how well it discriminates between the hypotheses. Categorization by Elimination can use various related ways of ordering cues from most to least useful (see chapter 6 for more on different types of cue orderings). In the version we present here, we order the cues based on how often they would make a correct categorization if they were used by themselves.

With regard to the second assumption, it has been demonstrated that people do not use all of the cues made available to them in a variety of decision-making tasks (see chapter 7). Saad and Russo (1996) investigated how many cues people would actively select to make a choice between two apartments in an experimental setting. When people were allowed to select cues in the order they wanted, they only used a quarter (median of

24%) of the possible cues; even when the experimenters controlled the cue presentation order, people still only requested about half (median of 52%) of the cues before making their decisions. In another decision task, people preferred to make a decision they were not completely sure of based on a limited number of cues, instead of accessing further information available to them (Jacoby et al., 1994). Perhaps most importantly for our purposes, it has also been found that people use fewer cues if they have high diagnosticity than if they have low diagnosticity (Van Wallendael & Guignard, 1992). These findings further indicate that when people can access cues in a particular desired order, they will typically use fewer of them.

Categorization by Elimination

To build a categorization model based on an elimination process, we begin with the following general assumptions: Objects to be categorized have perceivable cues with continuous or discrete values. For a given task, there is a set of possible categories in which objects can be placed based on their cue values. Unlike Tversky's EBA model of preference and probability-matching models of categorization, we are concerned here with problems where there is a correct answer to be determined, and where we can measure the performance of our algorithm against an external accuracy criterion. Our model is consequently deterministic rather than probabilistic (except where guessing is required). Further, because this is not an object identification task where we would look for an exact match of an object's cues with a cue profile stored in memory, there will be generalization. This means that there can be occasions on which the model will not predict an object's category correctly.

More specifically, we build the following components into CBE: To categorize an object, its values on the various cue dimensions are processed in a particular predetermined order. The same order is used for any object, but because of the eliminatory nature of the model, not all cues will be processed for all objects. Each cue processed restricts the set of possible categories left that could be ultimately chosen by removing some of them from further consideration—this is the elimination step. (Note that a given cue may also leave the set of possible categories unchanged, but it can never increase the pool of possibilities.) Processing of cues stops when a single category remains, or when no more cues are available, at which point a random choice is made from the remaining possibilities. Given these assumptions and components, we can now consider exactly how Categorization by Elimination operates and how well it performs.

An Example of Categorization by Elimination

To illustrate how the CBE model works, we can apply it to the task of determining a wine's variety—whether zinfandel, Pinot Grigio, or another of a prespecified set of possibilities—by using a set of cues that could be collected during a wine tasting. We begin with a list of categories to consider and a list of cues that can be used to place wines in those categories. The heuristic makes categorizations by processing a training set of wines whose categories (their varieties) and cue values are known. Out of the many possible cues we could use to assess the wines, we will consider here just four obvious ones: sweetness, color, aroma, and the presence or absence of added alcohol. First, the heuristic needs a rule that gives search a direction, that is, determines which cue is looked up first, second, and so on. As mentioned earlier, cues that make more correct categorizations when used by themselves will be ranked before cues that make fewer correct solo categorizations. For this wine-tasting task, imagine that it has already been estimated that color is the best single cue of wine type, followed by aroma, sweetness, and then added alcohol.

Second, the cue values of the known wines are analyzed to divide up each cue dimension into "bins" that correspond to specific variety categories. For example, the cue-value distributions of the wine categories in the training set may divide the "color" dimension into three bins: one with cue values from light yellow to gold, one with pink, and the last with red cue values. (We discuss how these bins are created from the training set data in the next subsection.) Each cue-value bin has a set of possible categories associated with it. For example, the bin spanning red color-cue values could correspond to the wine categories Beaujolais, Burgundy, Cabernet Sauvignon, Pinot Noir, zinfandel, port, and merlot. (Finer gradations of bins may increase categorization accuracy, but for now we will assume three bins are sufficient.) The "aroma" dimension might consist of several bins that correspond directly to cue values: woody, earthy, herby, fruity, and unassignable. Based on the known wines we have analyzed to construct these bins, the unassignable aroma bin could correspond to the categories sparkling wine, champagne, and Beaujolais. (Note that these categories could be present in other bins on the same cue dimension as well—for instance, if we had two types of Beaujolais in our known wine set, one fruity and one unassignable, then the Beaujolais category could fall into both the unassignable and fruity bins on the aroma dimension.)

Once the cues have been ordered and their value ranges divided into bins representing different categories, this knowledge can be used to categorize new wines. Imagine that we have a mystery glass poured in front of us, and we want to use CBE to figure out what kind of wine this is. We would proceed to check the cues in order. We first observe the color cue and see that the wine is red. We therefore know that this wine must be among the possible categories in the red color bin: Beaujolais, Burgundy, Cabernet Sauvignon, Pinot Noir, zinfandel, port, and merlot. This color cue has thus eliminated a number of wines from further consideration, such as golden Pinot Grigios and pink rosés. Next we take a sniff to assess the aroma of the wine, finding that it is not easily identifiable. Thus the aroma cue indicates that the wine's variety is one of those in the unassignable bin: a sparkling wine, champagne, or Beaujolais. We eliminate all but these wine varieties from the previous set of red-color possibilities, and see what choices we are left with. This is the same as taking the intersection between the two sets of wine categories that the two cues indicate. When we do this we find that only one wine variety remains that fits both cues: Beaujolais. So we conclude that the wine in question comes from this category. If there had been several possibilities that were both red and of unassignable aroma, we would have proceeded to check the next cue, sweetness, to see if that cut down the set of possibilities any further, and we would go on in this way with further lower-ranked cues until only a single category remained, or until we ran out of cues and had to guess among the categories still left in the running.

The Algorithm   •

Categorization by Elimination is a fast and frugal, noncompensatory, cue-based model of categorization. This means that it uses cues in a particular order to determine an object's category, and categorization decisions made by earlier cues cannot be altered (i.e., compensated for) by later cues. In CBE, cues are ordered and used according to their probability of success. We define probability of success as how accurately a single cue categorizes some set of stimuli, in percentage correct (see chapter 6 for more on this and other ways of ordering cues). This value can be calculated by running CBE using only the single cue in question and seeing what proportion of correct categorizations the algorithm makes. If using the single cue results in CBE being unable to distinguish between multiple categories for a particular stimulus, as will often be the case, the algorithm chooses one of those categories at random. For instance, if size alone is more accurate in categorizing birds (or more successful at narrowing down the possible categories) than shape alone, then the size cue would have a higher probability of success than shape, and so would be used earlier by CBE.

As described in the previous section, setting up CBE for a particular task involves identifying the relevant cue dimensions and then dividing up each dimension into bins. Each bin covers a continuous range of cue values (either nominal or numeric) that corresponds to certain categories. These bins form the knowledge base that CBE uses to map cue values onto their possible corresponding categories. Bins can either be fully constructed from a training set of objects before testing CBE's categorization performance (as we do here), or bin learning and categorization testing can be done incrementally. In both cases, bin construction proceeds by determining low and high cue value boundaries for each category on each cue dimension. These boundaries are then used to divide up each dimension into the cue-value ranges that form the bins (see figure 11-1). This means that CBE has very specific, and frugal, memory requirements: It

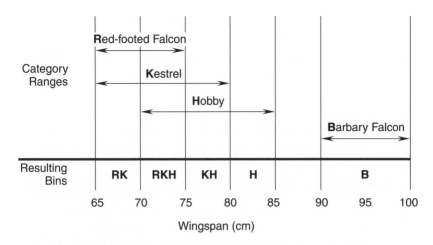

Figure 11-1: Construction of cue-value bins on one cue dimension. Here the wingspan dimension for four categories of birds is divided up into six bins (shown under the dimension line, with the categories they correspond to). The bin boundaries are determined by the upper and lower bounds of the distribution of wingspans of each category of bird, as shown by the vertical lines.

only needs to store two values per category per cue dimension, independent of the number of objects encountered.

We have explored two ways of determining the low and high cue-value bounds associated with each category. First, in cases where cue values for a particular category are assumed to be normally distributed, we can use a low cue bound that is one or two standard deviations below the distribution mean, and a high bound that is one or two standard deviations above the mean. This Gaussian binning (used in the first example in the next section with one-standard-deviation bounds) captures where the majority of members of a particular category will fall on a particular cue dimension—but objects in that category could be seen that have cue values outside of this range. This means that the binning structure will misclassify these noncentral objects on that dimension; however, other dimensions could still correctly categorize them.

Second, particularly if category cue values are thought to be uniformly distributed, then the low cue bound can simply be the lowest cue value seen for a particular category, and the high cue bound can be the highest value seen. In this case, the cue-value bins will map from a particular cue value to the entire set of possible categories associated with that value (in the training set), whereas the Gaussian bins only map to the most prevalent categories for a cue value. This "perfect binning" (also used in the next section) will not misclassify objects seen during training (bin construction), except when final guesses are required. Perfect binning thus generally yields a higher training-set accuracy than Gaussian binning.

How does CBE use the constructed cue-value bins to categorize a particular object? A flowchart of the processing steps used by CBE is shown in figure 11-2. Given a particular stimulus to categorize, we begin with an initial set of possible categories S and an ordered list of cue dimensions to be used. The categorization process begins by picking the cue dimension C with the highest probability of success. Next, the constructed bins are used to map the object's value on C to the corresponding set S^* of the possible categories for that cue value. If only one category corresponds to that cue value (that is, if S^* contains only one category), then the categorization process ends with this single category.

Usually, though, there will be more than one possible category in S^*. In this case, that set S^* of possible categories is intersected with the previous (full) set of possibilities, S, and the remaining possibilities in this intersection are saved as the new set S of possible categories for the next pass through the loop. This is CBE's elimination step: All those categories that are not in both the new and old set of possibilities are eliminated. In

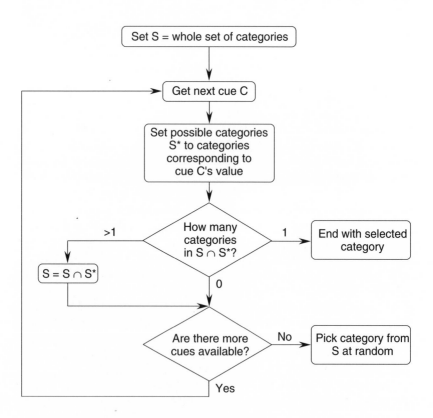

Figure 11-2: Flowchart for the Categorization by Elimination algorithm.

this way, only those categories that fit with all of the cues seen so far for this object will remain as possibilities. To continue the elimination process, the cue dimension with the next highest probability of success is chosen as the new C. The set of categories corresponding to the object's value on dimension C is assigned to S^*, and this new set is intersected with the previous set of remaining possibilities, S. Again if this intersection contains a single category, we are done. If not (and if there are still cues left to check), the intersection becomes the set of possibilities for the next round, and the process continues.

The Categorization by Elimination algorithm thus has a simple, straightforward stopping rule: If only one category remains in the newly formed set of possibilities, then this is the decision the algorithm ends with; or if all of the cues have been processed and more than one possible category remains, then a choice is made randomly from that set. As long as both of these conditions are not met, the algorithm continues, in one of two ways. If more than one possible category remains, then as indicated above, the next most successful cue is checked. Alternatively, if the intersection of S^* and S is empty, leaving no possible categories to choose among, then the present cue C is ignored, the prior set S of categories is retained, and the next cue is evaluated.

This algorithm has several interesting features. It is frugal in information, using only those cues necessary to reach a decision. It is noncompensatory, with earlier cues eliminating category-choice possibilities that can never be rescued by later cues. The binning functions used to associate possible categories with particular cue values are simple, use little memory, and can be easily learned. And the exact order of cues used does not appear to be critical: In preliminary tests, different random cue orderings vary the algorithm's categorization accuracy by only a few percentage points. But notably, the number of cues used with different orderings does vary more widely. This number is, however, kept low when the cues are used in order of their probability of success.

Categorization by Elimination is clearly related to Tversky's Elimination by Aspects model in several respects, though there are some important differences. First, EBA is a probabilistic model of choice while CBE is a deterministic model of categorization (but including the possibility of a final guess). Second, in CBE cues are ordered by our success measure before categorizing begins, so that the same cue order is used to evaluate each object. In EBA, aspects are selected probabilistically according to their weight, so that the order in which aspects are considered is not necessarily the same for each object. Third, as mentioned previously, EBA only chooses aspects that are present in the current set of remaining possible choices, and therefore the process never terminates with the empty set. However, this requires checking for the presence of each proposed aspect among the remaining choices. CBE does no such prescreening for appropriate cues to use, but rather takes the psychologically simpler route of dropping the last cue seen whenever it leads to an empty intersection of category sets.

CBE is also a relative of Gigerenzer and Goldstein's (1996a) Take The Best heuristic for two-alternative choice (see chapter 4). Take The Best makes its choices by going through a set of cues ordered by their ecological validity (see chapter 6); the first cue that allows a decision to be made will stop the search for further cues. CBE uses a similar stopping rule, ending the search for further cues as soon as a category choice can be made. Take The Best can be considered a special case of CBE, where the items to be categorized are now statements of the form "How does A compare to B?," the possible categories are "A is greater" and "B is greater," and the cues are ordered pairs (cue-x-of-A, cue-x-of-B). CBE extends Take The Best from discrete cues and two categories to continuous cues and multiple categories.

How Well Does Categorization by Elimination Perform?

Of course, all of these interesting features of our new algorithm make little difference if it does not actually perform well. How will the fast and frugal CBE compare to standard compensatory algorithms? We first tested CBE as a model of human categorization on motion trajectories that corresponded to different intentional actions (Blythe et al., 1996; see chapter 12 for a complete description). Participants in this experiment viewed recorded "movies" of two artificial bugs moving around on a blank background, and had to decide as quickly as possible whether a marked bug was pursuing, evading, fighting, courting, being courted, or playing with the other bug. We modeled the human performance on this intention-from-motion categorization task with four different algorithms: CBE, Dawes's rule (a linear model with unit weights—see chapter 4), Franklin's rule (a linear model with differential weights—see chapter 4), and a three-layer neural network, each of which could use seven basic motion cues to make a decision. CBE categorized the motion trajectories about as accurately as Dawes's rule and Franklin's rule on both training sets and testing sets (generalization), while using only half as many cues (see table 12-3). The neural network beat the other three algorithms, but suffered greatly on the test set when some of the cues were eliminated, indicating a lack of generalization robustness in comparison to CBE. All of the algorithms outperformed the human participants (in part because the algorithms were trained before they were tested, while the participants were purposefully given no practice). But the fact that CBE performed as well as the linear rules, even though it did not even consider half of the available information on average, supports its candidacy as a fast and frugal, psychologically plausible categorization algorithm.

To challenge CBE in a tougher competition, we next turned to data sets used as testbeds in the machine learning community[2]—the multidimensional object databases in the Irvine Machine Learning Repository (Merz & Murphy, 1996). We used three of these data sets (described below) to compare the performance of CBE using perfect binning with an exemplar model (Nosofsky's 1986 GCM) using variable dimension weights found by gradient descent, and a three-layer feed-forward logistic activation neural network trained with backpropagation. For each data set, we ran 10 trials in which we split the full data set in half, trained on one half (recording the fit to the training data), and tested generalization performance on the other half.

Table 11-1 shows the results of these comparisons for three data sets. The first is Fisher's (1936) famous iris flower database, containing 150 instances of flower measurements classified into three categories (different iris species) using four continuous-valued features (lengths and widths of flower parts). The next data set is made up of 178 wines from each of three particular Italian vintages, each with 13 associated continuous chemical-content cues. The third data set consists of 8,124 instances of two mushroom categories, poisonous and edible, with 22 nominally valued dimensions. For each data set, we show the three competing algorithms' accuracy and number of cues used (frugality) when fitting the training set, and their accuracy and number of cues used when generalizing to predictions about the test set. In addition, we include (in the two available cases) the average generalization performance of all machine learning systems reported in a survey by Holte (1993), and the best reported performance we have found for each data set in the machine learning literature.

Overall, CBE does quite well on these three sets of many-featured natural objects. It generalizes better than the exemplar model on two of the three data sets, and lags only a few points behind the average machine learning algorithm. We were not expecting CBE to outperform the various specialized machine learning algorithms; merely being in the same ballpark is a powerful indicator that this simple method's accuracy may extend to other more varied domains. The critical point of interest is that CBE performs similarly to its often more-complex competitors while using only a small proportion of the available cues. In fact, on average CBE can make accurate generalizations just using about a quarter of the information that the other methods use.

But perhaps the other methods do not really need all the information they are given—it could be that they too would perform just as well even when they only had as many cues to go on as CBE used. To test this, we ran the exemplar model and neural network on the three data sets again,

2. It is difficult to compare CBE to existing categorization models on human multiple-cue data, because few other experiments have been performed with more than three or four cues. We hope to see more researchers running such realistic multiple-cue categorization experiments in the future.

Table 11-1: Categorization Accuracy (Percent Correct) and Information Frugality (Number of Cues Used) for Various Models on Three Data Sets (Means Over 10 Runs)

| | Iris | | | | Wine | | | | Mushrooms | | | |
| | Fitting | | Generalization | | Fitting | | Generalization | | Fitting | | Generalization | |
	Frugality	Accuracy	Frugality	Accuracy	Frugality	Accuracy	Frugality	Accuracy	Frugality	Accuracy	Frugality	Accuracy
CBE	1.2	96%	1.2	93%	2.3	94%	2.2	87%	5.8	91%	5.7	91%
Exemplar	4.0	99%	4.0	92%	13.0	94%	13.0	84%	22.0	100%	22.0	100%
Neural network	4.0	99%	4.0	96%	13.0	100%	13.0	94%	22.0	100%	22.0	100%
ML average	—	—	—	94%	—	—	—	—	—	—	—	97%
ML best	—	—	—	98%	—	—	—	100%	—	—	—	100%
Frugal exemplar	—	—	1.2	88%	—	—	2.2	80%	—	—	5.7	52%
Frugal network	—	—	1.2	40%	—	—	2.2	54%	—	—	5.7	91%

Note. Fitting performance on the training set and prediction (generalization) performance on the test set are both shown. The fourth line (ML average) shows the average generalization ability of several machine learning algorithms (from Holte, 1993), while the fifth line (ML best) shows the best reported machine learning algorithm performance (James, 1985, for the iris data; Aeberhard et al., 1994, for the wine data; Holte, 1993, for the mushroom data). The last two lines show the generalization ability of an exemplar model and neural network when both are restricted to the cues used by CBE.

but this time we only let them use the same cues that CBE checked for each object. Thus, if CBE classified a particular wine after seeing just the first two cues, then we would let the exemplar model and neural network use only those two cues for their classification of that wine as well. With this restricted input, the two competitors suffered greatly, as can be seen in the last two lines of table 11-1 (the "frugal exemplar" and "frugal network"). On each data set the exemplar model typically dropped a few percentage points behind CBE, while the neural network was drastically hobbled, losing close to half its accuracy. Thus, CBE's virtue, frugally using as few cues as possible, can be another algorithm's bane.

Future Work

The results we have presented here indicate that a fast and frugal approach to categorization is a viable alternative to cue-integrating compensatory models. By only using those cues necessary to first make a category decision, CBE can categorize stimuli under time pressure. Moreover, if certain cues are missing (i.e., some feature values are unknown or cannot be perceived), CBE can still use the available cues to come up with a category judgment, in a way that has so far proven more robust than simple exemplar or neural network models (though further comparisons beyond those shown in table 11-1 are necessary, using different numbers of cues in training and testing). Yet, despite its limited use of knowledge, CBE still performs quite accurately and rivals the abilities of much more complex and sophisticated algorithms (not to mention human participants).

This research opens up many interesting avenues to be explored concerning the relationships between fast and frugal categorization methods and more traditional approaches. One important issue is how a categorization algorithm's accuracy is affected by the interaction between the number of cues it uses to make a decision and the amount of memory it needs to store its parameters. (We are primarily concerned here with the long-term memory needed to store the knowledge gained during learning or training, rather than the algorithm's working memory requirements as discussed by Smith et al., 1998.) These two factors can be used to divide categorization algorithms into four classes, which the algorithms in this chapter can be used to illustrate. For example, exemplar models typically use a large number of cues (all those available) to make their category decisions, and also require a large amount of memory to store all of their exemplars. Decision bound theory also uses a large number of cues, but has a low memory requirement. Holte's (1993) model only uses a single cue to categorize an object, but it needs a large amount of memory to store many small ranges of values on that cue dimension and the categories associated with each range. The only model with both minimal cue use and low memory needs is Categorization by Elimination. More systematic analysis of how accuracy, cue use, and memory requirements are inter-twined should yield new insights into how categorization algorithms can be designed to emphasize some of these factors more than others. Further-more, we expect that the information structure of different environments will allow different categorization algorithms to perform more or less ac-curately, and more or less frugally, and this aspect of the ecological ration-ality of fast and frugal categorization must also be explored.

Second, more data from human performance on categorizing multidi-mensional objects needs to be collected and analyzed to provide a testbed for comparisons between CBE and other categorization models. We are particularly interested in comparing the learning curves, patterns of mis-classifications, and decision times associated with CBE and human per-formance. The intriguing finding that CBE's categorization accuracy seems to vary little with changes in cue order should also be studied experimen-tally, although we expect that human behavior will not show this effect strongly, assuming that people have an absolute upper limit to the number of cues they will consider.

Third, category base rates and costs and benefits for incorrect and cor-rect classifications could be incorporated into the model. For example, if a mushroom remains uncategorized as poisonous or safe even after all the cues have been used, it seems reasonable to err on the side of caution and guess that the mushroom is poisonous. This extra information could not only be used to guide guesses in safer directions, but could also be taken into consideration earlier when the bin structure is set up, allowing costs and benefits to be incorporated throughout the decision process.

The very nature of categorization is to go from a limited amount of information to a greater body of knowledge—as soon as we can assign an object to a category, we are able to tap into our stored knowledge about (other) instances in that category, which we can then use to make smarter decisions regarding the object. A fast and frugal approach to categoriza-tion fits directly into this adaptive inference role, allowing that leap from a few features to more useful stored knowledge to be made all the sooner. It is not necessary to amass and combine all the available cues when tell-ing a hawk from a dove, or a Medoc from a Graves—fast and frugal does the trick.

Part V

SOCIAL INTELLIGENCE

12

How Motion Reveals Intention

Categorizing Social Interactions

Philip W. Blythe
Peter M. Todd
Geoffrey F. Miller

Do not go where the path may lead, go instead where there
is no path and leave a trail.

Ralph Waldo Emerson

If you should encounter a mountain lion while hiking in the Sierra Ne-
vada mountains of California, there are two things you must not do, according to the Mountain Lion Foundation: turn your back on the animal
or run away. Either of these behaviors would trigger the lion's predatory
chase behavior, transforming you from startled hiker into potential prey.
It is possible to avoid becoming prey by denying the lion's perceptual
system the cues that normally accompany being a mealtime animal.
Knowing how other creatures categorize behavior based on motion cues
could thus make the difference between life and death.

Humans are also very adept at making such behavioral judgments from
simple motion patterns: When two children run across a field, their parents can distinguish in a brief moment whether they are playing or fighting in earnest. When a pigeon twirls and struts before another, who ignores this display and turns away, we can quickly tell that the first is
trying unsuccessfully to court the second. In situations such as these, we
as outside observers can often decide what is going on—who is doing
what to whom—based just on the motions of the two organisms relative
to each other. Moreover, the human or animal participants in such cases
can also tell what kind of interaction they are having, again using motion
cues. How can organisms categorize behaviors based solely on observed
motion patterns? In other words, how can humans and other animals
translate from the domain of pure physical movement into the domain of

animate intentions and desires such as chasing, playing, and courting? What are the most important categories of behavior? What motion cues are most useful for distinguishing them, and how do we exploit these cues to achieve fast, accurate recognition of other agents' intentions?

The answers to these questions come in three stages. First, we must specify the major behavioral functions that an organism's whole-body motions can fulfill, such as chasing, fighting, or courting. Second, we must determine the observable motion cues that allow us to categorize which of these functions an organism is performing at a particular time. And third, we must find the cognitive algorithms that can be used to make this functional categorization based on motion cues.

These stages require very different research methods. The first stage entails an evolutionary task analysis of motion itself, asking what basic reasons animals have for moving at all, given the demands of survival and reproduction. The second stage requires analyzing the information structure of the environment, determining what useful motion cues can be recovered by observing a moving animal, and which motion cues are most useful in distinguishing the animal's reasons or intentions for movement. The third stage includes comparing the performance of different possible decision algorithms that map motion cues onto the basic functional categories of animal movement, to narrow the search for algorithms that animals and humans might actually use. Because many algorithms attain similar levels of accuracy when inferring intention from motion (see chapter 7 for more on this problem of algorithm comparison), we will not aim to be conclusive on this point. Rather, our main concern will be determining the functionally important motion categories and the available motion cues that can be used to distinguish between them.

It is not at all obvious how to get from motions to intentions. The difficulties are clear in comparing the standard dictionary definitions for motion terms with those for higher-level intentional behaviors. For example, the *Oxford English Dictionary* defines "run" as "to move the legs quickly (the one foot being lifted before the other is set down) so as to go at a faster pace than walking"; whereas it defines "chase" as "to pursue with a view to catching." Thus, "run" is defined by reference to observable motion cues, whereas "chase" is defined by unobservable intent with respect to a future goal concerning an unstated object. Nothing in the definition of "chase" suggests how a naive observer could distinguish chasing from any other intentional category of movement. Because we cannot directly perceive movement intentions and goals, and the targets of movement may even be hidden, we must infer them all indirectly using motion cues that can be directly perceived—a clear case of inference under uncertainty as described in chapter 1.

A general description of how we can infer goals and intentions from observable behavior would constitute a rather complete understanding of the human "theory of mind" (Baron-Cohen, 1995) and much of social psychology more generally. We are not attempting to provide that general understanding here—we focus only on the very simple case of using motion cues to categorize the most typical forms of intention-driven interaction between two agents. This special case is, nonetheless, biologically important to virtually every animal species, and psychologically important as the most elementary level of social cognition. Animal species differ in body structure, modes of locomotion, environmental constraints on motion, motion perception abilities, mating systems, and positions in the local food chain. However, by keeping our analysis of the special case of intention from motion sufficiently abstract, we hope to identify motion cues and intention categorization strategies that are general enough to apply to many species despite these differences.

We must still constrain the special case explored here by limiting the types of intentional motion categories, cues, and cue-processing algorithms we will consider. First, we assume that humans and other animals have domain-specific motion perception and intention inference adaptations that are attuned to ancestrally typical categories of motion patterns and intentions. These typical patterns, associated with intentions such as pursuit, evasion, fighting, courtship, and play, arise because there are just a few basic survival and reproductive goals for animate motion. The fact that there are only a few reasons why one animal moves relative to another animal makes our job as psychologists much easier, transforming an unconstrained inference task ("Why is that animal moving?") into a simple categorization decision ("Is that animal chasing, fleeing, fighting, courting, or what?").

Second, we limit our consideration of the vast range of possible information that could be used in judging the intentions of other agents. Potential cues include not only the motion of whole bodies in relation to other bodies—as when mountain lions infer edibility when humans turn from them—but also motions of one body part in relation to another, including threat and submission postures, facial expressions (e.g., snarling dogs or laughing children; see Darwin, 1872/1965) and those micromovements of throat, tongue, and lips that result in articulate human speech. Here we focus on just the first, simplest form of information for judging intentions: the overall motion trajectories of two whole organisms in relation to each other. Third, the inference algorithms that might use this motion information are also limitless, but again we are interested in simple possibilities: fast and frugal heuristics that use as little of the available information as they can to make their decisions and operate as quickly as possible. Particularly when judging the intentions of (possibly hostile) others, it is important to be able to make decisions quickly and with just the information at hand, rather than waiting until all possible evidence has been gathered and the mountain lion has pounced.

We begin this chapter with an evolutionary analysis of how animate intentions could be inferred from motion cues. We then develop a novel experimental method for studying how humans make these inferences. The first step is to gather ecologically representative examples of the six most typical animate motion patterns, by having participants play interactive computer games that require them to pursue, evade, fight, court, be courted, or play with each other. The participants control on-screen bugs with realistic motion physics using a mouse. The resulting motion patterns are recorded and presented to another set of participants, who try to infer what the bugs are trying to do to each other. We determine which intentions are confused most frequently with which other intentions. We then construct and test various models of how people could categorize these intentions given some simple motions cues that can be computed directly from the motion patterns. The goal is to identify both useful objective motion cues and simple heuristics that can process them to infer animate intentions. We view this intention-inference task as the foundation for more advanced forms of social cognition and attribution.

Previous Research on Inferring Intentions from Motion Cues

The question of how we infer intentions from motion cues seems fundamental for motion perception and social cognition, but it has rarely caught the attention of mainstream psychologists. The few exceptions are those who take an ecological view of perception, which motivates more direct study of the structure of the observable environment in relation to an agent's goals.

The earliest example was perhaps Fritz Heider, who set out to study the perception of social events by studying the particular stimuli that led to different attributions. His experiments in the 1940s with Simmel (Heider & Simmel, 1944) demonstrated that people spontaneously attribute intentions and personalities even to featureless geometric figures such as dots and triangles, if these figures move around in a cartoon film according to patterns reminiscent of animals courting and fighting. Heider and Simmel did not explicitly identify the motion cues that provoke these interpretations. But they had enough tacit knowledge of these cues that they could lead observers to view a roving triangle as a scheming villain, or a flitting disc as a fickle adulteress, through nothing more than relative motion in a simple environment.

Interest in this area fell dormant for a quarter of a century, aside from research in ethology specifically aimed at uncovering the motion cues that animals make to signal their intentions to each other, such as wolf pups bowing to signal playful intent (see Fagen, 1981). In the 1970s, J. J. Gibson's (1966, 1979) research on "direct" perception of ecologically important visual cues of motion inspired a number of studies on the perception of gait and other forms of biological motion by Kozlowski and Cutting (1977; Cutting & Kozlowski, 1977). These studies were aimed at identifying various dynamic and structural invariants in "point-light displays," films of people walking and acting in total darkness, with only small light sources affixed to their limbs and bodies. Even such impoverished stimuli, consisting solely of cues to movement, contained enough information to allow the visual system to make sophisticated inferences (e.g., that is a man lifting a heavy object, or that is a woman walking).

In a separate research tradition, French psychologist Albert Michotte investigated how people perceive cause and effect based on motion cues (Michotte, 1963). His project addressed mainly the psychology of causality (inspired by the philosophy of Aristotle and Hume), but Michotte was intrigued by his finding that people tend to interpret rectangles that interact without colliding as if they were animals or humans (Michotte, 1950), similar to Heider and Simmel's findings of rampant anthropomorphism. His work influenced modern studies on the innate preparedness of infants to perceive animacy (Premack, 1990; Spelke et al., 1995), and on the perception of animate motion more generally (Freyd & Miller, 1992; Gelman et al., 1995; McBeath et al., 1992). Michotte's emphasis on causation has been followed by recent studies that focus more on how people distinguish animate from inanimate motion, rather than how people distinguish between different types of animate motion.

This preoccupation with the animate-inanimate distinction is unfortunate because it stops short of what is arguably the more interesting question: Recognizing a moving object as animate is only the first step toward recognizing its intentions, which are what really matter for deciding what to do in response to it. Zebra herds have to live with lions hanging around at their watering holes, fleeing only when the lions show a real intention to chase them. The crucial distinction for a zebra is not between animate motion (a moving lion) and inanimate motion (a breeze stirring tawny grasses), but between animate motion that is relevant (a hungry lion at full sprint heading straight for you) and irrelevant (a fat lion chasing a fertile lioness). The point of animate motion perception is to guide one's own animate motion. The animate-inanimate distinction is just one relatively weak cue for deciding what to do; much stronger, more informative cues are available and so should be used to help determine other agents' intentions and one's own reactions. With that view, this chapter examines some basic goals of animate motion, some associated motion cues that may be general across species and ecologies, and some simple heuristics for categorizing intentions based on those motion cues.

The Basic Goals of Animate Motion

Moving has energetic costs, so animals are expected to move only when the fitness benefits of movement exceed these costs. The major fitness benefits of moving, as of any other behavior, are survival and reproduction. Thus, it is possible to deduce a few paradigmatic goals of animate motion from the fundamentals of natural selection and sexual selection.

Animals evolve to interact adaptively with various "fitness affordances" in their environments—things that are likely to affect the replication of their genes (Miller & Freyd, 1993; Todd & Wilson, 1993). Positive fitness affordances, such as food and sexual mates, promote survival or reproduction. Negative fitness affordances, such as predators, pathogens, parasites, and sexual competitors, interfere with survival or reproduction. Animals evolve sensory-motor systems to approach the positives and avoid the negatives. If two animals offer the potential of mutually positive yields, mutual approach usually results (e.g., in symbiotic relationships). If they threaten mutually negative yields, then mutual avoidance results. Movement patterns in these cases are just solutions to various positive-sum coordination games. The more interesting case is when animals present affordances of opposite sign to each other, that is, when one animal wants to be near the other, but the other wants to be far away. The zebra is a positive (food) affordance for the lion, but the lion is a very negative (death) affordance indeed for the zebra. Such conflicts of interest lead to more complex interactions, transforming simple approach into relentless pursuit, and simple avoidance into desperate evasion (Miller & Cliff, 1994).

From these arguments, it follows that the fundamental categories of two-agent animate interaction are mutual approach (boring), mutual avoidance (also boring), and pursuit and evasion (interesting). In the survival domain, pursuit and evasion usually occur between predators and prey, or between fighting conspecifics. In the reproductive domain, males usually pursue and females usually evade, at least for a while (Andersson, 1994; Darwin, 1871). Thus, almost every animal will need to master some subset of five basic categories of animate motion: pursuing, evading, fighting, courting, and being courted. To these categories we also add a sixth, play, which is widely used, especially by mammals, to learn mastery of the other five movement types. Although not all species need to exhibit the full set of these behaviors, they generally need to be able to recognize each of them. We will now consider the six behavior types in turn.

Pursuit   Animals move toward objects they desire. If the desired object is inanimate, we have a degenerate case of goal-directed behavior. But if the object is animate and does not want to be exploited as a fitness affordance (e.g., as food or as a mate), then it will move away (evade). The simplest pursuit strategy is to point one's front in the direction of the desired object and charge at top speed toward it, changing one's direction if the object deviates to the left or right of one's current heading. However, pursuit can be more efficient by predictively taking into account any environmental constraints on motion (obstacles and boundaries) and the pursued agent's own heading, movement, and intentions.

Evasion   Animals move away from things that threaten them. Again, if the threatening object is inanimate, we have a degenerate case of obstacle avoidance, or one-step "evasion." If the threat is animate, however, and does not wish to be evaded, then it will pursue, and sustained evasion becomes necessary. Evasion often favors strategies of deceptive feints and lunges and unpredictable, "protean" zigzagging (Driver & Humphries, 1988; Miller & Cliff, 1994), as well as avoidance of environmental traps or cul-de-sacs.

Fighting   Animals of the same species often fight over fitness affordances such as territories, resources, sexual mates, and social status. Fights can be tricky to decipher because both animals must combine pursuit and evasion, attack and defense, in a way that intimidates or overcomes the opponent, without injuring or killing themselves. Because animal bodies are heterogeneous, with some parts specialized for attack and other parts vulnerable to injury, fighting usually includes a great deal of precise, dynamic body positioning in relation to one's opponent.

Courting   Animals (usually males) move toward members of the opposite sex (usually females) with whom they wish to mate (Andersson, 1994; Darwin, 1871). But because selective mate choice is almost always imposed by the opposite sex (usually females), simple approach is almost never enough. Instead, mate-seeking animals often evolve extremely complex courtship behaviors with special features designed to display their health, strength, size, status, intelligence, or creativity (Andersson, 1994; Miller, 1998). These displays are usually produced close enough for the desired mate to perceive them, but not too close, lest the audience is scared off rather than enticed. After some display time, ranging from seconds (for some insects) to years (for some humans), if the desired mate signals her (or his) interest, the final approach and copulation can occur.

Being Courted   Animals sought after as mates (usually females) have strong incentives to select among their suitors quite carefully, because they usually have more at stake when mating than the suitors, and the genetic quality of the suitors they choose to mate with will determine half of the genetic quality of their offspring. Random mating is stupid mating (see chapter 13 for more on nonrandom mating and mate search). The task when being courted, then, is to express enough interest to elicit informative courtship behavior from various suitors so their mate quality can be assessed, but not so much interest that the courter skips courtship altogether and tries to move straight to copulation. Thus, being courted requires a delicate balance between interactive encouragement and coy reticence. Courted animals usually maintain enough proximity to their suitors that they can determine the suitor's quality, but do not get close enough to risk sexual harassment or rape.

Playing   Play often comprises a variety of actions through which young animals can practice all of the above movement types, using play signs to indicate that they are pursuing, evading, courting, or fighting without real lethal or sexual intent (Fagen, 1981). In basic play, animals repeatedly switch roles between pursuer and evader, or attacker and defender. In more complex play characteristic of large-brained primates, animals may interact in more abstract ways with imaginary partners or mutual mimicry.

These six goals for animate motion are not intended to be the building blocks in some sort of universal movement grammar. There are other movement goals that cannot be reduced to these categories, such as parental protection of vulnerable offspring from conspecifics or predators, foraging for inanimate food items or nest materials, migrating to new habitats, grooming oneself or others, flocking, mobbing predators, and so forth. We simply start with the most obvious basic cases of two-agent interaction. Future research will, we hope, analyze the motion cues that help distinguish these additional categories of behavior.

Eliciting Motion Trajectories for the Six Typical Behaviors

Following in the tradition of early work on attribution of intentional behavior to simple moving stimuli by Heider and Simmel (1944), we sought to study how people categorize the functional intentions of two interacting organisms based solely on their trajectories through space relative to each other. This required collecting some trajectories representative of each of our six functional categories that could be measured objectively to find useful motion cues, and that could be presented in a standard format as stimuli to human participants. But such trajectory data is rather difficult to come by. The literature in both biology and psychology offers many studies of long-range animal navigation, migration, and commuting on the one hand, and small-scale limb movements on the other. However, there is little publicly available data on behavioral trajectories between these extremes. So we decided to generate our own sample trajectories, using the animate agents we had in ready abundance: university students.

The question was how to obtain ecologically representative samples of the six typical behavioral categories. Despite generous research resources, it proved infeasible to attach radio tracking beacons to participants' heads, record them from satellite observations, and wait for some good examples of pursuit, fighting, courtship, and play. Though overhead video recordings from the Oktoberfest near our Munich laboratory would have captured instances of all of these behaviors, the trajectories would have appeared somewhat distorted by the potent Weissbier.

Instead, we had pairs of participants interact through a computer network, generating the trajectories by instructing them to play various movement games. Each participant sat before a computer and used a mouse to control the motions of a simple buglike creature displayed on the computer screen. Participants could see their own bug and another bug, which was controlled by another participant in another room at another computer. Both bugs are displayed on-screen in a featureless rectangular environment bounded by walls, without any obstacles, viewed from an overhead perspective (see figure 12-1). We engaged 10 pairs of participants to perform the six fundamental behaviors in this simple computer-mediated interaction game.

The bug did not act like an ordinary on-screen cursor that directly reflects hand movements across the mouse pad. Rather, the bug was constrained by some simulated physics. This included momentum, which produced slow acceleration and deceleration of the bugs; collision dynamics, which made the two bugs bounce off each other and the walls; and a top speed at which the bugs could travel. The participants' mouse movements were essentially treated as targets for where the bug should be heading next (for details, see Blythe et al., 1996). These semirealistic physics made the movement games challenging, enhanced the perception of animacy, and, we hope, made the resulting motion trajectories more ecologically representative of natural animal movement.

The bug form was chosen because it looked more interesting than a dot. As discussed earlier, previous experiments on motion perception suggested that the attribution of animacy to a moving object appears to be a natural tendency for humans, whether the object resembles a human form

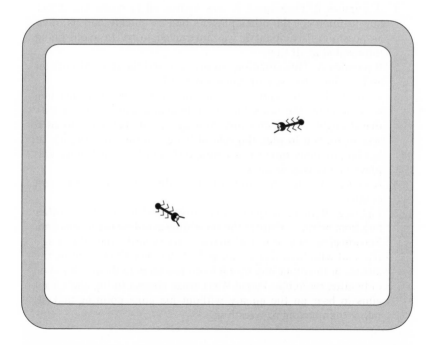

Figure 12-1: The two-bug view that each participant saw when generating motion trajectories, captured at a single instant in time. Each bug is a different color.

or a geometric shape (as found by Heider & Simmel, 1944; Michotte, 1963; Rimé et al., 1985). However, we thought the bug form would stimulate participants' interest without biasing their behavior in anthropomorphic ways, as a human-shaped icon might. It was also important to use a figure with a clear front and back end (as opposed to a circle, for instance) so that orientation would be unambiguous to both parties involved in the motion games. Furthermore, as biologist J. B. S. Haldane is reputed to have observed, "to a first approximation, all animals are beetles."

During each experiment, two participants unknown to each other were put into separate rooms with computers and were guided by on-screen instructions to practice and play the appropriate movement games in sequence. The participants were initially given a two-minute practice period to learn how to control their bugs using the mouse. Pilot studies showed this practice period sufficient for attaining a reasonable skill level, given that most participants had substantial experience with computer mouse controls. Following this, they participated in six trials of two minutes each.[1] The asymmetric trials of pursuit-evasion and courting-courted were duplicated with roles reversed, while fighting and play were only performed once by each participant pair.

The two participants, here A and B, were instructed to play the six movement games as follows:

1. A pursues B: Participant A was instructed to move his or her bug to intercept the other player's bug as quickly and as often as possible. Participant B was instructed to try to avoid being intercepted at all times.
2. B pursues A: This situation simply reversed the roles of pursuer and evader between participants A and B.
3. A courts B: Participant A was instructed to move his or her bug so as to court the other bug, by interacting with it in any way that it might find interesting, exciting, or enticing. Participant B was instructed to play the role of being courted, moving his or her bug to show interest or disinterest, and to elicit further displays in any way desired.
4. B courts A: This situation reversed the roles of courter and courtee.
5. Fighting: Both participants were instructed to attack the other bug from behind, while at the same time avoiding being attacked. Specifically, they were instructed to try to strike the other bug's rear end with their bug's front end, at the same time avoiding the attacks of the other bug trying to do the same to them. This type of fighting resembles World War I aerial combat (bring one's front guns to bear on the enemy without his guns pointing at you) rather than boxing or wrestling.

---

1. The courtship trials lasted three minutes as it is a slower, more gradual behavior that required more time with some participants. In real life, while fights and pursuits may be over in seconds, we expect courtship to take rather longer.

6. Playing: Both participants were instructed to play with the other bug in whatever manner they wanted.

These movement games were obviously underspecified: We gave no feedback, offered no monetary incentives for performance, and allowed almost no practice time. We were not interested in studying the long-term equilibrium strategies for these dynamic two-person games, but rather in using the games as a quick and easy way of generating ecologically representative motion trajectories for six typical kinds of animate interaction. We expected that participants would have relatively stable and readily applied notions about what movement in each category looks like, and this is the knowledge we wanted to elicit. For pursuit, evasion, and fighting it would have been possible to specify each participant's payoffs exactly, but for courting, being courted, and playing, such payoff specification would have been difficult.

Visualizing the Resulting Trajectories

In each motion category trial, the computer recorded the movement trajectory of each participant's bug at a high temporal and spatial resolution. We then analyzed the resulting fine-grained trajectories in various ways, to see if there were any motion cues that could distinguish one behavioral category from another. First, we used a simple visualization method to look at the trajectories of two bugs interacting during one two-minute motion trial. Figures 12-2 to 12-5 show space-time plots of typical pursuit-evasion, courtship, fighting, and play trajectories generated by pairs of participants. The horizontal plane of the plot represents the horizontal and vertical positions of the creatures in the two-dimensional environment, while the vertical axis represents time during one 90-second trial segment. These plots reveal some basic information about the trajectories. Higher velocities (more spatial distance covered per unit time) result in flatter trajectories. Bugs that are not moving result in vertical line segments in these plots. Smaller distances between the bugs result in tightly intermingled trajectories.

Several features are immediately apparent in the plots that result from different movement games. In pursuit and evasion (figure 12-2), one sees very flat (very high speed) movements extending over a great area of the environment, contrasting sharply with the slower, more restricted movements during courtship (figure 12-3). Both pursuit-evasion (figure 12-2) and fighting (figure 12-4) show high speeds combined with large amounts of turning and looping. Fighting (figure 12-4) is distinguished by a smaller average distance between the two bugs, and by more tightly intertwined looping, with frequent contacts between the bugs (where their trajectories meet). In courtship (figure 12-3), the courter moves much more than the often stationary courtee, sometimes circling, and occasionally engaging the courtee in little bursts of pursuit and evasion. Only a few body con-

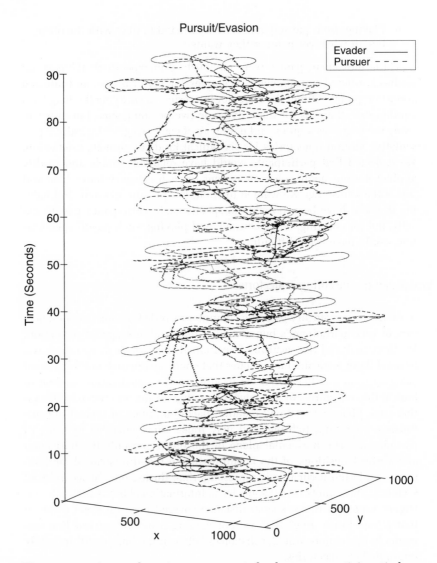

Figure 12-2: A sample trajectory generated when one participant's bug pursued the other, which evaded. Here, 90 seconds of interaction is represented, with time proceeding upward on the z-axis, and on-screen position of each bug plotted in the x-y plane. Note the generally high speed (flat segments) and large area covered.

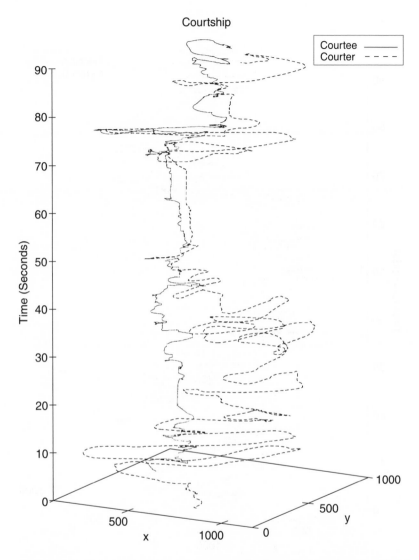

Figure 12-3: A sample trajectory generated when one participant's bug courted the other, which responded to the overtures. Note the more elaborate motions of the courter, and occasional rapid fleeing of the courtee.

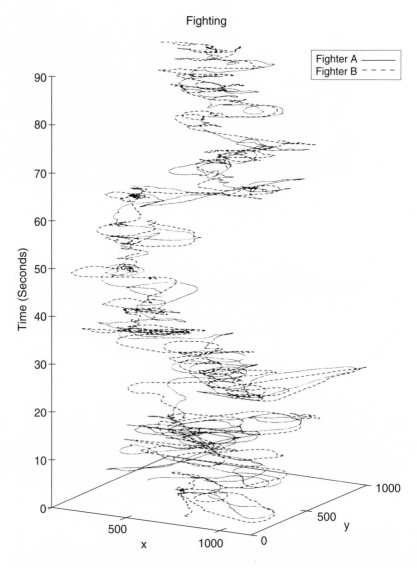

Figure 12-4: A sample trajectory generated when the two participants' bugs fought, trying to hit each other from behind. Note the high speed and high degree of looping.

Play

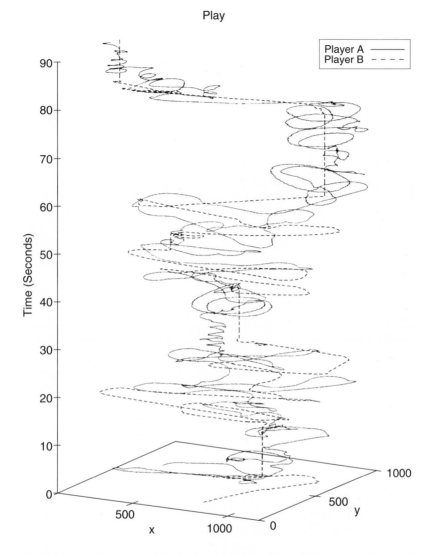

Figure 12-5: A sample trajectory generated when the two participants' bugs played with each other. Here, one bug looped while the other dashed.

tacts occur in courtship. Play (figure 12-5) looks like a combination of pursuit, evasion, fighting, and courtship, combining looping, rapid dashes, and long still pauses. We will use these observations later to suggest some motion cues for distinguishing among these behavioral categories.

How Do People Categorize the Trajectories?

Our goal is to find motion cues that can distinguish exemplars of the six behavior categories and that may be used by humans in making such categorizations. But before we analyze the motion trajectories we have collected for different intentional categories, we must be sure that these trajectories do in fact contain the cues necessary to make the proper categorical distinctions. To find out, we tested whether a new set of participants could categorize the motion patterns accurately. Given example trajectories, how good are untrained people at assigning them to the behavioral task for which they were originally generated? Knowing this provides a rough check on the ecological validity of the trajectories, and makes it possible to investigate which categories are easily confused and which are easily distinguished. A model of animate motion categorization might perform well, but unless it makes roughly the same pattern of judgments, both correct and incorrect, as real human participants, it would not qualify as a good psychological model. Also, we can see what happens when we present the trajectories of both bugs together, versus only one by itself (see next section), to check the relative importance of single-bug motion cues versus interactive, relational cues for trajectory categorization. That is, by systematically removing some motion cues and recording drops in categorization performance, we can see which cues matter.

The Two-Bug Case: Relational and Individual Cues

In this categorization experiment, 10 participants saw portions of 30 motion trajectories recorded from the first experiment presented in randomized order, with one bug displayed in blue and the other in red. Participants were instructed to decide which one of the six behaviors the red bug was engaged in, as quickly as possible. As soon as they felt they could decide whether the red bug was pursuing, evading, fighting, courting, being courted, or playing with the blue bug, participants were to stop the trajectory playback and make a choice. To clarify this six-alternative forced choice, these trajectory-categorizing participants were shown the instructions given to the original trajectory-generating participants. However, these participants were not shown any examples of the motion categories beforehand, nor given any feedback on their selections. Nonetheless, participants' categorization performance changed little if at all over the course of the 30 trials, with equal accuracy in the first and second halves of the trials, suggesting that there was no significant learning effect.

Table 12-1: Participants' Categorization Confusion Matrix for Two-Bug Trajectories

	Choice					
Actual	Pursuing	Evading	Courting	Courted	Fighting	Playing
Pursuing	**29**	1	1	0	9	17
Evading	5	**20**	0	5	6	7
Courting	2	0	**38**	2	4	8
Courted	0	2	5	**29**	4	6
Fighting	5	6	3	3	**10**	23
Playing	2	0	9	10	7	**21**
Totals	43	29	56	49	40	82

Note. Each entry shows how many times participants chose a particular (column) category for a trajectory generated in some actual (row) category. The main diagonal (in bold) shows correct categorizations.

(Response times were also recorded for each judgment for later comparison among different categorization models, but we will not discuss these data in this chapter.)

Overall, participants selected the originally intended motion category in nearly half (49%) of the trials. This is well above chance (about 17%) for six-alternative choice. (In comparison, three expert participants who were familiar with the task and had previously seen many trajectories—the three authors—achieved 72% matches.) To see where participants erred, we can construct confusion matrices showing which categories were most often confused with each other. Table 12-1 shows such a confusion matrix for the 300 participant categorizations. The rows denote the actual intention-category instruction given to the trajectory generators, and the columns denote the choice decisions made by the trajectory categorizers. Thus, the leading diagonal represents correct responses. With 10 participants each making 30 categorizations distributed across the six categories, each row contains about 50 responses.[2]

The column totals in table 12-1 (which would equal the row totals if participants matched all of the trajectory categorizations) show that participants overestimated the base rate of play by nearly 70%, and underestimated the amount of evasion by about 30%. (Participants also overestimated courtship and underestimated pursuit and fighting by smaller amounts.) These tendencies could reflect participants' underlying beliefs about the base rates of these motions in nature, particularly that play is more common than serious conflict, especially evasion. The play overesti-

2. Most rows in tables 12-1 and 12-2 do not have exactly 50 entries due to missing data and to the way in which randomly assigned trials were split between the pursuing-evading and courting-courted pairs.

mation could also indicate that participants use play as a default "catch-all" choice when no clear distinction can be made, in keeping with the argument mentioned earlier that play provides training for the other behaviors.

Reading across rows in the table, we also see some more specific sources of confusion. Pursuit was very often miscategorized as play, and fighting was miscategorized as play more often than it was accurately categorized as fighting. Fighting was often mistaken for pursuit and evasion, as well. In addition to the general tendency to mistake other behaviors as play, actual play was often mistaken for other behaviors such as courting, being courted, and fighting. This error can arise when participants first see a chasing component of play, for instance, and make a quick (wrong) decision of pursuit-evasion from this limited time window. In nature, other nontrajectory cues (such as laughing in humans) could be used to categorize play more accurately.

On the other hand, participants did often get the categorizations right: Pursuit and evasion were rarely confused with each other, and courting was rarely confused with being courted. As might be expected, pursuit and being courted were never mistaken for each other, and courting and evading were never mistaken for each other. This is consistent with the existence of similarities between pursuit and courting, and between evasion and being courted. However, important differences are clearly present as well, because pursuit was almost never perceived as courtship, courtship was almost never perceived as pursuit, and being courted was rarely mistaken for evasion. These differences and similarities should be reflected in the set of cues we ultimately settle on for categorizing motion trajectories.

While our data showed a high percentage of systematic errors (overestimating play, underestimating evasion) and many individual confusions, it must be emphasized that even with no feedback, no practice, and minimal instruction, naive participants can categorize behaviors into biologically important classes at far above chance levels, given nothing more than the recorded trajectories of two agents interacting. We have stripped away all environmental context, all gait and posture information about the agents, all facial expression, and all communication. Nevertheless, pure whole-body motion cues are sufficient to categorize the behaviors fairly accurately, from which we conclude that the trajectories we collected do in fact contain enough information to indicate intentional categories. We can therefore proceed to analyze just how that information is reflected in the trajectories: What are the cues we can use to judge intention from motion?

The One-Bug Case: Trajectories Without Relational Cues

One way to determine what sort of cues people (in particular, our participants) use to judge intention from motion is to eliminate part of the available information from the motion trajectories and see how this affects the categorization judgments made on the basis of the modified trajectories. In the first categorization experiment, participants saw all of the information captured in the complete trajectories of both interacting bugs. This made it possible for participants to use all of the motion cues that rely on the relative position, heading, and speed of the two creatures. To gauge the importance of this class of relational cues, we wanted to find out how well people could do at the categorization task if they were all stripped away. Such relative information can be removed by only playing back the recorded trajectory of one of the two bugs, so that participants cannot know what the other bug is doing.

To this end, we ran a second categorization experiment in the same manner as the first, but with 10 new participants, and with only one of the two bugs in an interacting pair being visible in each presented trajectory. Participants had to categorize what behavior the one visible bug was performing. Table 12-2 shows the confusion matrix from this experiment, presented in the same format as table 12-1. Now, overall percentage correct drops from the 49% level of the two-bug experiment to 30% (still well above the chance level of 17%). This large performance drop indicates that we should include relative motion information in our list of important cues in this domain. We can also learn something interesting from considering the patterns of errors made in this setting.

Inspecting the column totals in table 12-2 reveals that participants in this experiment selected all six categories more evenly; the play overestimation has disappeared, replaced by a slight tendency to overestimate the amount of courting going on. Most of the miscategorizations were due to strong confusions between certain behavior classes. Whereas pursuit was clearly distinct from evasion or courting if the second bug was visible (table 12-1), one-bug pursuit was very often confused with the latter two categories. Evasion was mistaken for pursuit as often as it was accurately categorized, perhaps because both entail high-speed, unpredictable loop-

Table 12-2: Participants' Categorization Confusion Matrix for One-Bug Trajectories

Actual	Choice					
	Pursuing	Evading	Courting	Courted	Fighting	Playing
Pursuing	**15**	8	12	3	7	7
Evading	13	**14**	9	1	5	6
Courting	2	5	**16**	17	5	9
Courted	5	7	4	**21**	2	5
Fighting	7	4	12	0	**13**	14
Playing	5	4	10	5	14	**10**
Totals	47	42	63	47	46	51

Note. Each entry shows how many times participants chose a particular (column) category for a trajectory generated in some actual (row) category, after seeing the motions of only one of the two bugs involved. The main diagonal (in bold) shows correct categorizations.

ing throughout the entire space. Courting was very often mistaken for being courted, but, strangely, being courted was still rarely mistaken for courting. Fighting was mistaken for courting and for play nearly as often as it was categorized accurately.

The differences between tables 12-1 and 12-2 indicate that relational cues are important in making some distinctions but not others. In particular, single-bug (nonrelational) information is usually sufficient to distinguish aggressive intentions (pursuit, evasion, fighting) from more passive intentions such as being courted. But relational cues seem to be necessary to decide whether the bug is the follower (pursuit or courtship) or the avoider (evasion or being courted). These two findings indicate that a different set (and number) of cues is needed to make different categorizations—in some cases, decisions can be made without using all of the available information. Our search for appropriate categorization algorithms later in this chapter will make use of this fact.

Identifying Useful Motion Cues Computable from Trajectory Information

The categorization experiments just described showed that, to categorize intentions from the motion trajectories of two interacting agents, we must consider both individually based cues computed from the motion of a single agent, and relational cues determined by comparing the motions of both agents together. To narrow in on the specific cues that could be used, we must consider the information embedded in the trajectories.

Some obvious cues might relate to the goals of the behavioral categories. For example, in our experiments the goal of pursuit was to intercept the other agent, and the goal of fighting was to strike the other agent's rear end with one's front end. Thus, one could just try to count up the number of successful interceptions and strikes to distinguish pursuit and fighting from play. However, the other agent does not want to be intercepted or struck. Successful evasion implies unsuccessful pursuit. Cues of success may be poor indicators of intention, particularly over short-term portions of an ongoing interaction, and in fact, such cues did not prove to be very diagnostic in our setting.

It is more useful to consider the simple, objective (nonintentional) cues that can be computed given an intentional motion trajectory. The trajectories recorded in our experiment took place in two spatial dimensions, so we can focus on some simple Newtonian cues. A trajectory can be measured in terms of the bug's position and velocity for each of the two linear dimensions. Because the bug figures have a head end and a tail end, they also have a rotational degree of freedom, captured in their orientation or heading, and a rotational velocity equivalent to the rate at which they are changing their orientation. Ignoring higher-order parameters such as acceleration, this yields six basic motion parameters for each agent: horizontal position, horizontal velocity, vertical position, vertical velocity, orientation, and rotational velocity. A two-agent system can thus be described with 12 independent parameters.

This might be fine for a physicist interested in modeling abstract changes in position in a two-body system, but is it useful for categorizing behaviors and intentions of animate agents? Intuition, and the results of our categorization experiments presented in the previous sections, suggest not. Information about one's absolute place in the world and that of some other organism does not matter to individuals nearly as much as comparison between oneself and others—social behavior, like evolution itself, is driven by relative differences. Absolute position information is largely irrelevant in perceiving how two agents are interacting (aside from the effects of special locations in the environment such as watering holes or shelter); what matters is their position relative to each other. Likewise, their individual orientations are not as informative regarding their intentions toward each other as are their relative orientations toward each other. From any one agent's perspective, the three position and orientation parameters that matter are likely to be the distance to the other agent (what we refer to as the *relative distance* cue), the angle between one's current heading and the other agent's location (*relative angle*), and the angle between one's current heading and the other agent's own heading (*relative heading*).

We can also reduce the six velocity parameters that describe a general two-agent system into four velocity parameters that matter to any given agent whose behavior we want to categorize: *absolute velocity* (how fast the agent is going forward, rather than in the two orthogonal spatial directions separately—as we will see, we can ignore the other velocity component corresponding to sideways motion), *relative velocity* (how fast the one agent is going relative to the other agent), *absolute vorticity* (how fast the agent is changing heading), and *relative vorticity* (how fast the one agent is changing heading relative to the other agent's heading change). We can eliminate two parameters by ignoring one's own sideways velocity (which is usually zero in nature and in our bug world), and relative sideways velocity (which is also usually zero). Thus, we are left with three relevant position parameters and four relevant velocity parameters. These can be converted into motion cues by averaging them over some temporal window. In accordance with the results of our second categorization experiment, which demonstrated the importance of relational information, five of the seven cues we have ended up with are relational (uncomputable given just one visible agent).

In summary, we propose seven simple, ecologically relevant cues that can be useful in categorizing the intentions of one (focal) agent interacting with another agent.

Relative distance: the distance between the two agents. Fighting and pursuit-evasion tend to produce smaller relative distances in the bug trajectories than do courtship and play.

Relative angle: the angle between the focal agent's current heading (the direction it is facing) and the other agent. This cue indicates whether the other agent is in front of or behind the focal agent. Pursuit can be distinguished from evasion most easily by relative angle.

Relative heading: the difference in heading between one agent and the other, indicating whether they are facing the same direction (more typical of pursuit and evasion), or facing each other (more typical of fighting, courtship, and play).

Absolute velocity: the forward velocity of the focal agent with respect to the background environment. Pursuit-evasion and fighting generate higher absolute velocities than do courtship and play.

Relative velocity: the difference between the velocities of the two agents. Pursuers and evaders tend to have nearly zero relative velocity across the duration of a chase, but courtship produces large differences in velocity between courter and courtee.

Absolute vorticity: the vorticity (change in heading) of the agent with respect to the background environment. Fighting and courting produce high vorticities, while play and being courted are associated with low vorticity.

Relative vorticity: the difference between the vorticities of the two agents. Pursuers and evaders tend to turn equally often, and so have zero relative vorticity, while courters and courtees often have a large vorticity difference.

Before settling on this set of seven cues distilled from the motion trajectories, we need to be sure that they contain at least enough information to make reasonably accurate intention categorizations. If we discover otherwise, then we would have to search for a different set of more appropriate cues. One way to test this question is to see whether a general-purpose pattern-associating algorithm can map from the particular values of these seven cues computed from portions of motion trajectories to the correct categories for those trajectories. We trained a simple logistic-activation three-layer neural network on the same 300 examples of motion trajectories that participants saw in our categorization experiments described earlier, using the values of the seven cues as inputs and the proper category as the target output. After training, the neural network correctly categorized 247 out of the 300 examples, or 82%. (When tested for generalization ability on 300 different examples, the network still got 200 correct, or 67%—see table 12-3.) Recall that participants only correctly categorized 49% of the 300 examples. Based on this, we concluded that these seven cues, while perhaps not fully capturing all of the distinguishing trajectory information, still distill enough information to allow us to create reasonable models of human performance in this task.

Solitary animals that only encounter a single other conspecific individual at any one time need only be able to categorize the behavior of those others relative to themselves, that is, from an egocentric viewpoint. For animals in more social species, where interactions between others are commonly witnessed, it can also be important to keep track of the inten-

Table 12-3: Categorization Accuracy of Participants and Competing Algorithms for One- and Two-Bug Trajectories, Along With Number of Cues Used by Each

			Competitor		
Criterion	Participants	CBE	Dawes's Rule	Franklin's Rule	Neural Network
% correct on training set with 7 cues	49%	65%	62%	68%	82%
% matches to participants' correct	—	73%	72%	77%	90%
Average number of cues used	?	3.6	7	7	7
% correct on testing set with 2 cues	30%	34%	33%	34%	26%
% correct on testing set with 7 cues	—	57%	60%	60%	67%

Note. Here, accuracy is shown in percentage correct (out of 300 trials), except for the second row, which shows percentage of matches to participants' (147) correct categorizations.

tions of different group members relative to each other. This is particularly true in species with dominance hierarchies and kin networks. Furthermore, between-species interactions often need to be judged accurately. For example, a gazelle should be able to tell if a lioness is chasing one of its herd mates, or if she is being chased herself, perhaps by another lion. Each of the seven cues listed above should be readily computable from either an egocentric viewpoint or from a third-party observer position. Although our experiments presented trajectories from a rather ecologically implausible (but computationally simple) top-down view, the seven cues could be computed almost as easily from a more realistic ground-level view.

The seven cues just described, like the 12 Newtonian parameters, are mostly independent in principle, but rather highly correlated in practice. That is, the structure of motion trajectories produced by organisms in nature will ensure that certain cue values co-occur. These natural intercorrelations between motion cues have two implications for categorizing intentions. First, only a few cues may suffice for making an accurate decision, because there is high overlap in information content between cues. Second, if one cue is unavailable, another may take its place: Correlated cues enable *vicarious functioning* (essentially, cue substitutability) in decision making (Brunswik, 1943).

Vicarious functioning is important because in many real-world situations some or most of the possible cues may not be perceivable at any given time. Furthermore, the speed with which a cue can be registered may be another crucial constraint on the decision-making process. For high-pressure problems, such as deciding whether a mountain lion is stalking you, it may not suffice to wait for all cues to become available before making a decision. Such time pressure may favor fast and frugal, noncompensatory decision heuristics that make the most efficient use of the motion information available (see chapter 7). These are the sorts of decision heuristics for categorizing behaviors from motion cues that we will now consider.

Decision Heuristics for Categorizing Behaviors

What sort of decision mechanism might people and other animals use to process motion cues into intention category judgments? As we have indicated, judging intention from motion is a critical task often performed under time pressure. Moreover, our categorization experiments indicated that different cues are useful for deciding on different categories. These observations led us to look for a simple fast and frugal decision mechanism that uses only as much of the information as is necessary to select a single category. The Categorization by Elimination (CBE) algorithm is just such a mechanism (see chapter 11 for a full introduction). CBE categorizes a given stimulus by starting with a full set of possible categories and then using the particular values of the cues for that stimulus to eliminate more and more categories until only a single possibility remains. Thus, different stimuli may require that more or fewer cues are processed before they can be categorized. This algorithm always checks the cues in a particular predetermined order, and only uses as few cues as it can get away with to reach category decision, rendering it fast and frugal. Yet its categorization accuracy on some standard test sets is still close to that of more traditional algorithms that combine all available cues (as shown in chapter 11).

To use CBE to categorize motion intentions, we first determined the order in which to use our seven cues, based on how well they can each distinguish among the six intentional categories in our training set of 300 trajectory examples. We found that the absolute velocity cue was the most accurate at categorizing these trajectories when used alone, so it was put first in the list, followed by relative angle, relative velocity, relative heading, relative vorticity, absolute vorticity, and relative distance. (We found that the exact cue ordering did not make much difference in overall categorization performance; however, it does have a large effect on the number of cues looked up by the algorithm.) Then, to categorize a particular trajectory, CBE starts with the full set of six possible intentional categories and considers the value of the absolute velocity cue for that trajectory to determine which categories to eliminate from the set of remaining possibilities. For instance, a relatively low velocity value of only 400 pixels per second indicates that the trajectory could correspond to the more leisurely categories of courting, being courted, or play, so that the other three more frenetic categories should be eliminated from the set of possibilities. Because more than one category remains after checking velocity, the next cue in the preordered list (relative angle) must be used to eliminate more categories. This process of checking further cues continues until a single category is left, which is the algorithm's final decision.

Categorization by Elimination has several interesting features as an algorithm for cue-based categorization. It is nonintegrative, using only those cues necessary to reach a decision. If each cue takes some time to assess, this makes CBE faster than algorithms that use all cues. It is also noncompensatory, with earlier cues eliminating category possibilities that can never be restored by later cues. Whether this is a reasonable feature depends on the type and number of errors CBE produces, and the consequences of those errors. For example, if CBE eliminates the category "fight" too readily, and stupidly mistakes fighting for playing, CBE would be maladaptive. Finally, CBE always uses cues in a particular order. Here we order the cues by their ability to make correct categorizations (cue success—see chapter 11). It is important to use cues in a good order, because this is what allows CBE to make a rapid decision. If the algorithm looked at cues starting with the *least* useful, for instance, it would take more cues (and hence more time) to reach a decision and would more often be incorrect.

We tested the performance of CBE on categorizing trajectory intentions using the seven motion cues against both the correct (originally intended) categories and the categories that participants actually chose (from table 12-1). These comparisons are shown in table 12-3. To see how this fast and frugal heuristic performs in comparison with more traditional decision-making methods, we also constructed two linear combination models (Dawes's rule, using unit weights, and Franklin's rule, using cue success as weights—see chapter 4), which process the cues in the usual integrative, compensatory fashion. As mentioned in the previous section, we also trained a three-layer neural network model on this task to see how a nonlinear, compensatory system would do.

The first row of table 12-3 shows the performance of the above four algorithms on 300 categorizations, along with participant performance on the same data set. (The cue values in each of the 300 trials were computed from the same time period of trajectory data that the participants saw in that particular trial, ensuring that no extra advantage was given to the algorithms over the participants.) Each of the algorithms outperformed the participants by a fair margin. But this is not surprising given that the algorithms were all trained with feedback on the data to make the proper categorizations, while participants were not given feedback and had to categorize each motion pattern the first time they saw it. What is more surprising, though, is that the fast and frugal CBE performs about as well as the more traditional linear information-integrating methods (see chapter 11 for more such surprises). Furthermore, CBE uses only half of the cues, on average, that the other algorithms do—and thus it achieves its good categorization performance with significantly less data.

How well do CBE and the other algorithms match the decisions made by our participants? For all trials that participants got right (147), we compare how many times each algorithm also chose the (same) correct category and show this as a percentage of the 147 trials in row 2 of table 12-3. (The different algorithms' matches to participant mistakes appeared largely random and uninformative—there are more ways to be wrong than to be right in this task—and so are not included here.) Here again CBE does as well as the other linear-integrative algorithms, matching nearly three-quarters of the participants' correct answers. Given that CBE is also faster and more frugal than the other two linear models, we have some reason for preferring it as a psychological model worthy of further investigation. (In comparison, the baseline neural network algorithm matched 90% of the participants' correct responses.)

But just how much more frugal is CBE in this task? In the third row of table 12-3, we show how many cues the different algorithms used to make each categorization, averaged across the 300 trajectories seen. For the linear models and the neural network, this average is rather straightforward: These algorithms always use all of the available cues, so their average cue use is 7. But CBE can use a different number of cues to categorize each trajectory, and in general uses as few as possible. On average, CBE uses only 3.6 cues per categorization, little more than half of the total number of cues available.

The benefits of CBE's minimal cue usage are indicated in the fourth row of table 12-3, where we have strictly limited the number of cues that participants or algorithms can use to make categorizations. Specifically, we showed participants only one of the interacting bugs in the trajectory (this is the data from the second categorization experiment reported earlier), and we allowed the algorithms to use only the two nonrelational cues that are computable from such a restricted single-bug trajectory (absolute velocity and absolute vorticity). CBE and the two linear algorithms again do at least as well as the human participants. But the powerful neural network model, which did so well on the full training set, is now relatively crippled by the lack of information it was expecting—it is the only decision model that makes fewer correct categorizations than the participants do. In the last row of table 12-3 we see further evidence about the ability of these models to adapt to situations with new information: Here we show their performance in generalizing to a different set of 300 trajectories. All lose a fair amount of categorization accuracy, with the neural network losing the most and the linear algorithms the least; CBE lies in the middle.

These results can help us put the superior performance of the neural network model on the full-cue categorization task in perspective. Certainly the greater number of free parameters in the neural network weights can help its fitting performance. Beyond this, perhaps nonlinear cue integration has an advantage in this domain, and perhaps compensatory cue use is more appropriate here as well, when all the cues are known. However, compensatory cue use requires simultaneous access to all relevant cues, and there may be situations where cues are naturally perceived at different times or in different orders. In such cases, standard neural network models may be at a relative disadvantage compared with fast and frugal competitors. CBE, by contrast, could use cues in the natural order in which they can be perceived, categorizing as far as possible given each piece of incoming information. For example, relative position information may often be easier to estimate than average velocity or vorticity information, and so could be used to make an initial estimate of the appropriate intentional category in a fast and frugal manner. These questions should be explored by creating on-line dynamic decision models that can appropriately categorize animate intentions under ecologically realistic time constraints.

In sum, the fast and frugal CBE heuristic performs about as accurately as more traditional linear cue-integrating mechanisms as a model of human categorization in the intention-from-motion domain.[3] It achieves this surprising performance despite using on average only half of the information that the other algorithms use. This frugality allows CBE to make faster decisions, especially in realistic situations where time is required to assess the value of each cue. Using fewer cues can also lend CBE added robustness in comparison to the plethora of parameters in the competing neural network model—several cues could be unobservable in the environment without affecting CBE's performance at all. These advantages may not make much of a difference in a laboratory setting, but they can be crucial in real-world life-and-death decisions. This leads us to propose CBE as an ecologically rational algorithm for determining an organism's intention from its motion alone.

A Motion Turing Test and Other Extensions

As an adjunct to our categorization work, we devised a pilot version of a motion-based Turing test, in which a robot bug replaces one of the human participants in the trajectory-categorization experiments described earlier. After the trial, we asked the lone human participants whether they thought they were interacting with another human-controlled bug, or with a computer-controlled bug. A pilot study suggested that even the simplest robot algorithms could be surprisingly convincing, especially when their actions respond to the human-controlled bug (as opposed to acting completely independently). That is, if one bug (e.g., a pursuer) is really controlled by a human and the other (e.g., an evader) is controlled by a simple

---

3. As is often the case, it is difficult to make an empirical distinction between the fast and frugal algorithm and other approaches based solely on comparisons to human choices. See chapter 7 for more on this difficulty, and for some approaches to distinguishing between algorithms using process data such as reaction times in addition to choice data.

computer program, the resulting motion pattern looks almost indistinguishable from that of two human-controlled bugs interacting. This simple test further indicates the power of limited motion cues to indicate animate intention. We can similarly test other proposed cues of intention from motion by building behaviors that generate those cues into new robot bugs and investigating which combinations are most convincing to human observers.

These sorts of animate motion experiments may provide some useful new methods for investigating human theory of mind—the attribution of intentions, beliefs, and desires to others based on observable behaviors. Some researchers suggest that autistic people have deficits in their theory of mind module, such that their attributions of intention are severely impaired (Baron-Cohen, 1995). If so, it would be interesting to see how autistics do on intention-from-motion categorization tasks: The types of animate intentions that different individuals can reliably categorize from motion trajectories may indicate the presence or absence of different kinds of empathic or social-attribution impairments.

Intention-from-motion heuristics could also be used in a variety of practical applications. Many countries are increasing their use of closed-circuit cameras to detect crime. Such crime detection is basically a problem of distinguishing criminal intentions and behavior patterns from benign patterns, given motion cues. Even our simple cue-based methods of distinguishing between pursuit, evasion, fighting, and play may find uses in such systems. Automated crime-detection systems would not have to be perfect on their own; they would only have to help security guards identify which screen to pay most attention to out of the many screens they are expected to monitor. Also, pharmaceutical companies often test drugs by recording their effects on animal behavior patterns. Algorithmic systems for categorizing rat behavior as aggressive, exploratory, or playful may help in automating such evaluations. The problem of inferring intentions from motion cues is so general that there are doubtless hundreds of other related applications of simple fast and frugal decision heuristics.

Conclusions

In this chapter we have succeeded in uncovering a set of motion cues that can be used to infer some major categories of adaptively important intentions. The set of seven cues we proposed appears sufficient to capture the major regularities of motion in the six intentional categories we investigated. We introduced a new simple algorithm, Categorization by Elimination, that could accurately categorize motion patterns using a minimal number of cues, showing that these adaptively important inferences can be made in a fast and frugal manner.

Our main goal has been to provide a basis for the concept of social rationality, by finding simple motion cues and fast and frugal cue integration mechanisms that humans and other animals may use to interact effectively with each other. Such mechanisms can exploit the fact that animate motion tends to fall into a few rather stereotyped categories that can be derived from basic evolutionary and ecological principles. We tested the competing decision algorithms on motion trajectories generated by human subjects in the course of playing various computer-mediated interaction games. We propose this methodological approach as a first step in examining how the basic building blocks of social cognition can be studied through a combination of evolutionary principles, ecologically representative stimuli, human experimentation, and computer simulation of how well different decision heuristics would perform against each other and compared with human data. Our guiding principle has been that natural environments offer a few key motion cues, a few typical kinds of animate motion, and a plethora of animals, including mountain lions, more than willing to eliminate others who fail to perceive the significance of their movements.

13

From Pride and Prejudice to Persuasion

Satisficing in Mate Search

Peter M. Todd
Geoffrey F. Miller

Wedding is destiny,
And hanging likewise.

John Heywood, Proverbs

I married the first man I ever kissed. When I tell this to my
children they just about throw up.

Barbara Bush, First Lady

In 1611, the first wife of astronomer Johannes Kepler (1571–1630) died of cholera in Prague. Liberated from an arranged and unhappy marriage, Kepler immediately began a methodical search for a replacement. Though short, unhealthy, and the son of a poor mercenary, Kepler had an MA in theology from Tübingen, succeeded Tycho Brahe as imperial mathematician of the Holy Roman empire, and had recently become famous for explaining how eyeglasses can correct myopia (*Ad Vitellionem Paralipomena*, 1604), documenting a supernova (*De Stella Nova*, 1606), and demonstrating that the orbit of Mars is an ellipse (*Astronomia Nova*, 1609). He was a good catch. Relentlessly courting, Kepler investigated 11 possible replacements in the two years after his wife's death. In a letter to Baron Strahlendorf written shortly after marrying candidate number five in 1613, Kepler described this methodical mate search. Friends urged Kepler to choose candidate number four, a woman of high status and tempting dowry, but she rejected him for having toyed with her too long, so Kepler was free to settle with his most-preferred number five. Kepler chose well: His new wife, though not of the highest rank or dowry, was well-educated, bore him seven children, and provided the domestic infrastructure for Kepler to publish four more major works laying the empirical foundations for Newton's law of gravity, and, incidentally, to save his mother from being burned at the stake as a witch in 1620 (see Ferguson, 1989; Koestler, 1960).

287

Kepler's experience illustrates some of the major themes in the literature on search strategies that has emerged over the past several decades in statistics, economics, and biology. So far in this book we have focused on decision problems where all of the alternatives are simultaneously presented, and one only needs to search through information to guide one's choice. In many real-world choice problems, though, an agent encounters options in a temporal sequence, appearing in random order, drawn from a population with parameters that are only partially known ahead of time. In this case, the search for possible options, rather than just for information about present alternatives, becomes central. For mate choice in particular, the structure of the search task requires that one choose a prospect that fits one's real criteria for success rather than irrelevant ideals suggested by well-meaning acquaintances, given limited time for investigating each possibility, and some risk that the prospect, being an agent in his or her own right, will reject one's offer of union. The three disciplines that have investigated search tasks most thoroughly have emphasized different subsets of these issues.

Statisticians have focused on the "secretary problem" (Ferguson, 1989; Gilbert & Mosteller, 1966), in which one must pick the very best secretary from a sequence of applicants that appear in random order drawn from an unknown distribution of quality. Once rejected, applicants cannot be recalled. The secretary problem seeks perfection, with a payoff of one for picking the very best applicant and zero for picking anyone else. It also ignores search costs such as time, ignores the problem of mutual choice (the possibility that the applicant you like will not like you), and assumes you know the exact number of applicants who will arrive. But it directly addresses what to do about the uncertainty that the next prospect one encounters might be far superior to the best seen so far. It can be shown that the solution to the secretary problem demands sampling a certain proportion of the applicants, remembering the best of them, and then picking the next applicant who is even better. The optimal number to sample is $1/e$ (37%). Following this "37% rule" finds the very best applicant about 37% of the time (see Ferguson, 1989).

Economists have developed models of job search for best salaries and consumer search for lowest prices, emphasizing the importance of search costs and the acceptability of less-than-perfect options (Lippman & McCall, 1976). These search models, like those of the statisticians, usually ignore mutual choice, but they do not assume the total number of prospects is known, nor do they assume that only the best will do. On the other hand, these models generally assume that you can backtrack to pick previously seen options. With assumptions differing markedly from those of the secretary problem, the solution is also quite different. The general solution to this type of search task is to set a "reservation price" at which the marginal cost of further search equals the marginal expected improvement over the best prospect seen so far. That is, one should keep looking for a better salary or a lower price until the effort of looking further is likely to be more costly than the amount of improvement you could achieve, and then return to the best seen. This in turn can depend critically on the standard deviation of the distribution of salaries or prices, which may need to be estimated from previously observed options (Martin & Moon, 1992). This type of solution, requiring involved computations to determine when to stop search, falls into the class of constrained optimization methods discussed in chapter 1.

Biologists spent considerable effort in the 1980s amassing support for Darwin's (1871) claim that animals engage in mate search with enough discrimination and persistence to impose sexual selection pressures on one another (see Andersson, 1994). Several researchers developed detailed models for search behavior (e.g., Johnstone, 1997; Wiegmann et al., 1996), often with less theorem-proving zeal than the statisticians or economists, but more attention to the empirical testability of their models. These models usually incorporate search costs, and sometimes lack of knowledge about the distribution of potential mates (Mazalov et al., 1996). Much recent effort has gone into distinguishing whether different species use a best-of-N rule or a threshold criterion rule in mate search (e.g., Fiske & Kalas, 1995; Forsgren, 1997; Valone et al., 1996). The best-of-N rule means sampling a certain number N of prospects and then choosing the best of those seen, whereas a threshold criterion rule, like the 37% rule and the reservation price rule, means setting an aspiration level and picking the first prospect that exceeds it. Simon (1990) has termed the latter aspiration-setting mechanism "satisficing," defined as "using experience to construct an expectation of how good a solution we might reasonably achieve, and halting search as soon as a solution is reached that meets the expectation" (p. 9). As indicated in chapter 1, Simon sees satisficing as one of the main forms of bounded rationality available in situations where the complete set of possible alternatives to choose from is not, or cannot be, known.

All of the above approaches tend to consider a single searcher assessing passive goods waiting to be chosen. But one of the major problems in mate search is coping with mutual choice. It is fairly easy to develop satisficing rules that work well for nonmutual search, for instance, shopping around for tomatoes or televisions that will not object to being bought. There has been much less research on finding satisficing rules for mutual search under uncertainty. One more literature is relevant in this regard: the tradition of economic game theory research on "two-sided matching" (Roth & Sotomayor, 1990), which is largely the study of mutual choice, but with certainty and complete knowledge.

As with most game-theoretic analysis, this tradition has focused on finding equilibria, or sets of strategies that are mutually optimal against one another. It can be shown that if a finite set of men and women have consistent, transitive preferences for one another, then there exists at least one "stable matching" in which no one who has a mate would prefer somebody else who would also prefer him or her in return. The two-sided matching literature also shows, however, that there are often multiple equilibria, or different possible stable matchings given a particular set of men and women with particular preferences. Although each is stable in the sense that there is no rational incentive for divorce and remarriage, different equilibria fulfill people's preferences to different degrees: Some are "male-optimal" (making men as happy as they could be given the actual preferences of women), some are "female-optimal" (making women as happy as they could be given men's preferences), and some are neither. There is a simple search method called the "deferred acceptance procedure" that is guaranteed to produce a stable matching efficiently given mutual choice and perfect and complete information about everyone in the population (Gale & Shapley, 1962). But whether such equilibria exist (or ever occur) for real populations, and whether any algorithms exist for finding them in realistic situations of imperfect, incomplete information, remains to be shown.

How do all these statistical, economic, and biological models illuminate Kepler's courtship plan, or more generally, human choice behavior when presented with a sequence of options? Mate search can be considered a rather difficult but extremely important type of decision making under uncertainty. The models mentioned above have identified some of the difficulties: uncertainty about the distribution of mate values one will encounter, ignorance of the order in which prospects will be met, difficulty of backtracking to previously rejected prospects, search costs, time limits and temporal discounting, and, above all, the mutual choice problem that mating must be mutually acceptable to both parties.

Different fields address or ignore these difficulties in different ways. Statisticians and economists tend to treat mate search as an interesting pretext for developing optimality theorems relevant to job search and consumer search, rather than treating mate search as a central adaptive problem in human life. Biologists view things differently, because mate search and mate choice drive sexual selection, an evolutionary process perhaps equal to natural selection in its power and creativity. With the resurgence of interest in sexual selection theory since the late 1970s (see Andersson, 1994; Bateson, 1983a; Cronin, 1991), and evolutionary psychology since the late 1980s (see Barkow et al., 1992; Buss, 1994; Miller & Todd, 1998), research has begun to focus on the role that sexual selection via mate choice has played in shaping many aspects of the human mind (Miller, 1998; Ridley, 1993; Wright, 1994). In studying mate search then, we are studying an interesting, difficult problem of decision making under uncertainty that, perhaps uniquely among such problems, is likely to have had a strong causal influence on human evolution.

As with so many problems of human decision making, the rationality and efficiency of human mate choice, including the process of search, has been questioned. Frey and Eichenberger (1996) argued that people do not search long enough when seeking a mate, taking the incidence of divorce and marital misery as indicators of insufficient search. Rapoport and Tversky (1970) questioned whether people adhere to the reservation price rule for searching given a known distribution of values and a known search cost. However, the sequential search literature is not dominated by these sorts of worries about the ways that people deviate from known optimal strategies, in part because the optimal strategies are not known for many realistic search situations, and in part because psychologists have paid much less attention to search tasks than to other decision-making tasks. Psychologists and economists who have studied search have often focused on the simple heuristics that people actually appear to use. Hey (1982, 1987) has identified a number of these rules, such as the "one-bounce rule," by which people seeking high values keep checking values as long as they increase, but stop as soon as they decrease and select the previous value. Martin and Moon (1992) used computer simulation to assess the relative performance of different simple strategies in a consumer search setting and found that some rules can come within 3% of the normative standard.

In this chapter, we follow in the footsteps of these researchers and look for simple satisficing search heuristics that perform adaptively in the specific domain of biologically realistic mate search problems. We also evaluate different heuristics in simulation across a variety of search conditions using a variety of performance measures. Following a similar historical trend in sexual selection theory in biology (see Cronin, 1991), we begin with the rather male-centered case of one-sided search, and then proceed to the more realistic case of mutual search, emphasizing female choice as well as male. (To keep our analyses simple, in this chapter we do not go into the effects of possible sex differences in mate search strategies, though these could certainly have interesting and important consequences.)

Through our analyses we find that, even for simple cost-free, nonmutual search as in the secretary problem, the 37% rule is outperformed on many criteria by heuristics that sample significantly fewer prospects. These heuristics do not even need to know the expected number of prospects one will encounter: A simple satisficing heuristic called "Try a Dozen" works well across a large range of numbers of prospects. We also find that when mutual choice enters the picture, these types of search strategies tend to perform very poorly. Only individuals who are very highly valued themselves can get away with applying the 37% rule or the Try a Dozen heuristic in mutual choice situations. (Kepler was lucky in this respect: His high mate value helped ensure that his "Try Eleven" strategy would yield good results.)

Instead, search heuristics that take into account one's own mate value perform much better in mutual choice, producing faster, more frequent, higher-quality matings for individuals. Even if one's own mate value is not known initially, good search efficiency can be attained using a simple adaptive heuristic that adjusts one's aspiration level based on the number of offers and rejections received from others during an initial sampling period. If one also pays attention to the mate values of those who do or do not show interest, it becomes easier to learn one's mate value, which can be used as a basis for effective search strategies that deliver close to the best mate that could be hoped for given mutual choice. In brief, search strategies such as the 37% rule and the Try a Dozen heuristic that work well without mutual choice perform extremely poorly given mutual choice, falling far behind mutual choice strategies that allow one to learn one's own mate value from others' reactions. In keeping with the idea of ecological rationality, we find that the satisficing heuristics for mate search that do best in a given environmental situation—whether one-sided or mutual search—are those that exploit the structure of the information in their environments, relying solely on mate values in the former case, and on expressions of interest or disinterest in the latter.

Algorithms for One-Sided Mate Search: The Dowry Problem

The idealized versions of search described in the previous section differ considerably from the situation that presents itself to men and women searching for a mate, at least in many modern Western cultures. This type of mate choice usually consists of a sequential search through successive potential mates in which each one is evaluated and decided on in turn in a process that can take minutes, hours, days, or years. (Here the decision can be thought of as whether to settle down and have children with a particular person, though other definitions are possible.) There are certainly costs associated with checking out each person during this search. But perhaps the most significant cost is that it is difficult, and often impossible, to return to a potential mate that has been previously discarded (because they remain in the "mating pool" and are likely to pair up with someone else in the meantime, as countless romantic tragedies attest). To further complicate matters, one does not know ahead of time what the range of potential mates may be: How can we know the first time we fall in love whether someone else might be able to incite still deeper feelings if we just keep searching long enough to find them? We cannot even tell how many more potential mates we may encounter. Given these restrictions on the search process and lack of knowledge about the space we are searching, finding a mate looks like a very daunting problem indeed.

We can consider this situation in more precise detail, and in a form more closely linked to mate choice, via an alter ego of the secretary problem mentioned in the previous section: the "dowry problem." This is a well-known puzzle from statistics and probability theory (Corbin, 1980; see also Gilbert & Mosteller, 1966; Mosteller, 1987), as the number of names it goes by attests (it is also known as the "beauty contest problem" and even "Googol"). In its dowry form, the story goes like this: A sultan wishes to test the wisdom of his chief advisor, to decide if the advisor should retain his cabinet position. The chief advisor is seeking a wife, so the sultan takes this opportunity to judge his wisdom. The sultan arranges to have 100 women from the kingdom brought before the advisor in succession, and all the advisor has to do to retain his post is to choose the woman with the highest dowry (marriage gift from her family). If he chooses correctly, he gets to marry that woman and keep his post; if not, the chief executioner chops off his head, and worse, he remains single. The advisor can see one woman at a time and ask her dowry; then he must decide immediately if she is the one with the highest dowry out of all 100 women, or else let her pass by and go on to the next woman. He cannot return to any woman he has seen before—once he lets them pass, they are gone forever. Moreover, the advisor has no idea of the range of dowries before he starts seeing the women. What strategy can he possibly use to have the highest chance of picking the woman with the highest dowry?

As mentioned earlier, it turns out that the algorithm the advisor should use to guarantee the highest chance of choosing correctly is the 37% rule, which in this case would work as follows: He should look at the first 37 women (or, more generally, 37% of any population of candidates he faces), letting each one pass, but remembering the highest dowry from that set—call this value D. Then, starting with the 38th woman, he should select the first woman with a dowry greater than D. (For derivations of this procedure, see Ferguson, 1989; Gilbert & Mosteller, 1966; Mosteller, 1987.) This 37% rule is the best the advisor can do—it finds the highest value more often than any other algorithm (again, 37% of the time), and thus is, in this sense, the optimal solution to this problem. With this rule, the advisor has slightly better than a one in three shot at picking the right woman and keeping his head. The other two-thirds of the time, the sultan has to look for another advisor.

The dowry problem is certainly an unrealistic reflection of human mate choice in many respects—it only involves one-sided (rather than mutual) search, it reduces search to a single dimension instead of appreciating the many facets by which we judge one another (Miller & Todd, 1998), it denies any possibility of comparing candidates simultaneously or returning to those previously seen, and so forth. But it gives us a reasonable starting point for testing some specific mate search mechanisms in a setting with at least some domain-specific structure. And we can modify some of its assumptions in useful ways to help us get a better understanding of more appropriate search mechanisms, as we will now show.

One of the major differences between the dowry problem and the real world is that in the latter, of course, our mating decisions are seldom so dramatic—we usually get to (or have to) live with whatever choice we make, even if it is not the "best" one. To the sultan's advisor, the performance of the 37% rule on those occasions when it did not pick the highest dowry did not matter—he was killed in any case. But to a population of individuals all using such an algorithm to choose their mates, what this rule does the other 63% of the time would matter a lot. For instance, if applied to a set of 100 dowries covering all integer values from 1 to 100, the 37% rule returns an average value of about 81 (i.e., the mean of all dowries chosen by this rule). Only 67% of the individuals selected by this rule lie in the top 10% of the population, while 9% fall in the bottom 25%. And it takes the 37% rule an average of 74 tests of potential mates (i.e., double the 37 that must be checked before selection can begin) before a mate is chosen. (These figures are all discussed in the next section.) If any of these performance figures could be improved upon by some other sequential choice algorithm, that algorithm could well prove more adaptive for a population of mate choosers, allowing them to pick better mates more often, or more quickly, or with a smaller chance of picking a total loser, and we might therefore reasonably expect it to evolve in preference to the 37% rule.

If the dowry problem itself is unrealistic, the 37% rule solution also has many characteristics that could make it an implausible model of how people actually choose mates. Here we will focus on two difficulties. First, it requires knowing how many potential mates, N, will be available, in order to calculate how many are in the first 37% to check and set one's aspiration level, D. Second, this rule requires checking through a large number of individuals before a decision can be made—74 out of 100 in the previous example. Even assuming a rather quick assessment of someone's mate potential, perhaps a few dates over a month's time, the search time involved becomes extensive.

Thus, using the 37% rule for human mate search may require information that is difficult to obtain (an accurate value for N), and a large number of individuals to be checked and consequently a long search time. On the other hand, Frey and Eichenberger (1996) argue that one of the paradoxes of marriage is that people search too little for their marriage partners, checking too few individuals before making a lifelong commitment to one of them. The evidence they cite argues against the use of the 37% rule in human mate search—but it also argues that, by not searching long enough, people are making worse mate choices than they might. If people are not using an algorithm as long-winded as the 37% rule, what might they be doing instead? Is it possible that there are any faster search rules whose performance can assuage Frey and Eichenberger's fears of poor mate choice behavior? If so, will these rules prove more complicated? In the next section, we explore the answers to these questions, and discover that we can in fact do more, in mate choice, with less.

The Consequences of Searching Less

To investigate whether any simple search heuristics exist that can outperform the 37% rule on various criteria in the standard secretary/dowry problem domain, we began by studying a class of satisficing rules derived from the original 37% rule. It turned out that even this small set of similar heuristics contained some that are better than the 37% rule on many dimensions, and so we restrict our discussion here to this class (though other types of simple search algorithms or rules will probably prove to have even better performance on some criteria). We have dubbed the class of search heuristics we consider here "Take the Next Best" (or TNB, named after the fast and frugal Take The Best decision heuristic described in chapter 4).

Take the Next Best rules work in direct analogy to the 37% rule as follows: For some specified C, the first $C\%$ of the N total potential mates are checked (without being selected), and the highest dowry D is remembered—this is the searcher's aspiration level. After the first $C\%$ of potential mates have gone by, the next potential mate with a dowry greater than D is chosen. (If no greater dowry turns up, then we assume that the searcher accepts the very last individual in the sequence, which is why our performance curves in the upcoming figures fall to a final nonzero value.) This simple heuristic (of which the 37% rule is one specific example) has minimal cognitive requirements: It only uses memory for one value at a time (the current highest dowry), only needs to know N and C and calculate $N \times C/100$, and only needs to be able to compare two dowry values at a time. We were interested in how the performance of these simple algorithms would change as we altered the percentage of potential mates they checked, C. Because we also wanted to be able to change the underlying assumptions of this problem, such as the distribution of dowry values, the cost of checking each potential mate, and whether or not N is even known, the mathematics quickly grew complicated, and we decided instead on a flexible simulation approach for answering these questions.

We tested the behavior of TNB search algorithms with values of C from 0% (corresponding to always choosing the first potential mate) to 15% in increments of 1%, from 20% to 50% in increments of 5% (except around the interesting 37% value, where we again increased the resolution), and from 60% to 90% in increments of 10% (because we believed most of the action—that is, good performance—would occur in the lower C ranges). We ran each rule with different numbers N of potential mates, each with 10,000 different randomly created dowry (or mate value) lists. We collected statistics on the distribution of mate values selected by each algorithm (including the mean, standard deviation, quartile distributions, and number of times the single best dowry value was chosen) and positions at which mates were selected (the mean and standard deviation). With these values in hand, we can answer the questions posed at the end of the previous section: Simply put, can the 37% rule be beaten?

Search Performance With 100 Potential Mates

The answer, even from the class of simple TNB rules, is a resounding "yes." Of course, the 37% rule picks the highest mate value most often. In figure 13-1, the "best" line shows how often the highest mate value was

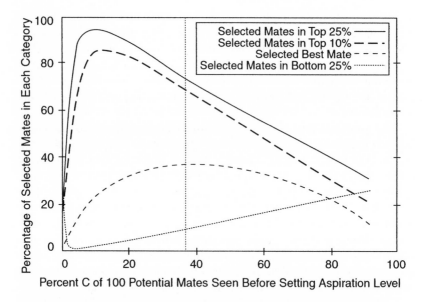

Figure 13-1: Chance of finding a mate in a particular value category, given different percentages of mates checked (out of 100 total possible mates) for setting the aspiration level before taking the next best candidate seen. The performance of the 37% rule on the various criteria is indicated by the broken vertical line.

picked by a TNB algorithm, for different percentages C of possibilities (potential mates) checked. (See Gilbert & Mosteller, 1966, figure 1, p. 42, for the mathematically derived equivalent of this function.) The greatest chance of choosing the highest mate value or dowry comes with a C of (about) 37%, as expected (the maximum in the figure is not at exactly 37%, because of the stochastic nature of the simulations we ran). But this curve also exhibits a flat maximum, so that it does not much matter what exact value of C is used—the results are largely the same for C between 30% and 50%. And the chance of finding the highest-value mate for any of these strategies is never higher than 37%, as mentioned in the first section—not very good odds.

   To an animal searching for a mate, this one in three chance of getting the "best" member of the opposite sex is probably not a bet worth taking—other "pretty good" potential mates will often be selected instead to save search time or energy (or even because the animal cannot perceptually distinguish between "best" and "pretty good"). In terms of having an adaptive advantage over other competing mate seekers, it may suffice to find a potential mate with a value in the top 10% of the population relatively quickly. In figure 13-1, we see that a low value of C, 14%, yields the highest chance, 83%, of selecting a mate in the top 10% of the value distribution. If one's standards are a bit more lax, just desiring a mate in the highest quartile (top 25%), then only $C = 7\%$ of the initial stream of potential mates need be checked to maximize this chance, yielding mates in that top quartile over 92% of the time. Finally, rather than being risk-seeking by searching for a mate in the top ranks of the population, an animal may be risk-averse, preferring only to minimize its chances of picking a mate in the bottom quartile of the population, where the mutants lie. From the line marked "bottom 25%" we can see that the way to achieve this goal is to use a much lower C of 3%, leading to a less than 1% chance of choosing a mate in the bottom (quarter) of the barrel. The 37% rule would pick these poor mates over 9% of the time, which is much worse performance by risk-averse standards.

Alternatively, an animal might gain the greatest adaptive advantage over its competitors by simply maximizing the expected value of its selected mate. Figure 13-2 indicates how to accomplish this goal, showing mean obtained mate value plotted against the percentage C of the potential mates that are checked to set the aspiration level D. Searchers using $C = 9\%$ in this environment of 100 potential mates with mate values from 1 to 100 will select mates with the highest average mate value, nearly 92. In contrast, if searchers were to use the 37% rule, their average would drop to 81.

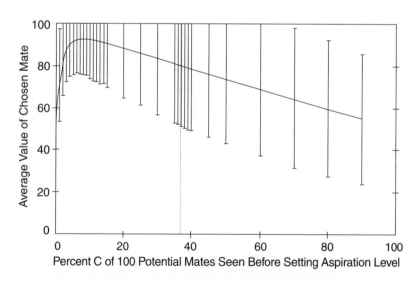

Figure 13-2: Average value of selected mate (bars indicate one standard deviation), given different percentages of mates checked (out of 100 total possible mates) for setting the aspiration level before taking the next best candidate seen. The performance of the 37% rule on this criterion is indicated by the broken vertical line.

The values of the mates selected by these search algorithms may not be the only criterion that matters to an organism seeking a mate—the time and energy spent searching may also strongly influence the adaptiveness of the algorithm used (see, e.g., Pomiankowski, 1987; Sullivan, 1994). In figure 13-3, we see how many total potential mates must be looked at, on average, before the final mate is chosen, varying as a function of the number of potential mates checked ($C \times 100$) to set the aspiration level before mate selection. The 37% rule must look at 74 potential mates on average before a final mate is selected. With lower values of C, the number of mates that must be looked at falls off rapidly, with increasing advantage as C decreases. The optimal value of C according to this criterion alone would be $C = 0$, that is, pick the first potential mate encountered. When combined with the other criteria, the importance assigned to this mean search length variable will determine the precise trade-off between finding a good mate and spending time and energy looking for that mate.

Search Performance With a Greater Number of Potential Mates

All of the criteria other than the chance of picking the single best mate favor Take the Next Best rules that set their aspiration levels by looking at less than 37% of the population. Checking about 10% of the population

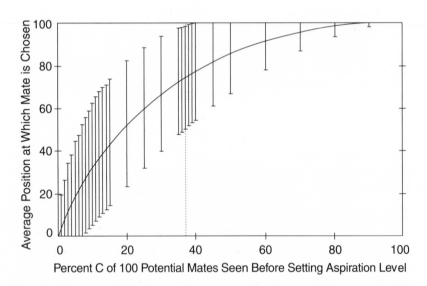

Figure 13-3: Average position at which a mate is selected (bars show one standard deviation), given different percentages of mates checked first (out of 100 total possible mates) for setting the aspiration level before taking the next best candidate seen. The performance of the 37% rule on this criterion is indicated by the broken vertical line.

of potential mates before selecting the highest individual thereafter will
result in about the highest average mate value possible, along with a high
chance of choosing mates in the top quartile and top 10%, and will require a search through 34 or so potential mates before the final selection
is made. This seems like quite reasonable performance, given that it only
requires checking 10 individuals initially out of a population of 100. But
ancestral humans may have had effective mating group sizes much larger
than this, and certainly in modern environments one can expect to meet
more than 100 people who could potentially become mates. So what happens with our simple search heuristics if the population size is increased
to 1,000, where checking 10% means testing 100 individuals, which may
start to seem less like fun and more like hard work? Because the number
of individuals that must be tested by a TNB rule with a $C\%$ parameter
goes up linearly with the total population size N, these rules may not end
up being so fast and frugal, at least for larger populations, after all.

But figure 13-4, which shows how TNB rules fare in a population of
1,000 potential mates with mate values from 1 to 1,000, proves that our
fears of linear time increase are unwarranted. As before, the greatest
chance of picking the single highest-value mate comes from first checking
37% of the population. But to maximize the chances of picking a mate in

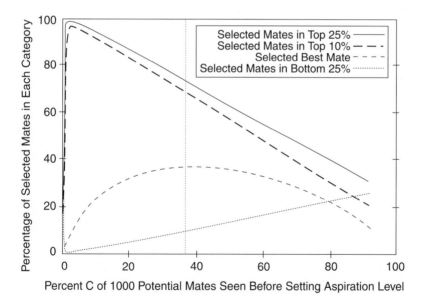

Figure 13-4: Chance of finding a mate in a particular value category, given
different percentages of mates checked (out of 1,000 total possible mates)
for setting the aspiration level before taking the next best candidate seen.
Note that a smaller percentage of potential mates need now be checked to
maximize the chances of getting a top mate. The performance of the 37%
rule on the various criteria is indicated by the broken vertical line.

the top 10% (with a 97% probability), only 3% of the potential mates need to be checked to set the aspiration level D; and for a mate in the top 25% (with a 98% probability), only 1% to 2% of the potential mates need be checked. Similarly, to minimize the chances (to 0.3%) of choosing a mate in the bottom 25%, only 1% of the population needs to be checked.

Thus, to maximize potential mate value and minimize risk in this population of 1,000 potential mates, somewhere between 1% and 3% of the population, or 10 and 30 individuals, must be checked first to come up with the aspiration level D. In the previous population of 100 individuals, checking about 10 of them also resulted in top search performance judged by these criteria. So despite the tenfold increase in population size, the number of individuals to check increases only slightly. This suggests that our TNB rules can be simplified. Instead of checking a certain percentage of the potential mates to come up with an aspiration level D, we only need to check a certain absolute *number* of potential mates. This number will work for population sizes varying over a wide range—for instance, Try a Dozen ($C = 12$) is appropriate for population sizes from 100 to several thousand. This simplified search heuristic escapes the criticisms raised earlier against the 37% rule: It performs better than the 37% rule on multiple criteria, it does not need knowledge of the total population size, and it does not require checking an inordinate number of individuals before a choice can be made. These results indicate that Frey and Eichenberger's (1996) pessimism about short-searching humans ever finding an appropriate mate may be unfounded—even a little bit of search may go a long way.

On to Mutual Sequential Mate Search

That is, a little search can go a long way, if you are a despot who can force a collection of hapless potential mates to parade past you until you choose one. While we may start out with adolescent fantasies about getting the person we most desire, most of us soon discover that the mating game operates a bit differently. Imagine that you enter the game with your brand-new egocentric Try a Dozen rule, all set to find that high-value mate. You dutifully consider the first 12 people you randomly encounter, eventually turning each one down but remembering how much you liked the best. Starting with the 13th, you look at a succession of further possibilities until finally, on person 20, you find what you have been looking for: someone better than all the others you have already seen. Your rule is satisfied, and so are you. You propose to your newfound mate—and are summarily rejected. What went wrong?

The problem is, at the same time that you are evaluating prospective mates, they are evaluating you in return. If you do not meet a particular other person's standards, then no amount of proposing on your part is going to win them over (in this restricted scenario, at least). And if you and everyone else in the population have been using the Try a Dozen rule to form an aspiration level, then you and everyone else will have rather high aspirations for whom you will agree to mate with. The trouble is then that if you do not yourself *have* a high mate value, then you will not be selected by anyone else as a potential mate, and will end up alone.

We can observe these effects by constructing a new simulation to explore how different mate search rules will work in a mutual search situation. We create a population of 100 males and 100 females, each with a distinct mate value between 0.0 and 100.0, and each with accurate knowledge of the mate values of members of the opposite sex, but not necessarily knowing his or her own mate value. We give each of the 200 individuals the same search strategy, and first let them assess some specific number of members of the opposite sex during "adolescence." During this time, individuals can adjust their aspiration level, if their search rule uses one. After this adolescence period, males and females are paired up at random, at which point they can either make a proposal (an offer to mate) to their partner or decline to do so. If both individuals in a pair make an offer to each other, then this pair is deemed mated, and the two individuals are removed from the population. Otherwise, both individuals remain in the mating pool to try again. This pairing-offering-mating cycle is repeated until every individual is mated, or until every individual has had the opportunity to assess and propose to every member of the opposite sex. We are interested in who gets paired up in this setting using different search rules; other criteria, such as how long this pairing process takes, are also of interest, but we will not discuss them here.

Figure 13-5 shows the number of mated pairs that will form in a population of 100 males and 100 females all using a particular mate-search strategy. If everyone uses Take the Next Best with $C = 1\%$, checking one individual to set their aspiration level, about half of the population will pair up. But as we increase the adolescence period (number of potential mates first checked), the number of mated pairs falls drastically. Thus if, instead, everyone uses the Try a Dozen variant and checks 12 potential mates for their aspiration level, only about eight mated pairs will be formed. The reason for this can be found in figure 13-6, where we can see the mean mate value of all mated individuals. For individuals using Take the Next Best rules, the longer the adolescence (number of mates to check, C), the higher the average mate value of all those who succeed in getting mated. That is, TNB rules give everyone in the population aspirations that are too high, so only the individuals who actually have the highest mate values will find mutually agreeing mates. Everyone else ends up spending Saturday night watching television.

But why not use TNB and check only a single individual? Then your aspiration level will not be too high, and nearly half of the population gets mated, which might be more reasonable. The problem lies in a third measure of population-level mating success: the average difference in mate value between partners in a mated pair. This is graphed in figure

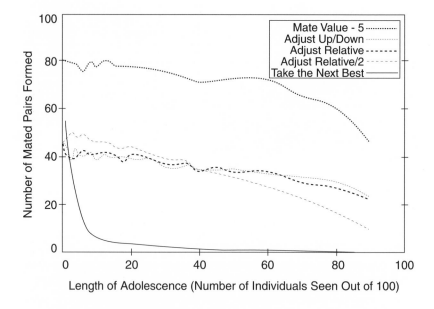

Figure 13-5: Number of mated pairs formed in a population with all individuals using a particular mutual sequential mate search strategy, graphed against the length of the adolescence period (during which an aspiration level can be learned). Higher values indicate more successful mate search strategies.

13-7. Here we can see that, even though TNB rules with very short adolescence periods do yield a good number of mated pairs, those pairs are rather mismatched—there is an average difference of nearly 25 between partners' mate values. Such a large difference would make the pairings formed very unstable in the game theory sense discussed in the first section: Many individuals would be inclined to switch partners. So how can we find a mutual sequential mate search rule that not only yields a high proportion of the population finding good mates (high values in figure 13-5), and finds mates for individuals from a wide and unbiased range of mate values themselves (values around 50 in figure 13-6), but also succeeds in pairing up individuals who are well matched to each other in terms of mate value (low values in figure 13-7)?

Now imagine that, considerably chastened by your earlier failure on the mating market, you reconcile yourself to be more realistic this time, and only aspire to a mate with a value similar to your own, rather than some lofty Hollywood-inspired ideal. In fact, out of humility you set a threshold five points *below* your own mate value, proposing to any individual with a mate value above this level. Now how will you fare, and how will everyone else do if they use similarly humble thresholds? In figure 13-5, we see that this strategy results in a high proportion of the

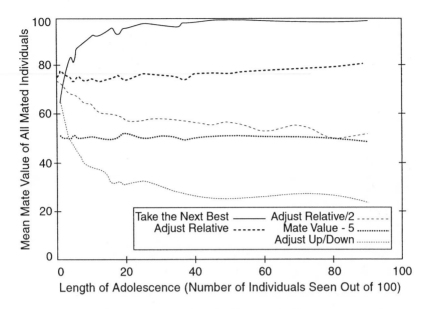

Figure 13-6: Mean mate value of all mated individuals in a population with all individuals using a particular mutual sequential mate search strategy, graphed against the length of the adolescence period. Middle values (around 50) indicate more successful egalitarian mate search strategies (for instance, those that enable more than just the elite to find mates).

population finding mates. In this case, adolescence does not involve learning or adjusting your aspiration level, because that value is fixed, but only represents an extended nonfertile period during which you meet people but cannot propose to them (and you still cannot go back to them later either). The length of adolescence has little effect on the performance of this humble mate search strategy. Only when adolescence gets very long does it start to reduce the number of mated pairs, simply because there is no longer enough of the population left to search through to ensure finding a good-enough partner.

This mate-value-based humble search strategy also does well on our other measures. Because most of the population gets paired up, the average mate value of those mated is around 50 (figure 13-6). It also succeeds in pairing individuals with very similar mate values (figure 13-7), making for a stable arrangement. That is, this strategy successfully sorts the population by mate value as it pairs the individuals. So this seems like a good mutual sequential mate search strategy to use. But there is a problem: Knowing one's own mate value is not necessarily an easy thing. We cannot be born with it, because it is both context sensitive (it depends on the others around us) and changes over time as we develop. We cannot simply observe ourselves to determine it, because we do not see ourselves in

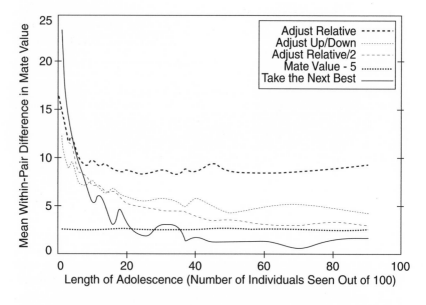

Figure 13-7: Mean difference between the mate values of partners in mated pairs formed in a population with all individuals using a particular mutual sequential mate search strategy, graphed against the length of the adolescence period. Lower values indicate mate search strategies that are more successful at forming well-matched pairs.

the same way that the others who judge us as potential mates see us. We do not even know the proper criteria on which to judge ourselves from the perspective of the opposite sex. Without this initial knowledge, then, we must somehow estimate our own mate value, if we are to use it to form our aspiration level.

Thus we must take another step toward making our mate search strategy less and less self-centered. We started by just considering what we thought of everyone else (Take the Next Best), then we used what we thought of ourselves (self-based aspiration level), and now we will look at what others think of us (adjusting our self-perception based on feedback). The first feedback-based method to try is to raise our aspiration level (the same as our self-perceived estimate of our own mate value) every time we get a proposal from someone else, and lower our aspiration level every time someone else does not propose to us. We will do this for a certain adolescence period again (i.e., use this feedback from a certain number of individuals we first encounter). The amount of adjustment we make to our aspiration level on each instance of feedback is inversely determined by the total length of our adolescence: If we have a short adolescence, we should make more adjustment (learn quickly) at each step, while if we have a long adolescence, we can learn more slowly. Thus, starting with an aspiration level of 50, we use $adjustment = 50/(1 + C)$

where C is the number of people we check out, and get checked out by, in adolescence. This rule pairs up about 40% of the population ("Adjust up/down" in figure 13-5), but preferentially in the lower half of the population (the mean mate value of mated individuals is about 25 in figure 13-6). What is happening here?

The problem with this aspiration-adjustment heuristic is that it is vain. Whenever a proposal comes from anyone, no matter what that person's mate value, the individual being proposed to gets excited and raises his or her aspiration level. Thus, individuals with mate values above 50 will get a lot of offers and then raise their aspirations to be too high, while those with mate values below 50 will more often get rejections, lower their aspirations, and as a consequence continue to boost the egos of the other half of the population. But individuals in the lower half, with the crushed aspirations, also succeed in finding mates, whereas those in the too-proud top half of the population often do not.

Instead of just taking someone else's word for it on whether you have a high mate value, you should also consider the source: What is the mate value of the other individual who is assessing you? If that person's mate value is higher than you think your own is, and he or she still proposes to you, then you should raise your own self-assessment, under the assumption that the other is well-calibrated and so is giving you accurate feedback about your own mate value. (You would always expect offers from individuals with mate values *lower* than your own self-image, so you should not use their offers to boost your self-image.) Similarly, if you get a refusal (lack of offer) from an individual with a mate value lower than your own self-perception, then this should make you think twice about your self-image, and lead you to lower your aspirations as well. (Again, lack of offers from those who are higher value than you think you are should not affect your self-image.)

If we make adjustments of the same size as the previous strategy, but now relative to the mate value of the other individual, we get about 40% of the population paired up again ("Adjust relative" in figure 13-5), but now it is the *top* half of the population that finds each other (mean paired mate value is about 75 in figure 13-6). However, they do not do a very good job of matching up—this strategy gives the worst mismatch between mated partners (about 10 points difference, in figure 13-7). The problem this time is that we are still using an adjustment that is independent of the mate values involved. The adjustment here is a fixed value depending only on the length of the adolescence period. But it does not make good sense to make the same upward adjustment both when someone with a mate value of 100 proposes to you, and when someone with a mate value of 60 proposes to you (assuming your self-image starts at 50, say). You should be much more excited about the former offer than the latter, and you should raise your self-estimate correspondingly higher. In the next strategy, we do just that.

As we have become less self-centered in our strategies, we have also added more information about the other potential mates we are interacting with. First, we looked at whether they proposed to us; next, we considered their proposals and the direction of their mate values relative to our own (i.e., we only needed to know if the values were bigger or smaller, not the exact values themselves); and now we consider their proposals, and the actual difference between their mate values and our self-estimate of our own mate value. If someone proposes to us whose mate value is higher than our self-image, then we raise our self-image (and hence our aspiration level) by half of the difference between the two. If a potential mate encountered during adolescence does not propose, and that person's mate value is lower than our self-image, then we lower our self-image by half of the difference. In this way, we put more weight on the feedback we get from individuals who are further away from our self-image.

When we do so, we end up with the best aspiration-learning strategy out of those we have considered so far. For short to medium adolescence lengths, this strategy pairs up about half of the population ("Adjust relative/2" in figure 13-5). The more learning it can do (i.e., the longer adolescence is), the closer it comes to pairing up an even distribution of individuals (figure 13-6). And with more learning, the mismatch between mated partners falls to near that of the humble mate-value-based strategy (figure 13-7).

Thus, we are getting close to a reasonable mutual sequential mate search strategy. It involves estimating one's own mate value by using the feedback of offers and refusals from members of the opposite sex, assuming that we know their mate values. But note that this kind of simple strategy does *not* assume that we know, or calculate, anything about the population as a whole. We do not have to keep track of means or standard deviations of the mate values encountered, for instance (as some of Martin & Moon's, 1992, strategies required). We also do not have to calculate optimal search times (as many of the approaches to the secretary/dowry problem required)—instead, most of the criteria seem to reach asymptote after checking about 20 individuals. And we do not need prior knowledge of the entire population, distinguishing this approach from that considered in two-sided matching problems (Roth & Sotomayor, 1990). Just seeing one individual after another, and learning about ourselves in the process, is enough.

Further Directions

We have presented here a collection of simple satisficing heuristics for one-sided and mutual search that can learn appropriate aspiration levels after checking only a few possible choices. As such, these heuristics fit into our overall framework of bounded rationality: They use as little of the available information as possible and still yield satisfactory performance.

These rules are also ecologically rational, relying on the structure of information in the environment—here, the pattern of proposals and rejections made by members of the opposite sex—to bootstrap their adaptive choice behavior.

Of course, we have still left much out of this discussion of mate search. Populations are never fixed, and the mating game does not proceed in discrete periods during which everyone in a predetermined set must pair up or give up—rather, new individuals are always being introduced, which has an effect on the overall mating success of different strategies (Johnstone, 1997). The distribution of mate values we have used here is uniform, but in the real world it is probably closer to a normal distribution. How will different distributions of mate values affect the performance of different strategies? We have given everyone in the population precisely the same impression of all the members of the opposite sex (all females rank all males the same way, and vice versa), but this is not realistic either: There will typically be some degree of agreement about who is a good catch and who is not, but there will also be a large amount of idiosyncracy in individual mate preferences. Some of these individual preference differences will be based on purely aesthetic criteria, but some will also have important fitness consequences (such as preferences for mating with distant, but not close, relatives—see Bateson, 1983b).

This leads to another issue we must address: What *are* the most important dimensions over which search algorithms such as these should be compared? Here we have argued that finding the absolute best individual in a population is not necessarily the most adaptive goal, if the search time, or mean chosen mate value, or distribution of chosen mate values, can be improved upon. Furthermore, finding a mate at all, in the mutual search case, could require selecting an individual with a mate value close to one's own. But we need to support these claims. One way to approach this problem is to create evolutionary simulations in which different algorithms compete with each other for mates and offspring, and see which types of algorithms win out over time. This approach, though, will only succeed in telling us something about real evolved human (or animal) behavior to the extent that we successfully incorporate the relevant ecological details (of how mate value maps onto number of offspring, for instance) into our model.

The ultimate goal is to look for evidence of particular strategies in the actual evolved search behavior that humans and other animals use, as others have done experimentally in settings including mate choice (e.g., Alatalo et al., 1988; Harrison & McCabe, 1996; Hey, 1982, 1987; Martin & Moon, 1992; Rapoport & Tversky, 1970; Sethuraman et al., 1994). There is always the concern that experimental situations may not tap into the mental mechanisms used in real-world behavior, though, so it is also important to look for evidence of different search algorithms in the real observed mate search behavior of people and other animals. Our simulations are intended to guide these investigations of real behavior, by indicating what kinds of psychologically plausible, simple but effective search rules we can reasonably expect, and so should look for.

All of this is not to say that love has no place in mate choice, that it is all down to percentages and aspiration levels and adaptive self-assessments. Love can be a way of making any particular choice stick, lessening or erasing any perceived mismatch between partners and making further search seem blissfully unnecessary, even unthinkable. Love and other emotions are important parts of behavioral mechanisms, rather than unique undefinable forces that are orthogonal or even antagonistic to adaptive behavior. But love can—and indeed may be designed to—obscure the operation of the decision mechanisms in mate choice, so that the entire process seems unfathomable when one is caught up in it. Choosing a mate should not be a scientific affair. But we hope that scientific research *can* be used to reveal some of the patterns in behavior underlying the way that people search for, and find, each other.

14

Parental Investment by Simple Decision Rules

Jennifer Nerissa Davis
Peter M. Todd

There was an old woman who lived in a shoe. She had so many children she didn't know what to do.

Traditional Nursery Rhyme

The old woman may not have had much to give her children, but somehow she still had to figure out how to divide the broth that she did have among them. How could she do this? How do parents decide how to divide their time, money, and energy among their children? They could try to perform some sort of complex analysis, estimating all the future costs and benefits from now until their children become independent for all possible current choices, if such a thing were realistically calculable. Although the task of figuring out "optimal" solutions to these sorts of problems may be terribly complex or even impossible, given the large amount of computation and prediction of uncertain future events required, this does not mean parents must perform complex calculations to invest wisely. Instead they can rely on simple rules to guide their investment in their children. In this chapter we present results of a study designed to test just how successful such simple rules can be.

Parental Investment

Economists and behavioral ecologists have both addressed the problem of how parents should divide investment among their children. The models they have created, however, typically require information that is at best difficult to calculate and at worst actually unknowable. For example,

Becker (1991) provides an economic analysis of how rational parents should distribute investment among their children, assuming that parents are trying to maximize total child quality as defined by the sum of all the children's wealth as adults. The quality of a child is a function of the resources invested in the child, the child's own skill and abilities, and any extra income he or she might earn as an adult through sheer luck. Becker assumes that there are diminishing returns on the payoffs for investing in a child, that is, that for each additional equal-sized increment of investment you give to a child, its effect on the child's quality is smaller. Becker's analysis indicates that so long as this payoff curve is the same for all children, parents should distribute investment such that each child produces the same payoff. However, if some children produce higher payoffs per unit investment than others, then parents should of course favor them.

Similar investment advice can be found in the biological literature on parental investment. There an individual's quality has typically been defined as the number of offspring it is expected to produce as an adult, that is, parents are expected to try to maximize their total number of descendants. As long as all offspring have identical expected reproductive output, parents should invest equally among them (Lacey et al., 1983; Real, 1980), but if differences exist that affect the expected return on investment to parents, then parents should pay attention to these differences and bias investment accordingly.

Although these conclusions may sound reasonable in general, they are of limited use in making predictions about actual parental behavior in specific situations. This is because both approaches assume that parents have some means of calculating the effects of each unit of investment on the future payoff they expect to gain from a child. In practice, however, this calculation can require involved manipulations of information that is itself difficult to obtain. In Becker's treatment, for example, the total capital of children is the sum of the value of the total investment parents have made in each child when this child grows up, the value of the endowment of each child when the child is an adult, and each child's capital gain due to luck in the market sector. The biggest problem with trying to adapt this form of analysis to make specific predictions about behavior is the intractability of determining the future values involved. Children do not come equipped with investment meters for their parents' convenience. To cash out investment mechanisms such as these, some method for accurately predicting future returns would have to be specified, but this is intractable, if not impossible.

Mechanisms of Parental Investment

Much of the research on parental investment decisions that has been carried out in the fields of behavioral ecology and evolutionary psychology has taken it as a given that parents could not possibly solve such complex equations. Instead these investigations have focused on finding much simpler decision rules parents could use to achieve success, with success once again defined as the maximum possible number of all future descendants. A common shorthand approximation of this is to measure success simply as the number of offspring raised to adulthood. As mentioned before, if all offspring will provide equal expected returns on parental investment, then parents should treat them all equally. Of course, even in this situation parents still need to make decisions about how much to provide at any one moment, and when to provide it. When the amount of investment per offspring that is required to reach a given level of fitness is identical for all offspring, then one parental solution would be to treat each on the basis of its need. Among birds, for example, chicks often beg for food when hungry. If amount of begging is an honest and accurate signal of need (e.g., Godfray, 1991), parents would then be expected to feed their chicks according to their begging intensity to achieve investment equality. This is clearly a very simple decision rule.

Of course, in reality, situations in which all offspring have identical expected returns are vanishingly rare. If the individual expected returns do differ among offspring, parents should be sensitive to this and use a decision rule that biases investment in favor of the offspring that will provide a bigger return. Again, behavioral ecologists have identified a simple decision rule parents could use that exhibits such a bias: Satisfy the oldest offspring first. To understand why it works it is first necessary to know a bit about what might cause such a difference in return on investment in the first place.

When Becker talks of children with greater rates of return he implies that these are children of especially gifted talent or ability who could achieve an especially large income as adults. When behavioral ecologists talk of greater return on investment they are referring to offspring that have a greater chance than their siblings of surviving to reproductive age and producing a greater number of offspring of their own. One major predictor of the probability of survival is the current age of offspring. The older they are, the closer they are to independence and reproduction, and the more likely they are to make it all the way there. Therefore, if parents are going to bias investment they should favor their eldest. Herein lies the simple decision rule: Invest preferentially in older offspring.

If we want to predict parental behavior, then we need to find some way of determining what sorts of situations parents face. Should they invest on the basis of need, or age, or perhaps on the basis of some other as yet unspecified variable? For instance, even if all offspring are the same age, they should not necessarily all be given equal resource investments if they differ in something such as size which could also be related to future success.

If resources are scarce and parents cannot successfully raise all of their offspring, then favoring the oldest makes adaptive sense. If you cannot save them all, save the ones most likely to make it to adulthood. However, the choices made in this situation may be fundamentally different from those parents make about how to partition investment among offspring when there is more than enough to go around. In this situation there is no a priori rationale for supposing that parents should achieve the greatest success by investing highly in some offspring and not in others. Rather than rearing one especially well-invested-in offspring and several who are less so, parents may, for example, receive greater returns by evening out resource distribution, or biasing it in favor of offspring who require more to reach the same levels as their siblings. Parents, then, might be expected to make environmentally contingent investment decisions. In poor environments they could choose the simple strategy of investing more in older offspring, while in more abundant environments they *might* do best to invest on the basis of something else.

The decision rules that parents use for investing can be very simple. In this chapter we discuss whether, given the intractable parental problems of explicitly determining the effects of investing in each offspring, there nonetheless exist simple decision rules that parents can use to guide their offspring investments without having to calculate the incalculable. We believe there are.

Determining the Decision Rules

We tackled the problem of finding successful parental investment strategies for different resource levels by constructing a computer simulation of the investment problem. Because human parental investment situations are difficult to characterize, and because we are investigating a broad theoretical question that should be applicable to a wide variety of organisms, we chose to model a simpler case: parental investment in birds. Like humans, many birds face the task of raising multiple offspring of different ages and different developmental stages simultaneously. Chicks in many species hatch a day apart from each other, and for birds this age difference translates into significant differences in size and developmental maturity. Parental investment in birds is easy to quantify, and investment strategies have already been measured in the field for a number of species. In contrast, in humans investment can take many forms, such as number of calories of food provided, amount of money spent, or quality of interpersonal interaction, therefore making it difficult to express as a single value. Furthermore, the variation in individual investment strategies has not been systematically measured.

More specifically, our study animal is the western bluebird (*Sialia mexicana*), or rather, an electronic replication of a western bluebird. Our simulation works by mimicking the hatching, feeding, growth, and nest-leaving (fledging) of chicks. We chose bluebirds because information is available about metabolic and growth rates for this species, which is necessary to build an accurate model. Equations for metabolic rate, digestion rate, and stomach size were derived from published field data on growth and metabolic rates of bluebird chicks across the nestling period (Mock et al., 1991). Values for calorie content of the insects the bluebird feeds to its chicks, and the percentage of metabolizable energy these items contain, were taken from Dykstra and Karasov (1993).

Our goal was to find out what sorts of parental investment strategies would work well for our simulated bluebird parents trying to raise a nest of chicks under various environmental conditions. For our birds, parental investment was limited to the amount of food a parent provides to a given chick. Parental success was measured by the total number of "grams of chick" that fledged from the nest. We used chick grams instead of merely the number of chicks that fledged because we expect increased weight at the time the chicks leave the nest to be monotonically associated with survivorship over the first year; that is, we expect that any increase in fledge weight will be associated with some increase in the ability of the chick to make it through its first year, and to its first breeding season. In the simulation, parents always did better to have more chicks fledge than to have fewer fatter ones, because the range of possible fledge weights was such that there was no possible overlap in total grams of chick for nests that contained different numbers of chicks (e.g., three chicks could weigh roughly between 78 and 84 grams in total, while two chicks could weigh between 52 and 56 grams).

Food comes in patches in our simulation, so that foraging parents can encounter several bugs in a row followed by a period with no bugs. To explore how different investment strategies would work under different environmental conditions, we constructed environments varying in two aspects of environmental quality: mean amount of food available, and the patch size of that food. These two parameters were chosen because they seemed to be the factors most likely to affect the outcome of various parental investment strategies. For example, feeding the oldest first, as mentioned above, may be best for situations of low food availability.

We tested six different parental decision rules. It has been suggested that in some species parents may preferentially feed their youngest or smallest chicks, so we tested both of these rules (feed from youngest to oldest, and feed from smallest to largest, e.g., Stamps et al., 1985). While this literature tends to equate these two rules with each other, from our standpoint they are quite different. If the smallest chick is always fed first, it may grow while its siblings do not, and hence the chick that is smallest may change over time. The youngest chick, however, will always be the youngest chick. Furthermore, the parental perceptual abilities necessary to distinguish the smallest chick differ from those necessary to distinguish the youngest. The former requires merely a size judgment, while the latter depends on individual recognition of offspring, something which parent birds may or may not be able to do.

We considered two more strategies: invest on the basis of need (feed the hungriest first), and invest more in older offspring (feed from oldest to youngest). We considered testing the opposite of feeding the smallest first, that is, feeding the largest first, but owing to the way chicks grow, as long as offspring differ in age this latter rule will always be equivalent to feeding the oldest first. We also tested a rule that would simply feed in fixed rotation, so that each chick would get the same number of feedings as its siblings. Again, this rule requires parents to be able to individually recognize their chicks, a perceptually more difficult task. Investing randomly was included as well to provide a benchmark for comparison. Parents are not expected to waste time with decision rules that give them outcomes worse than if they had invested randomly, and it is possible that in some environments investing randomly is the best thing to do.

More precisely, the six heuristics we tested were

1. Feed from youngest to oldest
   The parent first offers a bug to the youngest chick; then, if that chick is full, the parent offers the bug to the next youngest, and so on.
2. Feed from smallest to largest
   The parent first offers a bug to the smallest chick, then the next smallest, and so on. (Because chicks grow when they are fed, this rule can yield a different outcome from feeding the youngest.)
3. Feed the hungriest
   The parent gives a bug to the chick with the greatest proportion of empty space in its stomach relative to its stomach size.
4. Feed from largest to smallest
   The parent first offers a bug to the largest chick, then to the next largest, and so on.
5. Feed in fixed rotation (take turns)
   The parent offers a bug to chicks in a fixed order, that is, first to Chick 1, then to Chick 2, and so on. The fixed order is initially chosen at random.
6. Feed randomly
   The parent offers a bug to a randomly chosen chick. If it is full, another chick is chosen at random, and so on.

Although all of these strategies are computationally quite simple, they require varying degrees of perceptual abilities on the part of the parents. The strategies that feed the smallest first and feed the largest first require nothing more than that parents discriminate chick size. There is an even simpler way for parents to follow the strategy of feeding the largest: by creating an environment that does this sorting for them. In several species, parents set up a situation in which chicks physically compete for feeding positions in the nest (e.g., Koelliker et al., 1998). This competition leads to larger chicks being preferentially fed, and all parents need to do is consistently feed in the same part of the nest. Feeding on the basis of hunger can also be easy for parents to achieve, if it is assumed that begging is an honest signal of hunger. In this case, parents simply need to assess which chick is begging the hardest and feed that one. Of course begging may not always be honest, and there is the possibility that chicks could deceive their parents about their hunger level, but we do not consider this case here.

The strategies of feeding the youngest first and feeding in fixed rotation are perceptually more difficult, as they require parents to discriminate among individual chicks, and in the latter case, also remember who was fed previously. Given the success that field biologists generally have in swapping chicks between nests, it is not at all certain that parent birds have these perceptual abilities. Nevertheless, these two strategies were still tested, to see how well they fared against the others.

The Simulation

In this study we model only one feeding strategy per nest, because of the complexity of testing strategies where two parents differed in their choice of feeding heuristic. Each nest has four chicks, which hatch one day apart on four successive days. Each chick remains in the nest, is fed, and grows for 20 days, and then it fledges. Chicks thus fledge one day apart from each other. The goal of the parent is to keep as many of the chicks alive as possible and to make them as fat as possible before they have to leave the nest.

At the beginning of each simulation run, the parental decision strategy is set as one of the six listed in the previous section. The difficulty of the environment is set by designating the probability that a parent will be able to find a bug on any foraging trip given that it found one on its last trip, and by designating the probability that a parent will not find a bug on any foraging trip given that it did not find one on its last trip. These two probabilities allow us to vary both the mean food level of an environment and its patchiness.

The simulation is updated in 10-minute increments of simulated time. During each time period, a number of things happen:

1. Any egg due to hatch, hatches.
2. The parent searches for food.
3. The parent returns to the nest, and if she has returned with a bug, chooses a chick to feed and feeds it.
4. If a chick has been fed, the food item is added to its stomach. Each chick with food in its stomach digests some of it, burns calories in accordance with its metabolic rate, gains or loses weight accordingly, and its stomach capacity changes to accord with its new size.
5. If a chick's weight drops below a certain age-specific limit, it dies.

Parents are active between 6:00 A.M. and 8:00 P.M. As in the wild, during the night no food is gathered or distributed; however, chicks continue to maintain their basal metabolic rates, so that each chick burns calories, digests any food left in its stomach, and gains or loses weight accordingly during the night. When a chick reaches Day 20 it leaves the nest. The final fledge weights of all the chicks as they leave the nest are summed as the measure of parental success.

To investigate the success of the different decision rules in different environmental situations, we collected data from 500 electronic nests for each of the six feeding strategies, and we did this for each of 100 different environments, constructed from combinations of 10 levels of the probability of repeatedly finding food and 10 levels of the probability of repeatedly not finding food. From each set of 500 runs we computed the mean parental success score, that is, the mean total grams of chick fledged. The resulting mean parental success scores for each strategy were then compared to the success achieved by parents feeding randomly to determine in which environments each strategy exceeded this random baseline.

Simulation Results

Patch size in the environment accounted for almost no difference in the success of different feeding strategies. Instead, the mean amount of food available had the greatest impact on strategy success (figure 14-1).

Feeding the oldest first was the most successful decision rule in environments with low food availability (29% or less, figure 14-2). Feeding

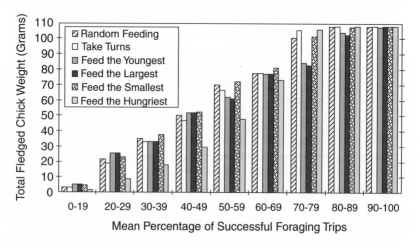

Figure 14-1: The mean number of "grams of chick" fledged from the nest for the heuristics we tested, across all amounts of food availability.

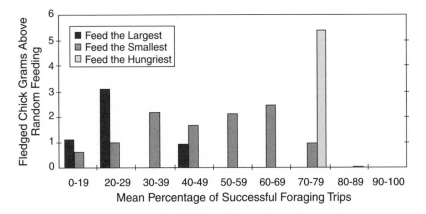

Figure 14-2: The mean number of fledged chick grams by which each of the three most successful strategies beat random feeding. Feeding the largest first is the most successful decision rule for conditions of up to 30% mean food availability. Feeding the smallest first does best in conditions of 30–69% food availability. Feeding the hungriest first does best in conditions of 70–79% food availability. Above 80% food availability all strategies perform more or less equally well, on par with random feeding.

the youngest first performed as well as feeding the oldest, but remember that feeding the youngest first requires more complex parental perceptual abilities, which it is not at all certain bird parents have. We therefore considered feeding the oldest to be a more ecologically rational decision rule than feeding the youngest, and have not plotted the data from the latter here.

Feeding the hungriest was the most successful strategy in conditions of moderately high food availability (70–79%, figure 14-2). Feeding in fixed rotation performed almost as well in this same range. Because of this and of questions about parental abilities to perform this strategy, we did not plot its performance here. When food was extremely abundant (80–100%) it ceased to matter how parents divided things up, as all six decision rules performed equally well. Parents in this environmental situation should therefore choose to feed chicks indiscriminately.

It was the middle range of food availability (30–69%, figure 14-2) that yielded the most surprising result. Between the point where feeding the oldest first did best and the point where feeding the hungriest was most successful, feeding the smallest first outperformed all other heuristics. Although data exists showing that this feeding pattern does occur in some species (as we discuss below), this result was not predicted by either economic or biological theory. Note one more time that feeding the smallest is not the same thing as feeding the youngest. Remember that as chicks are fed they grow, so that while the youngest chick will always be the youngest chick, the identity of the smallest chick can change.

"Optimal" Investment

We have so far compared five simple feeding rules with random feeding behavior. Of course we would also like to have a maximum possible parental success score with which to compare these simple decision rules. If a strategy beats random, but is still far from achieving perfection, this leaves open the possibility that some other as yet untested strategy might prove superior to those we have looked at so far. It is impossible to determine the optimal sequence of feeding decisions a parent bird should make, because this would require exact knowledge of the future, specifically, when all bugs will be found and how big they will be. This calculation could be approximated with guesses as to the arrival time of future bugs, but even in this case, the parent bird would have to try out all possible feeding sequences (e.g., give the first bug to Chick 1 and the next to Chick 3 . . . , give the first bug to Chick 2 and the next to Chick 3 . . . , and so on), and see which sequence resulted in the greatest total fledge weight in the end. This kind of search through the tree of possible sequences, as shown in figure 14-3, results in a combinatorial explosion of possibilities. There would be 4^{1680} paths to explore, by which time the waiting chicks would be very hungry indeed, and even this would only give a best-estimate solution. Still, we would like to know how much better that solution could be than the results of following our six simple feeding rules. Is there a way of approximating it more quickly? This sort of incalculability problem is often solved with dynamic programming, which starts at the desired end state of the system and works backward to find the best way to get there. Unfortunately, in this case it is the end state of the system that we are trying to determine, so this approach cannot be used.

What we can do is look at strategies that perform optimization under constraints, under the assumption that these will approach the success that long-term optimization calculations would achieve. We have looked at several such strategies with exactly this goal in mind. These maximization strategies are not designed as models of any decision-making process birds could actually use, because they involve complex computations using knowledge that may not even be assessable. All of these strategies require precise knowledge of the effects of feeding a given chick now on the total weight of chicks in the nest at some point in the future, that is, knowledge of chick metabolism and growth rates. One strategy also requires that parents know how long it will take a given chick to digest a given bug; the others require parents to be able to predict when the next bug is likely to be found.

In the first maximizing strategy, dubbed "bug digested," parents give the current bug to the chick whose eating of it will maximize the total weight of all chicks in the nest at the time that it finishes digesting the bug. The simulation runs as follows: Every time a bug is found, the program selects a chick and checks what would happen if it were to feed the bug to that chick. It calculates the number of time steps it would take for

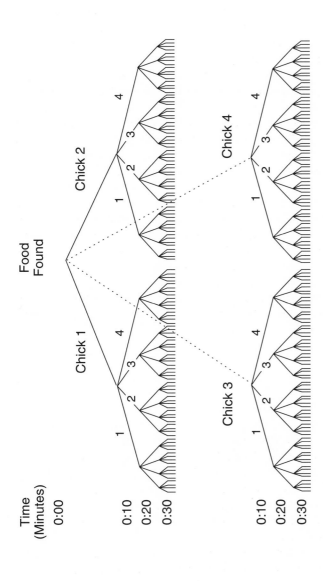

Figure 14-3: A schematic of the number of alternative feeding orders that must be checked to determine the best parental strategy for just half an hour's worth of feedings. Each final branch represents the states of all chicks in the nest at the end of the half hour.

that chick to digest that bug, then it calculates the weight of all chicks in the nest at the time that chick would finish digesting the bug and sums them. Next it checks the consequences of feeding the bug to another chick in the nest. This procedure is repeated until all chicks have been checked. The program then selects the chick that yields the highest summed weight at the time digestion is complete and actually feeds the bug to that chick.

The rationale for using this rule was simple: When deciding to whom the current bug should be fed, we reasoned that what should be maximized is the effect of that specific bug on the survival and growth of the chicks. This rule was inspired by similar computations in optimal foraging theory where the forager is assumed to be maximizing the net energy gained from its foraging activities, that is, the calories ingested minus the calories burned while finding and ingesting the food (Stephens & Krebs, 1986; see also chapter 15). The results of "bug digested" are presented in figure 14-4. Here we have graphed the performance of three constrained optimization approaches and the best of the simple rules from figure 14-2, all in terms of their difference from the performance of random feeding, for the full range of mean food availability in the environment. As you can see, it performed less than optimally. Not only was it worse than our simple decision rules, it was worse than random feeding in nearly all environments.

This outcome was completely unexpected. We began testing these types of strategies with the intention of seeing how closely our simple decision rules could approximate the performance of more complex maximization rules. We never expected to beat them. We hypothesized that our mistake might be that we were attempting to maximize the wrong

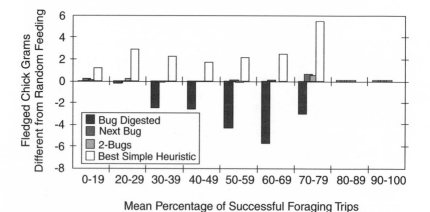

Figure 14-4: The performance of three strategies that attempt to optimize feeding, along with the best of the simple strategies, compared against random feeding. The "optimizing" strategies could not beat the best simple feeding rules.

thing. Perhaps the payoff from the current bug at the time when it is fully digested does not really matter. Instead, given that the chick is likely to have another chance to eat before digestion is complete, the important thing may be the payoff at the time when the next bug arrives.

In light of this, the second constrained maximization strategy we tested we dubbed "next bug." It works much like "bug digested" except that instead of calculating the payoff at the time when the current bug is digested, the program uses the environmental parameters specified for that run to calculate the expected number of time steps until the next bug will be found and chooses to feed the chick that maximizes the total weight of chicks in the nest at that time. Although it performed better than "bug digested," overall the "next bug" strategy still did rather poorly, essentially equalling random feeding across most environments, and never managing to outperform the best of the simple strategies.

Given the improvement of this strategy over "bug digested," we reasoned that perhaps we were on the right track but were still not making things complex enough. Maybe if we increased the number of feeding times the strategy checked we would see further improvement, so we created "2-bugs," which is identical to "next bug" except that it attempts to maximize the total chick weight in the nest at the time at which the second subsequent bug is found. It hypothetically feeds one chick, calculates the weight of all chicks at the time the next bug is expected to be found, hypothetically feeds each of these chicks the second bug in turn, calculates the total chick weight in the nest at the time the next bug after that should be found, and saves the maximum value for this second hypothetical as the total return for the first chick. This process is repeated for all chicks in the nest and the chick with the highest expected total return is actually fed. Unfortunately "2-bugs" also performs rather badly, essentially equaling the outcome of "next bug" (figure 14-4).

Obviously our attempts to find an upper limit to possible parental success has failed, but something even more interesting has emerged. All of these supposedly maximizing strategies are far more complex than our successful simple decision rules. They require knowledge of things such as current and projected future metabolic rates, digestion rates, and growth rates of all chicks, which actual parents are unlikely to know and could not directly assess. They integrate this information with knowledge of environmental conditions in an attempt to determine the best possible decision to make, in the tradition of biological optimality modeling, and yet, despite all that, they make terrible decisions. Our simple rules do not merely equal our more complex methods, they exceed them. What is going on here?

The aspects of the decision environment modeled in this chapter are different from those presented in the rest of the book, and from those for which standard optimality models are constructed. While each individual step requires a simple choice—pick one chick out of a set of no more than four—this choice must be made as many as 1,680 times before parental success is known. Each of these single choices affects the outcome of all future choices that must be made, making them interdependent. Finally, because the environment is probabilistic, at the time any given decision is made the timing and number of those future choices are unknown. Even this very simplified parental investment model is therefore not particularly simple. If it were possible to compute all potential outcomes we would be able to determine the perfect set of feeding decisions. Given that this is not possible we are forced to use strategies that make guesses about the future, and furthermore only guess about a very limited period of time, just to keep the strategies computationally tractable. This simplification is most likely what renders them impotent. It is in exactly this sort of uncomputable situation that Simon (1990) has indicated the importance of bounded rationality and satisficing heuristics.

Provisioning Rules for Birds

We do not yet have an upper limit with which to compare our simple decision rules, but we expect that the performance of these rules is, in fact, very close to the maximum possible. The process of natural selection has had a very long time to shape the investment decisions of parents and push them to optimality, so the investment strategies that real birds use should be close to the possible maximum performance. An examination of the literature on feeding patterns in birds reveals that the four simple decision rules shown by our simulations to be successful in different environments, and only those four strategies, seem to be used by bird parents faced with the task of raising a nest full of chicks. The strategies that lost out in the simulation, that is, feeding the youngest first and taking turns, do not appear to be used by any species. Coots (Horsfall, 1984), budgie mothers (Stamps et al., 1985), tree swallow mothers (Leonard & Horn, 1996), and pied flycatcher mothers (Gottlander, 1987) all preferentially feed the smallest chick. Pigeons (Mondloch, 1995) and budgie fathers (Stamps et al., 1985) preferentially feed the hungriest. Magpies (Redondo & Castro, 1992) may also feed on the basis of hunger. Arabian babblers (Ostreiher, 1997), pied-billed grebes (Forbes & Ankney, 1987), common swifts (Martins & Wright, 1993), yellow-headed blackbirds (Price & Ydenberg, 1995), blue-throated bee-eaters (Bryant & Tatner, 1990), stonechats (Greig-Smith, 1985), and tree swallows (Leonard & Horn, 1996) preferentially feed larger chicks. The degree to which the preference for larger chicks is a result of direct parental discrimination between chicks or is induced by parents setting the stage for chick competition over feeding position is unknown for these species, but using position in the nest to determine whom to feed has been observed in pallid swifts (Malacarne et al., 1994), great tit females (Koelliker et al., 1998), pied flycatcher males (Gottlander, 1987), and starlings (Kacelnik et al., 1995). Red-winged blackbirds (Clark et al., 1997), fieldfares (Ryden & Bengtsson, 1980), field sparrows (Best, 1977), and song sparrows (Reed, 1981) appear to feed randomly. Unfortunately, data on the food availability in the environments in which these birds were studied is not readily available. Nor were we able to obtain information on the feeding decisions of actual western bluebirds.

The few cases where a species of bird has been observed to switch provisioning rules in accordance with changing environmental conditions show shifts that agree with what we would predict based on our simulation results. Pied flycatcher females preferentially feed the smallest chicks under normal food conditions. When food availability is experimentally reduced, however, they switch strategies and instead preferentially feed the largest (Gottlander, 1987). When food is plentiful, sparrow hawk mothers allocate food resources equally among all chicks, although it is not clear whether they do this by means of feeding the smallest first or by random allocation. When food becomes scarce, however, they switch to a strategy that favors the largest chicks (Newton, 1978). Two studies of American robins have found different feeding strategies. Smith and Montgomerie (1991) found that parents fed on the basis of chick begging, while McRae et al. (1993) found chick competition for feeding position that resulted in older chicks being preferentially fed. Although information on food abundance is not reported in either paper, based on our results we hypothesize that this may explain the difference between them.

Provisioning Rules for People

Decision rules for parental investment can be simple and successful. The four best investment strategies are in fact actually used, at least by bird parents. Of what relevance are these results for human parental investment decisions?

Birds are a good model for the study of human parental investment. Like humans, and unlike most mammals, many bird species are faced with the task of simultaneously raising offspring of different ages, and the same basic biological principles that govern investment decisions in birds should govern them in all species faced with similar investment problems. We therefore expect these simulation results to be applicable to human parental investment decisions in much the same way that they are applicable to birds.

One example of how human investment patterns can be related to these results is through studies of inheritance practices in different cultures. Researchers have studied the division of land between children in agricultural communities and the ecological conditions that affect how it is divided in many different cultures across many different historical periods. They have found fairly consistent patterns (e.g., Hrdy & Judge, 1993) among wealthy landholders, who farm enough land to sustain their family. In low population densities, where land is plentiful, inheritance in such families is distributed relatively equally. This is akin to our simulated resource-rich environments where feeding the hungriest or feeding randomly, the two most egalitarian strategies, do best. In more crowded places, without so much room for expansion, and where subdividing existing holdings would eventually lead to farm sizes too small to support a family, parents have practiced primogeniture, channeling these resources into a single heir, typically the oldest son. This is similar to our simulation results in resource-poor environments where feeding the largest is most successful.

Given the recent resurgence of interest in birth order as an explanatory variable in psychology, knowledge of how parents distribute investment among their children has become increasingly important. Take, for example, Sulloway (1996), who has shown striking birth order effects in people's acceptance of scientific revolutions and radical ideas, and whose research is based on the hypothesis that the amount parents invest in a child varies predictably with birth order. He argues, from an evolutionary standpoint, that parents should value older children more than younger children. Older children, by virtue of simply having survived longer, are more likely to continue to survive and to reach an age where they can have children of their own.

Our results suggest, however, that this conclusion is not universally correct. Parents do not always do best by favoring their eldest. Sometimes they do best by favoring their smallest (i.e., the one that is farthest behind its siblings), and sometimes they may do best by treating offspring on the basis of need. Sulloway's analyses aside, birth order studies are notorious for giving null results, and, when significant effects arise, they are typically very small in magnitude. Our research suggests one possible cause for this: Birth order effects are elusive because the nature of the effect depends on environmental circumstance, a variable that none of these previous studies on humans have controlled for.

More to the point, unlike Becker's unboundedly rational parents, our results suggest that parents everywhere, be they avian or human, do not have to carry cumbersome investment equations in their heads. All they need are one or two simple rules and perhaps a way of telling when to use each one. Which rule is best depends on the harshness of the environment in which parents are attempting to raise their offspring, but the relation between the best rule and the environment also appears to be very simple. A problem that is very difficult to solve analytically can therefore be left unanalyzed, and parents can instead rely on simple strategies to make good investment decisions.

Part VI

A LOOK AROUND, A LOOK BACK,
A LOOK AHEAD

15

Demons Versus Heuristics in Artificial Intelligence, Behavioral Ecology, and Economics

Adam S. Goodie
Andreas Ortmann
Jennifer Nerissa Davis
Seth Bullock
Gregory M. Werner

[C]omplete representations of the external environment, besides being impossible to obtain, are not at all necessary for agents to act in a competent manner.

Rodney A. Brooks

How to model "rational," "intelligent," "adaptive," or "optimal" behavior? Disputes about the answer to this question have been fought in various disciplines, and with various vocabularies. In this chapter we consider the state of the unbounded versus bounded rationality debate as it pertains to the fields of artificial intelligence, animal behavior, and economics. What the disputes reveal is a tension between two visions of rationality. One vision starts with the default assumption that human, animal, or computational agents have unlimited computational powers, which they can use to derive "optimal" solutions to even the most difficult problems. Variants of this view can be found from *Homo economicus* to optimal foraging theory to the assumption that problems of artificial intelligence are computable. The alternative vision acknowledges that humans, animals, and computational systems do not have infinite capabilities, and investigates the simpler mechanisms that these minds actually use.

The alternatives to optimization in the three fields considered here each represent one of the dimensions that defined the ABC vision of rationality in chapter 1. Bounded rationality has been applied widely in the domain of artificial intelligence, where many problems have turned out not to be computationally tractable (Tsotsos, 1991), and relatively simple rules of thumb have often proved to be more successful. However, as we will see, this application has not always been carried out in the spirit of this book. Ecological rationality is perhaps nowhere better exemplified than in the study of animal behavior, where research programs from both field and laboratory studies are converging on the conclusion that unbounded rationality, in addition to being evolutionarily implausible, does not account for how real animals exploit the structure of their environments. The real-world success of such heuristics may also often approximate optimal strategies (when optimal strategies exist) remarkably closely. Finally, social rationality is exemplified by the study of gamelike interactions in economics, where the considerations of other people's strategies are leading to a recognition that even the simplest economic interactions can demand impossible calculations to find an optimal solution. This has begun to result in a consideration of simpler mechanisms that might serve similar functions.

In the following sections we illustrate the dispute between unbounded and bounded rationality by way of characteristic examples drawn from the three disciplines. Each section begins with a brief outline of the state of the dispute in its discipline, and concludes with speculative suggestions of future directions that each field might follow in pursuing fast and frugal strategies. Most environments in all the disciplines are too complex for an optimal approach to succeed, and as the task environment becomes more complex, human, animal, and computational minds must resort to boundedly rational strategies.

Bounded Rationality in Artificial Intelligence

Artificial intelligence (AI) is the enterprise of creating new systems that produce complex behavior—that is to say, smart computers. This contrasts with psychology, which studies already existing complex systems (people and animals). Since it is easier to imagine and theorize about a demon than it is to actually build one, it is unsurprising that practitioners of artificial intelligence have long been aware of the enormous problems involved in building unboundedly rational agents. Indeed, they have discovered that many problems cannot be optimally solved, even in principle (Garey & Johnson, 1979). As a result, the search for heuristics came to be a major theme of AI research, an important step toward slaying the demons of unbounded rationality. However, the initial success of the heuristic approach to creating artificial intelligence has led to the tacit assumption that certain heuristics are candidates for nearly universal application. Rather than considering heuristics to be fitted to certain problems but unsuitable for others, the ability of some to deal generally with a wide variety of problems has been feted. This perspective views the best heuristics as those that are able to deal with the widest range of problems. In this respect, AI treats heuristics as general-purpose demons. Although they are not expected to exhibit godlike perfection, they are admired for, and evaluated on, their ability to approach perfection in any given domain, regardless of the time and resources required.

Two approaches have emerged to respond when heuristic approaches no longer work well. Most "GOFAI" scientists (a term coined by Brooks, 1991a, which stands for "Good Old-Fashioned AI") use a two-pronged attack. First, they simplify the problem by creating "virtual" problems with limited and known dimensions that are to be solved by "disembodied" computers just by thinking about them. Then they use the latest and fastest computers to undertake the massive computational problems that still remain (Brooks, 1991b). The other approach, taken by a distinct minority of the community, is to find new heuristics for new situations. Practitioners in this tradition rigorously seek agents that capitalize on the structure of the environment they happen to occupy, which is often an environment in the real world (Brooks, 1991b). In this section we examine attempts in the AI community to find boundedly rational solutions to complex problems, in other words those drawn from the second tradition.

Getting Along in a Deceptively Simple Environment: Chess

In 1992, Herbert Simon wrote: "It is difficult to predict when computers will defeat the best human player. . . . It can only be a matter of a few years before technological advances end the human supremacy at chess" (Simon & Schaeffer, 1992, pp. 14–15). Simon's prediction was right, and five years later, in 1997, a computer called Deep Blue finally defeated Garry Kasparov, the world's best human chess player, in a tournament. This watershed event in the development of artificial intelligence was also a significant moment in the development of satisficing mechanisms. The game of chess occurs in a small field (an area of 64 discrete squares), with a limited set of alternative events at each point in the game (16 pieces per player, each with a defined set of legal moves), and a single goal (the capture of the opponent's king). What could be simpler? But as anyone knows who has attempted to play the game, or who has tried to program a computer to play it, finding the one best solution to the problem of putting an opponent in checkmate is unimaginably difficult. There are simply too many possible lines of play to simulate them all, even with the most powerful computers.

The game of chess, with its small field, its limited set of legal moves, and a single goal, is too complex a problem to be solved by any machine now imagined. While chess computers can easily consider millions of lines of play in their quest for the best move, this impressive power is dwarfed by the much greater number of possibilities to be considered. There are typically about 35 or so possible moves available to a player (de Groot, 1978), and the number of possible positions after n moves is approximately 35^n, which becomes a very large number very quickly. For example, 35^8 is more than 2.2 trillion. And even if chess computers could anticipate how the board will be arranged eight moves in the future, an ideal strategy would require them to search well beyond that point, all the way to the end of the game. Clearly, neither a computer nor a human player can consider all possibilities, and there are many ways to decide how to narrow the set. How do chess players and chess programmers cope with this problem?

At the most elevated level, the strategy of chess programmers is like that of expert players, namely to try to find lines of play that seem likely to lead to good outcomes short of checkmate. So, like humans, computers must try to evaluate the relative value of various positions that are available after some smaller number of moves. At a finer level, though, the methods used by programmers diverged long ago from those used by players, so that there is now more to be learned from differences between the two strategies than from their similarities.

The attempt to limit the scope of the search in chess dates at least to the work of Herbert Simon and George Baylor (Baylor & Simon, 1966), who produced some of the few true satisficing strategies in the artificial chess literature. They examined the performance of two programs that were designed to lead to checkmate, starting relatively late in the game and using simple decision rules regarding which lines of inquiry to follow. They reasoned that one major goal of the game is to reduce the opponent's mobility—indeed, the object of the game can be described as reducing the king's mobility to zero—and so paths were sought solely on the basis of how much mobility the opponent had following each move. In MATER I (Baylor & Simon, 1966), each possible first move was considered for how many moves the opponent could legally make in response, regardless of the quality of those responses. The move that left the opponent with the fewest moves was then examined for how many moves would be available to the opponent after the *second* move, and so on until checkmate was achieved. If checkmate was not possible, the program backtracked and traced the move with the second fewest possible responses. A second algorithm, MATER II, differed in emphasizing the mobility of the opponent's king. Moves that resulted in the king being unable to move, or able to move in only one or two directions, were given priority. Ties were resolved by recourse to the strategies of MATER I. While MATER I and MATER II were not designed to play entire games, and therefore cannot be evaluated in terms of games won, these early efforts began a quest to find simple but powerful, in other words boundedly rational, approaches to automated chess.

Since the introduction of MATER, programs have been written with an eye to winning complete games, making algorithms that are fast, frugal, and fit a greater challenge to devise. However, some characteristics of fast and frugal algorithms have remained cornerstones of chess programming. In general, all moves are evaluated according to a "static evaluation function" that gives a score to the positions they create. Since the expression is computed many millions of times, it must be very fast and use only information that is readily available in the board configuration. Typical chess evaluation functions use a few pieces of information, such as relative value of pieces remaining, number of pieces attacking the center of the board, and number of pieces attacking the opponent's pieces. Such strategies neglect a great deal of the remaining information. The function quickly calculates these values and integrates them into a single score, and moves are selected on the basis of their scores.

Clever design of the evaluation function is the difference between an artificial world champion and a machine that races toward bad outcomes. Indeed, the creators of Deep Blue credited their recent victory over the world champion to their much improved evaluation function. Much attention was paid to the speed of their machine, which had doubled since their previous attempt, but this improvement could have caused only minor improvements in playing ability. This is because a speed increase of up to 35 times is required to search one extra move ahead, meaning that a mere doubling of the speed of processing does not permit the machine even to look one move farther ahead in its computations in the allotted time. The key to improved chess is thus recognized to be clever algorithms—in other words, those that are fast, frugal, and accurate—rather than more powerful attempts at a Laplacean demon who can calculate the future from the present. These algorithms must find the cues that are subtle but available on the board and provide the most diagnostic information about the outcome of various moves; in other words, they must capitalize on the structure of the environment.

Still, the modern chess program is not an ideal model of satisficing techniques, since it is built on a long tradition of improving programs by waiting for the next generation of computer hardware to run yet more millions of computations per second, a feature of computers that is increasingly unrepresentative of human information processing (Brooks, 1990; Simon & Schaeffer, 1992). Deep Blue works as a high-speed computer, not as a human being, and while it undoubtedly possesses a sophisticated and clever evaluation routine, it also applies this evaluation to an inhuman number of positions in finding the next move. In contrast, the way expert humans play chess is to memorize approximately 50,000 positions, and good responses to them, and to consider approximately 100 paths of play prior to selecting a move in a real game (Simon & Schaeffer, 1992). The typical chess program memorizes no positions, except for a few well-studied opening moves, but searches millions of paths of play. The vision of the Laplacean demon has led chess research far away from Simon's vision of bounded rationality. Since the cleverness of the evaluation function, rather than the power of the computer, has proved to be a better road to improved chess, perhaps chess research in the future will return to the satisficing notions with which it began.

Losing Touch With Domain Specificity: Generalized Heuristic Search

Herbert Simon and his collaborators applied search techniques to the game of chess because the chessboard seemed like an environment where heuristic search would work well. The success of Deep Blue, which is based on a search engine that is partially restrained by its evaluation function, suggests that this intuition was correct. However, with the success of advancing generations of chess programs, the temptation mounted to apply heuristic search to increasingly disparate arenas of artificial intelligence. There is now a large class of problems that are approached under the rubric of heuristic search. A heuristic has come to be defined as a technique that decreases the time complexity of a process while possibly degrading the quality of the solution found (Aho & Ullman, 1992; Green & Knuth, 1982). This concept has clear ties to notions of bounded rationality. A search is simply the attempted acquisition of a specified goal, whether it be checkmate or the quickest route from home to work. Adding heuristics to search algorithms can eliminate unfruitful lines of search, and to the extent that heuristics are fast and frugal, the larger search algorithms that use them are fast and frugal as well.

Many decision-making problems can be characterized as search problems, which clarifies the appropriate subgoals along the path to the ultimate goal, and suggests satisficing strategies to achieve them (Pearl, 1984). Usually the goal is to find such a path with minimal cost. To find the absolute best solution, all possible paths from start states to goal states would need to be searched. For any problem with a nontrivial number of states, the number of possible paths is enormous; but heuristics can eliminate some paths or, preferably, classes of paths without actually testing them. For example, some search algorithms can be improved if they can determine approximately how far they are from a solution at a given intermediate state. Since they cannot know this exactly without knowing the entire solution, they need a heuristic that estimates the distance remaining to the goal. The better this heuristic, the more paths they can eliminate from the search, and the faster the search will run. For example, if a heuristic is known never to overestimate the distance to the solution, then many possible paths can be eliminated without sacrificing an optimal solution. In some cases, speed-ups can be attained with known properties of the degradation of solution quality. For example, if there is a heuristic that sometimes overestimates the distance to the solution, but never by more than a fixed amount, a bound can be placed on how far from optimal the final answer might be. The program will wrongly eliminate paths that may be the optimal solution, but the solution found will be no further away from optimal than the sum of the possible overestimates along the way.

Heuristic search is a powerful tool when applied to well-chosen domains. The trouble is that GOFAI has not been careful to choose domains well. Heuristic search has been applied to some problems where it is helpful, such as its original domain, chess, but also to many where it is not. In the wrong domain, a heuristic search algorithm, like any algorithm out of its proper environment, will not do the job well and needs to be accompanied by a demon that will do the heavy lifting.

In many domains, that heavy lifting amounts to conquering the well-known *frame problem* (McCarthy & Hayes, 1969). The frame problem arises when a system must decide what to do in a way that requires several steps. Each possible step that the system could take has certain consequences and sets up a new set of conditions and problems. This is the case in chess, where each move may simultaneously threaten an opponent's piece, expose or cover one's own piece, and so on. Each of these consequences also sets up new circumstances for the opponent, making the opponent's next move a particular problem that is different from the problem faced in a different move. For most problems, each possible step sets up new circumstances, and vast arrays of possible future circumstances, that make the computation of optimal solutions an enormous challenge. The problem is how to decide when to stop considering more possibilities, and make the primary decision that is supposed to be made.

However, this challenge is overcome more easily in some cases than in others. In chess, one can imagine ways to limit the impact of the frame problem, which are all possible because of the simplifying features of the chess problem that we noted above (small field, limited moves, and a single goal). Imagine, in contrast, the frame problem that confronts a robot whose mission is to search through a garbage dump to locate and remove recyclable materials. In addition to the goal-related consequences of its actions, such as finding and identifying aluminum cans, the robot must consider many other possibilities, such as moving an article that causes a pile of garbage to collapse on the robot, moving under a dripping can that short-circuits the robot, and so forth. It is easy to see that the frame problem is not equally daunting in all domains of artificial intelligence.

The frame problem illustrates one reason why bounded rationality must be applied in a domain-specific way (Cosmides & Tooby, 1987). While the techniques of heuristic search applied widely in AI are intended to reduce the need for demonlike computational capabilities, they often fail in this mission because the heuristics employed, while fast and frugal, are not fit in the environment on which they are unleashed.

The Ultimate Test: Robotics

In robotics, the limitations imposed by a domain-general application of heuristic search can literally walk up to their creators and bite them on the leg. However, these days they can do so only very slowly, and that is precisely the problem. Here is the way that GOFAI approaches have typically achieved robot behavior:

1. Have the robot collect data from cameras and a large number of sensors. Using these sensory data, and knowledge of physics, have the robot build a sophisticated model of the physical world. Include aspects of gravity, momentum, surface contours, and objects, as well as the robot's interaction with the world.
2. Generate a list of all possible things the robot can do next. This

list will include actions such as "turn 5 degrees left and move
1 inch forward."

3. Simulate the robot doing each of the things on the list in the
   world model. Assess whether the robot moves closer to its goal,
   crashes into objects, overturns, fails to climb a steep gradient,
   runs out of power, overheats, and so on.
4. Order all new states of the world according to some evaluation
   function, and pick the action from the list that produces the best
   resulting state.
5. Make the robot execute the chosen action in the real world.
6. Start again from step 1.

In practice, this approach is typically executed in environments carefully
engineered to be as easily represented by the robot as possible. Even so, a
supercomputer is typically required to build the world model and test
possible robot actions. Robots using this type of control strategy zoom
along at a few feet per day.

A different approach within AI has recently gained prominence. It employs simple, physically embodied systems that face and surmount real-
world tasks by employing simple task-dependent behaviors that exploit
the structure of the environment in which they operate. Brooks's (1991a,
1991b) robots, rather than building elaborate mental models, "use the
world as its own best model," exploiting regularities in their interaction
with the environment. For example, if an infrared detector spots a large
object ahead, the robot may assume that it is a dangerous obstacle and
steer away from it. A small rectangle in the visual field may be assumed
to be a can to be recycled, if recycling is the robot's mission, initiating a
grasping reflex. Robots that use this approach gain considerably in speed,
albeit at the expense of domain generality.

These systems are designed in the same spirit as the fast and frugal
heuristics discussed in this book. They are often described as "reactive"
in that their behavior is generated without periods of reflection or consideration. Analogously, the heuristics presented in this book are noncompensatory in that they do not compare or combine different pieces of
information. Brooks imagines a robot as a collection of separate competencies, or behavioral layers, that are selected among and triggered by specific environmental events. A robot thus conceived is redolent of the
adaptive toolbox outlined in chapter 1.

There are contrasts between the fast and frugal program presented here
and Brooks's robotic program, but these lie mainly in methods of implementation and not in the spirit of the enterprise. For example, Take The
Best searches for information before making an inference, a practice that
Brooks prefers to avoid. However, it is clear that Brooks does not disdain
search for its own sake, but rather the unlimited search that demands
computational demons. In this regard, the programs are entirely in agreement. Also, our heuristics, when simulated, are not embodied or situated
as Brooks advocates. In this regard they are similar to Braitenberg's (1984)

conceptual "vehicles" that use the simplest possible elements and strategies to create complex behavior. These robots were not actually built to
operate in the real world, but like our heuristics, they share Brooks's spirit
of power through simplicity.

The Future of Fast and Frugal Heuristics in Artificial Intelligence

Computers continue to increase in power at an astonishing rate, and so it
is likely that many people will continue to proceed as if a working Laplacean demon is just around the corner. While this approach may be popular, it will be a mistake; whereas the Laplacean demon has truly infinite
computational power, computers never will. The reason the Laplacean
demon must have infinite computational power is that the problems it
solves are infinitely difficult, marking the computer that finds unboundedly rational solutions as a chimera. Brooks's (e.g., 1991b) real robots and
Braitenberg's (1984) conceptual ones offer the beginnings of a more realistic alternative, while fast and frugal approaches to traditional artificial
intelligence challenges such as artificial chess might inspire a return to
the field's roots, which lie in domain-specific, satisficing approaches.

Ecological Rationality in Animal Behavior

Many roboticists and practitioners of the new artificial intelligence turn
to behavioral ecology for design tips from nature. Behavioral ecologists
study adaptations in living organisms, typically defined by evidence that
a particular behavior was designed by the process of natural selection for
a specific function in a specific environment. Because the fit between behavior and its environment is a central assumption of the field, it is normally taken for granted and seldom discussed. The phrase "ecological rationality" is not a standard expression of the behavioral ecology field, but
ecological rationality is what behavioral ecology is all about.

A good anatomical model of the fit between adaptations and environment is the vertebrate eye, which contains a single lens that focuses light
on the retina and a layer of photoreceptive cells that translate light patterns into neural impulses. Within this basic plan, however, there are
many variations in detail that allow particular organisms to see better in
their particular environments. Vertebrate eyes vary greatly in the distance
at which they can focus on objects, the colors that they are able to see,
and the light levels under which they are still able to make out their visual
world. For example, marine fish living in deep water where there is little
light have eyes with especially powerful lenses, and large multilayered
photoreceptors positioned with light reflectors under them that boost the
ability to sense light at low levels of illumination. Also, whereas the vertebrate eye allows for good resolution over large distances, insects, with

their large compound eyes, trade off the ability to focus clearly on objects at a distance for the ability to view their entire visual world simultaneously and maintain a large binocular field that aids in such activities as course control and navigation (Wehner, 1997).

The study of adaptations has taken two different but complementary forms in behavioral ecology. One approach focuses on the selection pressures an animal species is likely to have faced in its evolution and attempts to use these to specify what behavior the animal is likely to exhibit in its current environment, assuming that selection has shaped it to behave optimally in its natural setting. This approach captures the tradition of optimality modeling. A second approach examines how an animal expresses a given behavior and attempts to understand this in light of what selection is expected to have wrought. These researchers study the mechanisms of behavior. Both traditions have employed notions of bounds on rationality, but it is not surprising that the "optimality" approach has ventured only so far as to examine optimization under constraints; the mechanistic approach has begun to study true bounded rationality by examining the simple rules animals can use to succeed in their environments.

Unbounded Rationality in Behavioral Ecology

Optimality models have become a popular tool among behavioral ecologists because they help to formalize hypotheses about the design of adaptations and to clarify the adaptive problems that they solve. To the behavioral ecologist, the optimal solution is the one that gives the organism the best possible chance of surviving and reproducing. These optimal solutions specify the behavioral response that should ideally be observed in a given situation, but do not specify the mechanism by which the organism arrives at the response. These models are used primarily to test the results of the selection pressures thought to have acted on the organism. In other words, they are hypotheses about the way natural selection has acted on the creature under study.

Natural selection is expected to be an optimizing force. For example, take the problem of finding food, in which an organism must consume a certain number of calories every day to stay alive and must choose where to forage at each moment. How does it decide when it has eaten enough in one patch and should move on to another? An animal that forages too long in a depleted patch runs the risk of not finding enough food to survive, and even if it finds enough to survive another day, a nonoptimal forager will still not fare as well, in terms of survival and reproduction, as an animal that left the patch earlier in favor of a more abundant location. The animal in the depleted patch needs to spend more time and energy finding food than the animal who switched patches. This lost time and energy could have been spent caring for young, attracting mates, or storing energy for future days when food might not be so plentiful. For this reason, natural selection is expected to favor the proliferation of animals that maximize their net rate of energy gain by switching to new food patches at appropriate times. Animals that *almost* optimize, or that consume enough to survive, but do so inefficiently, would be supplanted by those who behave optimally. It would *seem* that as long as survival and reproduction increase continually as a function of performance (perhaps by way of the rate of energy gain) up to some maximal attainable value, organisms should be shaped by natural selection to attain that maximum value, and nothing less.

Optimization Under Constraints in Foraging Theory

But this picture is incomplete. Students of evolution, including optimality modelers, are well aware of the existence of constraints on perfection (e.g., Stephens & Krebs, 1986). Perhaps the most important for our purposes are phylogenetic or historical constraints, and constraints on time and materials. Phylogenetic constraints are limitations on the possible adaptive solutions placed on the organism by its previous evolutionary history. New behaviors are shaped in small increments, and each evolved point on the way from behavior A to behavior B must perform at least as well as the step before it. If an animal does not solve a problem optimally, the way a conscious designer would, this may be because there is no way to get "there" from "here." To borrow an analogy from Dawkins (1982), engineering by natural selection is like building a jet engine from a propeller engine by changing it one rivet, nut, or screw at a time. Furthermore, every prototype along the way must get off the ground and fly better than the one before it—obviously a daunting limitation. Limits on the amount of time and materials that an organism can devote to any given task constitute a second type of constraint. Every unit of energy that is used to help an animal find food, for example, is no longer available to be used caring for offspring, or evading predators, or doing any of the many other things necessary for survival, and because they are designed for their specific food-finding function the cognitive mechanisms that enable efficient foraging are similarly unavailable to be used for these other tasks.

If behavioral ecologists have always been aware that limits on optimality exist, they have not always taken them into account in trying to explain behavior. To illustrate we again turn to optimal foraging, a successful and highly model-driven area of behavioral ecology. Optimal foraging theorists have been concerned with determining whether various animals maximally exploit their food resources. An optimal forager faced with the task of deciding when to switch patches calculates the rate of caloric return of exploiting various patches, chooses the one that maximizes net energy gain, depletes it until its value falls below that of the next richest patch, switches to that one, and continues in this fashion. Early optimal foraging models assumed few or no constraints on the forager's abilities to compute how rich the various patches are. The models were endowed, for example, with perfect knowledge of the environment and perfect recall of that knowledge.[1]

The *ideal free distribution* (IFD) is an early optimal foraging model designed to predict how animals distribute themselves among patches of resources (Alexander, 1996; Fretwell & Lucas, 1970). In its simplest form it predicts that, given equal competitive abilities among individuals, the ratio of animals at different resource sites will be equal to the ratio of the amount of resources at those sites (Milinski & Parker, 1991). In this spatial distribution, each animal maximizes the resources it receives. To accomplish this feat, however, individual animals need perfect knowledge of the profitability of resources.

Experiments designed to test the IFD uncovered systematic deviations from its predictions, suggesting that some form of constraint may be affecting behavior (e.g., Abrahams, 1986). When deviations appear between the data and a theoretical model, foraging theorists assume that there are constraints preventing the optimal solution from being reached, and it is here that notions of constrained optimization begin to emerge. In parallel with AI, though, researchers in behavioral ecology have introduced such notions only when unbounded optimality models collapse. Early modelers took the lack of fit between theory and data largely for granted, and made little attempt to account for it. The unrealistic quality of their initial assumptions was acknowledged, and quantitative inconsistencies were often explained as the result of estimation errors on the part of the animal (i.e., as perceptual constraints of the organism). But these constraints were ignored in theorizing for the sake of generalizability, often because many constraints are species specific, and early modelers sought to create models that applied broadly across species. More recently, foraging theorists have taken deviations from the IFD as a starting point to determine the nature of the constraints and incorporate them into their models to allow greater accuracy in predicting behavior. If these "errors" are the result of perceptual or cognitive constraints, then they should appear as systematic, nonrandom deviations from optimal predictions.

An example of the systematic deviation between the data and the IFD model is that animals tend to underuse richer sites and overuse poorer sites. This led some theorists to believe that perhaps the assumptions of the original model were unrealistic; maybe animals do not have perfect knowledge of the profitability of different food patches. Gray and Kennedy (1994) have tested this in mallard ducks and shown that as the overall level of food drops, ducks find it increasingly difficult to discriminate between patches. As a result of this inability to discriminate, ducks ar-

---

1. It should be stressed that for the behavioral ecologist, assuming that the animal has perfect knowledge of these things does not mean believing that it is making conscious calculations following the formulas of the model. It is instead a shorthand way of saying that the animal is expected to behave as if it had perfect knowledge and abilities.

range themselves between patches in a manner inconsistent with the ideal free distribution, and consistent with the results of other, previous deviations from the IFD.

Bounded Rationality for Animals

The incorporation of constraints into optimality models should not be confused with true models of bounded rationality such as satisficing. While they are similar in accounting for suboptimal performance, the optimality models of behavioral ecology are continually refined to incorporate constraints and generate more accurate predictions of behavior, always assuming that the organism is optimizing given the tools available to it. After all, natural selection is expected to be an optimizing process. Satisficing techniques, on the other hand, do not attempt to achieve optimality. Instead they incorporate a minimum acceptable threshold (or aspiration level) that must be reached, and any improvement beyond this point is comparatively unimportant. In other words, a satisficer is concerned with doing well enough, while an optimizer is concerned with doing the best it can.

Stephens and Krebs (1986) have argued that if by some chance the trait under question increases in a step function (e.g., if a plateau exists along which increases in ability do not lead to increases in rate of food return), then some sort of satisficing mechanism would indeed be expected to be selected. Most modelers, however, have assumed that this situation is rare in biology, without ever testing this assumption.

This conception takes satisficing in particular, and bounded ecological rationality in general, to be an alternative to optimizing at the level of selection pressures. There is another way to conceptualize the role of bounded ecological rationality, however, and this is as the mechanism by which the behavioral expectations under optimality are achieved. The female *Trichogramma* wasp lays her eggs inside the eggs of other insects, and the optimum number to deposit is a function of the volume of the host egg. She could, perhaps, calculate the host egg volume using geometric methods of spherical trigonometry, and use the result to decide how many eggs she will lay. Instead, she estimates the volume by a fast and frugal mechanism. She adopts a particular body posture while standing on the egg, creating an angle between her head and the first segment of her antenna that is related to the radius of the sphere. By simply basing the number of eggs she lays on the acuteness of this angle, she can essentially "compute" the volume of the egg without engaging in a single complex calculation (Wehner, 1997).

Mechanisms of Ecological Rationality

Typically, optimality modelers do not claim that their models represent the means by which animals actually solve problems, and researchers who focus on understanding behavioral mechanisms start with the assumption that apparently complex behavioral decisions are mediated by simple processes. Furthermore, these processes are expected to be domain specific, that is, fitted especially to solve particular problems in the particular ecological environment in which they were selected. Simple heuristics can provide good solutions without a great deal of complex general purpose calculation. By stringing together a series of simple, special purpose heuristics, animals can perform some very sophisticated tasks. One illustration of this comes from Wehner's work on navigation in *Cataglyphis* ants of the Sahara desert (Wehner & Wehner, 1990; Wehner et al., 1996; Wehner, 1997). After foraging over great distances in a desert sand environment with almost no landmarks, the ants must be able to find their way back to the nest. They could try to memorize their path and retrace their steps exactly, but because they travel by circuitous routes while foraging, there is often a much shorter, more direct route home.

Cataglyphis solves its navigation problem by performing path analysis, though not with a calculator and a batch of complex equations as a mathematician might. Instead it relies on a number of simple subroutines that allow it to continually measure all angles it turns and distances it covers, and integrate this information into an updated vector that always points it roughly toward home. The angles are measured by reference to the pattern of polarized light in the sky (which, unlike humans, these ants can see). This skylight pattern is not stable but changes with the elevation of the sun over the horizon. *Cataglyphis* comes to the correct solution by template matching the pattern of light in the direction of its own orientation with a preprogrammed representation of the polarization pattern when the sun is at the horizon. This template is best matched with the external pattern when the animal is aligned with either the solar or antisolar meridian, providing the ant with an adaptive built-in compass by which to navigate. The path integration system is not without errors, and while it is sufficient to allow the ant to return to the general area of its nest, it does not usually lead it exactly to the entrance. *Cataglyphis* therefore uses a second template matching system once it arrives near its home. It creates a snapshot in its head of the visual location of various landmarks when standing in front of the entrance, and maneuvers around the area until the visual world matches the template in its head.

Navigation is not the only area in behavioral ecology where researchers have studied simple mechanisms that can perform as well as complex calculations. In addition to the optimal foraging models discussed earlier, some theorists have also built models of how a forager actually makes its decisions. These theorists have looked at a number of simple rules of thumb that make good foraging choices.

Green (1984) has examined rules of thumb that an animal could use to decide whether to leave its current patch to try its luck elsewhere, a problem that has been studied extensively. Perhaps the best-known approach to the problem is Charnov's (1976) marginal value theorem, which states that if the rate of finding food decreases over time as the forager searches, then it should leave for a new patch when its rate of finding food falls to equality with the highest possible rate it could achieve elsewhere. The problem with this notion is that although it allows us to predict when an animal should leave a patch, it does not tell us how an animal could know when that moment has arrived. As Green (1984) puts it, "It is like telling a gambler that he should stop playing just before he starts losing" (p. 30). Green tested several possible rules animals could use to make these sorts of decisions, such as the fixed-time rule (leave after a specified interval, regardless of success), the giving-up-time rule (leave if food has not been forthcoming over a specified interval), and the assessment rule (leave when the rate of food encounter falls below a specified level). Of these simple decision rules, the assessment rule achieved the highest return across the broadest number of environments, and experimental research has shown that at least one species, the parasitoid wasp *Nemeritis canescens*, appears to use the assessment rule in making foraging decisions (Waage, 1979).

This approach could be, and often has been, viewed as optimizing under constraints of information gathering ability, but as in the case of Wehner's work on ants, Green's analysis explicitly does not try to optimize. Instead it considers what sort of information would be readily available to a forager and from this tests various possible decision rules. There are no claims that this is the best an animal could possibly do, such as the marginal value theorem attempts. The aim is merely to show how well such simple rules of thumb can perform. In our terms, the optimizing equation belongs to the species of demon, and the rule of thumb to that of bounded rationality.

A Case History From the Lab: Matching Versus Maximizing

A related example comes from the field of animal learning, which has developed independently of behavioral ecology, but which shares an interest in the ways animals adapt to meet their survival needs. Animal learning researchers study how behavior can be changed in the laboratory, which is supposed to reflect how behavior changes in the wild, but in better-controlled conditions than can be obtained in the wild. We include this example because it provides a case study in simple heuristics that both describe real behavior better than models of unbounded rationality, and are also more plausible to suppose in the minds of real animals.

Imagine an animal living between two fruit trees that occasionally drop ripe fruit to the ground for the animal to eat.[2] Suppose that Tree 2 provides

---

2. This example is intended as an accessible model of concurrent variable interval (VI) schedules.

twice as much fruit as Tree 1, but the animal needs more food than can
be provided by either tree alone, and the animal must search for food from
both trees continuously. Clearly, it is better to spend more time looking
for fruit under Tree 2 than under Tree 1, but the animal should not leave
the fruit that drops from Tree 1 to rot on the ground either. It turns out
that the fruit the animal acquires is maximized if the time allocated to
each tree is proportional to the amount of fruit acquired there.[3] In mathematical notation:

$$\frac{B_1}{B_2} = \frac{R_1}{R_2} \tag{1}$$

where B is the behavior allocated to a particular source of food (either in
terms of time spent waiting at each source, or in terms of particular responses that must be made to obtain the food), and R is the food (or reinforcement) acquired from that source. This equation is known as the
matching law (Herrnstein, 1961) and is a staple of the literature of animal
learning. In addition to characterizing the optimal behavior in this situation, the matching law also provides a strikingly accurate picture of how
animals actually apportion their time and effort (Davison & McCarthy,
1988). The question is, do they calculate the optimal distribution of behavior, which happens to be equivalent to Equation (1) above; or do they
follow a simpler procedure that conforms to the matching law and find
that it performs well for them? There are several process models that have
taken the matching law as the fundamental output (Williams, 1988). What
they share in common is that they do not need to induce the structure of
the environment, then deduce the optimal behavior within that environment, before acting. All that is required is a mechanism to perceive reinforcers and behaviors, and then to find ratios among them.

To answer this question, we must first consider another kind of foraging situation. This time, imagine a bird that lives near two nut-bearing
trees, each of which provides more than enough nuts to sustain the bird.[4]
However, cracking the shell of a nut from either tree requires considerable
time and effort, and it takes twice as many pecks of the beak to crack the
shells of nuts from Tree A as to crack those from Tree B. Obviously, assuming the nuts from both trees provide equal nutrition, the bird would do
best to take nuts exclusively from Tree B. And in fact, this is what birds
do, an apparently different strategy from that of the fruit-seeking animal
that distributed its responses across both patches. However, this pattern
of behavior also conforms to the matching law. Consider what Equation

---

3. The exact location of the optimal choice proportions depends on one's model
of how an animal decides to change from one schedule to the other, but all theories
place the optimal proportion close to the matching proportion (Kagel et al., 1995).

4. This example is intended as an accessible model of concurrent variable ratio
(VR) schedules.

(1) would have to say about a bird that eats one nut from each tree. The ratio of reinforcers is $1:1$, but the ratio of behaviors required to eat those nuts is $2:1$ (because nuts from Tree A require twice as many pecks). If the bird eats one nut from Tree A and two from Tree B, the ratio of reinforcers is $1:2$, but the ratio of responses is now $1:1$ (because the effort to crack two nuts from Tree B is the same as is required to crack one nut from Tree A). If the bird eats one nut from Tree A and three from Tree B, the ratio of reinforcers is $1:3$, and the ratio of responses is $2:3$. It turns out that the only allocation that achieves equal ratios of responses and reinforcers is exclusive preference for the richer side, where both ratios are $0:1$.[5] Again the matching law both prescribes optimal behavior and describes real behavior, so again the question arises, do birds calculate their optimal behavior, or do they do something simpler to conform to the matching law?

To answer this, we need a situation where matching behavior and optimizing behavior are not the same, as they were in both the fruit trees and the nut trees. This is where the potential for creating artificial situations in the laboratory becomes especially useful. In a lab, we can place one of the fruit trees next to one of the nut trees, make them provide the same kind of food, control the rates at which they provide that food, and observe how much time and effort animals devote to each food source. Under these circumstances, optimal behavior requires a strong bias to work on the nuts, while only occasionally checking the fruit tree to see if something has fallen. This is optimal because the nuts require constant effort, while the fruit requires only waiting and occasional monitoring. However, the fruit tree can be manipulated to provide equal amounts of food over time as are acquired from the nuts, so that the matching law predicts little or no preference for the nut tree over the fruit tree. In fact, this matching law prediction is confirmed. When the matching law is experimentally pitted against optimality theory, the matching law does a better job of predicting the data (Williams, 1988).[6]

In this example, a simple rule of thumb—matching responses proportionally to obtained reinforcers—results in strategies that are identical to those of the optimal equation under choices between two fruit trees or two nut trees, and teasing them apart for theoretical reasons required us to introduce the somewhat artificial choice between the two kinds of trees. The matching law is thus an excellent example of a behavioral strategy that does very well in natural situations despite having a very simple structure. However, this point has sometimes been lost in the matching-maximizing debate. Those on the side of matching argue that pigeons are simple creatures obeying simple laws, suggesting that it was a mere coin-

5. Exclusive preference for Tree A would also conform to the matching law, but as is intuitively obvious, this does not happen. Melioration theory (Herrnstein & Vaughan, 1980) accounts for this effect.

6. This conclusion is not universally accepted (cf. Kagel et al., 1995), but is a majority opinion.

cidence that their behavior was optimal in many situations. To their credit, those on this side recognize the unlikelihood of the "demon in the pigeon" implied by optimality theory in an animal with only three grams of brain matter (these studies typically employ pigeons as subjects). But in describing the algorithms used by pigeons, "simple" seemed to mean "stupid," and the ingenuity of a simple mechanism that could do so well was often lost.

In response, those on the maximizing side were determined to demonstrate the cleverness of pigeons by insisting on increasingly complex (and, as a consequence, decreasingly plausible) models of what was really being optimized and what information was being used to optimize it. The defeat of optimality models seemed to be a defeat for conceptions of pigeon "intelligence." In fact, nothing could be further from the truth. The way that pigeons choose where to look for food is a marvel of ingenuity and adaptation.

The Future of Fast and Frugal Heuristics in Behavioral Ecology

After a long period of domination by the constrained optimization of selective pressures, the tide now seems to be turning toward the bounded rationality of behavioral mechanisms. A brief look at the last two editions of Krebs and Davies's edited volume *Behavioural Ecology* (1991, 1997), considered a standard book in the field, illustrates the change. The preface to the third edition acknowledges greater attention to mechanism than had been found in its pages previously. In the fourth edition, mechanism and individual behavior receive their own section of five chapters. Of course, as Kamil and Roitblat (1985) have pointed out, research is ideally a balance of both functional (selection pressures) and causal (proximate mechanism) rationales for behavior. Because of the earlier dominance by the former, the shift toward the latter represents a movement toward this balance.

Given the increased attention to mechanism, it is of course necessary to have an idea of how adaptations could function. Behavioral ecologists have thus far avoided the trap of trying to create mechanisms out of unbounded rationality or optimization under constraints. They have considered satisficing to some extent, but this has had limited impact, largely because of such assumptions as that plateaus of fitness are rare (e.g., Stephens & Krebs, 1986, but see also Ward, 1992). But other fast and frugal decision mechanisms have remained promising in the view of behavioral ecology, and a steadily growing body of research is attempting such approaches. Kin recognition mechanisms are instances of the recognition heuristic (chapter 2), as is the use of recognition in the social transmission of food choice in rats. Mate copying, mentioned in chapter 4, is another fast and frugal mechanism currently receiving a good deal of attention (e.g., Brooks, 1998; Dugatkin & Godin, 1998). And the mate choice algorithms and parental feeding mechanisms contained in chapters 13 and 14 of this book promise to add their own fast and frugal contributions to the behavioral ecology literature.

Social Rationality in Economics

In economics, success is not defined as navigating through an artificial environment, or finding food that is waiting to be gathered in a real but passive environment, but negotiating one's way to a living in an environment made up of other agents who are also trying to make a living. Suppose, in a small example of urban survival, that Sandy wants to buy a cup of coffee from Bill. To determine his profit-maximizing price, Bill needs to know not only how much the coffee cost him, but also what Sandy is willing to pay for it. For Sandy to maximize her utility, she must know the minimally profitable price that Bill is willing to accept. Even if we assume that Bill knows both his own costs and Sandy's willingness to pay, and Sandy knows both her willingness to pay and Bill's minimum acceptable price, the problem is clearly not easily solvable.

But usually information does not flow so freely: Sandy most likely will not reveal her willingness to pay, and Bill will not reveal his minimum acceptable price. The two of them are left with a "bargaining game" under incomplete information, which is even more complex than the problem with complete information. Other considerations enter in as well, such as how many people besides Sandy want a cup of coffee, how many people besides Bill have a cup of coffee to sell, whether Sandy would be just as happy with a glass of juice, whether Bill would like to sell coffee to Sandy every day for the next five years, and so on. If we proceed by this kind of analysis, for Bill to sell a cup of coffee to Sandy requires an ungainly amount of information and a large number of decisions, even for such a simple economic transaction. Clearly, this is not the way we normally go about buying coffee. Rather, institutions such as posted prices have arisen that allow fast and frugal decisions on the part of both the seller and the buyer of a cup of coffee. Sellers often construct posted prices on the basis of simple markup rules, although it is noteworthy that markup rules need to be sensible, since senseless rules would endanger the existence of a business. And buyers often use simple "take it or leave it" decision rules that to some extent arise in response to budgetary constraints.

History and Conceptions of Economic Rationality

The concept of rationality—unbounded, bounded, or otherwise—has a remarkably brief history in economics (Arrow, 1986; Vriend, 1996), if it is not confused with self-interest. The central idea of self-interest dates at least to the late eighteenth century with Adam Smith, whose most famous statement of the principle was: "It is not from the benevolence of the butcher, the brewer, or the baker, that we expect our dinner, but from their regard to their own self-interest. We address ourselves, not to their humanity but to their self-love, and never talk to them of our own necessities but of their advantages" (Smith, 1937, p. 14). The concept of self-interest is related to modern ideas of rationality, but there are fundamental differences. Self-interest, as it was conceived by classical economists, was not something that required the person possessing it to do any computation. The butcher, brewer, and baker need to make a living, and prefer to sell their wares for the greatest possible profit. How absurd to think that they do not automatically know this!

When Herbert Simon introduced the twin notions of satisficing and search in the mid-1950s, he also introduced two other ideas: that the mental state of economic agents matters, and that the assumptions made by economists about agents' mental states should not be unrealistic. Stigler (1961) introduced a different version of search theory, which modeled search as optimization under constraints. Search concerned extra information which was assumed to be costly, and that these costs should be taken into account in the final calculation of what is truly in the agent's best interest. These insights reintroduced the more general idea that the mental events of economic agents (in this case, their knowledge state) were important data in accounting for economic phenomena. Since Stigler's paper, a rich search literature has developed, but it shifted the emphasis from Simon's concern for bounded rationality to the ideal of optimal search with optimal stopping rules.

According to Vriend (1996), the pursuit of new questions raised by the relevance of agents' mental states took at least two paths. The first path, which includes the weighty tradition of expected utility theory (Ramsey, 1931; Savage, 1954; von Neumann & Morgenstern, 1944), seeks evidence for or against the proposition that people's decisions adhere to certain axioms. The axioms include such principles as completeness, invariance, dominance, and transitivity, and together are taken to be rationality itself. Not surprisingly, there is abundant evidence, some of it now bearing classic status, that in many situations, people do not adhere to these axioms (e.g., Allais, 1953; Ellsberg, 1961; Kahneman & Tversky, 1979). These results have been interpreted by some as demonstrating human irrationality, by others as demonstrating that the axioms were bad models of human rationality. But tests of axioms typically do not take into account the issue that Simon and Stigler addressed, namely the search for information, which people may or may not do in a manner perfectly consistent with their self-interest or with various axioms.

The other path taken to assess human rationality was to leave decisions aside and assess the thought processes that were supposed to underlie them. This question, whether people's mental operations allowed them truly to pursue their best interests, could be asked only after Simon and Stigler had introduced the importance of the mental state of the agents under consideration. It is from the emphasis on inference rather than preference that the question arises whether humans are intuitively capable of performing the complex calculations characteristic of economic analyses, to eventually arrive at "correct" inferences. Within this computational background Simon's (1955a, 1957, 1959) concept of bounded rationality came to influence economic thinking. People may not be able to calculate—without calculators or specialized training—the complex functions that economists have developed over the years, but they can make good inferences on the basis of simpler calculations that are well adapted to the inference (or decision) environment.

Models of bounded rationality have thus been present in the economics literature approximately as long as the concept of unbounded rationality (Mitchell, 1912; Sauermann & Selten, 1962; Selten, 1996; Simon, 1957), but their influence on the field has generally been minimal. For a long time the neoclassical paradigm of unbounded rationality, of " . . . contemplating all rates of substitution in n-space before buying a cup of coffee" (Leijonhufvud, 1996, p. 50), simply ruled supreme. With the comparatively recent arrival of experimental economics and game theory, however, this situation has changed dramatically, as these new approaches have compelled economists to examine the demands their models place on the people whose behavior they are trying to describe.[7] In response, economists have begun to come up with promising alternative models.

Game theorists now routinely distinguish the so-called eductive and evolutive approaches to noncooperative game theory. The first term derives from the word "education" and corresponds roughly to models that employ unbounded rationality and unlimited knowledge; the second term derives from "evolution" and corresponds to models that employ bounded rationality. Ken Binmore (1990) defines them as follows:

> The word *eductive* . . . describe[s] a dynamic process by means of which equilibrium is achieved through careful reasoning on the part of the players. Such reasoning will usually require an attempt to simulate the reasoning process of other players. . . . The word *evolutive* . . . describe[s] a dynamic process by means of which equilibrium is achieved through evolutionary mechanisms . . . adjustment takes place as a result of *iterated* play by *myopic* players. (p. 155)

---

7. Neoclassical theories explain, for example, consumer choices of commodity bundles as choices of "sure things" (cups of coffee, pieces of German chocolate cake, etc.). Consumer preferences are typically represented by "utility functions" whose construction requires certain heroic assumptions about the underlying consumer preferences. However, acknowledging that in most real and financial markets outcomes are risky or uncertain, game theorists model consumer preferences by way of von Neumann-Morgenstern utility functions. These utility functions represent outcomes of risky or uncertain nature as probability distributions over "prizes" (essentially the commodity bundles of neoclassical theories). Both neoclassical and von Neumann-Morgenstern utility functions are constructed under assumptions whose validity as a realistic description of choice behavior has been experimentally contested (see Kreps, 1990).

Let us illustrate the eductive and the evolutive approach to game theory by way of the example of symmetric bargaining games. These games attempt to formally model the incentive structure of the kind of haggling situation embodied in Sandy and Bill's coffee transaction. One example of a symmetric bargaining game is taken from the situation depicted in table 15-1, where two players ("Row" and "Column") can choose one strategy that is "fair and efficient," in other words that distributes all of the available money equally (e.g., each player gets 50¢). This strategy is risky, because if one player chooses it and the other does not, the one who chose it gets nothing. To avoid such an undesirable outcome, either player can choose a "safe" strategy that guarantees a payoff that is at least 30¢. For example, if Row chooses "safe" and Column chooses "fair and efficient," then Row gets 30¢ and Column gets nothing. Because Row went the safe route, a positive outcome was guaranteed, but this was exactly the possibility that made choosing the fair and efficient option risky. Notice that if either player goes the safe route, the fair and efficient outcome is impossible. A third and final strategy adds extra payoff to both players if (and only if) the other player has gone the safe route. This strategy is also risky because if it is played when the other player did *not* play it safe, neither player gets anything.

How would a rational player proceed in this situation, when the player is uncertain how the other player will act? The eductive approach predicts the outcome of such a game by determining a *Nash equilibrium*, which is a combination of actions such that, given other players' actions, no player has an incentive to change hers or his. Such a combination of actions can consist of one action for each player only, or a mix of action choices over many iterations of the game. A mixed strategy may be advantageous when there is something to be gained when the other player is uncertain what you will do next. Imagine a tennis player serving against an opponent. Even if she can serve faster to the left, she ought to serve to the right from time to time, to make her serve less predictable.

Unfortunately for a person seeking a unique, "rational" solution, there are five Nash equilibria in this game. Three of them are pure-action equilibria; they lie on the diagonal that runs from the lower left corner to the

Table 15-1: An Example of a Symmetric Bargaining Game

| | Column | | |
Row	Safe	Fair & Efficient	Third Way
Safe	30¢, 30¢	30¢, 0	60¢, 40¢
Fair & Efficient	0, 30¢	50¢, 50¢	0, 0
Third Way	40¢, 60¢	0, 0	0, 0

Note. The first number in each pair of payoffs denotes the payoff to the Row player; the second number denotes the payoff of the Column player.

upper right. If any one of these three pairs of strategies becomes established as a pattern, then neither player makes more money by switching to another strategy. The other two are mixed-strategy Nash equilibria.[8] As in the example of the tennis serve, these strategies capitalize on the uncertainty they create in the other player.

Even if experimental subjects could and did compute the five Nash equilibria, the eductive approach cannot identify a unique "best" equilibrium for the symmetric bargaining game above, and players would therefore have to take recourse to a general equilibrium selection theory (e.g., Harsanyi & Selten, 1988; Van Huyck et al., 1995, who discuss this bargaining example in more detail), using such criteria as symmetry (identical actions and payoffs for players), efficiency (maximal payoffs), and security (a certain nonzero payoff). For the symmetric bargaining game above, neither symmetry (which selects the 50¢,50¢ outcome and the two mixed-action Nash equilibria) nor efficiency (which selects the three pure-action Nash equilibria) makes a unique selection by itself; however, if we combine both properties the fair and efficient outcome (50¢,50¢) is selected.

Unfortunately, this is not what we find in experimental implementations of the symmetric bargaining game outlined above. Subjects most often choose the first action initially, and eventually approach the mixed-action equilibrium that employs the first action most of the time (Van Huyck et al., 1995).[9] It turns out that these experimental results can be explained by the evolutive approach, which predicts the outcome of a game by tracking the distribution of actions in repeated anonymous random-encounter games given an initial distribution of actions. In short, "fitter" mixes of actions gradually displace those that are less fit.[10] By modeling how iterated play of myopic players emerges, we can learn to what extent the heroic knowledge and rationality assumption of the eductive approach can lead to misleading predictions. These results and others in related games (e.g., coordination games, Crawford, 1997; Ochs, 1995) suggest that, indeed, economic agents make decisions in boundedly rational ways.

There are two problems, however, with the evolutive approach. The process of gradual displacement of actions is modeled by means of differential and difference systems, which by their very nature are backward-looking mechanisms. That is bothersome because in many economic con-

8. The mixed-strategy Nash equilibria are located at (6/7, 0, 1/7) and (2/5, 3/5, 0), where each triplet of numbers refers to the fraction of decisions allocated to the three options respectively.

9. That is, (6/7, 0, 1/7). This discussion refers to the one-population experiments reported in Van Huyck et al. (1995) only. The setting was a repeated anonymous random-encounter game, where subjects are randomly matched with one another at each stage to play the game repeatedly, without knowing who they are matched with.

10. See Erev & Roth, 1998; Friedman, 1991, 1996; Roth & Erev, 1995; Samuelson, 1997; Vega-Redondo, 1996; Weibull, 1995 for examples.

texts expectations about other agents' future behavior plays an important role. Furthermore, since dynamic systems typically track the distribution of actions in a population, the analysis takes place on the level of the population and not on the level of the individuals that make up the population. Reinhard Selten's learning direction theory (Selten & Buchta, 1994; Selten & Stoecker, 1986), overcomes these problems. It also turns out to use very simple—fast and frugal—adjustment rules.

Let us illustrate learning direction theory by a simple guessing game (Nagel, 1995). A large number of players simultaneously states a number between 0 and 100. The average (mean) of these numbers is determined and multiplied by a parameter p to determine a new target number. The person whose number is closest to this number is the winner, and is paid a fixed amount. If there is a tie, the prize is divided equally among all winners. The interesting case for our purposes is when $p < 1$. In this case, an eductive analysis determines that there is only one Nash equilibrium, which requires all players to choose 0. To illustrate this, if there were an equilibrium in which one player states a positive number with positive probability, then the mean would be a positive number. It is easy to show that there exists another number with the same probability that would be closer to the mean than the original number. Clearly, a lot of anticipatory thinking (and a lot of rationality) is required to get to the Nash equilibrium.

Nagel implemented this game in the laboratory. She had groups of players play the guessing game for four rounds. The groups did not manage to end up in equilibrium, although there was a clear tendency toward it (i.e., most subjects decreased their choices over time, using the previous round's target number as the reference point). Nagel also found that players often started around a reference point $50p$, suggesting that they did engage in anticipatory thinking, trying to predict other players' behavior. Crucially for our purposes, though, players seemed to adjust their guesses according to a simple adjustment rule that had them increasing their stated numbers if they were below the mean of the previous round, and reducing their stated numbers if they were above the previous mean. This strategy is an example of a fast and frugal mechanism. Similarly simple adjustment rules have been shown to be useful in other contexts; Nagel (1995) reviews some of this literature. Evidently, the simple heuristic embodied in Selten's learning direction theory achieves both descriptive and normative success: It accounts for people's real behavior, and also allows them to achieve near-equilibrium performance.

Since the field of economics is generally concerned with social interactions, its findings and theories, including notions of satisficing, can readily be applied to behavior within organizations. Herbert Simon first made his mark in organizational theory (e.g., Simon, 1947), and it is in this arena that the idea of satisficing first appeared. March and Simon (1993) say that "organization theories describe the delicate conversion of conflict into cooperation, the mobilization of resources, and the coordination of effort that facilitate the joint survival of an organization and its members" (p. 2). Essentially, organization theories are about games that convert the diverging interests of individuals into equitable and efficient outcomes (like the equal division outcome in the symmetric bargaining game) that mark the successful organization. However, human actors are unable to think completely through all contingencies, even in the simplest games (such as the guessing game) and increasingly in more complex task environments (such as bargaining games).

The Mediating Role of Decision Costs

One rationale for discounting theories of unbounded rationality is to claim that the cost of making an unboundedly rational decision exceeds what is gained over being boundedly rational. If the costs are greater than the benefits, then the boundedly rational agent will acquire more goods at the end of the day than the unboundedly rational agent, marking bounded rationality as the true rationality (Simon, 1987). For example, in bargaining games, that is, situations that confront players with the choice between a secure action and one or more risky actions, it makes a difference whether one gets to choose the risky strategy 10 times or 100 times. Economic theory suggests that, other things being equal, an increase in the number of periods lowers decision costs, increases the incentives for experimentation, and is likely to lead to different decision heuristics. Experimental economists have started to introduce such decision costs into their analyses (Pringle & Day, 1996; Wilcox, 1993), and there is the promise that we may have an empirically grounded understanding of the mediating role of decision costs in the not-too-distant future. The challenge faced by those who pursue this path is what happens when the agent needs to figure out whether to be boundedly rational. This problem is similar to the one noted by Green (1984) in knowing the premises of the marginal value theorem. The calculation to determine whether it is rational to be boundedly rational (i.e., the computations involved in determining whether expected costs exceed expected benefits) is itself costly, and this may nullify the advantage conferred by not being too rational (Leijonhufvud, 1996). Indeed, the cycle of decision costs could go on forever (Conlisk, 1996), and it is for this reason that Simon (1987) and Selten (1996) have chosen not to go this route, and instead recommend reference to aspiration levels or rules of thumb that may be gradually adjusted if they become too lax or binding a constraint. The challenges to this approach lie in defining what determines those aspiration levels and rules of thumb, if it is not the kind of rational calculation that can take forever. One promising explanation is that aspiration levels and rules of thumb them selves are the result of evolutionary selection. The question of how aspiration levels and rules of thumb emerge is currently a field wide open to inquiry.

The Future of Fast and Frugal Heuristics in Economics

Chapter 3 reported the successful (and lucrative) results of applying the recognition principle to investment decisions in real markets; and this and comparably fast and frugal approaches to investing may continue to perform well within existing markets. However, the question remains what sorts of algorithms might have operated in individual traders, prior to the entry of Borges et al. (chapter 3) into the market, that created the conditions that permitted the recognition heuristic to perform so well. In other words, what are the individual processes that combine to create the orderly and wealth-generating properties of markets that have fascinated economists for centuries?

Intriguingly, these processes might also be fast and frugal. Gode and Sunder (1993) have recently reported that simple programs with "zero intelligence" can converge on the maximal efficiency that is characteristic of humans in double auction situations. Gode and Sunder do not propose that people possess zero intelligence, but their findings suggest that fast and frugal strategies can produce behavior that is both highly effective in its intended environment, and conspicuously similar to what people actually do.

The Past, Present, and Future of Bounded Rationality

The demons of the behavioral sciences are formidable. Unbounded rationality is a strongly entrenched benchmark that continues to dominate the relevant fields in the sheer number of authors and articles that are influenced by it. We scanned titles, abstracts, and keywords in representative databases of publications in the life sciences for their representations of computational demons through words including "regression" and "Bayes," and for words connoting bounded rationality, namely "satisficing," "rule of thumb," "lexicographic," and "bounded rationality" itself. The databases are listed in table 15-2.

"Regression" was by far the most common of the concepts we examined. It appears in almost one-half of one percent of all publications scanned (some 104,000 out of almost 26 million), a figure that dwarfed all others. The next most common reference was to the other demon, "Bayes" with approximately 3,600 references. "Rule of thumb," which has been used primarily in satisficing-like contexts, had approximately one-fifth the prominence of "Bayes," with 731 references. All other terms with implications of bounded rationality appeared fewer than 400 times out of the 26 million articles and books over the entire period scanned. This is about 10% of the incidence of "Bayes," one-third of one percent of the incidence of "regression," and one-seventh of one percent *of one percent* of all citations. Figure 15-1 displays these incidence rates graphically by year, and shows that the trend has become worse over the years rather

Table 15-2: The Databases for the Quantitative Analysis of How Often the Term "Bounded Rationality" and Related Concepts Appeared in the Titles, Abstracts, and Key Words of Articles

Database	Years Active	Disciplines
Current Contents	1995–1998	All (journals only)
Dissertation Abstracts	1961–1998	All (dissertations only)
EconLit	1969–1997	Economics
Sociofile	1974–1998	Sociology
Psychinfo	1967–1998	Psychology
Biosis	1970–1998	Biology
Medline	1966–1998	Medicine

than better. Note that the data for the term "regression" are not even shown, since they would so profoundly overshadow all others.

Figure 15-2 displays the same data for the three disciplines we have considered here. There is approximately one order of magnitude difference between the proportion of articles that employ satisficing concepts in psychology and biology overall (a ratio of 8.7), and approximately one

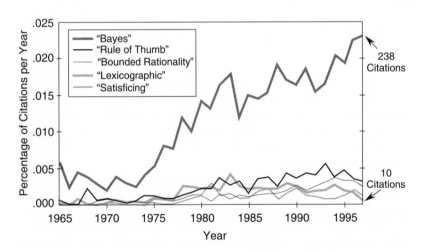

Figure 15-1: How often the term "bounded rationality" and related concepts (satisficing, rule of thumb, and lexicographic) appeared in the titles, abstracts, and key words of articles since 1965. (Sources are specified in table 15-2.) For comparison, the curve for the term "Bayes" is shown, as a representative of the class of demons. The data are presented as a percentage of all citations per year to control for the fact that the number of new articles and books has dramatically increased (by a factor of about seven) over the years.

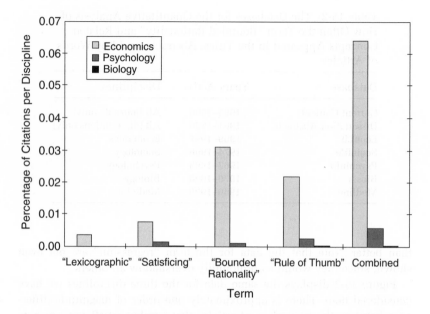

Figure 15-2: The contributions of the same concepts over the same period as in figure 15-1, this time separated by the disciplines in which they appear. The data are presented as a percentage of all citations per discipline to control for the fact that biology has produced approximately 10 times as many total books and articles over the years as psychology, which has produced approximately three times as much as economics.

order of magnitude difference between economics and psychology (a ratio of 11.3). In reversing the trend to model minds as demons, psychology may teach a thing or two to biology, but may need to learn a lesson from economics. As the analysis in figures 15-1 and 15-2 indicates, the expansion of the vision of bounded rationality is still in the future—this book may help to achieve it.

In this chapter we have examined how the tension between unbounded and bounded rationality is playing out conceptually in three fields outside of cognitive psychology: artificial intelligence, animal behavior, and economics. Heuristics have long been recognized as useful and necessary in artificial intelligence, a field whose success is defined by the performance of the minds it creates, but a drift away from domain specificity has made true fast and frugal strategies relatively scarce. In behavioral ecology, optimality theories generally dominate, but empirical failures of these theories demand a new way of theorizing about behavior in the wild, and such theories have begun to appear. Most take the form of optimization under constraints, but some have included fast and frugal strategies. The notion of ecological rationality is deeply embedded in the field, though, so that one may be optimistic about future developments. And in economics, the idea of bounded rationality confronts two centuries of classical theorizing, but its power has already paved the way to empirical justification and prompted important theoretical developments. In these three fields, we can see the idea of simple heuristics advancing conceptually; however, its quantitative impact remains small in comparison with older ideas of unbounded rationality. The seed ideas are present—the next step is for large numbers of theorists and experimenters to sprout them in their thinking and writing.

Bounded rationality will undoubtedly continue to be developed in all the disciplines we have discussed, either in coordination or in competition with each other. As the ideas grow in the various fields, the differences between them are likely to become sharper and more divisive, so we might do well to take a moment before this happens to reflect on what these notions have achieved so far in union, beginning to exorcise the beautiful but illusory ideal of omniscient and omnipotent beings from the behavioral sciences.

16

What We Have Learned (So Far)

Peter M. Todd
Gerd Gigerenzer

> At first it was thought that the surest way would be to take as a foundation for the psychological analysis of the thought-processes the laws of logical thinking, as they had been laid down from the time of Aristotle by the science of logic. These norms only apply to a small part of the thought-processes. Any attempt to explain, out of these norms, thought in the psychological sense of the word can only lead to an entanglement of the real facts in a net of logical reflections. We can in fact say of such attempts, that measured by the results they have been absolutely fruitless. They have disregarded the psychological processes themselves.
>
> *Wilhelm Wundt*

We have reached the end of our initial exploratory foray across the landscape of fast and frugal heuristics. Along the way, we have found unexpected vistas and surprising terrain. In chapter 1 we presented a rough map of the journey to come; now it is time to turn that map around and look at where we have been from different angles.

The heuristics in our mind's adaptive toolbox can be organized and accessed in a number of ways. They can be classified by type of decision task being faced, or according to the adaptive problem that needs to be solved—that is, in terms of a problem's domain-independent form or its domain-specific content. The first scheme divides heuristics into those for estimation, classification, two-alternative choice, and so on. The second organizes heuristics into those for food choice, mate choice, parental investment, inferring intentions from motions, and so on. In this book, we have taken both perspectives, and so can decision makers when seeking the appropriate tool for the problem at hand.

There is a third point of view: Heuristics can be categorized in terms of their building blocks—the particular heuristic principles they employ. In chapter 1 we described three classes of building blocks, namely principles for directing information search, for stopping that search, and for making a decision based on the search results. These can be used to define classes of heuristics that share one or more building blocks. These classes cut across decision tasks and adaptive problems. We now review the major classes of heuristics and the associated visions of rationality before ending this book with open questions still awaiting answers.

Classes of Heuristics

Ignorance-Based Decision Making

Good decisions need not require amassing large amounts of information; they can also be made on the basis of *lack* of knowledge. A basic cognitive adaptation is the ability to recognize faces, voices, smells, names, and other environmental features. There is a class of very simple heuristics based on this adaptation that share one building block: only search for recognition information. This may not sound like much for a decision maker to go on, but there is often information implicit in the *failure* to recognize something, and it can be exploited by these *ignorance-based heuristics*.

The simplest exemplar in this class is the *recognition heuristic*, for which we have found strong experimental evidence (chapter 2). Outside the laboratory, the recognition heuristic influences the behavior of organisms as widely varied as wild rats searching for food and humans deciding on a restaurant for lunch, and underlies the proliferation of identical fast-food chain outlets in much of the world (Schlosser, 1998). It can also be generalized to the task of choosing a subset of objects from a larger set, as in selecting a set of stocks based on recognition alone (chapter 3).

By analyzing and simulating the performance of the recognition heuristic, we arrived at a surprising prediction: Using this heuristic, a person who knows *less* than another can make systematically *more* accurate inferences. In chapter 2 we showed that this *less-is-more effect* is borne out by empirical data. Counterintuitive consequences such as this, which are not predicted by other theories or by common sense, are important indications of the empirical validity and theoretical significance of fast and frugal heuristics.

One-Reason Decision Making

Heuristics in the class of *one-reason decision making* search for reasons or cues beyond mere recognition, either in recall memory or in external stores of information. They use only a single piece of information for making a decision—this is their common building block. Therefore, they can also stop search as soon as the first reason is found that allows a decision to be made. We proposed and studied a variety of heuristics in this class, including the Minimalist, Take The Last, Take The Best (all in chapters 4, 5, and 6), and parental feeding heuristics (in chapter 14).

We were surprised by how accurate one-reason decision heuristics can be, for example outperforming multiple regression across 20 decision environments (chapter 5) and coming within a few percentage points of the accuracy of computationally complex Bayesian models (chapter 8). Thus there seem to be many situations without a trade-off between making a decision fast and frugally and making it accurately. Simplicity can come without a heavy price. The environmental conditions that explain this bargain are the topic of the study of ecological rationality.

There is growing empirical evidence that people actually use lexicographic heuristics such as Take The Best, particularly when time is limited (chapter 7). We have also investigated Take The Best as part of a memory-updating mechanism that underlies hindsight bias, successfully providing the first process model of this phenomenon (chapter 9). The quest for empirical evidence, however, is still burdened with a methodological problem. Policy-capturing methods for tracing thought processes still lack the power to distinguish exactly which heuristic an individual may be using—developing more sensitive methods is a challenge for further research.

Elimination Heuristics

Ignorance-based and one-reason decision heuristics (especially where the one cue has only two values) are most appropriate for tasks where one of two options must be selected. Other tasks call for a different class of heuristics. In categorization, for instance, one category must be chosen from several possibilities. For this type of task we can make fast and frugal, but still accurate, decisions by using an elimination rule rather than one-reason decision making. The class of elimination heuristics uses cues one by one to whittle down the set of remaining possible choices, stopping as soon as only a single category remains. QuickEst (chapter 10) can be seen as taking an elimination approach to estimation. The Categorization by Elimination heuristic (chapter 11) came within a few percentage points of the accuracy of traditional categorization algorithms including exemplar and neural network models, despite using only about a quarter of the available information. In chapter 12, we explored how Categorization by Elimination can be used to make rapid decisions about the intentions of other organisms from their motion cues alone, helping individuals avoid costly conflict or even predatory ingestion. In situations in which categorization must be performed quickly and cues take time to search for, this fast and frugal approach has clear advantages.

Satisficing

The previous three classes of heuristics are designed for situations in which all of the possible options are immediately available to the decision maker: For instance, the categories of possible intentions are all known, and the chicks to be fed are all sitting patiently in the nest (chapters 12 and 14). But a different class of heuristics is needed when alternatives (as opposed to cue values) take time to find, appearing sequentially over an extended period. In this type of choice task, a fast and frugal reasoner should limit not only the search for information (cues) about each alternative, but also the search for alternatives themselves. Herbert Simon (1955a, 1990) has used the term "satisficing" for heuristics that solve this problem by relying on an aspiration level to stop search.

We investigated satisficing heuristics for sequential mate search in chapter 13. Our focus was on simple mechanisms that limit both the time needed to determine a useful aspiration level, and the average number of potential mates considered before finding one who exceeded the aspiration. Simple learning heuristics can indeed find such adaptive aspiration levels, while still coming close to the mate choice performance of more "optimal" (and much slower) rules. The design of heuristics that search through *both* objects and cues, sequentially or simultaneously, is one of the unresolved issues for future research.

Visions of Rationality

We began this book with a triadic vision of bounded, ecological, and social rationality. The three are intimately linked: The success of boundedly rational heuristics depends on their ability to exploit the information structures in the ecological and social environment. Thus, the interaction of these three perspectives is essential for our notion of rationality.

Bounded Rationality

Our research program contributes to the study of bounded rationality on two levels. First, we have laid out a general framework for the construction of fast and frugal heuristics from a small set of building blocks. New heuristics can be formed through the combination of simple principles for guiding information search, stopping search, and reaching a decision. Second, we have explored a variety of specific heuristics that make accurate inferences despite being bounded by limited time, knowledge, and computation. These examples provide clear evidence that a demonic level of power and resources is not necessary for rationality.

Ecological Rationality

There are two reasons for the surprising performance of fast and frugal heuristics: their exploitation of environment structure and their robustness (generalizing appropriately to new situations as opposed to overfitting—see chapter 1). Ecological rationality is not a feature of a heuristic, but a consequence of the match between heuristic and environment. For instance, we have investigated the following structures of environments that can make heuristics ecologically rational:

Noncompensatory information. The Take The Best heuristic equals or outperforms any linear decision strategy when information is noncompensatory, that is, when the potential contribution of each new cue falls off rapidly (as defined in chapter 6).

Scarce information. Take The Best outperforms a class of linear models on average when few cues are known relative to the number of objects (as defined in chapter 6).

J-shaped distributions. The QuickEst heuristic estimates quantities about as accurately as more complex information-demanding strategies when the criterion to be estimated follows a J-shaped distribution, that is, one with many small values and few high values (as described in chapter 10).

Decreasing populations. In situations where the set of alternatives to choose from is constantly shrinking, such as in a seasonal mating pool, a satisficing heuristic that commits to an aspiration level quickly will outperform rules that sample many alternatives before setting an aspiration (as described in chapter 13).

By matching these structures of information in the environment with the structure implicit in their building blocks, heuristics can be accurate without being too complex. In addition, by being simple, these heuristics can avoid being *too* closely matched to any particular environment—that is, they can escape the curse of overfitting, which often strikes more complex, parameter-laden models. This marriage of structure with simplicity produces the counterintuitive situations in which there is little trade-off between being fast and frugal and being accurate.

Social Rationality

Some of the most challenging decisions faced by social species are those arising from an environment comprising the decisions of conspecifics. Social environments are characterized by the speed with which they can change and by the need to consider the decisions being made by others. These two features make social rationality an important and distinct form of ecological rationality. We have shown in this book that fast and frugal heuristics can guide behavior in these challenging domains, when the environment is changing rapidly as a result of others' behavior (e.g., in stock market investment—chapter 3), when the environment requires many decisions to be made in a successively dependent fashion (e.g., in parental investment—chapter 14), or when decisions must be made in coordination with other individuals (e.g., in mutual mate choice—chapter 13). These particular features of social environments can be exploited by heuristics that make rapid decisions rather than gathering and processing information over a long period during which a fleeter-minded competitor could leap forward and gain an edge.

These three perspectives on rationality are all defined in terms of an organism's adaptive goals: making decisions that are fast, frugal, accurate, and beneficial, in social and nonsocial situations. Thus, we see rationality as defined by decisions and actions that lead to success in the external world, rather than by internal coherence of knowledge and inferences. Theories of mind that focus on internal coherence have led, in artificial intelligence, economics, and elsewhere (see chapter 15), to models that assume that an individual must create elaborate representations of knowledge and solve impressive equations when making up its mind. The challenge ahead is not to construct models of omniscient minds, but rather of adaptive minds that can act quickly and reliably in their environments.

In *Walden* (1854/1960), Henry Thoreau thought deeply about the relationship that people have with their environment, albeit from a different perspective. His advice is equally appropriate for modeling minds in their environments: "Our life is frittered away by detail. . . . I say, let your affairs be as two or three, and not a hundred or a thousand. . . . Simplify, simplify" (p. 66). Such simplicity in models has a certain aesthetic appeal. The mechanisms are readily understood and communicated, and are amenable to step-by-step scrutiny. Furthermore, Popper (1959) has argued that simpler models are more falsifiable, and Sober (1975) deems them more informative. But the transparency, falsifiability, or informativeness of *models* are not the only grounds to argue for the simplicity of actual mental *mechanisms*. We have provided evidence that simple heuristics are also adaptive for those who actually use them (see also Forster & Sober, 1994). Simplicity can have both aesthetic appeal and adaptive value.

Looking Ahead

In this book we have proposed a variety of fast and frugal heuristics for making adaptive inferences and decisions. For each new heuristic we have endeavored to ask three main questions: How good is it—how well does it perform in comparison with decision mechanisms adhering to traditional notions of rationality? How is it ecologically rational—when and why does it work in real environments? And finally, do people or other animals actually use this heuristic? We certainly do not have all the answers to these queries. In fact, to date, most of our attention has been focused on the first (easiest) question, and while we are starting to gain some understanding about the second, our efforts to answer the third (very difficult and in some ways most significant) question are just beginning. This imbalance needs to be redressed. Looking ahead, there are many open challenges that follow from these three questions. Facing these challenges will not entail lone discovery of wholly new lands: Building on results already found by others, often in other fields and expressed in different languages, will accelerate the process of finding new answers.

Cognitive Tasks

The first challenge is to explore fast and frugal heuristics for solving tasks beyond those we have considered here. What other classes of decisions can be made by simple mechanisms? How can fast and frugal cognition help in tasks that extend over time such as planning or problem solving? Can simple heuristics be applied to perceptual mechanisms as well? A few researchers have called perception a "bag of tricks" (e.g., Ramachandran, 1990), full of quick and sometimes dirty mechanisms that evolved not because of their consistency but because they worked.

Adaptive Problems

The next challenge is to study how fast and frugal heuristics are applied to important adaptive problems—the second organizing scheme for the adaptive toolbox mentioned at the beginning of this chapter. The program of carving up an organism's life and behavior into separate adaptive domains, each containing several adaptive problems, has proved to be a great challenge (see Hirschfeld & Gelman, 1994, for the current plethora of approaches). But the discovery of domain-specific heuristics for important adaptive problems may help clarify some of the divisions—for instance, if heuristics used for sequential mate search differ from heuristics for sequential habitat search, this may indicate that mate choice and habitat choice are distinct domains with specialized mechanisms. What heuristics apply to adaptive problems such as food choice (including modern forms of dieting), health preservation (including visiting doctors and taking drugs), and navigation (including getting from one end of a city to another)? Why do people often prefer to solve adaptive problems using socially transmitted information, for instance, deciding what medical risks to take on the basis of hearsay rather than statistical evidence (while at the same time often obsessing about baseball statistics)?

Social Norms and Emotions

Simple heuristics can be advantageous for navigating the complexities of social domains, and can be learned in a social manner, through imitation, word of mouth, or cultural heritage. We suspect that social norms, cultural strictures, historical proverbs, and the like can enable fast and frugal social reasoning by obviating cost-benefit calculations and extensive information search. We have also speculated occasionally in this book that emotions may facilitate rapid decision making by putting strong limits on the search for information or alternatives, as when falling in love stops partner search and facilitates commitment. Where can we find further evidence for the decision-making functions of these cultural and emotional processes, and how can they serve as building blocks in precise models of fast and frugal heuristics? This is one of the most important areas still to be mapped out.

Ecological Rationality

We do not yet have a well-developed language for describing those aspects of environment structure, whether physical or social, that shape the design and performance of decision heuristics. Here one can turn for inspiration to other fields, including ecology and statistics, that have analyzed environment structure from different perspectives. For instance, the statistical measures of two-dimensional patterns developed in spatial data analysis (see, e.g., Upton & Fingleton, 1985) can be used when assessing heuristics for spatial search in foraging or habitat selection. Evolutionary psychology reminds us to reflect on possible differences between present and past environments, by considering the important adaptive problems our ancestors faced, the information available in their environment to solve those problems, and how these inputs have changed in the modern world (Cosmides & Tooby, 1987, p. 302).

Performance Criteria

How should the performance and usefulness of heuristics be measured? Ultimately, ecological rationality depends on decision making that furthers an organism's adaptive goals in the physical or social environment. How can measures of decision speed, frugality, and accuracy be augmented by and combined with measures of adaptive utility? We have tested the generalization ability of heuristics so far mostly in cross-validation tests. How can we measure predictive accuracy and robustness in environments that are in a state of continual flux, with new objects and cues appearing over time? Finally, we have focussed on adaptive goals in terms of correspondence criteria (e.g., accuracy, speed, and frugality) as opposed to coherence criteria (e.g., consistency, transitivity, additivity of probabilities) traditionally used to define rationality. Is any role left for coherence criteria? Should one follow Sen (1993) in arguing that consistency is an ill-defined concept unless the social objectives and goals of people are specified?

Selecting Heuristics

How does the mind know which heuristic to use? Following our perspective of bounded rationality, a fast and frugal mind need not employ a metalevel demon who makes optimal cost-benefit computations to select a heuristic. The fact that heuristics are designed for particular tasks rather than being general-purpose strategies solves part of the selection problem by reducing the choice set (see chapter 1). But we have not addressed how individual heuristics are selected from the adaptive toolbox for application to specific problems.

Multiple Methodologies

The combination of conceptual analysis, simulation, and experimentation has deepened our understanding of fast and frugal heuristics. However, more evidence must be amassed for the prevalence of simple heuristics in human and animal reasoning. This need not be done solely through laboratory experiments, where we often find that alternative mechanisms can equally account for the observed behavior (as discussed in chapter 7). Collecting data from the field—whether that field is a jungle habitat or an airplane cockpit—is also vital for discovering new heuristics and teasing competing mechanisms apart.

The Rational Meets the Psychological

Some years ago, sequestered in the hills overlooking Stanford, a gathering of economists and psychologists engaged in an animated conversation on the nature of reasoning. We argued over the latest stories about this or that paradox or stubborn irrationality until finally one of the economists concluded the discussion by throwing down the gauntlet. "Look," he said with the conviction of his field, "either reasoning is rational, or it's psychological." To him, this inviolable dichotomy implied an intellectual division of labor: Rational judgment is defined by the laws of logic and probability, and thus should be the domain of rigorous economists and mathematicians; what we know about the human mind is irrelevant for defining sound reasoning. Only when things go wrong should psychologists be called in to explain why people can be irrational.

We hope that the simple heuristics analyzed in this book exemplify a way to break down this unfortunate but widespread belief in an opposition between the rational and the psychological. This misleading idea has cursed the cognitive sciences since the antipsychologism of nineteenth-century philosophy, and it continues to obscure a realistic view of cognition to this day. A bit of trust in the abilities of the mind and the rich structure of the environment may help us to see how thought processes that forgo the baggage of the laws of logic and probability can solve real-world adaptive problems quickly and well.

Models of reasoning need not forsake rationality for psychological plausibility, nor accuracy for simplicity. The mind can have it both ways.

References

Abrahams, M. V. (1986). Patch choice under perceptual constraints: A cause for departures from an ideal free distribution. *Behavioral Ecology and Sociobiology, 19*, 409–415.

Abt, S. (1991). *Tour de France: Three weeks to glory.* San Francisco: Bicycle Books.

Aeberhard, S., Coomans, D., & de Vel, O. (1994). Comparative analysis of statistical pattern recognition methods in high dimensional settings. *Pattern Recognition, 27*(8), 1065–1077.

Aho, A. V., & Ullman, J. D. (1992). *Foundations of computer science.* New York: W. H. Freeman.

Alatalo, R. V., Carlson, A., & Lundberg, A. (1988). The search cost in mate choice of the pied flycatcher. *Animal Behaviour, 36*(1), 289–291.

Alba, J. W., & Marmorstein, H. (1987). The effects of frequency knowledge on consumer decision making. *Journal of Consumer Research, 14*, 14–26.

Albers, W. (1997). *Foundations of a theory of prominence in the decimal system.* Working papers (No. 265–271). Bielefeld, Germany: Institute of Mathematical Economics, University of Bielefeld.

Alexander, R. M. (1996). *Optima for animals.* Princeton, NJ: Princeton University Press.

Allais, M. (1953). Le comportement de l'homme rationnel devant le risque: Critiques des postulates et axioms de l'école americaine. *Econometrica, 21*, 503–546.

Allison, T., & Cicchetti, D. (1976). Sleep in mammals: Ecological and constitutional correlates. *Science, 194,* 732–734.

Ambady, N., & Rosenthal, R. (1992). Thin slices of expressive behavior as predictors of interpersonal consequences: A meta-analysis. *Psychological Bulletin, 111,* 256–274.

Anderson, J. R. (1990). *The adaptive character of thought.* Hillsdale, NJ: Erlbaum.

Anderson, J. R. (1991). The adaptive nature of human categorization. *Psychological Review, 98*(3), 409–429.

Anderson, J. R., & Milson, R. (1989). Human memory: An adaptive perspective. *Psychological Review, 96,* 703–719.

Anderson, J. R., & Schooler, L. J. (1991). Reflections of the environment in memory. *Psychological Science, 2,* 396–408.

Anderson, N. H. (1981). *Foundations of information integration theory.* New York: Academic Press.

Andersson, M. (1994). *Sexual selection.* Princeton, NJ: Princeton University Press.

Arkes, H. R., & Hammond, K. R. (Eds.). (1986). *Judgment and decision making: An interdisciplinary reader.* Cambridge, UK: Cambridge University Press.

Arrow, K. J. (1986). Rationality of self and others in an economic system. *Journal of Business, 59*(4, Pt. 2), S385–S399.

Arthur, W. B. (1994). Inductive reasoning and bounded rationality. *AEA Papers and Proceedings, 84*(2), 406–411.

Arthur, W. B., Holland, J. H., LeBaron, B., Palmer, R., & Tayler, P. (1997). Asset pricing under endogenous expectations in an artificial stock market. In W. B. Arthur, S. N. Durlauf, & D. A. Lane (Eds.), *The economy as an evolving complex system II* (pp. 15–44). Redwood City, CA: Addison-Wesley.

Ashby, F. G., & Gott, R. (1988). Decision rules in the perception and categorization of multidimensional stimuli. *Journal of Experimental Psychology: Learning, Memory, and Cognition, 14,* 33–53.

Ashby, F. G., & Maddox, W. T. (1992). Complex decision rules in categorization: Contrasting novice and experienced performance. *Journal of Experimental Psychology: Human Perception and Performance, 18,* 50–71.

Attneave, F. (1953). Psychological probability as a function of experienced frequency. *Journal of Experimental Psychology, 46,* 81–86.

Ayton, P., & Önkal, D. (1997). *Forecasting football fixtures: Confidence and judged proportion correct.* Unpublished manuscript.

Ayton, P., & Wright, G. (1994). Subjective probability: What should we believe? In G. Wright & P. Ayton (Eds.), *Subjective probability* (pp. 163–183). New York: Wiley.

Barkow, J. H., Cosmides, L., & Tooby, J. (Eds.). (1992). *The adapted mind: Evolutionary psychology and the generation of culture.* New York: Oxford University Press.

Barnett, S. A. (1963). *The rat: A study in behavior.* Chicago: Aldine.

Baron, J. (1990). *Thinking and deciding.* Cambridge, UK: Cambridge University Press.

Baron-Cohen, S. (1995). *Mindblindness.* Cambridge, MA: MIT Press.

Barsalou, L. W. (1992). *Cognitive psychology: An overview for cognitive scientists.* Hillsdale, NJ: Erlbaum.

Bartlett, F. C. (1932/1995). *Remembering: A study in experimental and social psychology.* Cambridge, UK: Cambridge University Press.

Bateson, P. P. G. (Ed.). (1983a). *Mate choice.* Cambridge, UK: Cambridge University Press.

Bateson, P. P. G. (1983b). Optimal outbreeding. In P. P. G. Bateson (Ed.), *Mate choice* (pp. 257–277). Cambridge, UK: Cambridge University Press.

Baylor, G. W., & Simon, H. A. (1966). A chess mating combinations program. In *AFIPS Conference Proceedings* 28, 1966 Spring Joint Computer Conference (pp. 431–447). Washington, DC: Spartan Books.

Beach, L. R., Barnes, V. E., & Christensen-Szalanski, J. J. J. (1986). Beyond heuristics and biases: A contingency model of judgmental forecasting. *Journal of Forecasting, 5*, 143–157.

Beach, L. R., & Mitchell, T. R. (1978). A contingency model for the selection of decision strategies. *Academy of Management Review, 3*, 439–449.

Becker, G. S. (1991). *A treatise on the family.* Cambridge, MA: Harvard University Press.

Benford, F. (1938). The law of anomalous numbers. *Proceedings of the American Philosophical Society, 78*, 551–572.

Ben Zur, H., & Breznitz, S. J. (1981). The effect of time pressure on risky choice behavior. *Acta Psychologica, 47*, 69–104.

Berretty, P. M., Todd, P. M., & Blythe, P. W. (1997). Categorization by elimination: A fast and frugal approach to categorization. In M. G. Shafto & P. Langley (Eds.), *Proceedings of the Nineteenth Annual Conference of the Cognitive Science Society* (pp. 43–48). Mahwah, NJ: Erlbaum.

Best, L. B. (1977). Patterns of feeding field sparrow young. *Wilson Bulletin, 89*, 625–627.

Bettman, J. R. (1979). *An information processing theory of consumer choice.* Reading, MA: Addison-Wesley.

Bettman, J. R., Johnson, E. J., Luce, M. F., & Payne, J. W. (1993). Correlation, conflict, and choice. *Journal of Experimental Psychology: Learning, Memory, and Cognition, 19*, 931–951.

Biggs, S. F., Rosman, A. J., & Sergenian, G. K. (1993). Methodological issues in judgment and decision-making research: Concurrent verbal protocol validity and simultaneous traces of process. *Journal of Behavioral Decision Making, 6*, 187–206.

Billings, R. S., & Marcus, S. A. (1983). Measures of compensatory and noncompensatory models of decision behavior: Process tracing versus policy capturing. *Organizational Behavior and Decision Processes, 31*, 331–352.

Billings, R. S., & Scherer, L. L. (1988). The effects of response mode and importance on decision-making strategies: Judgment versus choice. *Organizational Behavior and Decision Processes, 34*, 1–19.

Binmore, K. (1990). *Essays on the foundations of game theory.* Oxford, UK: Basil Blackwell.

Birnbaum, M. H., & Mellers, B. A. (1983). Bayesian inference: Combining base rates with opinions of sources who vary in credibility. *Journal of Personality and Social Psychology, 54*(4), 792–804.

Bjork, R. A. (1978). The updating of human memory. In G. H. Bower (Ed.), *The psychology of learning and motivation* (Vol. 12, pp. 235–259). New York: Academic Press.

Blum, A. L., & Langley, P. (1997). Selection of relevant features and examples in machine learning. *Artificial Intelligence, 97*(1–2), 245–271.

Blythe, P. W., Miller, G. F., & Todd, P. M. (1996). Human simulation of adaptive behavior: Interactive studies of pursuit, evasion, courtship, fighting, and play. In P. Maes, M. J. Mataric, J.-A. Meyer, J. Pollack, & S. W. Wilson (Eds.), *From animals to animats 4: Proceedings of the Fourth International Conference on Simulation of Adaptive Behavior* (pp. 13–22). Cambridge, MA: MIT Press/Bradford Books.

Böckenholt, U., & Hynan, L. S. (1994). Caveats on a process-tracing measure and a remedy. *Journal of Behavioral Decision Making, 7,* 103–117.

Böckenholt, U., & Kroeger, K. (1993). The effect of time pressure in multiattribute binary choice tasks. In O. Svenson & A. J. Maule (Eds.), *Time pressure and stress in human judgment and decision making* (pp. 195–214). New York: Plenum Press.

Boltzmann, L. (1968). Analytischer Beweis des zweiten Hauptsatzes der mechanischen Wärmetheorie aus den Sätzen über das Gleichgewicht der lebendigen Kraft. In F. Hasenöhrl (Ed.), *Wissenschaftliche Abhandlungen* (Vol. 1, pp. 288–308). Leipzig, Germany: Barth. (Original work published 1909)

Bourbaki, N. (1963). *Les élements des mathematiques.* Paris: Hermann.

Boyd, R., & Richerson, P. J. (1985). *Culture and the evolutionary process.* Chicago: University of Chicago Press.

Braitenberg, V. (1984). *Vehicles: Experiments in synthetic psychology.* Cambridge, MA: MIT Press.

Brase, G. L., Cosmides, L., & Tooby, J. (1998). Individuation, counting, and statistical inference: The role of frequency and whole-object representations in judgment under uncertainty. *Journal of Experimental Psychology: General, 127,* 3–21.

Brehmer, A., & Brehmer, B. (1988). What has been learned about human judgment from thirty years of policy capturing? In B. Brehmer & C. R. B. Joyce (Eds.), *Human judgment: The SJT view.* Amsterdam: Elsevier-North Holland.

Brehmer, B. (1994). The psychology of linear judgment models. *Acta Psychologica, 87,* 137–154.

Brehmer, B., & Joyce, C. R. B. (Eds.). (1988). *Human judgment: The SJT view.* Amsterdam: Elsevier-North Holland.

Breiman, L., Friedman, J. H., Olshen, R. A., & Stone, C. J. (1993). *Classification and regression trees.* New York: Chapman & Hall.

Brock, W., Lakonishok, J., & LeBaron, B. (1991). *Simple trading rules and the stochastic properties of stock returns.* Working Paper (91-01-00). Santa Fe, NM: Santa Fe Institute.

Brooks, L. R. (1978). Non-analytic concept formation and memory for instances. In E. Rosch & B. B. Lloyd (Eds.), *Cognition and categorization* (pp. 169–211). Hillsdale, NJ: Erlbaum.

Brooks, R. (1998). The importance of mate copying and cultural inheritance of mating preferences. *Trends in Ecology and Evolution, 13,* 45–46.

Brooks, R. A. (1990). Elephants don't play chess. In P. Maes (Ed.), *Designing autonomous agents: Theory and practice from biology to engineering and back* (pp. 3–15). Cambridge, MA: MIT Press.

Brooks, R. A. (1991a). *Intelligence without reason.* Massachusetts Institute of Technology A.I. Memo No. 1293. Cambridge, MA: MIT.

Brooks, R. A. (1991b). New approaches to robotics. *Science, 253,* 1227–1232.

Brown, N. R., & Siegler, R. S. (1992). The role of availability in the estimation of national populations. *Memory & Cognition, 20,* 406–412.

Brown, N. R., & Siegler, R. S. (1993). Metrics and mappings: A framework for understanding real-world quantitative estimation. *Psychological Review, 100,* 511–534.

Bruno, N., & Cutting, J. E. (1988). Minimodularity and the perception of layout. *Journal of Experimental Psychology: General, 117,* 161–170.

Brunswik, E. (1943). Organismic achievement and environmental probability. *Psychological Review, 50,* 255–272.

Brunswik, E. (1952). The conceptual framework of psychology. In O. Neurath, R. Carnap, & C. Morris (Eds.), *International Encyclopedia of Unified Science* (Vol. 1, No. 10). Chicago: University of Chicago Press.

Brunswik, E. (1955). Representative design and probabilistic theory in a functional psychology. *Psychological Review, 62,* 193–217.

Brunswik, E. (1956). *Perception and the representative design of psychological experiments.* Berkeley, CA: University of California Press.

Brunswik, E. (1957). Scope and aspects of the cognitive problem. In H. Gruber, K. R. Hammond, & R. Jessor (Eds.), *Contemporary approaches to cognition* (pp. 5–31). Cambridge, MA: Harvard University Press.

Bryant, D. M., & Tatner, P. (1990). Hatching asynchrony, sibling competition and siblicide in nestling birds: Studies of swiftlets and bee-eaters. *Animal Behaviour, 39,* 657–671.

Buffet, W. (1987, October 19). What can we learn from Philip Fisher. *Forbes.*

Busemeyer, J. R. (1990). Intuitive statistical estimation. In N. H. Anderson (Ed.), *Contributions to information integration theory* (Vol. 1: Cognition, pp. 187–215). Hillsdale, NJ: Erlbaum.

Buss, D. M. (1992). Mate preference mechanisms: Consequences for partner choice and intrasexual competition. In J. H. Barkow, L. Cosmides, & J. Tooby (Eds.), *The adapted mind: Evolutionary psychology and the generation of culture* (pp. 249–266). New York: Oxford University Press.

Buss, D. M. (1994). *The evolution of desire: Strategies of human mating.* New York: Basic Books.

Buzzell, R., Gale, B. T., & Sultan, R. (1975). Market share—A key to profitability. *Harvard Business Review, 53*(1), 97–106.

Campbell, D. T. (1959). Systematic error on the part of human links in communication systems. *Information and Control, 1,* 334–369.

Campbell, J. D., & Tesser, A. (1983). Motivational interpretations of hindsight bias: An individual difference analysis. *Journal of Personality, 51,* 605–620.

Charnov, E. L. (1976). Optimal foraging: The marginal value theorem. *Theoretical Population Biology, 9*, 129–136.

Chase, V. M., Hertwig, R., & Gigerenzer, G. (1998). Visions of rationality. *Trends in Cognitive Science, 2*(6), 206–214.

Chater, N., Oaksford, M., Nakisa, R., & Redington, M. (1997). Fast, frugal, and rational: Rational analysis and cognitive algorithms in human reasoning. Unpublished manuscript.

Chipman, H., George, E., & McCulloch, R. (1998). Bayesian CART model search (with discussion). *Journal of the American Statistical Association, 93*, 935–960.

Christensen-Szalanski, J. J. J., & Fobian Willham, C. (1991). The hindsight bias: A meta-analysis. *Organizational Behavior and Human Decision Processes, 48*, 147–168.

Clark, A. B., Wilson, D. S., Bjurlin, C., & Kagan, B. (1997). Red-winged blackbirds feed their young in (nearly) random order, with consequences for growth and sibling competition. *Animal Behavior Society Meeting*. College Park, MD: University of Maryland.

Clemen, R. T. (1996). *Making hard decisions: An introduction to decision analysis*. Belmont, CA: Duxbury Press.

Cohen, J. (1988). *Statistical power analysis for the behavioral sciences*. Hillsdale, NJ: Erlbaum.

Conlisk, J. (1996). Why bounded rationality? *Journal of Economic Literature, 34*, 669–700.

Connolly, T., & Gilani, N. (1982). Information search in judgment tasks: A regression model and some preliminary findings. *Organizational Behavior and Human Performance, 30*, 330–350.

Cooksey, R. W. (1996). *Judgment analysis: Theory, methods, and applications*. San Diego: Academic Press.

Cooper, G. (1990). The computational complexity of probabilistic inferences. *Artificial Intelligence, 42*, 393–405.

Cooper, G., & Herskovits, E. (1992). A Bayesian method for the introduction of probabilistic networks from data. *Machine Learning, 9*, 309–347.

Cootner, P. (Ed.). (1967). *The random character of stock market prices*. Cambridge, MA: MIT Press.

Corbin, R. M. (1980). The secretary problem as a model of choice. *Journal of Mathematical Psychology, 21*(1), 1–29.

Cosmides, L., & Tooby, J. (1987). From evolution to behavior: Evolutionary psychology as the missing link. In J. Dupré (Ed.), *The latest on the best: Essays on evolution and optimization* (pp. 277–306). Cambridge, MA: MIT Press/Bradford Books.

Cosmides, L., & Tooby, J. (1992). Cognitive adaptations for social exchange. In J. Barkow, L. Cosmides, & J. Tooby (Eds.), *The adapted mind: Evolutionary psychology and the generation of culture* (pp. 163–228). New York: Oxford University Press.

Craik, F. I. M., & McDowd, M. (1987). Age differences in recall and recognition. *Journal of Experimental Psychology: Learning, Memory, and Cognition, 14*, 474–479.

Crawford, V. P. (1997). Theory and experiment in the analysis of strategic interaction. In D. M. Kreps & K. F. Wallis (Eds.), *Advances in econom-*

ics and econometrics: Theory and applications (Vol. 1, pp. 206–242). Cambridge, UK: Cambridge University Press.

Cronin, H. (1991). *The ant and the peacock: Altruism and sexual selection from Darwin to today.* Cambridge, UK: Cambridge University Press.

Cutting, J., & Kozlowski, L. (1977). Recognition of friends by their walk. *Bulletin of the Psychonomic Society, 9,* 353–356.

Czerlinski, J. (1998). *Calculation costs of heuristics measured in EIPs.* Unpublished manuscript. Munich, Germany: Max Planck Institute for Psychological Research.

Darwin, C. (1871). *The descent of man, and selection in relation to sex* (2 vols.). London: John Murray.

Darwin, C. (1965). *The expression of the emotions in man and animals.* Chicago: University of Chicago Press. (Original work published 1872)

Darwin, C. (1969). *The autobiography of Charles Darwin, 1809–1882.* Edited by N. Barlow. New York: Norton. (Original work published 1887)

Daston, L. J. (1988). *Classical probability in the Enlightenment.* Princeton, NJ: Princeton University Press.

Davis, F. D., Lohse, G. L., & Kottemann, J. E. (1994). Harmful effects of seemingly helpful information on forecasts of stock earnings. *Journal of Economic Psychology, 15,* 253–267.

Davison, M., & McCarthy, D. (1988). *The matching law: A research review.* Hillsdale, NJ: Erlbaum.

Dawes, R. M. (1979). The robust beauty of improper linear models in decision making. *American Psychologist, 34,* 571–582.

Dawes, R. M., & Corrigan, B. (1974). Linear models in decision making. *Psychological Bulletin, 81,* 95–106.

Dawkins, R. (1982). *The extended phenotype.* Oxford, UK: Oxford University Press.

DeBondt, W. F. M., & Thaler, R. H. (1985). Does the stock market overreact? *Journal of Finance, 40,* 793–805.

Dedekind, R. (1987). Was sind und was sollen die Zahlen? *Gesammelte mathematische Werke* (3 Vols.). Braunschweig, Germany: Vieweg. (Original work published 1887)

de Finetti, B. (1937). La prévision: Ses lois logiques, ses sources subjectives. *Annales de l'Institut Henri Poincaré, 7,* 1–68. (Reprinted in 1964 in English translation as Foresight: Its logical laws, its subjective sources. In H. E. Kyburg, Jr. & H. E. Smokler (Eds.), *Studies in subjective probability.* New York: Wiley.)

Defoe, D. (1980). *Robinson Crusoe.* New York: Penguin. (Original work published 1719)

de Groot, A. D. (1978). *Thought and choice in chess* (2nd ed.). The Hague: Mouton.

Deutsche Börse AG (1997, June). *Vision & Money.*

DiFonzo, N. (1994). *Piggybacked syllogisms for investor behavior: Probabilistic mental modeling in rumor-based stock market trading.* PhD dissertation, Temple University, Philadelphia.

Doherty, M. E. (Ed.). (1996). Social judgement theory [Special issue]. *Thinking & Reasoning, 2,* 105–248.

Domingos, P., & Pazzani, M. (1996). Beyond independence: Conditions for the optimality of the simple Bayesian classifier. In *Proceedings of the*

13th International Conference on Machine Learning (pp. 105–112). San Mateo, CA: Morgan Kaufmann.

Driver, P. M., & Humphries, D. A. (1988). *Protean behavior: The biology of unpredictability.* Oxford, UK: Oxford University Press.

Dugatkin, L. A. (1996). Interface between culturally based preferences and genetic preferences: Female mate choice in *Poecilia reticulata. Proceedings of the National Academy of Sciences, 93,* 2770–2773.

Dugatkin, L. A., & Godin, J. J. (1998). How females choose their mates. *Scientific American, 278*(4), 46–51.

Duncker, K. (1945). On problem solving (L. S. Lees, Trans.). *Psychological Monographs, 58* (5, Whole no. 270). (Original work published 1935)

Dykstra, C. R., & Karasov, W. H. (1993). Daily energy expenditure by nestling house wrens. *Condor, 95,* 1028–1030.

Edland, A. (1994). Time pressure and the application of decision rules: Choices and judgments among multiattribute alternatives. *Scandinavian Journal of Psychology, 35,* 281–291.

Edwards, W. (1968). Conservatism in human information processing. In B. Kleinmuntz (Ed.), *Formal representation of human judgment* (pp. 17–52). New York: Wiley.

Edwards, W., Lindman, H., & Savage, L. J. (1963). Bayesian statistical inference for psychological research. *Psychological Review, 70,* 193–242.

Ehrenberg, A. S. C. (1982). How good is best? *Journal of the Royal Statistical Society A, 145,* Part 3, 364–366.

Einhorn, H. J. (1970). The use of nonlinear, noncompensatory models in decision making. *Psychological Bulletin, 73,* 221–230.

Einhorn, H. J., & Hogarth, R. M. (1975). Unit weighting schemes for decision making. *Organizational Behavior and Human Performance, 13,* 171–192.

Einhorn, H. J., & Hogarth, R. M. (1981). Behavioral decision theory: Processes of judgment and choice. *Annual Review of Psychology, 32,* 53–88.

Einhorn, H. J., Kleinmuntz, D. N., & Kleinmuntz, B. (1979). Linear regression and process-tracing models of judgment. *Psychological Review, 86,* 465–485.

Ellsberg, D. (1961). Risk, ambiguity, and the Savage axioms. *Quarterly Journal of Economics, 75,* 643–669.

Elster, J. (1979). *Ulysses and the sirens: Studies in rationality and irrationality.* Cambridge, UK: Cambridge University Press.

Erev, I., & Roth, A. E. (1998). Predicting how people play games: Reinforcement learning in experimental games with unique, mixed strategy equilibria. *American Economic Review, 88,* 848–881.

Ericsson, K. A., & Simon, H. A. (1993). *Protocol analysis: Verbal reports as data* (Rev. ed.). Cambridge, MA: MIT Press.

Estes, W. (1976). The cognitive side of probability learning. *Psychological Review, 83,* 37–64.

Estes, W. K. (1986). Array models for category learning. *Cognitive Psychology, 18,* 500–549.

Evans, J. St. B. T. (1989). *Bias in human reasoning.* Hillsdale, NJ: Erlbaum.

Fagen, R. (1981). *Animal play behavior.* New York: Oxford University Press.

Feigenbaum, E. A., & Simon, H. A. (1984). EPAM-like models of recognition and learning. *Cognitive Science, 8,* 305–336.

Ferguson, T. S. (1989). Who solved the secretary problem? *Statistical Science, 4,* 282–296.

Fischer Welt Almanach [Fischer World Almanac]. (1993). Frankfurt, Germany: Fischer.

Fischhoff, B. (1975). Hindsight ≠ foresight: The effect of outcome knowledge on judgment under uncertainty. *Journal of Experimental Psychology: Human Perception and Performance, 1,* 288–299.

Fischhoff, B. (1982a). Debiasing. In D. Kahneman, P. Slovic, & A. Tversky (Eds.), *Judgment under uncertainty: Heuristics and biases* (pp. 422–444). Cambridge, UK: Cambridge University Press.

Fischhoff, B. (1982b). For those condemned to study the past: Heuristics and biases in hindsight. In D. Kahneman, P. Slovic, & A. Tversky (Eds.), *Judgment under uncertainty: Heuristics and biases* (pp. 335–351). Cambridge, UK: Cambridge University Press.

Fischhoff, B., & Beyth, R. (1975). "I knew it would happen": Remembered probabilities of once-future things. *Organizational Behavior and Human Performance, 13,* 1–16.

Fishburn, P. C. (1974). Lexicographic orders, utilities and decision rules: A survey. *Management Science, 20,* 1442–1471.

Fishburn, P. C. (1988). *Nonlinear preference and utility theory.* Baltimore: Johns Hopkins University Press.

Fisher, R. A. (1936). The use of multiple measures in taxonomic problems. *Annals of Eugenics, 7,* 179–188.

Fiske, P., & Kalas, J. A. (1995). Mate sampling and copulation behaviour of great snipe females. *Animal Behaviour, 49*(1), 209–219.

Forbes, M. R. L., & Ankney, C. D. (1987). Hatching asynchrony and food allocation within broods of pied-billed grebes, *Podilymbus podiceps. Canadian Journal of Zoology, 65,* 2872–2877.

Ford, J. K., Schmitt, N., Schechtman, S. L., Hults, B. H., & Doherty, M. L. (1989). Process tracing methods: Contributions, problems, and neglected research questions. *Organizational Behavior and Decision Processes, 43,* 75–117.

Forsgren, E. (1997). Mate sampling in a population of sand gobies. *Animal Behaviour, 53*(2), 267–276.

Forster, M., & Sober, E. (1994). How to tell when simpler, more unified, or less ad hoc theories will provide more accurate predictions. *British Journal of Philosophical Science, 45,* 1–35.

Franklin, B. (1987). *Writings.* New York: The Library of America. (Original letter written Sept. 19, 1772)

Fretwell, S. D., & Lucas, H. J. Jr. (1970). On territorial behavior and other factors influencing habitat distribution in birds. *Acta Biotheoretica, 19,* 16–36.

Frey, B. S., & Eichenberger, R. (1996). Marriage paradoxes. *Rationality and Society, 8*(2), 187–206.

Freyd, J., & Miller, G. F. (1992). *Creature motion.* Technical Report 93-3. Department of Psychology, University of Oregon, Eugene.

Friedman, D. (1991). Evolutionary games in economics. *Econometrica, 59,* 637–666.

Friedman, D. (1996). Equilibrium in evolutionary games: Some experimental results. *Economic Journal, 106,* 1–25.

Friedman, N., & Goldszmit, M. (1996). Learning Bayesian networks with local structure. In *Proceedings of the 12th Conference on Uncertainty in Artificial Intelligence (UAI)* (pp. 252–262). San Mateo, CA: Morgan Kaufmann.

Gale, D., & Shapley, L. (1962). College admissions and the stability of marriage. *American Mathematical Monthly, 69,* 9–15.

Galef, B. G., Jr. (1987). Social influences on the identification of toxic foods by Norway rats. *Animal Learning & Behavior, 15,* 327–332.

Galef, B. G., Jr., McQuoid, L. M., & Whiskin, E. E. (1990). Further evidence that Norway rats do not socially transmit learned aversions to toxic baits. *Animal Learning & Behavior, 18,* 199–205.

Galef, B. G., Jr., & White, D. J. (1998). Mate-choice copying in Japanese quail, *Coturnix coturnix japonica. Animal Behaviour, 55,* 545–552.

Garey, M. R., & Johnson, D. S. (1979). *Computers and intractability: A guide to the theory of NP-completeness.* San Francisco: Freeman.

Gelman, R., Durgin, F., & Kaufman, L. (1995). Distinguishing between animates and inanimates: Not by motion alone. In D. Sperber, D. Premack, & A. J. Premack (Eds.), *Causal cognition: A multidisciplinary debate* (pp. 150–184). Oxford, UK: Clarendon Press.

Geman, S., Bienenstock, E., & Doursat, E. (1992). Neural networks and the bias/variance dilemma. *Neural Computation, 4,* 1–58.

Gennari, J. H. (1991). Concept formation and attention. In *Proceedings of the Thirteenth Annual Conference of the Cognitive Society* (pp. 724–728). Hillsdale, NJ: Erlbaum.

Gibson, J. J. (1966). *The senses considered as perceptual systems.* Boston: Houghton Mifflin.

Gibson, J. J. (1979). *The ecological approach to visual perception.* Boston: Houghton Mifflin.

Gigerenzer, G. (1981). *Messung und Modellbildung in der Psychologie.* Munich: Ernst Reinhard Verlag.

Gigerenzer, G. (1984). External validity of laboratory experiments: The frequency-validity relationship. *American Journal of Psychology, 97,* 185–195.

Gigerenzer, G. (1991a). From tools to theories: A heuristic of discovery in cognitive psychology. *Psychological Review, 98,* 254–267.

Gigerenzer, G. (1991b). How to make cognitive illusions disappear. Beyond heuristics and biases. In W. Stroebe & M. Hewstone (Eds.), *European review of social psychology* (Vol. 2, pp. 83–115). Chichester, UK: Wiley.

Gigerenzer, G. (1993). The bounded rationality of probabilistic mental models. In K. I. Manktelow & D. E. Over (Eds.), *Rationality: Psychological and philosophical perspectives.* London: Routledge.

Gigerenzer, G. (1994). Why the distinction between single-event probabilities and frequencies is relevant for psychology (and vice versa). In G. Wright & P. Ayton (Eds.), *Subjective probability* (pp. 129–161). New York: Wiley.

Gigerenzer, G. (1996). On narrow norms and vague heuristics: A reply to Kahneman and Tversky. *Psychological Review, 103*, 592–596.

Gigerenzer, G. (1997). Bounded rationality: Models of fast and frugal inference. *Swiss Journal of Economics and Statistics, 133*, 201–218.

Gigerenzer, G., Czerlinski, J., & Martignon, L. (1999). How good are fast and frugal heuristics? In J. Shanteau, B. A. Mellers, & D. A. Schum (Eds.), *Decision science and technology: Reflections on the contributions of Ward Edwards* (pp. 81–103). Norwell, MA: Kluwer.

Gigerenzer, G., & Goldstein, D. G. (1996a). Reasoning the fast and frugal way: Models of bounded rationality. *Psychological Review, 103*, 650–669.

Gigerenzer, G., & Goldstein, D. G. (1996b). Mind as computer: The birth of a metaphor. *Creativity Research Journal, 9*, 131–144.

Gigerenzer, G., & Hoffrage, U. (1995). How to improve Bayesian reasoning without instructions: Frequency formats. *Psychological Review, 102*, 684–704.

Gigerenzer, G., Hoffrage, U., & Kleinbölting, H. (1991). Probabilistic mental models: A Brunswikian theory of confidence. *Psychological Review, 98*, 506–528.

Gigerenzer, G., & Murray, D. J. (1987). *Cognition as intuitive statistics.* Hillsdale, NJ: Erlbaum.

Gigerenzer, G., & Richter, H. R. (1990). Context effects and their interaction with development: Area judgments. *Cognitive Development, 5*, 235–264.

Gigerenzer, G., Swijtink, Z., Porter, T., Daston, L., Beatty, J., & Krüger, L. (1989). *The empire of chance: How probability changed science and everyday life.* Cambridge, UK: Cambridge University Press.

Gilbert, J. P., & Mosteller, F. (1966). Recognizing the maximum of a sequence. *American Statistical Association Journal, 61*, 35–73.

Ginzburg, L. R., Janson, C., & Ferson, S. (1996). Judgment under uncertainty: Evolution may not favor a probabilistic calculus. *Behavioral and Brain Sciences, 19*, 24–25.

Gode, D. K., & Sunder, S. (1993). Allocative efficiency of markets with zero-intelligence traders: Market as a partial substitute for individual rationality. *Journal of Political Economics, 101*, 119–137.

Godfray, H. C. J. (1991). Signaling of need by offspring to their parents. *Nature, 352*, 328–330.

Goldstein, D. G. (1997). *Models of bounded rationality for inference.* Doctoral thesis, University of Chicago. Dissertation Abstracts International, 58 (01), 435B. (University Microfilms No. AAT 9720040).

Goldstein, D. G., & Gigerenzer, G. (1998). *Models of ecological rationality: The recognition heuristic.* Manuscript submitted for publication.

Gottlander, K. (1987). Parental feeding behavior and sibling competition in the pied flycatcher, *Ficedula hypoleuca. Ornis Scandanavica, 18*, 269–276.

Gray, R. D., & Kennedy, M. (1994). Perceptual constraints on optimal foraging: A reason for departures from the ideal free distribution? *Animal Behaviour, 47*, 469–471.

Green, R. F. (1984). Stopping rules for optimal foragers. *American Naturalist, 123*, 30–43.

Greene, D. H., & Knuth, D. E. (1982). *Mathematics for the analysis of algorithms.* Boston: Birkhäuser.

Greig-Smith, P. (1985). Weight differences, brood reduction, and sibling competition among nestling stonechats. *Journal of Zoology (London), 205*, 453–465.

Griggs, R. A., & Cox, J. R. (1982). The elusive thematic-materials effect in Wason's selection task. *British Journal of Psychology, 73*, 407–420.

Groner, M., Groner R., & Bischof, W. F. (1983). Approaches to heuristics: A historical review. In R. Groner (Ed.), *Methods of heuristics* (pp. 1–18). Hillsdale, NJ: Erlbaum.

Grüneis, F., Nakao, M., Yamamoto, M., Musha, T., & Nakahama, H. (1989). An interpretation of $1/f$ fluctuations in neural spike trains during dream sleep. *Biological Cybernetics, 60*, 161–169.

Gulliksen, H. (1950). *Theory of mental tests.* New York: Wiley.

Hamel, G., & Prahalad, C. K. (1994). *Competing for the future.* Boston: Harvard Business School Press.

Hamilton, W. R. (1995). Political polling: From the beginning to the center of American election campaigns. In J. A. Thurber & C. J. Nelson (Eds.), *Campaigns and elections American style* (pp. 161–180). Boulder, CO: Westview Press.

Hammond, K. R. (1955). Probabilistic functioning and the clinical method. *Psychological Review, 62*, 255–262.

Hammond, K. R. (1966). *The psychology of Egon Brunswik.* New York: Holt Rinehart & Winston.

Hammond, K. R. (1996a). *Human judgment and social policy: Irreducible uncertainty, inevitable error, unavoidable injustice.* New York: Oxford University Press.

Hammond, K. R. (1996b). Upon reflection. *Thinking & Reasoning, 2*, 239–248.

Hammond, K. R., Steward, T. R., Brehmer, B., & Steinmann, D. O. (1975). Social judgment theory. In M. F. Kaplan & S. Schwartz (Eds.), *Human judgment and decision processes* (pp. 271–312). New York: Academic Press.

Harrison, G. W., & McCabe, K. A. (1996). Stability and preference distortion in resource matching: An experimental study of the marriage problem. In R. M. Isaac (Ed.), *Research in experimental economics* (Vol. 8). Greenwich, CT: JAI Press.

Harsanyi, J. C., & Selten, R. (1988). *A general theory of equilibrium selection in games.* Cambridge, MA: MIT Press.

Hartley, D. (1749). *Observations on man, his frame, his duty, and his expectations* (Vols. 1, 2). London.

Hasher, L., Goldstein, D., & Toppino, T. (1977). Frequency and the conference of referential validity. *Journal of Verbal Learning and Behavior, 16*, 107–112.

Hasher, L., & Zacks, R. T. (1979). Automatic and effortful processes in memory. *Journal of Experimental Psychology: General, 108*, 356–388.

Hasher, L., & Zacks, R. T. (1984). Automatic processing of fundamental information: The case of frequency of occurrence. *American Psychologist, 39*, 1372–1388.

Haubensack, G. (1992). The consistency model: A process model for absolute judgments. *Journal of Experimental Psychology: Human Perception and Performance, 18,* 303–309.

Hawkins, S. A., & Hastie, R. (1990). Hindsight: Biased judgments of past events after the outcomes are known. *Psychological Bulletin, 107,* 311–327.

Heider, F., & Simmel, M. (1944). An experimental study of apparent behavior. *American Journal of Psychology, 57,* 243–259.

Hell, W., Gigerenzer, G., Gauggel, S., Mall, M., & Müller, M. (1988). Hindsight bias: An interaction of automatic and motivational factors? *Memory & Cognition, 16,* 533–538.

Henss, R. (1996). The attractiveness of prominent people. Unpublished manuscript, University of Saarbrücken, Saarbrücken, Germany.

Herrnstein, R. J. (1961). Relative and absolute strength of response as a function of reinforcement. *Journal of the Experimental Analysis of Behavior, 4,* 267–272.

Herrnstein, R. J., & Vaughan, W., Jr. (1980). Melioration and behavioral allocation. In J. E. R. Staddon (Ed.), *Limits to action: The allocation of individual behavior* (pp. 143–176). New York: Academic Press.

Hertwig, R. (1996). Temporal dynamics of hindsight bias: The effect of retention interval. Unpublished manuscript, Max Planck Institute for Psychological Research, Munich, Germany.

Hertwig, R., & Chase, V. M. (1998). Many reasons or just one: How response mode affects reasoning in the Linda problem. *Thinking & Reasoning, 4,* 319–352.

Hertwig, R., Gigerenzer, G., & Hoffrage, U. (1997). The reiteration effect in hindsight bias. *Psychological Review, 104,* 194–202.

Hertz, J., Krogh, A., & Palmer, R. G. (1991). *Introduction to the theory of neural computation.* Redwood City, CA: Addison-Wesley.

Hey, J. D. (1982). Search for rules for search. *Journal of Economic Behavior and Organization, 3,* 65–81.

Hey, J. D. (1987). Still searching. *Journal of Economic Behavior and Organization, 8,* 137–144.

Hintzman, D. L. (1984). MINERVA 2: A simulation model of human memory. *Behavior Research Methods, Instruments and Computers, 16,* 96–101.

Hintzman, D. L. (1988). Judgments of frequency and recognition memory in a multiple-trace memory model. *Psychological Review, 95,* 528–551.

Hirschfeld, L. A., & Gelman, S. A. (Eds.). (1994). *Mapping the mind: Domain specificity in cognition and culture.* Cambridge, UK: Cambridge University Press.

Hock, H. S., Malcus, L., & Hasher, L. (1986). Frequency discrimination: Assessing global-level and element-level units in memory. *Journal of Experimental Psychology: Learning, Memory, and Cognition, 12,* 232–240.

Hoffman, P. J. (1960). The paramorphic representation of clinical judgment. *Psychological Bulletin, 57,* 116–131.

Hoffrage, U. (1995). *The adequacy of subjective confidence judgments: Studies concerning the theory of probabilistic mental models.* Doctoral thesis, University of Salzburg, Austria.

Hoffrage, U., Hertwig, R., & Gigerenzer, G. (1999). *Hindsight bias: A by-product of knowledge updating.* Manuscript submitted for publication.

Hoffrage, U., Martignon, L., & Hertwig, R. (1997, August). *Does judgment policy "capturing" really capture the policies?* Poster presented at the 16th conference on Subjective Probability, Utility and Decision Making, University of Leeds, Leeds, UK.

Hogarth, R. M. (1981). Beyond discrete biases: Functional and dysfunctional aspects of judgmental heuristics. *Psychological Bulletin, 90,* 197–217.

Hogarth, R. M. (1987). *Judgement and choice: The psychology of decision* (2nd ed.). Chichester, UK: Wiley.

Hogarth, R. M., & Makridakis, S. (1981). Forecasting and planning: An evaluation. *Management Science, 27,* 115–138.

Holmes, W. G., & Sherman, P. W. (1983). Kin recognition in animals. *American Scientist, 71,* 46–55.

Holte, R. C. (1993). Very simple classification rules perform well on most commonly used datasets. *Machine Learning, 3*(11), 63–91.

Holton, G. (1988). *Thematic origins of scientific thought* (2nd ed.). Cambridge, MA: Harvard University Press.

Holyoak, K. J., & Spellman, B. A. (1993). Thinking. *Annual Review of Psychology, 44,* 265–315.

Horsfall, J. A. (1984). Brood reduction and brood division in coots. *Animal Behaviour, 32,* 216–225.

Hrdy, S. B., & Judge, D. S. (1993). Darwin and the puzzle of primogeniture. *Human Nature, 4,* 1–45.

Huber, O. (1979). Nontransitive multidimensional preferences: Theoretical analysis of a model. *Theory and Decision, 10,* 147–165.

Hume, D. (1975). *A treatise of human nature.* Oxford, UK: Clarendon Press. (Original work published 1739)

Jacobs, L. R., & Shapiro, R. Y. (1996). Presidential manipulation of polls and public opinion: The Nixon administration and the pollsters. *Political Science Quarterly, 110,* 519–538.

Jacoby, J., Jaccard, J. J., Currim, I., Kuss, A., Ansari, A., & Troutman, T. (1994). Tracing the impact of item-by-item information accessing on uncertainty reduction. *Journal of Consumer Research, 21,* 291–302.

Jacoby, L. L., Kelley, C., Brown, J., & Jasechko, J. (1989). Becoming famous overnight: Limits on the ability to avoid unconscious influences of the past. *Journal of Personality and Social Psychology, 56,* 326–338.

Jacoby, L. L., Woloshyn, V., & Kelley, C. (1989). Becoming famous without being recognized: Unconscious influences of memory produced by dividing attention. *Journal of Experimental Psychology, 118,* 115–125.

James, M. (1985). *Classification algorithms.* New York: Wiley.

Jameson, D., & Hurvich, L. M. (1959). Note on factors influencing the relation between stereoscopic acuity and observation distance. *Journal of the Optical Society of America, 49,* 639.

Jensen, F. (1996). *An introduction to Bayesian networks.* London: UCL Press.

Johnson, E. J., & Meyer, R. J. (1984). Compensatory choice models of noncompensatory processes: The effect of varying context. *Journal of Consumer Research, 11*, 528–541.

Johnson, E. J., & Payne, J. W. (1985). Effort and accuracy in choice. *Management Science, 31*(4), 395–414.

Johnson, E. J., Payne, J. W., Schkade, D. A., & Bettman, J. R. (1991). *Monitoring information processing and decisions: The mouselab system.* Unpublished manuscript, Center for Decision Studies, Fuqua School of Business, Duke University, Durham, NC.

Johnson, M. K., Peterson, M. A., Yap, E. C., & Rose, P. M. (1989). Frequency judgments: The problem of defining a perceptual event. *Journal of Experimental Psychology: Learning, Memory, and Cognition, 15*, 126–136.

Johnson, M. K., & Sherman, S. J. (1990). Constructing and reconstructing the past and the future in the present. In T. Higgins & R. M. Sorrentino (Eds.), *Handbook of motivation and cognition: Foundations of social behavior* (Vol. 2, pp. 482–526). New York: Guilford Press.

Johnson, M. P., & Raven, P. H. (1973). Species number and endemism: The Galapagos Archipelago revisited. *Science, 179*, 893–895.

Johnstone, R. A. (1997). The tactics of mutual mate choice and competitive search. *Behavioral Ecology and Sociobiology, 40*(1), 51–59.

Jonides, J., & Jones, C. M. (1992). Direct coding for frequency of occurrence. *Journal of Experimental Psychology: Learning, Memory, and Cognition, 18*, 368–378.

Julesz, B. (1971). *Foundations of cyclopean perception.* Chicago: University of Chicago Press.

Juslin, P. (1993). An explanation of the hard-easy effect in studies of realism of confidence in one's general knowledge. *European Journal of Cognitive Psychology, 5*(1), 55–71.

Kacelnik, A., Cotton, P. A., Stirling, L., & Wright, J. (1995). Food allocation among nestling starlings: Sibling competition and the scope of parental choice. *Proceedings of the Royal Society of London, 259*, 259–263.

Kadlec, D. (1997, January 27). Why U.S. funds aren't up to par. *Time*, 32–33.

Kagel, J. H., Battalio, R. C., & Green, L. (1995). *Economic choice theory.* Cambridge, UK: Cambridge University Press.

Kahneman, D., Slovic, P., & Tversky, A. (1982). *Judgment under uncertainty: Heuristics and biases.* Cambridge, UK: Cambridge University Press.

Kahneman, D., & Tversky, A. (1979). Prospect theory: An analysis of decision under risk. *Econometrica, 47*, 263–291.

Kahneman, D., & Tversky, A. (1982). On the study of statistical intuitions. *Cognition, 11*, 123–141.

Kahneman, D., & Tversky, A. (1996). On the reality of cognitive illusions: A reply to Gigerenzer's critique. *Psychological Review, 103*, 582–591.

Kamil, A. C., & Roitblat, H. L. (1985). The ecology of foraging behavior: Implications for animal learning and memory. *Annual Review of Psychology, 36*, 141–169.

Kass, R., & Raftery, A. (1995). Bayes factors. *Journal of the American Statistical Association, 90*(430), 773–779.

Keeney, R. L., & Raiffa, H. (1993). *Decisions with multiple objectives*. Cambridge, UK: Cambridge University Press.

Kelley, H. H. (1967). Attribution theory in social psychology. In D. Levine (Ed.), *Nebraska symposium on motivation* (Vol. 15, pp. 192–238). Lincoln: University of Nebraska Press.

Kerstholt, J. H. (1995). Decision making in a dynamic situation: The effect of false alarms and time pressure. *Journal of Behavioral Decision Making, 8*, 181–200.

Klayman, J. (1985). Children's decision strategies and their adaptation to task characteristics. *Organizational Behavior and Human Decision Processes, 35*, 179–201.

Klayman, J., & Ha, Y. (1987). Confirmation, disconfirmation, and information in hypothesis testing. *Psychological Review, 94*, 211–228.

Klein, G. (1998). *Sources of power: How people make decisions*. Cambridge, MA: MIT Press.

Kleinmuntz, D. N., & Kleinmuntz, B. (1981). Decision strategies in simulated environments. *Behavioral Science, 26*, 294–305.

Koelliker, M., Richner, H., Werner, I., & Heeb, P. (1998). Begging signals and biparental care: Nestling choice between parental feeding locations. *Animal Behaviour, 53*, 215–222.

Koestler, A. (1960). *The watershed: A biography of Johannes Kepler*. Garden City, NY: Anchor Books.

Koriat, A. (1993). How do we know that we know? The accessibility model of the feeling of knowing. *Psychological Review, 100*, 609–639.

Kozlowski, L., & Cutting, J. (1977). Recognizing the sex of a walker from a dynamic point-light display. *Perception and Psychophysics, 21*, 575–580.

Krebs, J. R., & Davies, N. B. (1991). *Behavioural ecology: An evolutionary approach* (3rd ed.). Oxford, UK: Blackwell.

Krebs, J. R., & Davies, N. B. (1997). *Behavioural ecology: An evolutionary approach* (4th ed.). Oxford, UK: Blackwell.

Kreps, D. M. (1990). *A course in microeconomic theory*. Princeton, NJ: Princeton University Press.

Krüger, L., Gigerenzer, G., & Morgan, M. (Eds.). (1987). *The probabilistic revolution. Vol. II: Ideas in the sciences*. Cambridge, MA: MIT Press.

Kruschke, J. K. (1992). ALCOVE: An exemplar-based connectionist model of category learning. *Psychological Review, 99*, 22–44.

Kusch, M. (1999). *Psychological knowledge: A social history and philosophy*. London: Routledge.

Lacey, E. P., Real, L., Antonovics, J., & Heckel, D. G. (1983). Variance models in the study of life history. *American Naturalist, 112*, 114–131.

Laplace, P. S. (1951). *A philosophical essay on probabilities* (F. W. Truscott and F. L. Emory, Trans.). New York: Dover. (Original work published 1814)

Legendre, G., Raymond, W., & Smolensky, P. (1993). Analytic typology of case marking and grammatical voice. *Proceedings of the Berkeley Linguistics Society, 19*, 464–478.

Leibniz, G. W. (1951). Toward a universal characteristic. In P. P. Wiener (Ed.), *Leibniz: Selections* (pp. 17–25). New York: Scribner's Sons. (Original work published 1677)

Leijonhufvud, A. (1996). Towards a not-too-rational macroeconomics. In D. Colander (Ed.), *Beyond microfoundations: Post Walrasian macroeconomics* (pp. 39–56). Cambridge, UK: Cambridge University Press.

Leonard, M., & Horn, A. (1996). Provisioning rules in tree swallows. *Behavioral Ecology and Sociobiology, 38*, 341–347.

Lichtenstein, S., Slovic, P., Fischhoff, B., Layman, M., & Combs, B. (1978). Judged frequency of lethal events. *Journal of Experimental Psychology: Human Learning and Memory, 4*, 551–578.

Lippman, S. A., & McCall, J. J. (1976). Economics of job search: A survey. *Economic Inquiry, 14*(2), 155–189.

Locke, J. (1959). *An essay concerning human understanding.* A. C. Fraser (Ed.). New York: Dover. (Original work published 1690)

Loftus, E. F. (1997). Memory for a past that never was. *Current Directions in Psychological Science, 6*, 60–65.

Lopes, L. L., & Oden, G. D. (1991). The rationality of intelligence. In E. Eels & T. Maruszewski (Eds.), *Poznan studies in the philosophy of the sciences and the humanities* (Vol. 21, pp. 225–249). Amsterdam: Rodopi.

Lucas, R. E., Jr. (1980). *Studies in business cycle theory.* Cambridge, MA: MIT Press.

Luce, R. D. (1956). Semiorders and a theory of utility discrimination. *Econometrica, 24*, 178–191.

Luce, R. D. (1995). Four tensions concerning mathematical modeling in psychology. *Annual Review of Psychology, 46*, 1–26.

Luchins, A. S., & Luchins, E. H. (1994). The water jar experiments and Einstellung effects. Part II: Gestalt psychology and past experience. *Gestalt Theory, 16*, 205–270.

Lynch, P. (1994). *Beating the street.* New York: Simon & Schuster.

MacKay, D. (1995). Developments in probabilistic modelling with neural networks—Ensemble learning. In B. Kappen & S. Gielen (Eds.), *Neural networks: Artificial intelligence and industrial applications* (pp. 191–198). Heidelberg: Springer Verlag.

Makse, H. A., Havlin, B., & Stanley, H. E. (1995). Modelling urban growth patterns. *Nature, 377*, 608–612.

Malacarne, G., Cucco, M., & Bertolo, E. (1994). Sibling competition in asynchronously hatched broods of the pallid swift (*Apus pallidus*). *Ethology, Ecology, and Evolution, 6*, 293–300.

March, J. G., & Simon, H. A. (1993). *Organizations* (2nd ed.). Oxford, UK: Blackwell.

Martignon, L., & Hoffrage, U. (1999). *Fast and frugal heuristics can be fit.* Manuscript submitted for publication.

Martin, A., & Moon, P. (1992). Purchasing decisions, partial knowledge, and economic search: Experimental and simulation evidence. *Journal of Behavioral Decision Making, 5*(4), 253–266.

Martin, G. L., & Pittman, J. A. (1991). Recognizing handprinted letters and digits using backpropagation learning. *Neural Computation, 3*(2), 258–267.

Martins, T. L. F., & Wright, J. (1993). Brood reduction in response to manipulated brood sizes in the common swift. *Behavioral Ecology and Sociobiology, 32*, 61–70.

Massaro, D. W. (1988a). Ambiguity in perception and experimentation. *Journal of Experimental Psychology: General, 117*, 417–421.

Massaro, D. W. (1988b). Some criticisms of connectionist models of human performance. *Journal of Memory and Language, 27*, 213–234.

Maule, A. J. (1994). A componential investigation of the relation between structural modelling and cognitive accounts of human judgement. *Acta Psychologica, 87*, 199–216.

Mazalov, V., Perrin, N., & Dombrovsky, Y. (1996). Adaptive search and information updating in sequential mate choice. *American Naturalist, 148*(1), 123–137.

McAllister, D., Mitchell, T. R., & Beach, L. R. (1979). The contingency model for selection of decision strategies: An empirical test of the effects of significance, accountability, and reversability. *Organizational Behavior and Human Performance, 24*, 228–244.

McBeath, M., Morikawa, K., & Kaiser, M. (1992). Perceptual bias for forward-facing motion. *Psychological Science, 3*(6), 362–367.

McCarthy, J., & Hayes, P. J. (1969). Some philosophical problems from the standpoint of artificial intelligence. In B. Meltzer & D. Michie (Eds.), *Machine intelligence* (Vol. 4, pp. 463–502). Edinburgh, UK: Edinburgh University Press.

McClelland, A. G. R., & Bolger, F. (1994). The calibration of subjective probabilities: Theories and models 1980–1994. In G. Wright & P. Ayton (Eds.), *Subjective probability* (pp. 453–482). Chichester, UK: Wiley.

McCormick, J. (1987, August 17). The wisdom of Solomon. *Newsweek*, 24–25.

McDonald, G. C., & Schwing, R. C. (1973). Instabilities of regression estimates relating air pollution to mortality. *Technometrics, 15*, 463–482.

McGonigle, B., & Chalmers, M. (1992). Monkeys are rational. *Quarterly Journal of Experimental Psychology, 45B*, 189–228.

McKenna, P., & Warrington, E. K. (1980). Testing for nominal dysphasia. *Journal of Neurology, Neurosurgery and Psychiatry, 43*, 781–788.

McKenzie, C. R. M. (1994). The accuracy of intuitive judgment strategies: Covariation assessment and Bayesian inference. *Cognitive Psychology, 26*, 209–239.

McRae, S. B., Weatherhead, P. J., & Montgomerie, R. (1993). American robin nestlings compete by jockeying for position. *Behavioral Ecology and Sociobiology, 33*, 101–106.

Medin, D. L., & Schaffer, M. M. (1978). Context theory of classification learning. *Psychological Review, 85*, 207–238.

Medin, D. L., Wattenmaker, W. D., & Michalski, R. S. (1987). Constraints and preferences in inductive learning: An experimental study of human and machine performance. *Cognitive Science, 11*, 299–339.

Mellers, B. A., & Birnbaum, M. H. (1982). Loci of contextual effects in judgment. *Journal of Experimental Psychology: Human Perception and Performance, 8*, 582–601.

Mellers, B. A., & Cooke, A. D. J. (1994). Trade-offs depend on attribute range. *Journal of Experimental Psychology: Human Perception and Performance, 20*, 1055–1067.

Merz, C. J., & Murphy, P. M. (1996). *UCI repository of machine learning databases* [http://www.ics.uci.edu/~mlearn/MLRepository.html]. Irvine, CA: University of California, Department of Information and Computer Science.

Metzger, A. (1975). *Gesetze des Sehens*. Heidelberg: Graupert Verlag.

Michotte, A. (1950). The emotions regarded as functional connections. In M. L. Reymert (Ed.), *Feelings and emotions* (Mooseheart Symposium) (pp. 114–126). New York: McGraw-Hill.

Michotte, A. (1963). *The perception of causality*. London: Methuen.

Milinski, M., & Parker, G. A. (1991). Competition for resources. In J. R. Krebs & N. B. Davies (Eds.), *Behavioural ecology: An evolutionary approach* (3rd ed., pp. 137–168). Oxford, UK: Blackwell.

Miller, C. S., & Laird, J. E. (1996). Accounting for graded performance within a discrete search framework. *Cognitive Science, 20*, 499–537.

Miller, G. A. (1956). The magical number seven, plus or minus two: Some limits on our capacity of processing information. *Psychological Review, 63*, 81–97.

Miller, G. A., Galanter, E., & Pribram, K. H. (1960). *Plans and the structure of behavior*. New York: Holt, Rinehart & Winston.

Miller, G. F. (1998). How mate choice shaped human nature: A review of sexual selection and human evolution. In C. Crawford & D. Krebs (Eds.), *Handbook of evolutionary psychology: Ideas, issues, and applications* (pp. 87–129). Hillsdale, NJ: Erlbaum.

Miller, G. F., & Cliff, D. (1994). Protean behavior in dynamic games: Arguments for the coevolution of pursuit-evasion tactics in simulated robots. In D. Cliff, P. Husbands, J.-A. Meyer, & S. W. Wilson (Eds.), *From animals to animats 3: Proceedings of the Third International Conference on Simulation of Adaptive Behavior* (pp. 411–420). Cambridge, MA: MIT Press/Bradford Books.

Miller, G. F., & Freyd, J. (1993). *The interplay among evolutionary, cognitive, and behavioral dynamics*. Technical Report CSRP 290. University of Sussex, Brighton, UK: School of Cognitive and Computing Sciences (COGS).

Miller, G. F., & Todd, P. M. (1998). Mate choice turns cognitive. *Trends in Cognitive Sciences, 2*, 190–198.

Mises, R. von (1957). *Probability, statistics, and truth* (H. Geiringer, Trans.). London: Allen and Unwin.

Mitchell, W. C. (1912). The backward art of spending money. *American Economic Review, 2*, 269–281.

Mock, P. J., Khubesrian, M., & Larcheveque, D. M. (1991). Energetics of growth and maturation in sympatric passerines that fledge at different ages. *Auk, 108*, 34–41.

Mondloch, C. J. (1995). Chick hunger and begging affect parental allocation of feeding in pigeons. *Animal Behaviour, 49*, 601–613.

Montgomery, H., Gärling, T., Lindberg, E., & Selart, M. (1990). Preference judgments and choice: Is the prominence effect due to information integration or information evaluation? In K. Borcherding, O. I. Larichev, & D. M. Messick (Eds.), *Contemporary issues in decision making* (pp. 149–157). Amsterdam: Elsevier-North Holland.

Montgomery, H., & Svenson, O. (1989). A think aloud study of dominance structuring in decision processes. In H. Montgomery & O. Svenson (Eds.), *Process and structure in human decision making* (pp. 135–150). Chichester, UK: Wiley.

Moore, J. A. (1975). *Total biochemical oxygen demand of animal manures.* Unpublished doctoral dissertation, University of Minnesota.

Morton, F. B. (1995, February). Charting a school's course. *Chicago,* 86–95.

Mosteller, F. (1987). *Fifty challenging problems in probability with solutions.* New York: Dover. (Reprint of the 1965 Addison-Wesley edition.)

Muth, J. F. (1961). Rational expectations and the theory of price movement. *Econometrica, 29,* 315–335.

Nagel, R. (1995). Unraveling in guessing games: An experimental study. *American Economic Review, 85,* 1313–1326.

Narula, S. C., & Wellington, J. W. (1977). Prediction, linear regression, and minimum sum of relative errors. *Technometrics, 19,* 185–190.

Newell, A. (1973). You can't play 20 questions with nature and win: Projective comments on the papers of this symposium. In W. G. Chase (Ed.), *Visual information processing* (pp. 283–308). New York: Academic Press.

Newell, A., & Simon, H. A. (1972). *Human problem solving.* Englewood Cliffs, NJ: Prentice Hall.

Newton, I. (1978). Feeding and development of the sparrowhawk, *Accipiter nisus,* nestlings. *Journal of Zoology (London), 184,* 465–487.

Nisbett, R. E., & Wilson, T. D. (1977). Telling more than we can know: Verbal reports on mental processes. *Psychological Review, 84,* 231–259.

Norman, D. A. (1993). *Things that make us smart: Defending human attributes in the age of the machine.* Reading, MA: Addison-Wesley.

Nosofsky, R. M. (1986). Attention, similarity, and the identification-categorization relationship. *Journal of Experimental Psychology: General, 115*(1), 39–57.

Nosofsky, R. M., Palmeri, T. J., & McKinley, S. C. (1994). Rule-plus-exception model of classification learning. *Psychological Review, 101,* 53–79.

Oaksford, M., & Chater, N. (1994). A rational analysis of the selection task as optimal data selection. *Psychological Review, 101,* 608–631.

Ochs, J. (1995). Coordination problems. In J. H. Kagel & A. E. Roth (Eds.), *Handbook of experimental economics* (pp. 195–252). Princeton, NJ: Princeton University Press.

Ostreiher, R. (1997). Food division in the Arabian babbler nest: Adult choice or nestling competition? *Behavioral Ecology, 8,* 233–238.

Parducci, A. (1965). Category judgment: A range-frequency model. *Psychological Review, 72,* 407–418.

Pascal, B. (1962). *Pensées.* Paris: Editions du Seuil. (Original work published 1669)

Payne, J. W. (1976). Task complexity and contingent processing in decision making: An information search and protocol analysis. *Organizational Behavior and Human Performance, 16,* 366–387.

Payne, J. W., Bettman, J. R., & Johnson, E. J. (1988). Adaptive strategy selection in decision making. *Journal of Experimental Psychology: Learning, Memory, and Cognition, 14,* 534–552.

Payne, J. W., Bettman, J. R., & Johnson, E. J. (1990). The adaptive decision maker: Effort and accuracy in choice. In R. M. Hogarth (Ed.), *Insights in decision making: A tribute to Hillel J. Einhorn* (pp. 129–153). Chicago: University of Chicago Press.

Payne, J. W., Bettman, J. R., & Johnson, E. J. (1993). *The adaptive decision maker.* New York: Cambridge University Press.

Payne, J. W., Bettman, J. R., & Luce, M. F. (1996). When time is money: Decision behavior under opportunity-cost time pressure. *Organizational Behavior and Human Decision Processes, 66,* 131–152.

Payne, J. W., Braunstein, M., & Carroll, J. (1978). Exploring predecisional behavior: An alternative approach to decision research. *Organizational Behavior and Human Performance, 22,* 17–44.

Pearl, J. (1984). *Heuristics: Intelligent search strategies for computer problem solving.* Reading, MA: Addison-Wesley.

Pearl, J. (1988). *Probabilistic reasoning in intelligent systems.* San Francisco: Morgan Kaufmann.

Pearson, K. (1897). On the scientific measure of variability. *Natural Science, 11,* 115–118.

Penrose, K. W., Nelson, A. G., & Fisher, A. G. (1985). Generalized body composition prediction equation for men using simple measurement techniques. *Medicine and Science in Sports and Exercise, 17*(2), 189.

Persson, M. (1996). *Flexible and accurate reasoning with an exemplar-based algorithm: An examination of Gigerenzer and Goldstein (1996), based on a more realistic learning model.* Unpublished undergraduate thesis, Uppsala University, Uppsala, Sweden.

Peterson, C. R., & Beach, L. R. (1967). Man as an intuitive statistician. *Psychological Bulletin, 68,* 29–46.

Pfennig, D. W., Gamboa, G. J., Reeve, H. K., Reeve, J. S., & Ferguson, I. D. (1983). The mechanism of nestmate discrimination in social wasps. *Behavioral Ecology & Sociobiology, 13,* 299–305.

Pinker, S. (1997). *How the mind works.* New York: Norton.

Planck, M. (1958). Zur Theorie des Gesetzes der Energieverteilung im Normalspectrum. In M. Planck, *Physikalische Abhandlungen und Vorträge* (Vol. 1, pp. 698–706). Braunschweig, Germany: Vieweg.

Polya, G. (1954). *Mathematics and plausible reasoning. Vol. 1: Induction and analogy in mathematics.* Princeton, NJ: Princeton University Press.

Pomiankowski, A. (1987). The costs of choice in sexual selection. *Journal of Theoretical Biology, 128,* 195–218.

Popper, K. (1959). *The logic of scientific discovery.* London: Hutchinson.

Posner, M. I., & Keele, S. W. (1968). On the genesis of abstract ideas. *Journal of Experimental Psychology, 77*(3), 353–363.

Prahalad, C. K., & Hamel, G. (1990). The core competence of the corporation. *Harvard Business Review,* May-June, 79–91.

Premack, D. (1990). The infant's theory of self-propelled objects. *Cognition, 36,* 1–16.

Price, K., & Ydenberg, R. (1995). Begging and provisioning in broods of asynchronously hatched yellow-headed blackbird nestlings. *Behavioral Ecology and Sociobiology, 37,* 201–208.

Prince, A., & Smolensky, P. (1991). *Notes on connectionism and harmony theory in linguistics.* Technical Report No. CU-CS-533-91. Boulder, CO: University of Colorado, Boulder, Department of Computer Science.

Pringle, M., & Day, R. H. (1996). Modes of economizing behavior: Experimental evidence. *Journal of Economic Behavior and Organization, 29,* 191–209.

Quinlan, J. R. (1986). Induction of decision trees. *Machine Learning, 1*(1), 81–106.

Quinlan, J. R. (1993). *C4.5: Programs for machine learning.* San Mateo, CA: Morgan Kaufmann.

Raimi, R. A. (1976). The first digit problem. *The American Mathematical Monthly, 83,* 521–538.

Ramachandran, V. S. (1990). Interactions between motion, depth, color and form: The utilitarian theory of perception. In C. Blakemore (Ed.), *Vision: Coding and efficiency* (pp. 346–360). New York: Cambridge University Press.

Ramanujam, V., & Venkatraman, N. (1984). An inventory and critique of strategy research using the PIMS database. *Academy of Management Review, 9*(1), 138–151.

Ramsey, F. P. (1931). Truth and probability. In F. P. Ramsey (Ed.), *The foundations of mathematics and other logical essays* (pp. 156–198). London: Routledge & Kegan Paul.

Rapoport, A., & Tversky, A. (1970). Choice behavior in an optional stopping task. *Organizational Behavior and Human Performance, 5,* 105–120.

Ratcliff, R. (1978). A theory of memory retrieval. *Psychological Review, 85,* 59–108.

Real, L. (1980). Fitness, uncertainty, and the role of diversification in evolution and behavior. *American Naturalist, 115,* 623–638.

Redondo, T., & Castro, F. (1992). Signaling of nutritional need by magpie nestlings. *Ethology, 92,* 193–204.

Reed, J. R. (1981). Song sparrow "rules" for feeding nestlings. *Auk, 98,* 828–831.

Regier, T. (1996). *The human semantic potential: Spatial language and constrained connectionism.* Cambridge, MA: MIT Press.

Restle, F. (1961). *Psychology of judgment and choice.* New York: Wiley.

Revusky, S. H., & Bedarf, E. W. (1967). Association of illness with prior ingestion of novel foods. *Science, 155,* 219–220.

Reynolds, V. (1973). Ethology of social change. In C. Renfrew (Ed.), *The explanation of culture change: Models in prehistory* (pp. 467–480). Pittsburgh: University of Pittsburgh Press.

Rice, J. A. (1995). *Mathematical statistics and data analysis* (2nd ed.). Belmont, CA: Duxbury Press.

Ridley, M. (1993). *The red queen: Sex and the evolution of human nature.* London: Viking.

Rimé, B., Boulanger, B., Laubin, P., Richir, M., & Stroobants, K. (1985). The perception of interpersonal emotions originated by patterns of movement. *Motivation and Emotion, 9*(3), 241–260.

Rivest, R. J. (1987). Learning decision lists. *Machine Learning, 2,* 229–246.

Rodkin, D. (1995, February). 10 keys for creating top high schools. *Chicago*, 78–85.

Rosch, E. (1978). Principles of categorization. In E. Rosch & B. B. Lloyd (Eds.), *Cognition and categorization* (pp. 27–48). Hillsdale, NJ: Erlbaum.

Roth, A. E., & Erev, I. (1995). Learning in extensive-form games: Experimental data and simple dynamic models in the intermediate term. *Games and Economic Behavior, 8*, 164–212.

Roth, A. E., & Sotomayor, M. (1990). *Two-sided matching: A study in game-theoretic modeling and analysis.* Cambridge, UK: Cambridge University Press.

Rozef, M. S., & Kinney, W. R. (1976). Capital market seasonality: The case of stock returns. *Journal of Financial Economics, 3*, 379–402.

Rumelhart, D. E., & Todd, P. M. (1993). Learning and connectionist representations. In D. E. Meyer & S. Kornblum (Eds.), *Attention and performance XIV* (pp. 3–30). Cambridge, MA: MIT Press/Bradford Books.

Runeson, S. (1977). On the possibility of "smart" perceptual mechanisms. *Scandinavian Journal of Psychology, 18*, 172–179.

Runeson, S., & Costall, A. P. (1991). *The ecological concept of information versus the traditional notion of cue.* Unpublished manuscript.

Russo, J. E., & Dosher, B. A. (1983). Strategies for multiattribute binary choice. *Journal of Experimental Psychology: Learning, Memory, and Cognition, 9*, 676–696.

Ryden, O., & Bengtsson, H. (1980). Differential begging and locomotory behavior by early and late hatched nestlings affecting the distribution of food in asynchronously hatched broods of altricial birds. *Zeitschrift für Tierpsychologie, 53*, 291–303.

Saad, G., & Russo, J. E. (1996). Stopping criteria in sequential choice. *Organizational Behavior and Human Decision Processes, 67*(3), 258–270.

Saffran, J. R., Aslin, R. N., & Newport, E. L. (1996). Statistical learning by 8-month-old infants. *Science, 274*, 1926–1928.

Samuelson, L. (1997). *Evolutionary games and equilibrium selection.* Cambridge, MA: MIT Press.

Sandberg, J. S., Basso, M. J., & Okin, B. A. (1978). Winter rain and summer ozone: A predictive relationship. *Science, 200*, 1051–1054.

Sargent, T. J. (1993). *Bounded rationality in macroeconomics.* Oxford, UK: Oxford University Press.

Sauermann, H., & Selten, R. (1962). Anpassungstheorie der Unternehmung. *Zeitschrift für die gesamte Staatswissenschaft, 118*, 577–597.

Savage, L. J. (1954). *The foundations of statistics.* New York: Dover.

Schacter, D. L. (Ed.). (1995). *Memory distortions: How minds, brains, and societies reconstruct the past.* Cambridge, MA: Harvard University Press.

Schacter, D. L., & Tulving, E. (1994). What are the memory systems of 1994? In D. L. Schacter & E. Tulving (Eds.), *Memory systems 1994* (pp. 1–38). Cambridge, MA: MIT Press.

Schlosser, E. (1998, September 3). Fast-food nation. Part one: The true cost of America's diet. *Rolling Stone*, 58–117.

Schmidt, F. L. (1971). The relative efficiency of regression and simple unit predictor weights in applied differential psychology. *Educational and Psychological Measurement, 31,* 699–714.

Schmitt, M., & Martignon, L. (1999). *Improving the performance of Take the Best.* Technical Report. Graz, Austria: Institut für Informatik, University of Graz.

Schonfield, D., & Robertson, B. (1966). Memory storage and aging. *Canadian Journal of Psychology, 20,* 228–236.

Schwarz, N., Bless, H., Strack, F., Klumpp, G., Rittenauer-Schatka, H., & Simons, A. (1991). Ease of retrieval as information: Another look at the availability heuristic. *Journal of Personality and Social Psychology, 61,* 195–202.

Sedlmeier, P., Hertwig, R., & Gigerenzer, G. (1998). Are judgments of the positional frequencies of letters systematically biased due to availability? *Journal of Experimental Psychology: Learning, Memory, and Cognition, 24,* 754–770.

Selten, R. (1991). Evolution, learning, and economic behavior. *Games and Economic Behavior, 3,* 3–24.

Selten, R. (1996). *Aspiration adaptation theory.* Discussion Paper No. B-389. Bonn, Germany: University of Bonn.

Selten, R., & Buchta, J. (1994). *Experimental sealed bid first price auctions with directly observed bid functions.* Discussion Paper No. B-270. Bonn, Germany: University of Bonn.

Selten, R., & Stoecker, R. (1986). End behavior in sequences of finite Prisoner's Dilemma supergames: A learning theory approach. *Journal of Economic Behavior and Organization, 7,* 47–70.

Semenza, C., & Sgaramella, T. M. (1993). Production of proper names: A clinical case study of the effects of phonemic cueing. In G. Cohen & D. M. Burke (Eds.), *Memory for proper names* (pp. 265–280). Hove, UK: Erlbaum.

Semenza, C., & Zettin, M. (1989). Evidence from aphasia for the role of proper names as pure referring expressions. *Nature, 342,* 678–679.

Sen, A. (1993). Internal consistency of choice: *Econometrica, 61,* 495–521.

Sethuraman, R., Cole, C., & Jain, D. (1994). Analyzing the effect of information format and task on cutoff search strategies. *Journal of Consumer Psychology, 3*(2), 103–136.

Shannon, C. (1948). A mathematical theory of communication. *Bell Systems Technical Journal, 27,* 379–423, 623–656.

Shanteau, J. (1988). Psychological characteristics and strategies of expert decision makers. *Acta Psychologica, 68,* 203–215.

Shanteau, J. (1992). How much information does an expert use? Is it relevant? *Acta Psychologica, 81,* 75–86.

Sharpe, W. (1964). Capital asset prices: A theory of market equilibrium under conditions of risk. *Journal of Finance, 19,* 425–442.

Shepard, R. N. (1964). Attention and the metric structure of the stimulus space. *Journal of Mathematical Psychology, 1,* 54–87.

Shepard, R. N. (1967a). On subjectively optimum selections among multiattribute alternatives. In W. Edwards & A. Tversky (Eds.), *Decision making* (pp. 257–283). Harmondsworth, UK: Penguin.

Shepard, R. N. (1967b). Recognition memory for words, sentences, and pictures. *Journal of Verbal Learning and Verbal Behavior, 6,* 156–163.

Shepard, R. N. (1990). *Mind sights.* New York: Freeman.

Shields, M. D. (1983). Effects of information supply and demand on judgment accuracy: Evidence from corporate managers. *The Accounting Review, 58,* 284–303.

Shleifer, A., & Summers, L. H. (1990). The noise trader approach to finance. *Journal of Economic Perspectives, 4,* 19–33.

Simon, H. A. (1947). *Administrative behavior.* New York: Macmillan.

Simon, H. A. (1955a). A behavioral model of rational choice. *Quarterly Journal of Economics, 69,* 99–118.

Simon, H. A. (1955b). On a class of skew distribution functions. *Biometrika, 42,* 425–440.

Simon, H. A. (1956a). Rational choice and the structure of environments. *Psychological Review, 63,* 129–138.

Simon, H. A. (1956b). Dynamic programming under uncertainty with a quadratic criterion function. *Econometrica, 24,* 19–33.

Simon, H. A. (1957). *Models of man: Social and rational.* New York: Wiley.

Simon, H. A. (1959). Theories of decision-making in economics and behavioral science. *American Economic Review, 49,* 253–283.

Simon, H. A. (1982). *Models of bounded rationality.* Cambridge, MA: MIT Press.

Simon, H. A. (1987). Rational decision making in business organizations. In L. Green & J. H. Kagel (Eds.), *Advances in behavioral economics* (Vol. 1, pp. 18–47). Norwood, NJ: Ablex.

Simon, H. A. (1990). Invariants of human behavior. *Annual Review of Psychology, 41,* 1–19.

Simon, H. A. (1991). Cognitive architectures and rational analysis: Comment. In K. VanLehn (Ed.), *Architectures for intelligence* (pp. 25–39). Hillsdale, NJ: Erlbaum.

Simon, H. A. (1996, February 19). Interview with Bruce Weber, A mean chess-playing computer tears at the meaning of thought. *New York Times,* pp. A1, A11.

Simon, H. A., & Schaeffer, J. (1992). The game of chess. In R. J. Aumann & S. Hart (Eds.), *Handbook of game theory* (Vol. 1, pp. 1–17). Amsterdam: Elsevier.

Skov, R. B., & Sherman, S. J. (1986). Information-gathering processes: Diagnosticity, hypothesis-confirmatory strategies, and perceived hypothesis confirmation. *Journal of Experimental Social Psychology, 22,* 93–121.

Sloman, S. A. (1996). The empirical case for two systems of reasoning. *Psychological Bulletin, 119,* 3–22.

Smith, A. (1937). *The wealth of nations.* New York: Modern Library.

Smith, E. A. (1991). *Inujjuamiut foraging strategies: Evolutionary ecology of an Arctic hunting economy.* New York: de Gruyter.

Smith, E. E., Patalano, A. L., & Jonides, J. (1998). Alternative strategies of categorization. *Cognition, 65,* 167–196.

Smith, H. G., & Montgomerie, R. (1991). Nestling American robins compete with siblings by begging. *Behavioral Ecology and Sociobiology, 29,* 307–312.

Smyth, A. H. (Ed.). (1907). *The writings of Benjamin Franklin, Vol. 10.* New York: Macmillan.

Sober, E. (1975). *Simplicity.* Oxford, UK: Oxford University Press.

Soros, G. (1994). *The theory of reflexivity.* New York: Soros Fund Management.

Spelke, E. S., Phillips, A., & Woodward, A. L. (1995). Infants' knowledge of object motion and human action. In D. Sperber, D. Premack, & A. J. Premack (Eds.), *Causal cognition: A multidisciplinary debate* (pp. 44–78). Oxford, UK: Clarendon Press.

Sperber, D., Cara F., & Girotto, V. (1995). Relevance theory explains the selection task. *Cognition, 57,* 31–95.

Squire, L. R., Knowlton, B., & Musen, G. (1993). The structure and organization of memory. *Annual Review of Psychology, 44,* 453–495.

Stamps, J., Clark, A., Kus, B., & Arrowood, P. (1985). Parent-offspring conflict in budgerigars. *Behaviour, 94,* 1–40.

Standing, L. (1973). Learning 10,000 pictures. *Quarterly Journal of Experimental Psychology, 25,* 207–222.

Stephens, D. W., & Krebs, J. R. (1986). *Foraging theory.* Princeton, NJ: Princeton University Press.

Stigler, G. J. (1961). The economics of information. *Journal of Political Economy, 69,* 213–225.

Stigler, S. (1986). *The history of statistics.* Cambridge, MA: Harvard University Press/Bellknap Press.

Sullivan, M. S. (1994). Mate choice as an information gathering process under time constraint: Implications for behaviour and signal design. *Animal Behaviour, 47*(1), 141–151.

Sulloway, F. (1996). *Born to rebel: Birth order, family dynamics, and creative lives.* New York: Pantheon.

Svenson, O. (1979). Process description of decision making. *Organizational Behavior and Human Performance, 23,* 86–112.

Svenson, O. (1992). Differentiation and consolidation theory of human decision making: A frame of reference for the study of pre- and post-decision processes. *Acta Psychologica, 80,* 143–168.

Svenson, O., & Maule, A. J. (Eds.). (1993). *Time pressure and stress in human judgment and decision making.* New York: Plenum Press.

Synodinos, N. E. (1986). Hindsight distortion: "I-knew-it-all-along" and I was sure about it. *Journal of Applied Social Psychology, 16,* 107–117.

Tanner, W. P., Jr., & Swets, J. A. (1954). A decision-making theory of visual detection. *Psychological Review, 61,* 401–409.

Tetlock, P. E. (1983). Accountability and complexity of thought. *Journal of Personality and Social Psychology, 45,* 74–83.

Thaler, R. H. (1991). *Quasi rational economics.* New York: Russell Sage Foundation.

Thaler, R. H. (1992). *The winner's curse: Paradoxes and anomalies of economic life.* New York: Free Press.

Thaler, R. H. (Ed.). (1993). *Advances in behavioral finance.* New York: Russell Sage Foundation.

Thoreau, H. (1960). *Walden.* New York: Signet. (Original work published 1854)

Timmermans, D. (1993). The impact of task complexity on information use in multi-attribute decision making. *Journal of Behavioral Decision Making, 6*, 95–111.

Todd, P. M. (1997). Searching for the next best mate. In R. Conte, R. Hegselmann, & P. Terna (Eds.), *Simulating social phenomena* (pp. 419–436). Berlin: Springer-Verlag.

Todd, P. M., & Miller, G. F. (1993). Parental guidance suggested: How parental imprinting evolves through sexual selection as an adaptive learning mechanism. *Adaptive Behavior, 2*(1), 5–47.

Todd, P. M., & Miller, G. F. (1997). Biodiversity through sexual selection. In C. G. Langton & K. Shimohara (Eds.), *Artificial Life V: Proceedings of the Fifth International Workshop on the Synthesis and Simulation of Living Systems* (pp. 289–299). Cambridge, MA: MIT Press/Bradford Books.

Todd, P. M., & Wilson, S. W. (1993). Environmental structure and adaptive behavior from the ground up. In J.-A. Meyer, H. L. Roitblat, & S. W. Wilson (Eds.), *From animals to animats 2: Proceedings of the Second International Conference on Simulation of Adaptive Behavior* (pp. 11–20). Cambridge, MA: MIT Press/Bradford Books.

Tooby, J., & Cosmides, L. (1990). The past explains the present: Emotional adaptations and the structure of ancestral environments. *Ethology and Sociobiology, 11*, 375–424.

Tooby, J., & Cosmides, L. (1992). The psychological foundations of culture. In J. Barkow, L. Cosmides, & J. Tooby (Eds.), *The adapted mind: Evolutionary psychology and the generation of culture* (pp. 19–136). New York: Oxford University Press.

Tooby, J., & Cosmides, L. (1998). *Ecological rationality and the multimodular mind.* Manuscript submitted for publication.

Toscani, O. (1997). *Die Werbung ist ein lächelndes Aas.* Frankfurt: Fischer.

Townsend, J. T., & Ashby, F. G. (1982). Experimental tests of contemporary mathematical models of visual letter recognition. *Journal of Experimental Psychology: Human Perception and Performance, 8*(6), 834–864.

Trope, Y., & Bassok, M. (1982). Confirmatory and diagnosing strategies in social information gathering. *Journal of Personality and Social Behavior, 43*(1), 22–34.

Tsotsos, J. K. (1991). Computational resources *do* constrain behavior. *Behavioral and Brain Sciences, 14*, 506.

Tucker, W. (1987, September 25). Where do the homeless come from? *National Review*, 34–44.

Tuddenham, R. D., & Snyder, M. M. (1954). Physical growth of California boys and girls from birth to age 18. *Calif. Publ. Child Develop., 1*, 183–364.

Tversky, A. (1972). Elimination by aspects: A theory of choice. *Psychological Review, 79*, 281–299.

Tversky, A., & Kahneman, D. (1973). Availability: A heuristic for judging frequency and probability. *Cognitive Psychology, 5*, 207–232.

Tversky, A., & Kahneman, D. (1974). Judgment under uncertainty: Heuristics and biases. *Science, 185*, 1124–1131.

Tversky, A., & Kahneman, D. (1981). The framing of decisions and the psychology of choice. *Science, 211*, 453–458.

Tversky, A., & Kahneman, D. (1983). Extensional versus intuitive reasoning: The conjunction fallacy in probability judgment. *Psychological Review, 90*, 293–315.

Upton, G., & Fingleton, B. (1985). *Spatial data analysis by example. Volume 1: Point pattern and quantitative data.* Chichester, UK: Wiley.

Valone, T. J., Nordell, S. E., Giraldeau, L.-A., & Templeton, J. J. (1996). The empirical question of thresholds and mechanisms of mate choice. *Evolutionary Ecology, 10*(4), 447–455.

Van Huyck, J., Battalio, R. C., Mathur, S., Van Huyck, P., & Ortmann, A. (1995). On the origin of conventions: Evidence from symmetric bargaining games. *International Journal of Game Theory, 24*, 187–212.

Van Wallendael, L. R., & Guignard, Y. (1992). Diagnosticity, confidence, and the need for information. *Journal of Behavioral Decision Making, 5*, 23–37.

Varey, C. A., Mellers, B. A., & Birnbaum, M. H. (1990). Judgments of proportions. *Journal of Experimental Psychology: Human Perception and Performance, 16*, 613–625.

Vega-Redondo, F. (1996). *Evolution, games, and economic behavior.* Oxford, UK: Oxford University Press.

von Neumann, J., & Morgenstern, O. (1944). *Theory of games and economic behavior.* Princeton, NJ: Princeton University Press.

Vriend, N. J. (1996). Rational behavior and economic theory. *Journal of Economic Behavior & Organization, 29*, 263–285.

Waage, J. K. (1979). Foraging for patchily-distributed hosts by the parasitoid, *Nemeritis canescens. Journal of Animal Ecology, 48*, 353–371.

Walberg, H. J., Strykowski, B. F., Rovai, E., & Hung, S. S. (1984). Exceptional performance. *Review of Educational Research, 54*, 87–112.

Wald, A. (1947). *Sequential analysis.* New York: Wiley.

Waldmann, M. R., & Martignon, L. (1998). A Bayesian network model of causal learning. In M. A. Gernsbacher & S. J. Derry (Eds.), *Proceedings of the Twentieth Annual Conference of the Cognitive Science Society* (pp. 1102–1107). Mahwah, NJ: Erlbaum.

Wallsten, T. S. (1980). Processes and models to describe choice and inference behavior. In T. S. Wallsten (Ed.), *Cognitive processes in choice and decision behavior* (pp. 215–237). Hillsdale, NJ: Erlbaum.

Wallsten, T. S., & Barton, C. (1982). Processing probabilistic multidimensional information for decisions. *Journal of Experimental Psychology: Learning, Memory, and Cognition, 8*, 361–384.

Wang, X. T. (1996a). Domain-specific rationality in human choices: Violations of utility axioms and social contexts. *Cognition, 60*, 31–63.

Wang, X. T. (1996b). Framing effects: Dynamics and task domains. *Organizational Behavior and Human Decision Processes, 68*, 145–157.

Ward, D. (1992). The role of satisficing in foraging theory. *Oikos, 63*, 312–317.

Warrington, E. K., & McCarthy, R. A. (1988). The fractionation of retrograde amnesia. *Brain and Cognition, 7*, 184–200.

Wason, P. C. (1983). Realism and rationality in the selection task. In J. S. B. T. Evans (Ed.), *Thinking and reasoning: Psychological approaches* (pp. 44–75). London: Routledge & Kegan Paul.

Wehner, R. (1997). Sensory systems and behaviour. In J. R. Krebs & N. B. Davies (Eds.), *Behavioural ecology: An evolutionary approach* (4th ed., pp. 19–41). Oxford, UK: Blackwell.

Wehner, R., Michel, B., & Antonsen, P. (1996). Visual navigation in insects: Coupling of egocentric and geocentric information. *Journal of Experimental Biology, 199*, 129–140.

Wehner, R., & Wehner, S. (1990). Insect navigation: Use of maps or Ariadne's thread? *Ethology, Ecology and Evolution, 2*, 27–48.

Weibull, J. W. (1995). *Evolutionary game theory.* Cambridge, MA: MIT Press.

Weisberg, S. (1985). *Applied linear regression.* New York: Wiley.

Westenberg, M. R. M., & Koele, P. (1992). Response modes, decision processes and decision outcomes. *Acta Psychologica, 80*, 169–184.

Wiegmann, D., Real, L. A., Capone, T. A., & Ellner, S. (1996). Some distinguishing features of models of search behavior and mate choice. *American Naturalist, 147*(2), 188–204.

Wilcox, N. (1993). Lottery choice: Incentives, complexity and decision time. *Economic Journal, 103*, 1397–1417.

Wilks, S. S. (1938). Weighting systems for linear functions of correlated variables when there is no dependent variable. *Psychometrika, 3*, 23–40.

Williams, B. A. (1988). Reinforcement, choice, and response strength. In R. C. Atkinson, R. J. Herrnstein, G. Lindzey, & R. D. Luce (Eds.), *Stevens' handbook of experimental psychology* (Vol. 2, pp. 167–244). New York: Wiley.

Williams, K. W., & Durso, F. T. (1986). Judging category frequency: Automaticity or availability? *Journal of Experimental Psychology: Learning, Memory, and Cognition, 12*, 387–396.

Wilson, T. D., & Schooler, J. W. (1991). Thinking too much: Introspection can reduce the quality of preferences and decisions. *Journal of Personality and Social Psychology, 60*, 181–192.

Wimsatt, W. C. (1987). False models as means to truer theories. In M. Nitecki & A. Hoffman (Eds.), *Neutral models in biology* (pp. 107–166). London: Oxford University Press.

Wimsatt, W. C. (in press). *Re-engineering philosophy for limited beings: Piecewise approximations to reality.* Cambridge, MA: Harvard University Press.

Winter, S. G. (1975). Optimization and evolution in the theory of the firm. In R. H. Day & T. Groves (Eds.), *Adaptive economic models* (pp. 73–118). New York: Academic Press.

Winterfeldt, D. von, & Edwards, W. (1973). *Costs and payoffs in perceptual research.* Unpublished manuscript, University of Michigan, Engineering Psychology Laboratory.

Winterfeldt, D. von, & Edwards, W. (1986). *Decision analysis and behavioral research.* Cambridge, UK: Cambridge University Press.

Woodley, W. L., Simpson, J., Biondini, R., & Berkeley, J. (1977). Rainfall results 1970–75: Florida area cumulus experiment. *Science, 195*, 735–742.

Wright, R. (1994). *The moral animal: Evolutionary psychology and everyday life.* New York: Pantheon.

Wundt, W. (1973). *An introduction to psychology.* (R. Pintner, Trans.). New York: Arno. (Original work published 1912)

Yaniv, I., & Foster, D. P. (1995). Graininess of judgment under uncertainty: An accuracy-informativeness trade-off. *Journal of Experimental Psychology: General, 124,* 424–432.

Zacks, R. T., Hasher, L., & Hock, H. S. (1986). Inevitability and automaticity: A response to Fisk. *American Psychologist, 41,* 216–218.

Zajonc, R. B. (1968). Attitudinal effects of mere exposure. *Journal of Personality and Social Psychology Monograph Supplement, 9,* 1–27.

Zeigarnic, B. (1927). Das Behalten erledigter und unerledigter Handlungen [The retention of completed and uncompleted tasks]. In K. Lewin (Ed.), Untersuchungen zur Handlungs- und Affektpsychologie [Psychological studies of action and effect]. *Psychologische Forschung, 9,* 1–85.

Zipf, G. K. (1949). *Human behavior and the principle of least effort.* Cambridge, MA: Addison-Wesley.

Author Index

Subject Index